Are You So Foolish?

A Commentary on Galatians

Jeff Amsbaugh

ISBN# 978-1-61119-135-6

Printed in the United States of America.
Printed by Calvary Publishing
A Ministry of Parker Memorial Baptist Church
1902 East Cavanaugh Road
Lansing, Michigan 48910
www.CalvaryPublishing.org

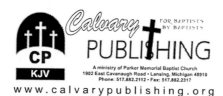

Calvary PUBLISHING
FOR BAPTISTS BY BAPTISTS
CP
KJV
A ministry of Parker Memorial Baptist Church
1902 East Cavanaugh Road • Lansing, Michigan 48910
Phone: 517.882.2112 • Fax: 517.882.2317
w w w . c a l v a r y p u b l i s h i n g . o r g

Are You So Foolish?

A Commentary on Galatians

Jeff Amsbaugh

TABLE OF CONTENTS

One Hundred and One Galatians

Galatians 1:1-5

I have a vision for the world and a burden for my city. I want to see people come to know the Lord Jesus Christ as their personal Saviour. The Apostle Paul must have felt that same thing when he went into places like Galatia and preached. Paul, pardon the pun, when he went into Galatia, was probably thankful to have a hundred and one Galatians. Do you want a hundred and one people in your town to accept the Lord as their Saviour? We have a great message to present to a lost world. We have a wonderful opportunity to help people find the answer to life's dilemma in the Lord Jesus Christ. I want to share with you several things about this Gospel that we preach.

The Content of the Gospel

The Death of Christ (v. 4a)

First, the Gospel includes the death of Christ. He gave Himself – that is a very picturesque way of referring to the crucifixion of Christ. Immediately, this shows us that the cross of Christ was no accident. The death of Christ did not take God by surprise. No, Jesus came for the express purpose of giving Himself upon the cross of Calvary. Indeed, no man took His life but He willingly laid it down. The cross of Christ is so much a part

9

of Christianity that if you were to remove the cross from Christianity, you would no longer have Christianity. The cross is so central that we do not have our faith without it.

The cross is magnified in so many areas. It's magnified at Bethlehem. The reason that those little hands were fashioned in Mary's womb was that one day nails might be driven in them. The reason those little feet were fashioned was that one day they might take a trip up Golgotha's hill. The reason that sweet little infant brow was fashioned was so that one day it might be crowned with thorns. The reason that little abdomen was made was so that one day a soldier might drive a spear into the side of the God man. I submit to you that the cross was magnified at Bethlehem.

The cross is also magnified in the Bible. Look at how many times the death of Christ is referred to in Scripture. Every time you cut the Bible, it bleeds. It is absolutely red with redemptive truth. The cross is magnified at Bethlehem and it's magnified in the Bible.

It's magnified in the by-and-by. Some day when we all get to Heaven and gather around the throne of God, we will be singing, "Worthy is the Lamb that was slain." It will take all of eternity to exhaust the praise that we give to Jesus for dying upon the cross to save us from our sins. It's the central truth of the Gospel.

In the opening verses of I Corinthians 15, the Apostle Paul states that the very first plank of our belief, the very first thing that we deliver to people, is the fact that Jesus Christ died upon the cross of Calvary for the sins of the world. I submit to you that when we talk about the ultimate good news, we are talking about the fact that Jesus died for sinners. We are talking about the death of Christ.

The Resurrection of Christ (v. 1b)

Not only do I see the death of Christ as part of the content of the Gospel, but I also see the resurrection of Christ as part of the Gospel. God the Father raised Jesus from the dead. If Jesus was raised from the dead, then He really died. His lungs stopped breathing. His heart stopped beating. He had no pulse. It's clearly obvious that Jesus really died. That's why they put Him in a tomb; you only bury dead people. When the soldier came, he was going to break Jesus' legs but he saw that Jesus was dead already and pierced His side instead with a spear. Out came blood and water. Cardiologists tell us this is only possible if a person has already died.

Why did the women go to the tomb? They went to anoint what they thought was a dead body that first resurrection morning. Jesus Himself said that He was dead when He said, "I am He that is alive and was dead and behold I am alive forevermore." He really died. But after He really died, He really rose from the dead. The very word *resurrection* translates the Greek term *anastasis* which means to stand up. Spirits don't stand up; bodies stand up. It was a bodily resurrection. It was His body that came out of the tomb.

Many cults and some liberal Christian denominations teach that it was His glorious spirit or His glorious influence that came out of the tomb. He dismissed His spirit to the Father while He was still hanging on the cross. What they put in that tomb was a body and what came out of that tomb was a body, which was demonstrated by the empty tomb. How could you say, "Come see the place where the Lord lay" if you're only referring to a spirit? Why would Jesus say, "Look at my hands and my feet that it is I" if you're only talking about a spirit?

This is also central to the Gospel because the Apostle Paul says, " I delivered unto you that which I first also received how that Christ died for our sins according to the Scriptures and that He was buried and that He rose again the third day according to the Scriptures." So the Resurrection is just as central to the truth of Christianity as is the death of Christ. If you gut the resurrection out of Christianity, you no longer have Christianity. This is why Jesus predicted that He would rise again; this is why the Apostles preached that Jesus had risen again. More than one hundred times in the Bible the resurrection is referred to. I submit to you that when we go out and preach the good news of Jesus Christ, we are preaching the death, the burial, and the resurrection of Christ. That is the content of the Gospel.

The Purpose of the Gospel

Think with me secondly about the purpose of the Gospel. There are at least three purposes that are outlined in this passage.

To Deal with Past Sins (v. 4b)

Many times we say that Jesus died for burdens and for heartaches, and all of that may be true. But predominantly when Jesus died, He died to deal with the sin issue. The Bible uses many terms to describe how this was done. First, He paid the ransom for our sin. When people wrong you, they're in debt to you. That's why they come to you and say, "Oh, please forgive me." They want you to cancel that debt. If our sins put us in debt to other people, they ultimately put us in debt to God. All of us are bankrupt at the court of Heaven. We owe God more than we could ever repay Him because of all the sins that we have committed against Him. We do not have the resources to pay that debt that we owe at the court of Heaven. But when Jesus died upon the cross, everything that you owed God was completely paid for by Jesus Christ. He paid your ransom.

Not only did He pay the debt for your sins but He also propitiated an angry God. Let's not forget the fact that sin angers God. Holiness is offended by sin, and God, who is ultimately and perfectly Holy, is really angry at sin. No one by their good works can appease the wrath of a Holy God. It took the supreme sacrifice of Jesus Christ upon the cross of Calvary to do that. When God saw the blood that was shed there upon Calvary's cross, His anger was assuaged, His wrath was appeased, and He was satisfied. He paid the ransom for our sin and propitiated an angry God.

The cross also reconciled us to God. Sin is a great separator. It divides people, but ultimately sin separates us from God. God and we are on opposing sides because of our sin, but when Jesus died upon the cross, He brought us near to God.

The cross is also described as a substitution. We are under the sentence of death, but when Jesus died for our sins, He took the penalty that our sins deserved. No matter whether you view sin as a debt that needs to be paid, as an offense that needs to be appeased, as a separation that needs to be bridged, or as a penalty that needs to be paid, God dealt with sin when Jesus died upon the cross. Everything that you've ever done that caused you to be in debt to God, separated you from God, everything that you've ever done that angered God, everything that you've ever done that was sending you to death and hell, everything that your sin ever did, Jesus paid the price in full when He died upon Calvary's cross. All your infractions were dealt with at the cross. It paid for your sin.

To Change Our Present Environment (vv. 4c , 3)

The purpose of the Gospel is not only to deal with past sin but also to change our present environment. Jesus died to deliver us from this present evil world. He died to deliver us from this present evil system in which we are trapped.

You and I are part of a system, the world's way of thinking that is opposed to God. You and I follow the herd. We think the way we're conditioned to think. It is difficult when you're in the break room and everybody says, "Oh, it's this way." Even if you know it's not that way, you have a difficult time standing up and saying,

"Oh, it's not that way." People say, "What do you think?" And you've got forty people whose thoughts are opposed to a holy God. This world tells us how to think, it tells us what to do, and we blindly follow it as if we are dumb, brute beasts.

The sad thing is the world tells us, "You Christians just can't think for yourselves." Really? Most people opposed to Christ are the herd followers. People who are without Christ are trapped into thinking the way they have been conditioned by the world to think. We are slaves to a mentality that is anti-God. And it causes us great anxiety of heart to know we're that way. We are trapped in a way of thinking that causes us to be ungracious to other people; it causes us to lack a peace deep down in our hearts. But when we embrace the Gospel, that way of thinking is abolished. At the very moment that we accept Christ, we're liberated from that mental bondage.

What a wonderful thing it is to be able to think the way God wants you to think! Some people say that Christians are brainwashed, and that's not a bad deal if your brain is dirty. My brain was dirty before I became saved; I needed someone to wash it. And when I became a Christian, I was delivered from following the world just because people said that was the thing to do. So the cross dealt with my past sin, but it also dealt with my present environment.

To Give Us Future Direction (v. 4d)

At the moment of conversion, we became aligned

with the will of God. Getting saved is not just a neat idea; it's something that God commands us to do. And therefore, when you become born again, you are following the command of God and aligning yourself at that very moment with the will of God. But the will of God doesn't get exhausted at the moment of conversion; it starts the will of God for us. When a man is lost, his life is aimless. It is directionless. We are lost. Have you ever been lost? Men don't usually admit it: "No, we're just taking the scenic route." But men do get lost.

When I was a little tot, a mall opened in our hometown, and that was a big deal. We had never had a mall before. My mother took me to this new mall. When I was little, I used to sit under the clothes and play with the tags while my mom shopped. So I'm sitting underneath the clothes playing with the tags and I peak out from underneath the clothes and Mom is nowhere to be found. I did what any three-year-old boy would do, I started bawling, "I want my mama!" The sales lady came over and picked me up and took me up to the office there in the department store. The next thing you heard was, "Janet Amsbaugh, your son can be found at the Lazarus mall office. Please come pick him up." My mama came and got me and oh, what a joy it was to be found.

Have you ever felt lost? What do you do? I go to work every day. Why? So I can get a paycheck. Why do you want a paycheck? So I can put food on the table. Why do you want to put food on the table? So we can eat. Why do you want to eat? So I can live. Well, why do you want to live? So I can go back to work tomorrow. Here we go round the mulberry bush. Many people have no direction. But the moment I received Christ, my life had purpose. My life had meaning. It had direction. I was no longer aimless. I was no longer lost. I was aligned with the will of God.

I'm saying that the purpose of the Gospel is to deal with my past sin, to deal with my present environment, and to deal with my future direction. Past, present, and future were all taken care of at the cross. That's the purpose of the Gospel.

The Results of the Gospel

Notice finally the results of the Gospel. What are the results of the Gospel? We have seen what the Gospel is, why we need it. But what's going to happen if we embrace it? There are several results of the Gospel listed here.

People Become Christians (v. 2a)

In verse 2, Paul refers to the brethren. Do you know what that means? When you receive Christ, you become part of the family. Oh, I like that. There's no initiation, no probationary period to make sure you cut the mustard. You're part of the family.

It's been my privilege to get together with some of the new babies at our church. And none of the parents of these new babies said, "We're going to wait just a few weeks and see if he or she measures up. And then if they measure up, we'll officially induct them into the family." No, the moment you're born, you're part of the family. You know it's interesting how a mother and a father can love all their children. It seems like when you have a child, you can't imagine your family without that child. At the very moment I was saved, I received all the rights and privileges of being a son. I was taken out of an orphanage of abuse and adopted into the family of God with all its attendant blessings. I became one of the brothers.

Churches Are Planted (v. 2b)

Notice that all the brothers are with the Apostle Paul. It is natural for Christian people to want to hang out with other Christian people. I get a little scared of people who make professions of faith and don't want to hang out with Christians. I get a little leery when I lead someone to the Lord and when I go back the next week they're peeking out from behind the blinds but won't answer the door.

An inevitable result of people getting saved is they start hanging out with one another. And when Christian people start hanging out with one another, the inevitable result of that is that churches get started because they provide an arena where people who are believers can hang out with one another. Any kind of Christian life without church life is the wrong life. Why do we get together? We get together for several purposes. One is to worship and tell God how great He is. We get together for instruction, to learn out of the Word of God. We get together to fellowship with other people. We also get together so we can organize ourselves to go attack our city for Christ and evangelize more people. So people become Christians and then churches are planted.

Missionaries Are Sent (v. 1a)

As Christians develop, they become sensitive to the Holy Spirit. They desire to know what it is that God wants them to do. And the Spirit says, "I'd like to start some churches in some other areas." And He calls people out of these churches to go repeat this process around the world.

I love to preach at new church plants. Why? I love to see God send even more people to go out and repeat the process. This is the thrust of what Paul is saying in verse 1. God reaches down and puts it in man's heart to go and preach the Gospel in an area where people have never heard or an area that desperately needs the Gospel. The man answers that call and says, "Lord, here am I. Send me." And when he goes out, the church lays their hands on him and says, "Amen, we support what the Holy Spirit is doing." So people are saved. Churches are planted. And then out of those churches, missionaries are sent around the world to proclaim the Gospel of Jesus Christ.

God Is Glorified (v. 5)

The final thing that happens in all of this is that God is glorified. What's the ultimate goal of the Christian life? The ultimate goal of the Christian life is to bring glory to God. And nothing brings more glory to God than people being saved and churches being started and missionaries being sent. God just sits up there in Heaven and He says, "Oh, I like that." And He's glorified.

When I was dating my wife, I made a conscious effort to try to bring glory to her. I wanted to brag on her, to tell people and to tell her how wonderful I thought she was. I still try to do that. I don't know if I'm as successful as I was when we were dating, but I still like to tell my wife from time to time how much I think of her. My wife's a very hard-working woman. When I look at Proverbs 31, I don't know of a principle in that passage that my wife violates. I looked at her last week after she had done a lot of hard work for us. I looked at her and I said, "I appreciate that hard work that you do for us to make this family work." I heap glory upon her. I submit to you that heaping glory upon someone you love is easy to do.

And our heart ought to want to heap glory on God because this family would not survive if God was not doing what He is doing. Every Christian who has been saved, every church that has been started, every missionary who has been sent is the direct result of the movement of Almighty God. You and I ought to look up to Heaven and say, "I appreciate you. To you be glory forever and ever. Amen." Do you appreciate God? Do you honor God? Nothing honors God more than souls being saved and churches being started and missionaries being sent. God sits up in Heaven and says, "I like that."

Let me conclude with one illustration. Let's say that someone came to me and said, "Pastor, I want to honor you. I want to give you two tickets to the Columbus Ballet." Now obviously that person doesn't know me, because I don't believe men in leotards dancing around an ice rink is really skating. But if you see a man who's wearing a full set of pads and he gets checked into the boards, and he's still standing, that's skating. Hockey players know how to skate. So if someone were to honor me with tickets to skating, they wouldn't give me tickets to the Ballet. They'd give me hockey tickets because they know that's what I like. Here we are doing all this talking about honoring God, but we do things He doesn't like. When you honor God, you honor God by doing the things that God likes. And what God likes is people getting saved. What God likes is churches getting started. What God likes is missionaries being sent. That is the heart of God. That is the desire of God. That is the passion of God. And if you and I really want to honor Him you'll honor Him with things that He likes, not with things He dislikes.

If I were going to honor my youngest daughter, I wouldn't say, "I'm going to give you a three-year supply of Brussels sprouts." She doesn't like Brussels sprouts. If I want to honor her I say, "Hey, once a month for the next year, I'm going to take you to get some ice cream" because I know that's what she likes. If you want to honor God, you ought to honor God with the things that God likes and there's nothing that God likes better than people getting saved. The best way we can honor God is to have a hundred and one people come to know the Lord before the end of the year. That's the best way we can honor God. The best way we can exalt Him up is by getting passionate about the things that God is passionate about and contributing to those causes.

CHAPTER TWO

The Subtle Dangers of Pastor Appreciation Sunday

Galatians 1:6-10

At one church where I ministered the congregation had an annual "Pastor Appreciation Sunday." This was a particular Lord's Day every year where they took time to honor their pastor, but there is a subtle danger of Pastor Appreciation Sunday. The subtle danger is that people might get the idea that ministry is all about men. The thought may be that we wouldn't be able to do what we do were it not for certain men. We could even go so far in some cases as to say, "The worship goes to the pastor rather than God." If that ever happens, we are in trouble. If Jeff Amsbaugh or any other preacher is your god, you're in trouble. It's right to appreciate, it's even right to honor spiritual leadership, but we have to be careful because any time we honor human leaders for what they mean to us or what they've done for us, at that very moment there are subtle things that can sneak in there that can be very undermining to our faith. Let's talk about what these things are. There are three major dangers in Pastor Appreciation Sunday.

The Danger of Forgetting God (v. 6a)

The word *marvel* is a word that means to be astounded. It's a strong word carrying with it the idea of being bewildered. The Apostle Paul is absolutely bewildered that people would leave God. When people leave God, it ought to marvel us. It ought to astound us. It ought to bewilder us that people would leave God. And the fact that he is bewildered is in part because he says it happened so soon. He says, ". . . ye are so soon removed. . ." The idea is that of quick departure. In that word *soon* you have the idea of both easy and quick. Isn't it amazing how easily and how quickly people can remove themselves from God?

The word *remove* is a strong word that was used of military desertion. Men in the Army, especially men who fought in Vietnam and have been in harm's way, probably don't have anything in their heart for a deserter. If there's a Benedict Arnold in the group, if there's a traitor in the group, if there's someone who can't take the heat, a guy who is absent without leave, I've got a sneaking suspicion that if you're a red-blooded American, you would be repulsed by him.

But there is a greater desertion than that and it is when people leave God. In Bible times, military desertion was punishable by death; it was very serious. This verb indicates that this desertion was a voluntary action. In spite of the fact that there were false teachers leading them to do it, they chose to do it. They with their own volition decided to remove themselves from God. And this is all the more astounding when you see that God is the one who decisively called them into the Gospel of Christ. That's what makes it special.

Notice two things about this calling. One is the fact that He calls it the Gospel of the grace of Christ. There's only one name that can save you and it's the name of Christ. The Bible says in Acts 4:12, "Neither is there salvation in any other: for there is none other name under Heaven given among men, whereby we must be saved." In John 14:6 Jesus said, ". . . I am the way, the truth, and the life: no man cometh unto the Father, but by me."

To our United Nations eclectic culture, that seems so narrow-minded, so bigoted, and it may not be politically correct; but it is Biblically accurate. People can only become saved through Jesus Christ. I've heard many people say that going to Heaven is like going to New York: Some people take a train, some people take a plane, some people take a boat, some people walk but we're all going to the same place; we're just going different ways. The Bible, however, is clear that there aren't many ways to God. There is only one way, and that way is "the grace of Christ."

Second, there is not only one name that saves, but there is only one means that saves. That means is grace. The Bible says in Ephesians 2:8-9, "For by grace are you saved through faith; and that not of yourselves: *it is* the gift of God: Not of works, lest any man should boast." Thus, when we preach the Gospel of Christ and we preach the Gospel of grace, no man can ever get credit for saving people. Christ alone saves and grace alone saves; there's something missing in that equation and it is men. Men don't save people. God's grace saves people. Specifically, Christ's grace saves people.

Several years ago, I was preaching a Bible conference in Ohio. The pastor and I were out on visitation and went to a house where we led a young man to the Lord. When the sinner finished praying for salvation, he looked up with tears running down his face and said, "I want to thank you for saving me." The pastor and I both simultaneously blurted, "We didn't save you; God did." When it's by grace, through faith, there's only one person who can get the credit for salvation. It's God.

Everything we possess is because of Christ and the grace of Christ. Don't be so appreciative of your pastor that you miss God in the equation. God has done much more for you than any pastor has ever done. Fall in love with God. I'm not saying that you shouldn't love people, but I am saying that if your faith is anchored to a man, you're going to set yourself up for a downfall. Humans often fail us. In the history of many churches, men who were highly respected and revered have let people down, but God will never let you down. So don't get so appreciative of men that you lose sight of God because that would be a mistake.

The Danger of Forgetting the Gospel (vv. 6b-9)

There's a second danger. Not only is there the danger of forgetting God, but notice second the danger of forgetting the Gospel. There are two different Greek words in this passage, both translated *another*. The first is a Greek word that means another of a different kind. Paul says, "I marvel that ye are so soon removed from that him that called you into the grace of Christ unto another gospel:" – another of a different kind. Then in verse 7, Paul uses a different Greek word for the word *another* and that word means another of the same kind. He is saying, "I marvel that you have so soon removed unto another gospel of a different kind which is not another of the same kind." The apostle is essentially saying there is only one Gospel. There are things out there that claim to be the good news but are not the good news at all. It claims to be a gospel but it's a gospel of a different kind; it's not the gospel of the same kind that we preach. He's saying that there are some things that purport to be good news but those things don't provide any consolation of good news to the heart at all; those things actually trouble the heart.

The word translated *trouble* is a strong word. It was used of things like trees that were shaken in dramatic storms. It was often used of great emotional disturbance. It's the same word that Jesus used in John 14 where He said, "Let not your heart be troubled. . ." Here's the point: the true Gospel has a way of settling the heart, but false gospels based on human effort have a way of unsettling the heart. To put it another way, if God is completely responsible for my salvation, it takes a great deal of worry off of me.

If salvation is by works, however, I'm greatly troubled. If I become saved by walking old ladies across the street and buying boxes of Girl Scout cookies and giving pints of blood to the Red Cross, how do I know when I've done enough? When salvation is all up to me, I'm frazzled. We must remember that when Jesus died on the cross He said, "It is finished." Everything that was necessary for us to be saved was accomplished. That is a great comfort to know. It is not up to me to earn salvation. All I need to do is accept what has already been done.

We must be very careful lest people pervert the Gospel. Different kinds of people can pervert the Gospel, and Paul gives you two examples when he says, "But though we, or an angel from heaven preach any other gospel unto you than that which we have preached unto you, let him be anathema." It might be somebody who is loved and respected like the Apostle Paul. It may be somebody who has done much in your life. It may be somebody for whom you have great admiration, like a fellow pastor or previous minister. Maybe it was a dear man who prayed with you in the hospital or helped you in a time of crisis. It may even be somebody spectacular like an angel. Angels, of course, are very good orators. They give divine messages in glorious manifestation. But whether a minister or an angel, Paul states that if the message is a different kind of Gospel, the messenger is to be accursed. This is hard for us to believe because in our technological society we tend to accept people based on their appearance rather than their content. When, however, we accept people based on how they look or on their demeanor rather than on the content of their message, we err.

The Bible ought to be preached with clarity. It ought to be preached powerfully and interestingly, and I don't deliberately set out on Sunday mornings to bore anyone. But the bottom line is that preaching cannot be judged on how funny it is or how interesting it is. You have to judge messages on how Biblically accurate they are. If anyone is preaching another gospel, he is to be rejected. Paul says again in verse 9 just we don't miss it, ". . . If any *man* preach any other gospel unto you than that ye have received, let him be accursed."

There are many times that preachers are judged or evaluated based on how nice they are, what their appearance is, or how kind they've been, and preachers ought to be all of that. But what makes a pastor beneficial to you in the final analysis is his ability to open the Bible and accurately preach the truth.

Thus, another potential problem with a Pastor Appreciation Sunday, is not only does it sometimes undermine God, but sometimes if we're not careful it can undermine the very Gospel because we are not here to elevate the personality of men, but to embrace the content of the Gospel. We have to be very careful that we keep our affections where those affections ought to be centered. The central thing is God and His message. So we have to be careful that we don't undermine God, and we have to be careful that we don't undermine the gospel.

The Danger of Forgetting the Goal (v. 10)

Third, not only is there a danger of forgetting God and a danger of forgetting the Gospel, but there is also the danger of forgetting the goal. The goal of the preacher is not the praise of men. That is not the goal of the preacher. The goal is pleasing God. That's the reason why we center on Jesus and that's the reason we center on grace. It's because when you center on Jesus and center on grace, you're centering on two things that always please God. God is always pleased when Jesus is magnified and He's always pleased when grace is magnified. So here's our goal. We're out to please God. We're out to please Him accurately and we're out to please Him absolutely. We are His bond slaves, as Paul says here. We are at His beck and call. We are here to do exactly what God wants us to do, when God wants us to do it, in the way that God wants it to be done. We are to preach Christ the way that Christ Himself would want Himself preached. We do so for one simple reason: We're out to please God and that's the goal.

When I first started preaching, I was a 22-year-old man straight out of college. When I took my first church, there were people in that church who were very affluent. It was a rich church with many wealthy people. I knew that what I was preaching on Sunday morning was cutting across the grain of that church. But I wanted those people to be happy. I wanted them to think they had hired the best man they had ever hired. But often I stood in the pulpit and offended them. Thus, there was great tension inside of me. I had this great desire to be accepted but yet at the same time, I knew that what I had to do wasn't going to be pleasing to many of the people who were listening.

In all of this, there was a subtle temptation for me to believe that the goal was pleasing people. I'm not saying that there's anything wrong with churches honoring men of God. But if a pastor ever gets to the point where he thinks that that's the goal of his ministry, he has sorely undercut himself. The goal is not pleasing men; the goal is pleasing God. So there's a danger of forgetting God, there's a danger of forgetting the Gospel, and there's a danger of forgetting our goal.

In summary, we cannot have misplaced affection. God means more than the messenger. We cannot have misplaced attention. The Gospel means more than personality. And we cannot have misplaced achievement. God's praise must mean more than man's praise.

One day we're all going to stand before God, and when do, the thing that's going to make our life really significant is to hear one simple statement from the lips of our Master, "Well done, thou good and faithful servant." Pastors need to live every day for the approval of God. God must be lifted up, the Gospel must be lifted up, and the goal of pleasing God in all that we do must be lifted up. I'm appreciative of the pastors who have lifted up God in my thinking and who have lifted up the Gospel in my thinking and who have kept before me the constant goal of living for that praise from God, "Well done thou good and faithful servant."

CHAPTER THREE

Looking Forward

Galatians 1:11-24

Every day we have an opportunity to look forward. This is the first day of the rest of your life. And because it is, you and I must be concerned with personal development. There are some things that I want to be true of me. As I read this passage of Scripture today, I cannot help but be in awe of some of the things that were true of the Apostle Paul. These are the things that I'd like to be true of me.

I Want to Be Factual (vv. 11a, 20)

You will notice in verse 11 that Paul says, "But I certify you, brethren..." And then in verse 20 he says, "Now the things that I write unto you, behold, before God, I lie not." The word *certify* means to make known with certainty. We could put it this way: I want to make one thing perfectly clear. That's the idea. When you and I present things to people, we ought to be very clear about what we mean. We ought not to be double-tongued; we ought to say what we mean and mean what we say. We ought not to be ambiguous when we talk to people; we don't want to say things in such a way that people could take it different ways. We ought to be absolutely clear in what we are saying.

It's hard for leaders to be treated as leaders if they're not honest people. When some people die, others may say, "There lies the body of truth because it never came out while that person was alive." We must be characterized by forthrightness and transparent honesty.

I've often stated to staff members that honesty cannot be debated. Lying is always wrong. In other words, when someone agrees to work for an institution and says, "If I assume this position, I'm going to dress a certain way, then they ought to dress that way because they said they would." While we may be able to debate dress standards to some degree, we cannot debate lying. The same thing is true if someone agrees to attend church. If someone agrees to attend church as a condition to employment, then he ought to attend church on Sunday morning, Sunday night, and Wednesday night. Someone may say, "Well, Wednesday night's not in the Bible." Yes, but not lying is in the Bible. So if you say you're going to go to church on Wednesday night, you ought to go to church on Wednesday night simply because you agreed to do that.

In the future, you and I ought to strive to be honest. We ought to strive to be factual in everything that we do. As a pastor of a church, truth has to be important to me. The Bible says that the church of Jesus Christ is the pillar of truth. No institution stays in business long if it doesn't practice the truth. If you go to a restaurant and order a steak well done and it comes back in a pool of blood, you probably won't go back to that restaurant. You expect well done to be well done. If you go to a shipping store and pay for second day air and the package doesn't get there until six days later, you probably won't use that company as a courier in the future because you expect that institution to be characterized by truth. If we expect the post office to be characterized by truth and the local restaurant to be characterized by truth, then obviously the church of Jesus Christ ought to be characterized by truth. Truth was important to the Apostle Paul. In verse 20 he says, "Now the things which I write unto you, behold, before God, I lie not." If only that statement would be true of every one of us so that in the future no one would be able to point a finger at us and say, "He or she is a liar."

I ought to tell the truth and before God I ought not to lie. All of us should strive to be factual, honest people who say what we mean and mean what we say.

I Want To Be Biblical (vv. 11b-12)

Notice what Paul says in the latter part of Verse 11. The apostle is very upfront here that he preached a message that was from God, not from man. This put him in great opposition to the Judaizers who were causing all kinds of trouble at this time. These Jews were people who memorized what other men said about the Bible. They didn't study the Bible for themselves. They rather studied what other men said about the Bible. They looked to human interpretations and what respected men said more than they looked at what God Himself said in the Word of God. They gave supernatural reverence to it but they never studied it. It's kind of like that family today who has the Bible sitting on the coffee table collecting all kinds of dust. It's a relic that's never opened. Or it is like the Christian who runs to the local bookstore to find out what an author has to say about the Word of God and yet never reads the Word of God directly.

We Baptists believe in individual soul liberty. That means that you can pick up the Bible because you have the Holy Spirit in your heart. The Holy Spirit can teach you by Himself what the Word of God has to say. We study the Bible as the Bible. Paul was not one who would run around memorizing or trying to find out what other people had to say about the Bible – that was not his tactic. Paul was highly trained in rabbinic schools. He sat at the feet of Gamaliel and other well-known rabbinic teachers. Thus, he could have said, "I sat at the feet of famous teachers." But that's not the issue.

God has given me the privilege of sitting at the feet of some great Bible teachers. Richard Young, my Greek teacher, wrote a grammar that is widely used all around the United States. The Hebrew teacher at our seminary was one of the executive editors of the New King James Version. Obviously, he knew Hebrew. I sat at the feet of Warren Wiersbe who is one of the greatest Bible teachers alive today. But that's not the issue. God doesn't want us to brag about who we sat under. God wants us to be Biblical. That's the issue. And the question is not, Who do I know? The question is not whether what I'm saying is or isn't supported by famous scholars; it's whether what I say is in line with the sacred text of the Word of God. That's the key issue. In the future, it's not who I know as far as my ministerial associations are concerned as much as am I bound by the sacred text of Scripture, am I a person who is motivated and governed and driven by the Word of God? Am I Biblical? The Apostle Paul says that he wants to be factual; he also says that he wants to be Biblical.

I Want to Be Humble (vv. 13-14)

When Paul started off in Judaism, he was steeped in the oral tradition of his fathers. It was a family matter. And this is one of the hardest reasons even today that it is difficult to lead a person in Judaism to the Lord; they would have to break with their family to accept Christ. The same thing is true with many people who are steeped in Roman Catholicism today. They're Catholics and yet many times they never even go to mass at all. They are Catholic simply because they were born into a Catholic family. There are many Protestants who are the same way. We follow the traditions of our fathers.

Paul was so entrenched in this family heritage that he used to persecute the church of God. And when he says that he persecuted it, he uses an imperfect tense verb, which suggests that in the past it was a persistent, continual harm that he was seeking to bring to the cause of God. He also says that he "wasted" the church. That's a very strong word that was used of an army ravaging a city, and once again, he uses that imperfect tense verb, meaning this is something that characterized his previous life habitually and consistently. Paul was committed to moving up Judaism's ladder. That word *profited* was often used of blazing a trail, and was usually said of someone who would go through with a machete and cut a path for somebody else.

Paul was a trendsetter within the scope of Judaism. He was ahead of the rest. Now if you're ahead of the rest and you're moving up the corporate ladder, it's a very sobering thing to wake up one day and say "I was wrong." When Paul was going to Damascus that day to arrest Christians, God arrested him, and Paul said, "Who art thou, Lord?" And God said, "I am Jesus whom you persecute." Paul had been zealously fighting against Jesus Christ, when Jesus Christ is the one that he should have been embracing. Paul had a decision to make. He either had to accept the truth and embrace Christ admitting his wrong, or ignore the truth and be wrong because he did not want to be embarrassed. Paul was humble enough to recognize that he was wrong and that he needed to change. I am thankful for that. If only we had more men concerned with being right than protecting their reputation.

We must be people who are willing to admit when we are wrong. And when we are wrong, we have to be humble enough to turn in the other direction. When I think about this, I think about a man many years ago who made a vow that he would not eat any live organism. So he determined to eat nothing but rice. Then one day someone bought him a microscope and he said, "I'm going to look at a grain of rice under the microscope." So he put the piece of rice on a slide and slid it under the microscope, and to his horror he discovered that there was microscopic life inside of the rice.

He did the only logical thing: he destroyed the micro-scope. There are many people like that. They want to destroy the evidence because they don't want to admit that they're wrong. The Apostle Paul was a humble man, and when he came face to face with the truth of Jesus Christ, he said, "I'm sorry, I was wrong." In a word, he was humble. That's the kind of man I want to be.

I Want to Be Sensitive (vv. 15-16a)

God had a plan for Paul's life. That plan was that one day Paul would preach the glorious gospel to the heathen. It pleased God to call the Apostle Paul to preach the very Christ that he so vehemently hated. He now had the privilege of preaching that very Christ to the heathen. What grace it is that God allows us to advance His cause when at one time we fought against it. But this job of preaching Christ is not mere words, though, of course, words are involved in it. Paul says here that God wanted to reveal His Son in me. That's a sobering statement. When you and I preach the gos-pel, people should not merely hear our words; they must see Christ in us.

I had a Bible professor who used to say that if you go up to somebody, spit in their face, stomp on their feet, and quote John 3:16, you haven't preached the Gospel. Many people don't hear what we have to say until they see the principles of Christianity demonstrated in our life. I think it was Gandhi who said that he would have been a Christian but for one thing: He met too many Christians. People need to see Jesus in us so that when we present the propositional truth of the gospel, it rings true in their heart because they've seen it implemented and practiced in our lives. I want to be so sensitive to the will of God and the call of God on my life that people can literally see Jesus in me. Oh, that you and I would be sensitive to the call of God and sensitive to what God wants to do not merely with us but in us.

It pleases God to reveal His Son in me. What a wonderful prospect that is. Oh, I want to be sensitive to what God wants me to do so that when I act, people see Jesus in my actions. I want to be sensitive.

I Want to Be Independent (vv. 16b-19, 21-24)

I am an independent Baptist by conviction. What does that mean? Well, after conversion, Paul stays several days in Damascus, but even then he didn't confer with flesh and blood. That is, he didn't talk to Ananias and other people about the revelation that he received from Jesus to see if it had any validity or not. He rather went to Arabia and there was prepared for the ministry. After he left Arabia, he went back to Damascus. Do you know what happened when he went back to the city of Damascus? They basically tried to kill him.

Because the king wanted to kill him, he must have known something about the Apostle Paul. The Apostle Paul probably wasn't merely being trained in Arabia; he was probably doing some preaching there as well. He was in Damascus, he went to Arabia, and then he came back to Damascus. And only after a three-year period of time did he travel to the city of Jerusalem. And when he went to the city of Jerusalem, he tells us that he was only there for fifteen days. He'd been saved for three years before he went to Jerusalem, and when he went to Jerusalem, he was only there for fifteen days. And the only Christians he met while there was the apostle Peter and James, the Lord's half brother. And from there he went to the regions of Syria and Cilicia.

Why did he even go to Jerusalem? They were trying to kill him. Remember, they let him down the city wall in a basket and sent him to Jerusalem. When he left Damascus, he was running for his life. He went to Jerusalem three years after his conversion, he was only there for fifteen days, and the only reason he went there was because his life was in jeopardy. From there, he went to the regions of Syria and Cilicia. His hometown, Tarsus, was in Cilicia. And once again, he only went there because his life was in danger. He stayed in those regions for several years. During that time, he was unknown by any of the Judean churches. They didn't even know him by face; all they knew was that he used to persecute the church of Jesus Christ and was now preaching the very gospel that he tried to snuff out.

Why would he live in obscurity in Arabia? Why would he go to these unknown regions? Why wouldn't he hang out with the local ministers in Jerusalem? Paul tells us why. He was not concerned with his own glory. He was concerned with the glory of God. He makes that plain in the last verse where he says, "And they glorified God in me."

God spare us from politics. There are so many ministers who are trying to drop their name and move up the corporate ladder. When I graduated from Bible College, we went from Chattanooga to Philadelphia. Philadelphia was nowhere near the Bible Belt. I lived a life of obscurity. But one passage of Scripture that always meant much to me was that of Saul being picked to be king of Israel. He was hiding out in the standing corn but God knew where he was. God always knows where you're at. You don't have to play politics to advance the cause of Christ. God knows where you are.

Those who are so concerned about manipulating others to get where they want to be need to stop and humble themselves under the mighty hand of God so that He'll exalt them in due time. What a wonderful thing it is to know that God knows where you are. When Paul was in Arabia, and again when he was in Cilicia and Syria, he was probably tempted to think that nobody would ever hear about him. Question: have you ever heard about the Apostle Paul? I've heard about him, haven't you? Why? Because God knew where he was. And God knows where you are. And God takes notice of what you're up to and what you're doing this year. You don't have to blow your own horn. God knows where you are.

I want to be independent. This is not only true of ministry. If you want to move up the ladder at your secular corporation, God knows where you're at. You don't have to stab people in the back at your local establishment to achieve advancement; God knows where you are. We need to be content in the place where God wants us to be, knowing that whatever our future holds, it is in the hands of God. We can trust Him.

I want to be factual; honesty is the best policy. I want to be Biblical; I want my life to be governed by the Book. I want to be humble; I want to be the type of man who has the ability to admit that he's wrong when he is. I want to be sensitive; I want to do exactly what God wants me to do in the way that God wants me to do it so that people can see Jesus in me. And I want to be independent; I don't want to be a person who's going around trying to manipulate all kinds of things to get where I need to be. God knows where we're at.

CHAPTER FOUR

Becoming a World-Famous Soul Winner

Galatians 2:1-2

The Apostle Paul's activity as a soul winner is world famous. If you were to ask, "Who in the New Testament was one of the most famous soul winners?" I think you'd have to say the Apostle Paul is right up there on the list. When we talk about missions, when we talk about reaching the world for Christ, we may ask, "Who out of anybody in the New Testament was most effective at reaching their generation for Christ?" I think you'd have to say the Apostle Paul was right up there on the list. Indeed, his soul-winning ability became so great that the people who were in Jerusalem were skeptical of him. So they called him up to Jerusalem and wanted to know exactly what was going on.

It reminds me of a former pastor of mine, Jerry Caswell. Out of all the preachers that I knew, Jerry was the best soul winner. There are people in my hometown today who owe their spiritual life to Jerry Caswell because he didn't just preach about soul winning; he did it. He knocked on people's doors. He shared the Gospel – not just for flashy reasons or numbers or statistics – but because he loved people. He was interested in seeing people saved. He was gifted at sharing the faith. He was so conscious about souls that he invited a world-famous soul-winning instructor to conduct a soul-winning seminar in our home church. We were all thrilled because we all wanted to become soul winners like Pastor Jerry.

This instructor came and taught his seminar. Pastor Caswell was so impressed with the seminar that asked the instructor to go soul-winning with him. The teacher said he'd be honored to do so, and so they went out one afternoon together. They knocked on many doors, and the guy tried every way he knew how to lead somebody to Christ that afternoon; but he was largely ineffective. Finally, toward the end of the afternoon, he looked at Pastor Caswell and said, "Well, Jerry I've struck out all afternoon; the next home is yours." So they knocked on the door, and Jerry led that person to Christ. The famous instructor returned to our church and said, "I don't know why you people paid all of this money to bring me in for this seminar. The best soul winner I've ever seen is your pastor."

Something like that is what is happening in this passage. All these famous teachers at Jerusalem are surprised at this fellow that nobody's ever heard of. Paul is leading people to the Lord. And they want in on this. They're asking him to come up to Jerusalem and to explain to them why he is such a great soul winner. Now in hindsight, hundreds of years after the fact, you and I look back on the fact and think those fellows didn't know who they were dealing with. They were dealing with a world-famous soul winner, and they didn't know it.

That's what I want to be; I want to be a world-famous soul winner. If I'm known for anything, I want to be known for having a love for people. I want to see people born again and saved. I want to shed tears over people's souls. I want to go after people. I want to be a soul winner. Let's discuss several things that can help us be great soul-winners.

He Had Consistency (v. 1a)

From the very first time that Paul went to Jerusalem until this visit to Jerusalem, there was a space of fourteen years. During that fourteen years, what had the Apostle Paul done? I'll tell you what he'd done during that fourteen years: He had stayed at it. He preached the Gospel to Jews and Gentiles alike, and for fourteen years he stayed at the stuff – through good times and through bad times. He was consistent at getting the Gospel out and helping people become saved. The Bible says in Psalm 126:6, "He that goeth forth and weepeth, bearing precious seed, shall doubtless come again with rejoicing bringing his sheaves *with him*." That phrase "bearing precious seed" is very important. Literally, it carries the idea of a trail of seed. Wherever we go, we ought to leave a trail of seed.

In the story of Hansel and Gretel, they left bread crumbs to find their way back home. You and I ought to be able to retrace our steps by the seed of the Word of God that we have left behind. Most of us go protracted periods of time without attempting to win souls. Then the pastor preaches about soul winning and we get a big handful of seed, which we sow all at once. We declare this method to be ineffective and quit within a brief period of time, until the preacher preaches on soul winning again. That's not the way God wants us to soul win. God wants it to be a way of life with us – constantly leaving a trail of seed wherever we go. That's consistency.

You and I have to stay at this thing. We don't catch fish every single time we go fishing. So we must continue to put our line in the water habitually. For fourteen years the Apostle Paul continued to be a soul winner. He had consistency.

He Had Compassion (v. 1b)

The Bible says that fourteen years after his first visit, Paul went up again to Jerusalem with Barnabas. Let's examine Paul's first visit there (Acts 9:26). The church was afraid of him. Why do you suppose they were afraid of him? The week previous he had been persecuting Christians. They were not sure whether his conversion was genuine or not.

But Barnabas took up the case of Paul. The disciples did not want to accept this new convert without a probation period. They were fearful of him, but one man by the name of Barnabas encouraged them to take the risk. He did not view the new convert as a threat; rather he viewed the new convert as somebody to be welcomed. Barnabas was a man of great compassion; that's why they called him the son of consolation. Is it no wonder that the Apostle Paul brought him up to Jerusalem. If there was anybody who could help settle the dispute between Paul and the Jerusalem church, it was Barnabas. He accepts new converts upon their profession of faith.

My sister was three-and-a-half years old when I was

born. She was the first grandchild on my mom's side of the family, and she was spoiled. When mom became pregnant with me, Debbie wandered into the kitchen and said, "Mom, when the new baby comes and you have to give me away, will you give me to Grandma?" My mom said, "Debbie, we're not going to give you away. What in the world are you thinking?" Debbie said, "Well, parents can only have one child at a time and you've got this new baby coming, so I'm going to have to be given away. I want you to give me to Grandma." Mom said, "Honey, people can have more than one child. And we're going to love you just as much as the new baby."

But when I was born, it was a big adjustment for Debbie because she was accustomed to having all the attention. She was used to having things her own way. And now she had to share space, and a new baby demands a lot more attention. Toddlers can hold their own sippy cup. Newborn babies have to have the bottle held for them. And the older child often has to stand and watch.

We have a video of Amy, our second daughter, when she celebrated her first birthday. Our oldest daughter Ashley was about two and a half at the time. We're giving all these presents to Amy, and there's video footage of Ashley standing to the side looking on. It's an image I'll always remember. People who have been saved for a while do not need as much attention as somebody who just been birthed into the family. The temptation is to be jealous of the attention that new converts receive. God, however, wants us to exercise compassion on the newly regenerated.

Dr. Lee Roberson, my mentor, was a big fan of compassion. This in part made him a very effective soul winner. Soul winners are compassionate people.

He Had Credentials (v. 1c)

Many people say that soul-winning doesn't work. It's a method of the past and has lost its effectiveness. People just aren't getting saved today. We live in the last days. Perilous times are here prohibiting the conversion of souls. Here's one thing for sure: If you don't attempt to lead anyone to the Lord, you won't win anybody to the Lord. This argument is often just a copout for people who are too lazy to share the faith. The people who claim that soul winning is ineffective are the people who aren't doing it.

The leaders in Jerusalem were saying that God is not saving Gentiles. So Paul brought Titus along to prove that this was not the case. Here is a Gentile who has been transformed by the Gospel. Paul is essentially saying, "Look at Titus and tell me that it doesn't work." Here's a man who has been saved by the grace of God. Don't tell me it doesn't work; I've got proof. My souls are my credentials.

Many people have deluded themselves into thinking that God saved all He's going to save. No, until the trumpet sounds, you and I ought to be handing out tracts and sharing our faith. Tell that new convert that he is really not born again. The proof of the pudding is in the eating. We don't see everybody become saved when we share the Gospel, but one thing's for sure: If we don't share our faith, nobody will get saved. Paul had credentials.

He Had a Commission (v. 2a)

When he went to Jerusalem, Paul went by revelation. He went because God told him to. That's something we often lose sight of. Many times we judge whether we should go or not based on effectiveness, on whether we will see results. How many people become saved as a result of visitation? But the issue is not how many people got saved. The issue is obedience to what God has told us to do. We're supposed to water, we're supposed to plant, and God's supposed to give the increase. Let me do my job and let God worry about His. We need to share our faith.

In our society, we're largely success-oriented rather than biblically-oriented. There's a big difference. We ought to be doing something just because it's right, not necessarily because of the results of it. We do what we do because we want to be obedient. We go and speak because God commands it. By revelation we go. I know of a Baptist church were a Jehovah's Witness lives right next door. A while back, the pastor of that church was talking with that Jehovah's Witness about methods of proselytizing used by the Jehovah's Witnesses. The man said that his group goes door to door sharing their message. The pastor asked, "Do you find that effective?" The Jehovah's Witness looked back at him and said, "What's that got to do with it? We believe Jehovah told us to go and we go. What difference does it make whether we're effective or not?" Sadly, we have the truth, and we're less committed. If a cultist feels that way, how much more should you and I who believe the truth feel that way? God said go and we go because God told us to. What more do we need? We have a commission.

He Had Carefulness (v. 2b)

Paul communicated the Gospel. The Greek word translated *communicated* means to lay something before somebody for their consideration. Paul carefully delineated the contents of the Gospel. If we are going to communicate the Gospel, it helps to know what the Gospel is. That's why we train people in knowledge and presentation. We want people to know how they can effectively communicate their faith and what the content of the gospel is. We send people out to carefully lay before other people the contents of the Gospel for consideration. And then we let the Spirit of God take the Word of God and do His work. The power is not in our technique. The power is in the Gospel that we present to people. It's the power of God unto salvation.

I have noticed some surprisingly untalented people become great soul winners. It amazes me. There are certain people that I would guess to be ineffective in witnessing. Yet they are effective because the power is in the Gospel itself. The power is in the truth of the Word of God. If we know that truth and carefully present that truth, we give God's Holy Spirit a chance to work.

Years ago we knew a lady who was having problems with her daughter. Her daughter at one point was a very spiritual girl, and then they moved out of the area and sent their daughter to a public school. The daughter did not choose her friends wisely and was introduced to drugs. She was arrested and placed in a halfway house. The family called from the location where they had moved and asked me to go see their daughter, which we gladly agreed to do.

Upon our arrival, I zeroed in on that girl and talked to her about her dedication to Christ. I began to share Bible verses with her. As I was zeroing in on the girl, the counselor was zeroing in on me. She was watching my technique to see if my technique was effective. And when it was all over, she looked at me and said, "That was a rather interesting technique; what do you call that?" And to be honest with you, I had no name for it. She thought I was – through some type of human manipulation and technique – trying to accomplish something with that girl. I was trying to do nothing of the kind. I was trying to present God's Word to her and let that Word provide conviction. Our job is to concentrate on the Bible and let the Word of God do its work. We carefully present the Gospel and then we let God do what He does best with His Word.

He Had Consideration (v. 2c)

When Paul communicated unto them the Gospel which he preached among the Gentiles, he did it privately to them which were of reputation. Notice that the Apostle Paul discussed the Gospel privately and part of the reason was because the men that he was talking to were men of reputation. They had a name. He didn't want the truth that he was presenting to them to embarrass them. Paul was not doing this privately because he was scared he was wrong. He's doing it privately because he's scared they're wrong. And he doesn't want to show them up in front of everybody else. Thus, he does it privately so if there's any error on their part, they can correct it behind closed doors.

On occasion, I have shared the Gospel with men who have a blurred understanding. They believe that salvation is faith plus works. I attempt to show them that salvation is by grace through faith alone. Salvation is ours exclusively through the work of Christ. And I believe that if I had such men alone they stand a greater chance of being saved. But often men don't want to admit wrong in front of others. To be quite honest, sometimes we must exercise consideration in these matters. Don't walk into the break room where there are forty-two people and shout from one end of the break room to the other, "Hey, Bill, have you made your decision for Christ yet?" That's not tactful. Respect people. Respect their dignity. The Gospel is a fixed body of truth, but we've got to present it in such a way that people will listen to it. You can be so obnoxious that people don't listen. Be a gentleman. Paul was. He had consideration.

He Had Consequences (v. 2d)

The reason that Paul did all of these things was because he believed there was a distinct possibility that he could run in vain. There are consequences of what we do. Paul uses this same phrase in Galatians 4:11 where he says, "I am afraid of you, lest I have bestowed upon you labor in vain." There are eternal ramifications of what we do.

I had and uncle by the name of Homer. Homer was perhaps the vilest man that I ever met. He was blasphemous. He said if there was a Hell, he'd take his chances. He was having too much fun in sin to quit. Homer was a mechanic. One night Homer was in his shop and that shop was not properly ventilated. The carbon monoxide fumes came in on Homer's life and he went out into eternity. For decades now Homer, my uncle, has been crying for one drop of water to cool his tongue. And it has not been forthcoming. Is there a Hell? If we believed there is, there are consequences of what we do.

What's the driving force of your life this week? What motivates you? What are you praying for? What's in the forefront of your thinking? When you think about big things that have to be accomplished this week, are the souls of men on the forefront of what you're doing? Why would God leave us here on planet earth after we got saved? Why would He leave us here to experience all the heartache and disappointment of this life if we're already assured of Heaven? Why? There are other people who aren't on their way to Heaven. That's why we've been left here. And it's our job to get them out of Hell and into Heaven. That's our job. That's why we're here. If you're going to be big at something, be big at that.

Years ago, I knew of a Christian high school that had a pretty good sports team, but that sports team was not known for their athletic ability, even though they were good ballplayers. They were known for their soul-winning. When that sports team would travel to away games, they would pack up with tracts to distribute at the restaurant where they dined. They hoped to win the game, but they weren't on that trip to win ballgames; they were on that trip to win souls. That's what we're after; that's where true winning is. If we are going to be famous at something, let's be famous at that.

CHAPTER FIVE

A Soldier Worth Remembering

Galatians 2:3-14

As we fight this war on terror, there is something inside of me that wishes politicians would get out of the way and let the military be the military. Sometimes politics can do much to make a war unsuccessful and in the same way, I feel it would be good in Christianity if pastors were less concerned about politics and more concerned about fighting the war.

I heard a story not long ago about a military family. They were a strong, proactive military family, and they sat at the dinner table and discussed military maneuvers. They decided that it was about time their family got involved in church so they packed up the family one Sunday morning and went to Sunday school. For the first time the little boy in the family heard the story of Jesus and how Jesus died on the cross to save the world from sin. As that little boy was sitting there, the teacher waxed eloquent on how there was no greater sin in history than people taking their very own Creator and nailing Him to the tree. She said it was horrible what the world did to Christ, and the little boy finally had enough of this and raised his hand. The teacher said, "Do you have a question?" And the little boy said, "Yes. While they were doing all this to Jesus, where were the Marines?"

It seems like the cause of Christ is suffering some casualties. It seems like people are crucifying afresh the very Son of God. It seems like Jesus Christ is not getting His due these days, and my question to you is this: Where are all the soldiers of Jesus Christ? When I stand before God, I want to be a soldier worth remembering.

Many years ago when I was a little boy, there was a fellow in our home church by the name of Freddie Welch. Freddie was a little slow and wasn't the most gifted person on the face of the earth. Freddie Welch was challenged in a lot of ways, but he had one desire and that was to fight for his country at the height of the Vietnam War. As soon as Freddie was old enough, he registered for the draft and was accepted. Many people believed that Freddie was not intelligent enough to fight for his country. Most of the people at our church knew that if Freddie was drafted, he would come home in a body bag. Sure enough, Freddie was drafted by the Army and he went to Vietnam. In just a brief period of time, Freddie's parents received word that he had given his life for his country. As a little boy, I can still remember that Freddie was not intelligent by the world's standards; he was not a gifted person, and we might go so far as to say that he was slightly retarded. But I could not help but think as I went to his memorial service that he was a soldier worth remembering.

I may not be the brightest person that has ever graced God's green earth – I'm challenged in a lot of ways – but everything that I've got, I want to give it for my God. I want to die with my boots on and when I stand before God, I want to be a soldier worth remembering. What are the characteristics of a soldier worth remembering?

A Soldier Worth Remembering Practices Loyalty (v. 3)

There were false teachers in Paul's day. They were called Judaizers and they taught that you had to be circumcised to be saved. There was at least one fellow on the face of the earth who was not buying that teaching, and his name was Titus. Titus was not going to submit to this error. Though there was great pressure on him to be circumcised and though there was a great pressure on him so succumb to this false way of teaching, Titus was not buying it. He had embraced the pure Gospel of Jesus Christ, and was going to remain extremely loyal to that Gospel message. No one could move him. No one could change him. No one could cause him to drift from the Gospel that was once for all delivered to saints. He was not adding one solitary work of man to it. It is all of grace and that is where Titus stood. He was loyal to the Gospel.

No amount of peer pressure in our society and no amount of political correctness ought to cause us to move from the pure Gospel of Jesus Christ. In our society today with its United Nations mentality, people want us to believe that there are all kinds of ways to Heaven. They think as long as one is sincerely following one of those paths, he is going to make it to Heaven, but that is not what the Bible says. Jesus says in John 14:6, ". . . I am the way, the truth and the life: no man cometh unto the Father, but by me." No amount of human effort or human ingenuity can create a better plan of salvation than that which is revealed in the pure and precious

Word of God. The Gospel of grace, the Gospel of Jesus Christ demands our absolute loyalty.

In 1995 the United States Congress was debating some tax measures and in the House of Representatives, they were discussing how they could crack down on people who were avoiding taxes by changing their citizenship. They called these people "Benedict Arnold Billionaires" because these rich people were giving up their United States citizenship so they didn't have to pay taxes to the United States government. And the representatives were trying to make a way that they could get these people to remain loyal to America and pay their taxes.

There are some things that are worth being loyal to regardless of how much it costs us. American citizenship is one of those things. I may not like taxes, but I'd rather pay taxes to America than to any other government. The Gospel of Jesus Christ is another thing that I want to remain loyal to regardless of the cost.

We're an anchor for those who are hurting,
We're a harbor for those who are lost.
Sometimes it's not always easy bearing Calvary's cross.
We've been ridiculed by those who don't know Him,
And mocked by those who do not believe,
Still I love standing up for my Jesus,
'Cause of all that He's done for me.

I am not ashamed of the Gospel of Jesus Christ. I am loyal to that. A soldier worth remembering is a soldier who practices loyalty.

A Soldier Worth Remembering Practices Liberty (v. 4)

Anybody who teaches that you can work your way to Heaven is a false teacher, a false brother. The Greek word here in verse 4 is *pseudadelphos* from *pseudo* meaning "fake" and *adelphos* meaning "brother". He is a sham – he is a fake Christian. Sometimes people who are fake Christians slide into churches undetected because they have this *pseudo* or token relationship to Jesus Christ. Paul says that they have come in for the purpose of sabotage; they want to bring people into slavery, and the word here is a very intense Greek word: *katadouloo*. It carries with it the idea of an intense bondage, a very tenacious form of slavery.

A works salvation is always intense slavery because if you are working your way to Heaven, you don't know how much good work is enough good work. If I get to Heaven by walking old ladies across the street, how many old ladies do I have to walk across the street? If I get to Heaven by buying boxes of Girl Scout cookies, how many boxes of cookies do I have to buy? If I get to Heaven by giving pints of blood, how many pints of blood do I have to give? If working to get to Heaven is all up to me, I am always under the bondage of wondering how much work is enough to merit the smile of a holy God.

But then I come to an old rugged cross and I see a man hanging there in agony and shame. When He raises His head to die, He says, "It is finished." I know now that everything I need to be right with a holy God was accomplished there. Jesus paid it all. Therefore, when I come to an old rugged cross, I am released from that bondage. As John 8:36 says, "If the Son therefore shall make you free, ye shall be free indeed." Soldiers are people who believe in liberty for all. I believe that everybody is worth being free – I don't care whether they live in Korea or Vietnam or Iraq – I think freedom works for everybody. Therefore, any system that tries to keep people in bondage is a system worth fighting.

In the same way, false religion is slave-oriented. It wants to keep people in bondage. Why do you think all these religions exist that try to insist upon human works? It is because such mentality holds people in bondage. We are soldiers who fight systems that keep people in bondage because we believe in liberty – we believe in freedom. I was told as one of the soldiers went into Iraq and met one of the young children that he was liberating, the child looked up at the soldier and said, "Hello, freedom man." I want to be a freedom man. I want to find people in bondage all around the world tell them of the liberty found in the pure Gospel of Jesus Christ. Wouldn't it be great to find someone who has an addiction to alcohol or an addiction to drugs or an addiction to elicit relationships – or whatever bondage they may be in – and to preach the Gospel to them this week? Then they can say, "Hello, freedom man." Soldiers worth remembering believe in liberty.

A Soldier Worth Remembering Practices Tenacity (v. 5)

The truth of the Gospel is something that is eternal. It is something that Paul says must continue. That being the case, we don't give in to false teachers – not even for an hour. We fight doctrinal error.

In 1937 Pat Magee played high school basketball and did something unique that I don't think has ever been done in the history of basketball before or since. Every member of his team fouled out at the end of the game except him. He was the only one playing basketball against five guys, and he stayed in. Believe it or not, his team won. I have been in church my entire life, and I have seen a lot of good players foul out. I've seen a lot of good men ruin their testimony and get involved in things that they shouldn't be involved in. I have seen a lot of people foul out and become castaways.

As long as I'm able to put on a pair of sneakers, I'm still in the game. My whole team may have fouled out, but I am tenacious enough that I am going to stay in there and fight for a victory even if the rest of the team is gone. Even if there is only one person left in the game, I have some fight left in me and I hope you do too. A soldier worth remembering has that type of tenacity.

A Soldier Worth Remembering Practices Teamwork (vv. 6-10)

People in the church have different jobs to do. Paul

was sent to the Gentiles. The Bible tells us here that Peter was sent to the Jews. But the great thing is the same Spirit that worked in Paul as he went to the Gentiles was the same Spirit that worked in Peter as he went to the Jews. They had different jobs but they had the same Holy Spirit working inside them. They worked for the same reason and that was to get people saved. What a great picture that is of the church. There are people in the church who just don't understand one another because they are involved in different ministries. Every person thinks that his ministry is the most important job.

The great thing about it is that we all have different jobs and sometimes we can't understand why somebody would want to do that other job when there is this job to do. But the great thing about it is that even though we are all involved in different jobs, the same Spirit that works in them is the same Spirit that works in us. Even though Peter, James, and John were famous in the church of Jerusalem, they didn't look down their noses at Paul and Barnabas as the new kids on the block. As a matter of fact, not only did they not look down on Paul and Barnabas for being new kids, they encouraged these new preachers to search for the downtrodden. Of course, Paul was more than willing to do that. Getting the Gospel out is a team effort. You and I will only get the job done if we decide to quit our bickering and get along with one another to accomplish the task that is before us.

The story was told of a ship captain who was arguing with his chief engineer over who was the most important person on the boat. And the captain said, "I'm the captain. I'm the one who gives the orders to steer the ship in a certain direction. I'm the most important." And the chief engineer said, "You couldn't even guide this ship if I wasn't running the engine properly. I'm the most important person." So they were fighting with each other and they decided to do what husbands and wives erroneously decide to do from time to time – they decided to switch places. So the captain went down in the boiler room and the engineer went up to the crow's-nest. Finally, after a brief period of time, the captain emerged from the boiler room covered with dirt and oil, and he looked up in the crow's-nest and said, "Will you get down here in the boiler room? I can't get this engine to go." And the engineer shouted back from the crow's-nest, "Of course you can't get it to go, we've run aground."

Many times we try to be better than others rather than depending upon one another. In the church of Jesus Christ, it's not for us to try to be better than the person next to us. We all depend upon one another to get this vessel down the road in the direction that it should go with the power that it needs to get there. We're never going to win the war if we don't practice teamwork.

A Soldier Worth Remembering Practices Bravery (vv. 11-14)

Paul was not easily moved by those of reputation. He wanted their approval or he wouldn't have sought it.

But their approval or lack of approval didn't change the call of God that was upon his life, and in that sense, what they said made no difference to the apostle Paul. It's like an ordination council. Usually at the end of an ordination, the council will ask, "What would you do if we refused to ordain you?" The candidate usually responds, "If you don't ordain me, I'm going to preach anyway because that is what God has called me to do." We desire the recognition of other godly men but even if we don't get it, we must do what God has asked us to do.

Bravery is necessary because we have to stand up to people. There is going to be confrontation along the way, and sometimes people are going to have to be corrected. No human being is beyond making mistakes, and because that is true, it takes bravery to engage in confrontation. I'm sure that Paul had a very difficult time correcting Peter. It took courage to do that. The hypocrisy and favoritism that Peter was practicing was having an effect on people – the Bible says even Barnabas was carried away with it. Peter was not living according to the Gospel he preached – he was not walking uprightly. The word used here is very interesting. It's the word *orthopdoeo* from which we get our word "orthopedics". It carries with it the idea of straight feet. He was not walking straightforward; he wasn't walking the line as he ought to.

Peter was a Jew and yet he did not separate from Gentiles. He ate with those Gentiles as he should and acted more like a Gentile than a Jew. But then he went to the Gentiles and said, "You ought to act more like

Jews." Here was a Jew acting like a Gentile telling Gentiles they ought to act like Jews. The entire thing didn't make any sense. He was inconsistent and Paul called him on the carpet for it. He confronted him publicly. I'm sure that it took a lot of bravery for the new kid on the block to do that. If you want to be a soldier, you are going to have to be brave.

A nurse was assisting a doctor in surgery. It was her first day, and the doctor was trying to decide if he was going to keep her. The doctor had used twelve sponges during that surgery and it was one of the jobs of the nurse at the end of the surgery to count the sponges to make sure that they did not leave any sponges in the patient. At the end of the surgery the nurse looked at the doctor and said, "There are only eleven sponges here." The doctor looked back at her and said, "I have been doing this for years. I got them all out." She said, "Doctor, I'm telling you there are only eleven sponges here." He said, "I'm telling you that I am a chief surgeon and they are all out of the patient." She said, "Doctor, there are only eleven sponges here." At that moment, he lifted his foot off the twelfth sponge that he had purposely put on the floor and hid, and then looked at the nurse and said, "You're hired." All of us need people who are brave enough to tell us when we're wrong. That's the nature of being a soldier. A soldier has to be a brave person to be able to stand up in the conflict.

When I die, I may not be decorated with military honors. There may be no firing of guns or blasts of trumpets, but I hope that in the service of the Lord I have lived a life that will commend me as a soldier. I want to be a man who has been loyal to the Gospel of Christ. I want to be a man who believes in liberty and freeing people from the tyrannical grip of sin. I want to tenaciously continue to do the things God has called me to do. I want to be practicing teamwork that brings people together. And I want to bravely be able to confront people when they are wrong – even when it is going to cost me something.

That is my job as a soldier. And if we do these things, we will be soldiers worth remembering. By God's grace, all of us ought to seek to be that kind of a soldier.

CHAPTER SIX

The Danger of Working Your Way to Heaven

Galatians 2:15-21

The key word in this passage is the word *justify*. You'll notice how frequently that word is used in verses 16 and 17. This is the big question. How am I going to justify myself when I stand before God someday? Have you ever caught your kid red-handed doing something and then had him or her try to justify the activity? Someday you and I are going to stand before God, and when we stand before Him, the question is, how are we going to justify ourselves in that day? Most of the time when people give an answer to this question, it is some type of a works answer. They say, "I'm a pretty good guy and I don't intentionally hurt anybody." Sometimes people will say something like, "I am just trying to live by the golden rule. I am trying to do good by my fellow man." Others say that they are trying to get to Heaven by keeping the Ten Commandments. And that is interesting because they probably couldn't list five of them but they are trying to get to Heaven by keeping the Ten Commandments or by doing the best they can do.

The danger of this is clearly evident. If you and I get to Heaven by the good works that we do, then the question we have to ask ourselves is this: How much work is enough? How much good work does it take to make me good enough to go to Heaven? If I go to Heaven by walking old ladies across the street, how many old ladies do I have to walk across the street? If I go to Heaven by giving pints of blood to the Red Cross, how many pints of blood does it take for me to get to Heaven? If I go to Heaven by buying boxes of Girl Scout cookies, how many boxes do I have to buy? So consequently, at the very moment that I determine that I get to Heaven by good works, then I am in trouble because I don't know exactly how much I have to do to get myself into Heaven. If we are justified by working, then we are clearly indecisive about how much work it takes for a person to go to Heaven. I want to suggest to you four dangers of trying to work your way to Heaven.

Irrational (vv. 15-16)

Paul in this passage is writing to Jewish believers. He is talking to Jews who have believed in Jesus Christ. And Paul says that they have discovered something to be true – there is something that they know to be a fact. No man can be justified by the works of the law. He contrasts what he says with Gentiles who are sinners, people who are living in raw paganism. People who are Jewish by nature were raised within Judaism. They heard the stories about Adam and Eve, Abraham, and Noah and the flood. They memorized verses out of the Old Testament, and they were very religious. Gentiles who were raised in raw paganism knew nothing about those things. They just went out and did their sinning. They didn't hear the Bible stories and they didn't memorize the verses. If the Jewish people who were raised with

Judaism and who heard the Bible knew that they could not get to Heaven by the good works that they did, then how in the world could the Gentiles work their way to Heaven when their lives weren't as moral and when they knew nothing of the Bible? It was irrational to think so.

I was born on a Tuesday and on Sunday morning I was in church. When I was born, I was so little that the doctor told my mother not to take me out into a crowd because I was liable to catch something, and the doctor said if I caught something, I might die. We went to such a small Baptist church that mom and dad didn't consider it a crowd, so Sunday morning I was in church and from that moment I was in church Sunday morning, Sunday night, Wednesday night, revivals, missionary conferences – you name it and I was there. When the janitor cleaned, we showed up at church because every time the church doors were open, we thought we were supposed to be there. I memorized Bible verses, I heard Bible stories, I was raised within Christianity and I discovered something to be true – I wasn't good enough to go to Heaven.

If a guy who was raised in church from infancy discovered that to be true, then how in the world can I expect someone who was raised in a crack house to go to Heaven by his good works? If being raised in the church house is still not good enough, if being raised around the Bible and the things of the Bible is still not good enough, then how in the world can I piously sit back and look at somebody who is raised in the throes of a dysfunctional, pagan home and say, "You have to try to be good enough to go to Heaven"? Even people who are raised in moral homes cannot work their way to Heaven, so if moral people can't work their way to heaven, we certainly know that the immoral crowd cannot. It is preposterous to even think anyone can work their way to Heaven.

Just so we don't miss the point, Paul says it three ways. He says it generally, he says it personally, and he says it universally. You can't get to Heaven by good works. You can't get to Heaven by keeping the deeds of the law. In order for us to be saved, we have to abandon all hope of trying to work our way to Heaven. We have to trust exclusively in what Jesus did on the cross to save us from our sins because even a man raised within the confines of religion knows self-righteousness cannot save. Thus, if that man knows it to be true, it is irrational for him to think anybody else could be saved by working himself or herself to Heaven. Salvation by works is irrational.

Iniquitous (vv. 17-18)

Paul says we have been saved by faith in Jesus Christ. When you say that you're saved by faith in what Jesus did independent of good works, people will say, "My goodness, if you are just saved by believing in what Jesus did on the cross, you can live any way you want to and still go to Heaven as long as you put your faith in Jesus." People think that if you're saved by faith alone, you can sin any way you want to. The impression that people have is that because we are for faith alone, that means we are for sin. If you and I kowtow to that kind of thinking and we began to put a little bit of works into salvation, then we are actually saying that Christ is guilty of sin because Christ came to this earth and taught that He was the way, the truth, and the life and that no one comes to the Father but by Him. When Jesus went to the cross and died, and there shed His blood as an eternal sacrifice, if my good works would get me to Heaven, then what Jesus did was an unnecessary way to get to Heaven. So if by my good works I am saved, I am really saying that what Jesus did was false religion, what Jesus taught was false, what Jesus said was bogus, and that I can work my way to Heaven. I'm saying that Jesus is not the only way – I can work my way to Heaven, so there was no need for Him to die. I am basically saying if I believe in a works salvation that Jesus Christ was guilty of heresy.

I've got to tell you that there is no greater sin in the entire world than devaluing Jesus Christ. When a person says that Jesus doesn't know what He is talking about and that Jesus' work was not sufficient to pay the penalty for a man's sin, that person has done the worst injustice imaginable. The whole reason that Jesus came to this earth was to destroy the idea of a works salvation, and if you begin to rebuild again those very things that Christ by His teaching and work knocked down, you are wrong. Liberal churches that think and teach that people can get to Heaven by doing good works, and think and teach that as long as you are a friend to your fellow man, you will make it, are wrong. Churches that teach those things are basically saying that Jesus Christ didn't know what He was talking about. I don't care if they have the word *Christian* on their sign, if they are fighting against the teaching and the work of Jesus Christ and they are trying to make Jesus Christ a heretic, they are committing the worst iniquity imaginable. They are saying that Christ was not right and that is the height of iniquity. I would hate to stand before God on Judgment Day having been a preacher who told my congregation that what Jesus said was not really true. How would you like to stand before Jesus some day and look Him in the eye and say, "You know, I kind of thought you were wrong"? When you and I try to claim that you can get to Heaven by good works, it is not only irrational, but it is also iniquitous. We are saying that Jesus Himself was a minister of sin.

Impossible (vv. 19-20)

Paul begins to articulate in verses 19 and 20 that when we trust Jesus Christ as our personal Saviour, the old man that was in sin and on his way to Hell dies. As an eleven-year-old boy, when I received the Lord Jesus Christ as my personal Saviour, the man who knelt down there was a sinner on his way to Hell. When I got up off my knees, that sinful man on his way to Hell didn't exist anymore. God killed him and God raised a brand-new man to take the place of the old man. That is what we picture in baptism. When somebody is baptized beneath baptismal waters, they are not merely saying that Christ died, was buried, and rose again; they are saying that it was a co-death, a co-burial, and a co-resurrection.

When Jesus died, my old life died with Him; when Jesus was buried, my old life was permanently put away; and when Jesus walked out of the tomb, I was raised to walk in newness of life. I am not the man I used to be; the old man is dead.

It reminds me of that scene in *Oklahoma* where the fellow sings that poor Judd is dead.

> Poor Judd is dead, poor Judd Fry is dead.
> All gather around his coffin now and cry.
> He had a heart of gold and he wasn't very old.
> Why did such a feller have to die?

> Poor Judd is dead, poor Judd Fry is dead.
> He's looking all so peaceful and serene.
> He's all laid out to rest with his hands across his chest
> And his fingernails have never been so clean.

The day that I became saved, the old man that was in sin was killed; he doesn't exist anymore. Thus, the law can't touch them. Many people may remember when John F. Kennedy was shot and killed. Lee Harvey Oswald pulled the trigger and killed the President. They arrested Lee Harvey Oswald and were going to bring him to trial. While he was being brought to the trial, Jack Ruby shot Lee Harvey Oswald. They didn't prosecute Lee Harvey Oswald. Why? Because he was dead. What the court was going to do to him had already been done. The law can't touch a dead man because he is dead. At the very moment that I became saved, the old Jeff Amsbaugh died. Thus, the law cannot touch him. The law can't do anything to him because he is dead.

This new life that I have, Paul says, is by the faith of the Son of God who loved me and gave Himself for me. It is a brand-new life that courses through me, and the me that you now see is not the me that used to be because God killed the old me and created a new me to take the place of the old me. Therefore, the law can't touch me. The law can't touch a dead man. I heard a true story about a policeman in Los Angeles who was walking down the street one day and saw a car parked in a No Parking zone. The cop went over and wrote the man sitting in the driver's seat a ticket and stuck it on the dash; however, the man didn't move. The man in the driver seat couldn't move because three hours earlier he had been shot through the head. The cop didn't even notice that the man was dead. They could not arrest the guy for not paying his parking ticket because he was dead. How are you going to prosecute a dead man? You can't.

I have a relative who makes it his goal in life to make enemies with everybody he meets, and he is very successful at it. He tries to inflame everybody he comes in contact with. One of my friends who knows this relative said, "I am not dealing with him anymore" and he refers to my relative as "the dead man." He'll come by and say, "Hey I saw the dead man today." What does he mean by referring to my relative as "the dead man"? He means that he is having nothing to do with him; as far as he is concerned, that man is dead. As far as God's law is concerned, your old life is dead to God. God can't prosecute that old man because he doesn't exist anymore. Now that I am saved, for me to think that I have to add good works to salvation is absolutely ridiculous. I can't do the time for the crime because I am dead. It is impossible for a dead man to be put on a work release program because he is already dead. Because I am already dead, the law can't reach me, and it would be impossible for me to work my way to Heaven.

Irritating (v. 21)

Jesus died on the cross to save me. If I could go to Heaven by my good works, then Jesus died in vain. That is very important. If you can go to Heaven by your works, then why did Jesus die? If I get to Heaven by the good works that I do, then Jesus died in vain. There was no reason for Him to die if I can work my way to Heaven. A works salvation frustrates the grace of God. Jesus came to do for us what we cannot do for ourselves. If you could do it for yourself, there was no need for Jesus to come and do it. Yet people want to try it on their own.

This frustrates God's offer of help. God wants to offer you His grace, His unmerited favor. God wants to do it for you, but when you say, "No thank you," you're frustrating the very grace of God. You are irritating the God of Heaven. The very thought that you could work your way to heaven is an irritant to the heart of God.

I heard a story on the radio about a little boy who went to the Washington Monument and was impressed with it. He looked up at the guard and he said, "I'd like to buy the Washington Monument." The guard played along with him and asked, "How much have you have?" The kid reached in his pocket, pulled out a quarter, and handed it to the guard. The guard said, "I don't think that is quite enough, young man." The little fellow reached in his pocket and pulled out the remaining nine cents that he had been holding out and gave that in addition to the quarter. The guard said, "I'm afraid that's still not enough." He told the little boy, "You see, we've got three problems. Number one, the Washington Monument is not for sale. Number two, if it were for sale, you wouldn't have enough to buy it. And Number three, if you are a United States citizen, it is already yours. All you have to do is use it."

I say to you that Jesus died on the cross to save you from your sin and your salvation is not for sale. Even if it were for sale, you wouldn't have enough to buy it. And it is already yours; all you have to do is use it. This idea that you and I by our own righteousness could work our way to Heaven is irrational, iniquitous, impossible, and irritating to the very heart of God.

Let's say that one of my daughters was outside making mud pies and decided to come in and give her dad a glass of water. Without washing her hands, she reaches and grabs a glass, and as she does, the mud just sticks to the side of the glass. She then sticks that glass under the faucet and fills it with water. She sticks her muddy fingers over the brim of that glass and a big clod of mud slides down into the water. Then she comes into the living room and presents that glass of water to me and says, "Dad, I brought you a glass of water." I appreciate her noble intention but I am not drinking that water because it is polluted.

The Bible says that all of our righteousness is nothing more than filthy rags in the sight of God. Many people are trying by good works to gain the favor of God, and though God may appreciate the sentiment behind that, God cannot accept those works because they are tainted with the unbelief of rejecting His Son Jesus Christ and what He did on Calvary's cross. The only way that a person can go to Heaven is by accepting what Jesus did as payment in full. When you and I try to put our human ingenuity and good works into the salvation equation, we are involved in a futile exercise. Salvation is by grace through faith. Don't add anything to that. There is great danger in trying to work your way to Heaven.

CHAPTER SEVEN

Self-Revelation at the Front Door

Galatians 3:1

Several decades ago, there was a debate in evangelistic circles about the nature of salvation. Out of that debate, three books were written. John MacArthur wrote a book called *The Gospel According to Jesus*, Charles Ryrie wrote a book called *So Great Salvation*, and Zane Hodges wrote a book called *Absolutely Free*. Each of these books took a different position on the nature of repentance in the salvation experience.

Zane Hodges in his book *Absolutely Free* wrote that repentance was not necessary for a person to be saved. He stated that all a person has to do is believe in Jesus. A person does not have to change his mind about his sin or his self. He can be saved by faith independent of repentance.

John MacArthur, on the other hand, says just the opposite. In *The Gospel According to Jesus*, he states that for a person to be saved, he has to put his faith in Christ and feel sorry for his sin recognizing that he needs a change in his life. He says that people have to change their mind about sin and themselves to be saved.

Charles Ryrie in his book *So Great Salvation* takes a middle-of-the-road position and says that repentance is necessary but not about sin or self. He says that a person has to change his mind about Jesus and accept Him as God. He says that repentance is necessary but that repentance is only about Jesus and God, not about sin and self.

This debate is still going on today in evangelical circles. I want to go on record, not necessarily as agreeing with any one of these men as much as agreeing with the Bible. When I look at the Bible, it seems to me that the Bible indicates that people do have to change their mind about their sin and themselves to be saved. I don't think that Charles Ryrie's position holds up under the scrutiny of Scripture. For example, in the passage in the Bible where the tower of Siloam fell, Jesus said to the people who were there, "Do you think that these people were worse sinners than you? I tell you that except you repent, you shall all likewise perish." There He is talking about perishing or not perishing. Jesus and His deity are not under discussion in that passage. What is under discussion is sin, and Jesus says, "Except you repent of your sin, you shall all likewise perish." This is crucial because as that great Puritan preacher Thomas Watson said, "When a person becomes saved, he must see himself as a sinner and only as a sinner."

The problem is that many times when we knock on someone's door and ask that person how he knows for sure he is on his way to heaven, he may say, "Well, I've been a good person. I've never intentionally tried to hurt anybody. I've never murdered anybody, and I try to live by the Ten Commandments and the Golden Rule. Most of my neighbors would say that I'm a moral person, so I think that my good works outweigh my bad works and someday, when I stand before God, I think God is going to let me into Heaven based on my own morality." If a person says that – no matter how sweet a person they are, no matter how nice a grandmother they may be, no matter how wonderful, and warm and cozy and kind that person may be – if that person does not see himself or herself as a Hell-deserving, Hell-bound sinner, there will be no hope of salvation for that person.

When Jesus died on the cross, he died to save us from our sin, and if we don't think that our sin is sending us to Hell, then what did Jesus die on the cross for? Every single person who is confronted about their need of Christ must have a self-realization that they are a sinner, they deserve judgment, and they deserve to go to Hell. That is why I must call out to God and ask Him to save me. When you think that you can get to Heaven by your good works, when you think that you are okay by yourself, independent of Christ, you reveal several things about yourself. This may seem unkind, but it really is charitable because you have to have this self-realization to go to Heaven.

You Reveal That You Are Brainless (v. 1a)

The word *foolish* in verse one carries with it much emotion. It carries the idea of anger – Paul is mad about it. It carries the idea of love – he is concerned about them. It carries the idea of surprise – he's shocked that a person could actually think such a thing. In other words, Paul is simply saying, "I cannot believe what you people believe." When Paul uses that word *foolish*, he is not so much referring to mental deficiency as much as he is referring to mental laziness. They had a brain – they were just choosing not to use it.

I've met a lot of people like that. They have a brain – they are simply choosing not to use it. They were not using their heads, and they were exercising poor judgment. Frequently when the word foolish is used in the Bible, it is used of people who have allowed their emotions to take over their brain and are functioning according to what they feel and sense rather than according to objective truth as it is revealed. In 1 Timothy 6:9, for example, Paul uses the word foolish of people who are after money, people who have made materialism the number one pursuit of life. Because they are charged with emotion about the pursuit of money, they have put their brain on hold about what really is important – lust blurs judgment.

Any man who has ever cheated on his wife reveals this same type of thing. It's a different kind of lust – it is a sexual lust instead of financial lust – but it is lust nevertheless. If a man who is contemplating sexual infidelity talks to himself long enough, he will make statements like, "My wife is not really meeting my needs. After all, I deserve this." He will give himself emotional justification. Because he has allowed his emotions to kick in, he will become emotionally charged so much so that he has put his brain on hold.

The same idea is found in Luke 24:25 with regard to the men on the road to Emmaus. These men had allowed their emotions to blur the judgment of the Word of God. Jesus had already predicted that He would die, that He would be buried, and that He would rise again the third day. The Old Testament had predicted that in several passages. They should have known that Jesus was going to rise from the dead and that everything was going to be okay. But because of the trial and the crucifixion, and all the emotion of that day, they had allowed the emotions of what they had seen to blur their judgment of the Word of God. And because of that, Jesus called them foolish.

You and I are not to follow whims and circumstances. Paul calls them "foolish Galatians" because they were following their feelings and senses rather than the Word. You and I are to never follow our whims; we are to follow the truth of the Bible. We are not saved based on what we feel is right or what we sense God is going to do in the Day of Judgment. It is not a matter of being saved by a self-oriented mind but a Scripture-oriented mind. They had accepted false doctrine not because they had been intellectually persuaded that it was correct, but rather they had accepted it because their emotions had been victimized.

Anybody who is trying to work his way to Heaven has become filled with ego, and he thinks he can do it himself – that is a pride issue. That is exactly what Paul was alluding to in Ephesians 2:8-9, when he said, "For by grace are ye saved through faith; and that not of yourselves: *it is* the gift of God: Not of works, lest any man should boast." If I can work my way to Heaven, then I accomplished it and can brag about it. There is great emotional pride in that. I have to come to the realization that salvation is based on what the Word of God declares to be true and everything else has to be set aside. The problem is that many people want the Christian life to be an emotional adventure. God never intended us, when we get saved, to put our minds on hold in search of an ecstatic good feeling. The man who is trying to work his way to Heaven reveals that he has put all of the truth of the Word of God aside so that he can function according to what he believes in his heart, what he senses in his heart and what inclinations he has, rather than what he Word of God objectively declares to be true. In so doing, he puts his brain completely on bypass and reveals he is brainless.

You Reveal That You Are Bewitched (v. 1 b)

Whenever you put your brain on hold, you are gullible. When you don't think, you are susceptible, and because these people had become foolish in their thinking, they left themselves open to being bewitched by false teaching. The word *bewitched* means "to charm or fascinate in a misleading way." Have you ever been flipping through the channels and stumbled across a television preacher who looked like the devil incarnate? He looked like a slick used-car salesman. Many of us have sat there and looked at such a preacher and thought, "How in the world could some little old lady give that guy thousands of dollars? What in the world are people thinking?" It's clear they are not thinking and because they have put their mind on hold, they have become gullible. Specifically, they have become gullible to flattery.

We tend to think that people who flatter us are intelligent. When my wife flatters me, I think, "What a smart woman she is." People are susceptible to flattery and false promises like "just give a little seed money and you will get tens of thousands of dollars back." The only people getting rich off that seed money are the people who are receiving it – not the people who are giving it. Consequently, false promises exist and sometimes the word *bewitched* is not only used to describe people who are duped by flattery or false promises but sometimes even the idea of a cult or satanic power is embedded in that word *bewitched*. All of that is true of a salvation based on works – it flatters me because I am responsible for my own salvation and it makes a false promise because I think I can be saved by myself. That flattery is energized by Satan himself.

We have a definition of the term *bewitched* in Ephesians 4:14. When you put your brain in neutral, you are able to be duped. You flip and flap and flutter from one thing to another like a silly dove. You go from wire to wire of doctrine, from one thing to another, trying to embrace the newest fad or fashion. People like that are tricked by Satan-energized men who are constantly scheming. You have been sold a bill of goods.

One day while my dad was at work, a salesman peddling encyclopedias stopped by our house. My sister Debbie was four and I was six months old. The salesman told my mother how wonderful these encyclopedias would be for her children's education and she bought it, hook line and sinker, and he told her how these encyclopedias could be hers for a hundred and forty-two easy monthly payments. Dad came home from work and here we have the 1965 edition of World Book Encyclopedia. Mom began to tell Dad in glowing terms how wonderful these encyclopedias would be for our education. Dad looked at her and said, "Janet, Debbie is only four and Jeff is only six months old. By the time they can read those encyclopedias, they will be obsolete." Dad called the salesman, and chewed him out for taking advantage of a vulnerable woman without allowing her to talk to her husband first. He said, "What kind of salesman are you anyway?" The shamed salesman came back and got the encyclopedias and we've never heard from him since. My mother historically is an intelligent woman. She graduated from high school with a four-year Latin scholarship but on that day, she put her mind on hold and when she put her mind on hold, she was standing there with a bill of goods that were of no value to her.

Lest you are thinking that I am only applying this to women, let me incriminate myself. One day when Karen and I were in Chattanooga, I was the pastor of a chapel in Dalton, Georgia. I didn't have two nickels to rub together. My fiancé, Karen, and I were walking through the mall and this guy stopped us and said, "My goodness, y'all are the best-looking couple I have ever seen in my life." He was a photographer and was selling pictures. Before he was done, I had signed my life away and had bought all these pictures. Then it dawned on me that I couldn't pay for those pictures. In the mall that afternoon, because of my lust, I was foolish and because I was foolish, I was bewitched. That is what many people do when it comes to salvation. They have put their mind on hold and because they have put their mind on hold, they are highly susceptible to the enticing snares of false teachers.

You Reveal That You Are Blind (v. 1c)

The phrase "evidently set forth" is a phrase that was used of posting public notices in the marketplace. This is how Paul describes his preaching. Paul was a dynamic preacher – he was not ambiguous about who Jesus was and what Jesus could do. He stressed over and over again the significance of Christ's atoning death. They were under conviction for their sin and knew that Jesus was the answer. This was all done publicly – it was not done under the shadow of darkness – it was done publicly in the marketplace for everybody to see. Jesus is exclusively the only way to Heaven and it was so public that if you couldn't see it, you must be blind. It is terrible enough to be blind but it is even more terrible to be willfully blind. These guys had put their minds on hold, and they had become gullible, and they had chosen to be blind to the truth.

When I was twelve years old, Mom asked me to go to the local store and get a half gallon of milk. I had done this numerous times and it was no big deal. I started walking toward the store, which meant I had to go up Ferndale Road and make a right on Malone and go up to the corner where the convenience store was located.

I decided to do something different on this particular day and walk to the store with my eyes closed because I wanted to see what it was like to be blind. I was a curious young man who wanted to know what it was like to live in total darkness. Believe it or not, I made it all the way up Ferndale Road with my eyes closed. My mom was probably wondering what was taking me so long.

When you turn onto Malone Road, there is a bridge that crosses over the Route 13 bypass in Mansfield, and as I went up on the bridge, because my eyes were closed, I slipped and fell face first into the concrete embankment of that bridge and hit teeth first and broke half of my front tooth off. My face was bleeding and the nerve of my tooth was exposed and I went running home in pain. I was rushed to the dentist and he capped that tooth. All that happened because I decided to close my eyes and walk in darkness. I know you are probably thinking that I was stupid and you are right – I was stupid. It is always stupid to close your eyes and be blind when you can just open them and see. I learned as a 12-year-old boy that when you walk in willful blindness, you can injure yourself like nobody's business.

There is one thing worse than choosing to walk in physical blindness and that is choosing to walk in spiritual blindness because when you walk in physical blindness, you may break a tooth and have to go to the dentist but when you walk in spiritual blindness, you will end up in an eternal Hell. There is greater danger in being spiritually blind than there is in being physically blind.

You Reveal That You Are Bound (v. 1d)

The word *crucified* that closes this verse is a past perfect participle, which basically means that it is a finished act with an abiding result. In other words, the crucifixion of Christ will never have to be repeated and it has an abiding result that will last for all eternity. There is no ceremony or ritual that you can devise to add to the cross of Christ. You never have to pick up where the cross of Christ leaves off because the cross of Christ does not leave anything off. It is a continuing eternal payment for all sin. This one act of Christ being crucified conclusively proves that men cannot save themselves. If this is the permanent way by which men are saved, then it remains that there is no other alternative by which man can be saved. Yet you see many religions using the name of Christianity that say you have to do this or that to be saved. If a religion says you have to do anything else to be saved, that religion is rejecting the complete sufficiency of the cross, and anything that rejects the complete sufficiency of the cross is heresy (cf. Act 13:39). When you try to do for yourself what only Christ can do, you're in great bondage. Every person has to come to the humbling realization that "I can't do it."

When I was between my freshmen and sophomore years of college, my dad secured a job for me at the local steel plant where he worked. This was a highly prestigious thing. During the summer they hired college kids who were the children of company personnel, but they never hired the kids of union workers to work during the summer. In the whole history of the steel plant, as far as I know, I was the only child who was ever hired as the son of a union worker to work during the summer. The reason that I was hired was simply because my dad had such a good work record at that plant that they wanted somebody who could work like Art Amsbaugh, and so they thought, "Let's hire his son."

There was only one problem with that situation – my dad is incredibly strong and I cannot beat my way out of a wet paper bag. One of the things they had me do one night, or at least attempt to do, was to pull the scraps of steel out of the reversing mill. These scraps of steel would get stuck and it was my job to pull those scraps of steel out. I saw guys go up there with one hand and pull out the scraps with relative ease. I went over there and tried to pull one out and it wouldn't even move in spite of the fact that I was using two hands. Finally, one foreman said to me, "I need to see you tomorrow." I went into his office and he read me the riot act. He said, "Son, I don't know what you think this is, but this is no Sunday school picnic. This is hard work and you can't just fool around with those scraps; you've got to put your all into it." I didn't know what to say except, "Sir, I did put my all into it but my all wasn't strong enough." When I was released from the steel plant, one of the bosses wrote, "What others could do with relative ease, Jeff did with reckless abandonment." It was a sobering realization to go home that night knowing that I couldn't do it. I longed to have the strength of my father, but I didn't.

When it comes to salvation, you have to come to the

realization that your Heavenly Father has more strength than you have. There are certain things that you would love to be able to do for yourself, but you can't because it takes the power of your Heavenly Father to accomplish it.

Am I waking from dreams like a child in the night?
Am I moving from darkness out into light?
Am I turning from wrong and embracing the right?
Is that why there are tears in my eyes?

What a fool I have been to have lived all alone,
As a rule I have lived with no cares but my own.
I have needed no love and no love have I shown,
Is that why there are tears in my eyes?

Am I living again, am I living as when,
I was young with the trust of a child?
Am I learning to see why Christ anguished for me
And that through His death and life we're reconciled?

Am I turning around, am I changing my course?
Can God cancel my past? Can there be such divorce?
Am I being compelled by the Spirit's great force?
Is that why I am stunned with surprise
At these tears, tears of joy in my eyes?

That realization has to occur in the life of every person. Every person must recognize that he or she can't do it – they can't get to Heaven on their own. At the very moment you say that you can't, that's when God steps in and He does what you can't do. When I was pastor of the Hillview Baptist Chapel in Dalton, Georgia, as a 21-year-old pastor, there was a girl who came to that chapel virtually every Sunday. She struggled with sexual temptation and one day she was standing there at the door of that church with tears rolling down her face and she said to me, "I just can't live the Christian life." I said to her, "It's about time that you realized that you can't live it. The only way anybody can live the Christian life is for God to come and live it through them."

The problem with many of us is we think that somehow we can do enough good works to appease a holy God and that is what differentiates Christianity from every other religion on the face of the earth. Religion is man trying to do something for God. Christianity is God doing something for man that man cannot do for himself. It is only when you come to the realization that you can't but God can that you have hope to be saved. That is the revelation that you have to have at the front door.

CHAPTER EIGHT

Tell Me about Yourself

Galatians 3:2-5

As the pastor of a multi-staff church, I have often had to interview prospective employees. In each one of these incidents I've said to people, "Tell us a little bit about yourself." I like to hear people describe themselves. I ask them specific questions like, "How did you get saved? What's your home life like? How did you respond to your parents? When you were in college, who was your favorite professor and why?" These are important questions.

If you will permit me, I would like to interview you. I would like to ask you some questions and then ascertain if the way you respond measures up to the Word of God.

How Were You Saved? (v. 2)

There are many different ways that we can describe salvation. Theologians tell us that over five hundred things happen to a person the moment he receives the Lord Jesus Christ as his personal Saviour. Paul cuts to the chase in this verse and says that he only wants to know one thing. In effect, he is saying, "If I could know nothing else about you, here is what I want to know. How did you get the Spirit?" Out of all the ways you could describe salvation, this is a significant thing. Salvation at its core is a matter of receiving the Holy Spirit of God. There are many people who have walked away from a salvation proposal still not possessing the Spirit of God.

How many of you have led somebody to Christ that you really didn't lead to Christ, if you know what I mean. You may have gotten them to pray the sinner's prayer but subsequent history proves that whatever was going on at that time, that person did not get it because there was no invasion of his humanity by the sweet Spirit of God. When the Bible defines salvation, it really cuts to the chase by informing us: if you have the Spirit of God inside of you, then you are saved. If you do not have the Spirit of God inside of you, then you are not saved (cf. Romans 8:9).

Do you understand that this is the defining hallmark of a person who is really a child of God? This defines a person who really belongs to Jesus Christ. A person who really belongs to Jesus Christ will possess the Holy Spirit. The great thing about that Spirit is that when He moves into our hearts, He bears witness with us that we are the children of God. God's Spirit communicates with our spirit that we really do belong to Him – we know that we have passed from death unto life because of the Spirit that dwells within us.

The question that we ask ourselves is this: If the Spirit lives within the body of all believers, how do we get that Spirit?" That is the question under discussion in Verse 2. Paul lays out two possibilities on how they became saved. First, was it by keeping the rules of the Bible? Second, was it by hearing the gospel and responding to it in simple faith? Paul wants to know which way the person got saved. Was it by hearing the rules of the Bible and trying to keep them? Or was it by hearing the gospel message and responding to it in faith? What is the proper message of salvation?

We don't even have to wonder what the correct answer is because in 2:16 Paul has already answered it. You would have to be very bullheaded to miss the point of that verse. With great repetition, we see that no one is ever saved by the good works he performs. The only way a person can be justified, made right, in the eyes of God is to respond in faith to the simple gospel message. We are justified by faith – not by our own rule-keeping. That is the message of the whole book of Galatians

Yet as simple as this is, and as much as the Bible hammers it, unfortunately there are still many people who don't get it. Frequently, when I am on visitation and talk to people about their eternal destiny, it is amazing how many people will say, "I'm just trying to do the best I can," or "I'm trying to keep the Ten Commandments." Or they will say, "I'm not a bad person. I haven't murdered anybody. I'm as good as the next guy." But no one is ever going to make it into Heaven by keeping the rules of the Bible. People only get to Heaven by responding to the gospel message in simple childlike faith.

There is a story of a Native American who was trying to tell somebody how he became saved. He put some leaves on the ground in a circle and then he poured gasoline on those leaves and lit those leaves on fire so there was a circle of fire on the ground. In the middle of that circle, he placed a caterpillar and that caterpillar would start to move toward the fire and then back up and move in a different direction. This caterpillar attempted several times to escape the fire. Finally, after a few seconds of desperation, that caterpillar raised its head and when it did, the Indian reached down his finger for the caterpillar to crawl out and said to his friends, "That is how I got saved."

Before you and I were saved, we used to think that if we just went in a certain direction, we could save ourselves, only to discover that all of those paths led to the fire of Hell. When we realized there was nothing we could do, we looked up to God in simple childlike faith and when we did, that's when the hand of God reached down for us. That's how we become born again.

A physician in the greater Chicago received a call in the middle of the night that a boy had been involved in a horrific accident and was not expected to live. He needed emergency surgery if he was going to survive. Dr. Winters was one of the most accomplished physicians in the type of surgery the boy needed in the whole city of Chicago. He was asked to get to the hospital as quickly as possible to perform the necessary surgery to save this boy's life. From Dr. Winter's house, the closest route to the hospital was through some of the roughest sections of Chicago. When Dr. Winders got to one intersection and stopped at a stop sign, a fellow opened the door of Dr. Winter's car and said, "Sorry, buddy, I need your car." Dr. Winters tried to explain but before he could explain what was happening, the man had already grabbed him and thrown him from the car and jumped in the car and sped off.

Dr. Winters caught a taxi and tried to make it to the hospital but it took him much longer to get there. When he arrived, he was informed that thirty minutes before his arrival the young man had died. Dr. Winters said, "Is there any member of the family that I can talk to and apologize to?" They said there was only one family member, the father of the young boy, and he was down at the end of the hall in the waiting room. Dr. Winters went down the hall to see the man, and to his horror, when he walked into the waiting room, he found that the father of the boy was the one who had pulled him from his vehicle. Dr. Winters realized that the father was trying to get there as fast as he could so that somehow he could make a difference, and in his effort to be there, he had robbed his son of the only hope of being saved. He had thrown the great physician out of the way.

Every single time people try to work their way to Heaven through their own efforts, when they try to accomplish salvation through their own means, they have thrown the Great Physician out of the way. He is the only one who can truly bring salvation to those who are critically ill. There is only one way a person can be saved and that is by responding in simple faith to the Gospel, and if you are trusting in anything else – whether it be baptism, church membership, or your own efforts – you will not make it. There is only one way that a person receives the Gospel and it is not by keeping rules; it is rather by responding in simple faith to the glorious gospel message. That's how we get the Spirit. So I ask you,

"How were you saved?"

How Are You Sanctified? (v. 3)

After we become saved, there are still some rough edges that need to be knocked off; there is still some work that needs to be done. At the moment you and I trust the Lord Jesus Christ as our personal Saviour, we are saved from the penalty of sin but we are not saved from the power of sin. At the very moment we become saved, we have all the power that we need to have victory every day, but the problem with many of us is we don't avail ourselves of that power. So consequently, though we have trusted the Lord Jesus Christ as our personal Saviour, although we have the capacity, we don't avail ourselves of that capacity to live a victorious Christian life.

Therefore, some people become saved and do not have immediate victory over enslaving habits. Some of the things that they used to do in their pre-Christian days carry over into their Christian days, and sometimes people struggle to live a victorious Christian life. New Christians do not always avail themselves of all the power that they have to live victoriously. But, praise God, when some people become saved, they immediately quit enslaving habits. For example, my dad was an alcoholic, and from the very moment that my dad trusted the Lord Jesus Christ as his personal Saviour to this very hour, he has never touched a drop of alcohol again.

I have a friend who was a hippie strung out on pot, and he stumbled into a Baptist church and trusted the

Lord Jesus Christ as his personal Saviour on a Wednesday night. From that moment to this, he has never taken another hit of marijuana again. Some people become saved and immediately cease with all enslaving habits. Unfortunately, for some people, complete victory does not come in all areas of life instantaneously. There are some things that people still struggle with. For example, my dad immediately gave up alcohol but it was a long time before my dad gave up cigarettes. He struggled with that addiction for some time.

Why do some people possess instantaneous victory while others struggle? And why do some people have victory in some areas but not in other areas? The reason that Christians still sometimes battle enslaving habits is because they have a fundamental misunderstanding about how victory comes. That is what the apostle Paul implies in verse 3 when he asks, "Are you so foolish?" The word *foolish* translates the normal Greek word for *wisdom* and puts a negation in front of it. Paul is saying, "How do you have no understanding? How is it that you have no perception about what needs to be done? Why is it that your thinking is fundamentally flawed?" There is something that we have not perceived. You have not perceived how it is that a person becomes sanctified, for sanctification happens just like salvation happens.

The Christian is in a pursuit of perfection. He is in pursuit of living a victorious life that does not succumb to the enslaving habits of his pre-Christian days. He is in the process of bringing himself to full maturity, but how does that happen? It does not happen by grit and determination. Salvation is always by simple childlike faith in the Gospel of Jesus. We understand this when it comes to the penalty of sin, but sometimes we do not understand this when it comes to having power over sin in our daily lives. We still think that through grit and determination, we are going to be right with God.

I have this enslaving habit and I determine that I am not going to do that anymore. I have made up my mind. I'm going to pull myself up and by sheer grit and determination, I'm not going to do that again - only to find that three days later, I am doing the very same thing again. I have failed to understand that people get sanctified the same way people get saved. They get victory over the power of sin the same way they got victory over the penalty of sin and that is by faith in God rather than by human effort and achievement. You cannot save yourself from the power of sin any more than you can save yourself from the penalty of sin. You are not made perfect by the flesh - you are rather made perfect by faith in God.

Vain and fruitless is the struggle;
Self to sanctify,
God alone can cleanse and keep you;
Wherefore should you try?

Oh, the needless cares and conflicts;
You had never known,
If you'd learned the simple lesson,
Let yourself alone.

Let your eyes keep looking upward;
Cease to look within,
All your introspection
Cannot cleanse a single sin.

You will find your best self-effort vain;
And worse than vain,
As the touch of soiled fingers,
Only leaves a stain.

Leave your rights and reputation;
In the Master's hands,
What, though men misunderstand you;
Jesus understands.

He can shield and vindicate you;
Right your every wrong,
Turn the hate of men and devils,
Into joy and song.

All the springs of power and blessing,
Flow from yonder throne;
If you'd have them fill and flood you,
Let yourself alone.

My associate pastor in Philadelphia was a great, godly man. Many years before Pastor Al Johnson trusted the Lord Jesus Christ as his personal Saviour, he was a famous Jazz musician in the city of Philadelphia. He played numerous gigs and could really tickle the ivories of a piano. One day, Al Johnson had a heart attack and was forced out of work. He had to lay on his back recuperating. He had several cousins who were saved and were taking classes at Philadelphia College of the Bible. They said, "Al, since you are sick, could you help us study for our Bible test?" They knew exactly what they were doing. Al would read the questions and they would answer them. What does the Bible teach about human nature? Answer: All have sinned and come short of the glory of God. What does the Bible teach is the remedy for sin? Answer: God commended his love toward us in that while we were yet sinners, Christ died for us. How does a person receive the gift of salvation? And they would go on and quote verses about being justified by faith alone.

Al Johnson, in helping them study for their Bible test, came under deep conviction while lying on that bed of affliction. There was nothing he could do in that hour except look up to Heaven. He received the Lord Jesus Christ as his personal Saviour on the bed of affliction. After he became saved, God healed him and he was able to go back to work. Al Johnson had an enslaving habit to nicotine - he loved to smoke. He said that he could not tell you how many times he went to the toilet and took those cigarettes and threw them into the toilet and said, "Never again. I'm through. I'm not going to smoke again." Then he'd go outside and would be next to somebody who was smoking, and he said he was just like a bloodhound and would say, "God doesn't want me to be fanatical about this," and would start smoking all over again.

He said finally one day after all of those months of trying to quit through grit and determination, he fell on his face before God and said, "Oh, God, I want to be rid of this filthy habit. God, I can't have victory. Please take this from me." And he said at that exact moment, the desire to smoke was gone. No tapering off, no gum, no patch - total victory by trusting God to do for him what he was unable to do for himself. I think this is the problem with many Christians. Some people are trying to do the ten-step program to get victory in some area, but God is looking for us to take one step, one step to Him.

As you trust God and as you depend upon Him, He changes human desires. The Bible says to trust in the Lord and He will give you the desires of your heart (cf. Psalm 37:4). This does not mean if I want a motorcycle, I trust in God and He gives me a motorcycle. It rather means that when I trust God, He puts in me the desires that He wants me to have. I will begin to desire the things that are compatible with His Word - God will change my "want to." You say, "I don't want to go to Church." Trust in the Lord, and you will want to go to church. As you trust in God, illicit desires are taken away and replaced with healthy desires that come from God. You and I need to put our faith in a divine Saviour who is able to change internally the way we desire to do things.

This is the big difference between legalism and true sanctification. *Legalism* is not merely trusting yourself for salvation through rules; it is also trusting yourself for sanctification through rules. Let's say, for example, that

I have a problem with anger. That is an illicit desire. The wrath of men never works the righteousness of God. I can put up some rules in my life and eradicate all the things that irritate me. But all I've done is cage that anger and limited its opportunity to come to the surface. It is caging the animal but it has not destroyed the animal.

For example, I may have lust. I may have this lustful urge that I desire to eliminate. So, I do things in my life like refrain from movies and carefully monitor my TV set. This causes the lustful urges to be caged, but the lust is still there resident within me. I have fenced it to some degree with certain rules but the lust is still there waiting to leap out at any moment when I least expect it. When I avail myself of the grace of God, however, I do not merely cage those animals - I kill those animals. Those things no longer have an ability to leap out for they no longer exist. God has come in, and by my trust in Him, He has completely changed those desires and replaced them with wholesome desires. Victory has taken place - not through human effort but rather through faith in God. The same way that I am saved (by faith) is the same way that I am sanctified (by faith).

How Are You Successful? (v. 4)

The word *suffer* in verse four carries the idea of *allow* - have you allowed these things? It carries with it the idea of experience - have you experienced so many things in vain? In other words, when you and I try to sanctify ourselves, when we try to pull ourselves up by our own boot straps and say, "I'm not going to do that anymore," when that is our method of sanctification, the apostle Paul asks us a question. Let me paraphrase it for you: "How's that working out for you?"

When you say, "This is the way I'm going to get right. I'm just going to vow that I'm not going to do it anymore" and I vow all of these things and through my human effort, I just say, "I'm not going to do that," let me ask you a question: How is that working out for you? Is that successful? Or if you are honest with yourself, is that vain? Paul implies that this method of sanctification is never successful. It does really work at all. To the contrary, it is exasperating.

How many of you have infuriated yourself? How many of you have said, "Hey, I'm not going to do that again" and there you go, doing it again? You keep exasperating yourself because you are trying to sanctify yourself instead of letting God do it. Here is the only way that self-help is beneficial - it's beneficial when it helps you realize that it is not beneficial. When you try to do it yourself, you fail and become exasperated, and because you are exasperated, you look to God. The only way self-help is beneficial is that it deliberately exasperates us so that we will look to God, which is what we should have done initially.

When I was a sophomore in Bible college, I knew it all. After all, I had passed two semesters of Bible doctrines class. Thus, when a famous evangelist wrote something in a periodical with which I disagreed, I wrote him a letter and said, "I disagree with you on this and here is the reason why." I then quoted one of my professors.

Well the famous evangelist wrote me back, which I expected him to do, but he also sent a copy of his letter to the professor I had quoted, which I did not expect him to do. A couple of days after I had received my letter, I went to Dr. Phillip's office and when I did, he said, "Oh, Brother Amsbaugh, I am so glad you stopped by. Have a seat." I sat down and he said, "I just want to tell you one thing. I'm not going to talk about what is in the letter or what's not in the letter; I just want to tell you something. Don't be a letter-writing preacher."

That is the only piece of advice he gave me. He said, "If you respond in print to everybody that you disagree with, you will be writing letters the rest of your life." If I could paraphrase him, he said, "Writing letters - how's that working out for you?" Well, it didn't work out. I didn't straighten out the evangelist; the evangelist tried to straighten me out. And instead of anything going well in my life, it went terrible. I realized that it was pretty foolish to write that letter. Letter writing was not working out too well.

Dr. Phillips said this after he was done: "This will be a beneficial experience if you learn something from it. If you walk out of my office today and have learned something about letter-writing, the rest of your ministry will be helped. If you will forever change, this will be a milestone day in your life." Well, I never wrote another letter again so that day was a very good day. It was a bad day - I was completely exasperated, but it was a good day in the sense that I learned a valuable lesson.

Something like that is being said in verse four. If

you're tried to pull yourself up by your own boot straps and tried to make yourself right by just your own human self-effort, only to fall flat on your face, and it's not working out too well for you, then you have learned a valuable lesson. You can't make yourself better - only God can make you better. Therefore, if you've learned something from your self-improvement plan, you're well-served.

The story was told of a little boy who was climbing a ladder. He was halfway up the ladder when his mommy saw him. There was a guy on top of the roof who was doing construction. The mother said to the construction worker, "Look at my son." The construction worker, however, silenced the mother. He got the little boy's attention and said, "Come on, boy, keep climbing. Look at me. Keep your eyes on me. Keep climbing higher." Within a few steps, the little boy was safely in the arms of the construction worker who brought the boy down to his mother. The construction worker knew that if the little boy had looked down, he was going to fall, but as long as the boy kept his eyes up, he was going to succeed. The problem is that you and I are looking to a very inadequate agent to take ourselves higher. We need to keep our eyes focused on God. When we keep our eyes focused on God, we can climb to new heights because of whom we are focused on. This is the only way that you and I can be successful. The Psalmist said, "I will lift up mine eyes unto the hills, from whence cometh my help. My help *cometh* from the LORD, which made heaven and earth."

(Psalm 121:1-2) Experience teaches us that the only way we can be better in our Christian life is by faith.

How Are You Supernatural? (v. 5)

When you and I look to God for salvation and sanctification, at that moment, we are looking to a God who does miracles. Our God is a miracle-working God. This is the same God who stepped out of eternity past and said, "Let there be light" and there was light. God calls things into existence out of nothing; He is a miracle-working God.

When Jesus walked this earth, He multiplied food. He turned water into wine. He miraculously healed infirmed individuals. Jesus raised people from the dead. He walked on water. Our God is a miracle-working God. He's not limited by the natural; He conquers the natural. God is not bound by natural laws; He is a supernatural God. This is the same God who ministers the Spirit to us. Therefore, it makes sense to trust Him for sanctification rather than yourself.

Years ago, when we were living in Philadelphia, I decided that I was going to help Karen by making one meal per week. I went to the cookbook and found extravagant dishes. I wasn't content to throw hotdogs in the pot and let them boil - I wanted to do something big. Finally, after about three weeks of this, the kids said, "Mommy, could you please not let Daddy cook anymore." Here's the deal - they understood what daddy's abilities were in the kitchen, and they said, "Mommy, could you keep him from himself?" When you put your trust in yourself for sanctification, you are putting your trust in something that is natural, but when you put your trust in God for sanctification, you are putting your trust in something that is light years beyond you. You are putting your trust in Someone who is supernatural, and there's a big difference.

In counseling, people often say, "Well, that's just the way I am." We come from a German background and the people in our family have always been hotheads; that's just the way I am." For example, my Mom was from West Virginia and she is a great cook. She is insulted if you don't eat everything on your plate and then some. That's why my dad weighs what he weighs. Now I can explain my gluttony away by saying, "Hey, that's just the way I am. That's the way I was brought up."

My dad was raised in the home of an alcoholic. That may be true, but that has nothing to do with victory because sanctification is not a natural thing. You don't want to live a life that can be explained by you. The same God who turned water into wine is able to turn beer into furniture.

For example, we often hear talk that homosexuals are born this way, and we fundamentalists want to fight that. To me, it doesn't matter if you are born that way - all you prove is that you have the nature of Adam in you. Even if you were born that way, all you've proven is that you a sinner by birth. So what? We are all sinners by birth. What you need is the grace of God to overcome what you are.

Years ago, there was a lawyer in Philadelphia, a

drunken lawyer, who was confronted by a business-man, and the businessman asked him if he was saved. The drunken lawyer admitted that he was not and the businessman asked him one question: "Why not?" The lawyer thought for a good long period of time and didn't have a good answer so there in Philadelphia Center City, that lawyer trusted the Lord Jesus Christ as his personal Saviour. That drunken lawyer's name was C. I. Scofield. Many of you may use a Scofield Reference Bible. Do you know what God wants to do in all of us? He wants to take us from our dependency on the bottle to making us addicted to the Bible. The only way you can get out of debauchery and be a living copy of the Word of God is by allowing the grace of God to become operative in your life. That's what takes us out of the natural and puts us into the realm of the supernatural. God wants your life to be a living miracle.

When I was sixteen years old, I had a doctor walk into my hospital room and tell me that by the time I was eigh-teen, I was going to be in a wheelchair. And by the time I was thirty-five, I was going to be bedridden. At the time of that diagnosis, I could not take more than ten steps without falling down. Mom and Dad, however, believed that God could do a miracle. They asked numerous pas-tors in our hometown to come over to our house and pray that God would make Jeff Amsbaugh a miracle. As far as I know, in all the history of Friedreich's Ataxia, there has only been one person cured of that disease, and I am that person. I'm telling you that I am a living miracle.

On a spiritual plane, we all are crippled and cannot

take ten steps without falling down. You know what we need, don't you? We need a miracle, and the miracle that we need is no less miraculous than the miracle that I needed as a crippled teenager. Indeed, I think the miracle to conquer sin is greater than the one I received as a teen. Oliver Greene said that the greatest miracle since the virgin birth is the new birth. There is a lot of validity to that. It's not within us to live what needs to be lived. We have to have complete dependency on God. We feel that we can manage our lives quite independent of God. But the fact is that we all need a miracle to live a victorious life. Yet, somehow, we want to get our humanness into it and humanness always fails. I heard a famous preacher say that if the devil can get you to do righteousness in the flesh, it is just a step until he can get you to do unrighteousness in the flesh. You and I should not do anything in the flesh - we should do everything in the power of the Spirit of God.

CHAPTER NINE

The Exclusive Inclusion of Christianity

Galatians 3:6-9

In the previous section, we saw that men are justified and saved by faith. In Verse 2, Paul asks the question, ". . . Received ye the Spirit by the works of the law, or by the hearing of faith?" And the obvious answer is you received the Spirit by receiving the gospel by faith. You heard the gospel and you put your faith in it, and that's what caused the Holy Spirit to move inside you. You did not work to become acceptable to God and thereby received the Spirit. You didn't receive the Spirit by keeping a bunch of rules, no matter how good those rules were. You received the Spirit because there was one day when you heard the gospel and you put your trust in it - that's how you became saved.

That is not only how you are saved, but it is how you are sanctified (v. 3). You begin in the Spirit, but you are not made perfect by the works of the flesh. You don't reach maturity by works any more than you are saved by works. You are sanctified the same way - by putting your faith in God and allowing God to sanctify you. God is the one who not only gives you the power over the penalty of sin but He is also the one who gives you the power over the daily defilement issues that you confront when you are tempted.

So we are saved and sanctified by faith, and we are successful by faith (v. 4). If you don't trust God for your sanctification, you're going to be a failure. If you try to muster up enough sweat to be a spiritual person, you are going to be a failure, and your Christian life will always be one of repentance and sorrow, and of being unsuccessful because you're not good enough to live the Christian life. You need God to live it through you.

So you are saved by faith, sanctified by faith, successful by faith, and supernatural by faith. The reason you have to trust God is because God is a miracle-working God. God is a God who does the impossible and being good is impossible apart from Him. It's not in us to do right We need the supernatural power of God. And all of this is accomplished by faith.

We are saved by faith, sanctified by faith, successful by faith, and supernatural by faith. We live the Christian life by faith and without faith it is impossible to please God. We live by faith rather than by sight. To help us out with this, Paul gives an illustration.

The Illustration (v. 6)

The Bible states, "Even as Abraham believed God, and it was accounted to him for righteousness." In a Jewish lore, if there was anybody who could work his way to Heaven, it would have been Abraham. Abraham was the dean of Judaism. Abraham was the father of the nation. In a word, Abraham was "the man." So, if there was anybody who could by his own effort be saved and sanctified and successful and supernatural merely by human effort, it would have been Abraham.

Let's trace some things that Abraham did. Abraham

was living with his idolatrous father in Ur of the Chaldees. He didn't come from a believing home; he came from the home of an idolater. His dad worshipped idols. God, however, came to him in his home of dysfunction and told him to leave without giving him a specific destination of arrival. Abraham went out and he didn't even know where he was going. He broke with that idolatrous background and left it behind.

He took his nephew, Lot, with him. A division developed, however, between Lot's herdsmen and Abraham's herdsmen, and Abraham had to break with more family members. Some of us accept Christ but we're scared to push it too hard because it might lead to a break with some of our family members. Abraham said the friction was too great so he told Lot they were going to separate. After Lot left, he got himself in a bunch of trouble, which you would expect him to do, and Abraham had to go up against four powerful nations and defeat them with an army of his own servants to rescue Lot.

After that was all over, the king of Sodom offers Abraham a gift. But Abraham refuses to take the gift and rather pays tithes to the king of Salem. Abraham went to the place God told him to go, separated from the people God told him to separate from, fought the people God told him to fight, and paid the people God told him to pay. Yet none of that is what gave Abraham a proper standing before God. What gave Abraham a proper standing before God was one day Abraham heard God's revelation and put his faith in it.

There is only one reason that any of us have righteousness credited to our account and that is because we have placed faith in the revelation of God. If anybody could have claimed works as a means of justification, Abraham would have been that man.

Abraham's morality was on a much higher plane than yours or mine, and yet Abraham was justified by one reason and one reason alone - he put faith in the Word of God. The only way that you and I are saved is the same way. If Abraham can't make it by his works, then certainly you and I can't make it by our works. If anybody in the world illustrates the fact that you are justified by faith and faith alone, Abraham is that man. He is the pinnacle picture of the fact that there is no other way to please God other than by a life of faith.

The Insight (v. 7)

Because this is true of Abraham, we know something: "Know ye therefore that they which are of faith, the same are the children of Abraham." The predominant characteristic of the life of Abraham was not his ability to fight and conquer people. His predominant characteristic was not even the fact that he was a separatist or the fact that he was a giver. The predominant characteristic of the life of Abraham was that he was a man of faith. Whatever Abraham did, it was an act of faith. This was the prevailing, predominant characteristic of his life. As a matter of fact, in verse nine, he is called "faithful Abraham." That was his defining character trait.

Nobody acts more like Abraham than the person who is exercising faith. If you want to act like Abraham, if you want to be known as a little Abraham, then the only way that you can do that is to be characterized by a life of faith because Abraham's predominant characteristic was faith. There is nobody upon the face of the earth who shows that he's more like Abraham than a person who exercises faith.

My mom has one biological daughter and one daughter by marriage. My sister, my mom's biological daughter, acts nothing like my mother. She doesn't keep a home like my mother, she doesn't practice organization like my mother, and she doesn't manage things like my mother. My sister is nothing like my mother. Good, bad, or indifferent, my sister doesn't act like my mom. My wife, Karen, however, acts like my mother. The way she organizes a home, the way she raises her kids, the strict disciplinarian that she is - Karen acts like my mom.

If you were to walk into Debbie's home, you would say, "This is nothing like Janet Amsbaugh's house." If you were to walk into my wife's home, you would say, "This is just like Janet Amsbaugh's house." My wife is not a biological descendant of Janet Amsbaugh, but she acts like Janet Amsbaugh. On the other hand, there is a girl who is a biological descendant of Janet Amsbaugh but acts nothing like her. More than once my mother has said, "Karen acts more like my kid than my kid acts like my kid."

That is what Paul is saying here. When people exercise faith, they look more like they are Abraham's kid than people who are physical descendants of Abraham and exercise no faith. According to the Bible, what really makes you look like you are a descendant of Abraham is when you put faith in the good news of God - that's what makes you really look Jewish.

It's funny sometimes that people who are steeped in Judaism are scared to put faith in the gospel because they are scared it will insult their Jewish heritage. There is nothing that makes you look more like you came from Abraham than when you exercise faith.

If you have girls, you have probably seen *Anne of Green Gables*. *Anne of Green Gables* tells about an orphan who comes to live with two old people in Canada. She always looks for a kindred spirit because she is an orphan. She doesn't have any genetic connection with which to bond so she is always looking for a kindred spirit. What Paul is saying to these Jewish people is that it is more important to have a kindred Spirit with Abraham than to share genes with Abraham. It is better for someone in heart to agree with the principles of Abraham than to just be a genetic descendant of Abraham. He is saying that nobody acts more like Abraham than the people who are willing to put faith in the revelation of God.

Kindred spirits are closer than kindred genes. This is the insight that God wants us to have. It is more Jewish to be a man of faith than to be circumcised or have a bar mitzvah. The illustration is that Abraham is a man of faith. The insight is that I am more like Abraham when I exercise faith.

The Interracial (v. 8)

The Bible says, "And the scripture, foreseeing that God would justify the heathen through faith, preached before the gospel unto Abraham, *saying*, In thee shall all nations be blessed." If it is true that nobody can act more like Abraham than by putting faith in the revelation of God, then that means the heathen can be saved. The heathen can act Jewish. Gentile people can act Jewish by exercising faith in the revelation of God. They can look more like Abraham's seed if they exercise faith and one doesn't have to be of a certain genetic descent for this to happen. It can happen to anybody, to any heathen. After all, it's not a matter of coming from the right stock - we all came from the wrong stock - it's a matter of putting faith in the Word of God.

As early as Genesis, we see that the gospel was intended to be an interracial thing. Abraham's faith was supposed to be an example to the whole world and to all nations upon the face of the earth. Even Abraham himself was saved from the home of an idolater. It wasn't like Abraham was practicing Judaism when God showed up. He wasn't running to the synagogues - he was in the home of a no-good idolater and God appeared to him and gave him good news. He accepted it and put his faith in it, and that's what made him a child of God. In the same way, it doesn't matter what home you came from - what matters is that you have put faith in God's Word.

Aren't you glad that God doesn't hold us responsible for the homes we come from? Probably some of us could write a book on the dysfunction that we experienced growing up. But the Word of God came to us, and we put our faith in it and as heathen people, God counted us righteous. Abraham, this child from the home of an idolater, sets an example for the whole world. This is the way God wants everybody upon the face of the earth to know. What matters is that we put faith in the revelation of God. The only reason Abraham was saved was not because of his gene pool - it was because God gave him good news and he believed it.

The only way a person is saved is through the gospel. The great thing about the gospel is that it is available to any idolater who will take it. It doesn't matter what your background is. God will save you.

The gospel is both an inclusive thing but at the same time it is an exclusive thing. It's inclusive in the sense that it reaches out to people all over the world. God will save people tonight in Africa if they will put faith in Him. God will save people in Asia if they will put faith in Him. God will save people in Europe if they will put faith in him. God will save people in South America and Central America and even North America if they will put faith in Him. There is no nation upon the face of the earth that God says He won't save. God has an open immigration policy. There are no fences, no towers, and no surveillance camera. God doesn't say, "Watch out! Here come those Japanese" or "Watch out! Here come those Mexicans." God is willing to take anybody from any ethnic background and in that sense Christianity is very inclusive.

In another sense, however, it is exclusive because though God will take people from any nation, He won't take them any way. The only way they can come is by faith in the gospel and in that sense, Christianity is very exclusive. In many people's minds, the Christian message is bigoted because it is narrow. But understand that we're not discriminating against people's culture - we want every Middle Eastern person to be saved. We're not discriminating against people's culture. What we are practicing is theological discrimination because there are certain belief systems that are sending people to Hell. Love for people of various cultures can best be shown by offering them the exclusive good news of Christianity, which will include them in the family of God. All the people of the world have to come by the narrow gate that Jesus talked about.

When I was young, there was a swimming pool club in our hometown and Dad wanted to join it. We filled out all the paperwork and sent it to this place and paid the fee, and they said we needed to have an on-site interview. We went for the on-site interview but they didn't ask us any questions, they just looked at us and said, "Okay, you're good." When we went home, we knew exactly what had happened. They were making sure we weren't black. That's what you call bigotry. We don't do that with Christianity. You are a candidate for Christianity regardless of your skin color.

Let's suppose that my family is African American and we went to that pool club and they said, "You can all come in" and my dad said, "There is just one problem - we don't have the money." If those people said, "I'm sorry, you can't join if you don't have the money," at that point, they wouldn't have been discriminating or bigoted - they would have just been functioning according to their rules. Salvation cost the blood of the Lord Jesus Christ and when people are excluded, they are not excluded because of their skin color - they are excluded because they haven't come by way of the price. They haven't come by that salvation that is exclusively purchased through the work of Christ. The offer is extended to all but people have to accept God's terms of payment. People may say that salvation is inclusive or exclusive but it's both. It will include anybody who will come by way of the cross, but if you don't come by the way of the cross, you can't come in.

The Inclusion (v. 9)

"So then they which be of faith are blessed with faithful Abraham." Whoever that person is who exercises faith, he's in along with Abraham. Heaven is going to be a culturally diverse place. Revelation 7:9 states, "After this I beheld, and, lo, a great multitude, which no man could number, of all nations, and kindreds, and people, and tongues, stood before the throne, and before the Lamb, clothed with white robes, and palms in their hands;" If you have a bigoted mindset and believe that people of divergent races should not live in the same neighborhood, you will not like Heaven. If racial diversity is what lowers property value, then Heaven is not as glorious as we have been told. When we all get to Heaven, it is going to be one diverse neighborhood standing around the throne. People of all nations and kindreds will be there.

Let us not go to Heaven with bloody hands because we ceased to warn, ceased to tell, and ceased to share because we were too concerned about being accepted by an American society that will split Hell wide open. Let's go after these people with the exclusive message that will make them included them in the redeemed throng of Heaven.

CHAPTER TEN

Four Problems with a Works Salvation

Galatians 3:10-14

I think all of us in our lives may have had a brilliant idea only to discover after we talked to people about it that wasn't so brilliant after all. I think anybody who is married can relate to this. You come home and you have a great idea and you talk to your spouse about it, and you discover it's not such a great idea after all.

Most people, when you talk to them on the street, are trying to work their way to Heaven. On visitation virtually every week we discover people who believe that salvation is earned by good works. The vast majority of people are trying to work their way to Heaven. Indeed, I think this is the fundamental difference between Christianity and all the rest of the religions in the world. *Religion* is man trying to do something to gain the smile of God. *Christianity* is God doing something for man that man can't do for himself. That's the difference between religion and true faith.

At first glance, it might seem that working your way to Heaven is a good idea. After all, there is an emphasis on morality, there is an emphasis on doing good, and certainly, if you are justified by faith, you can live any way you want to. It almost seems that justification by faith is against morality to some degree - it doesn't encourage people to live right, so the argument goes.

But if that person thought it through, he or she

would realize that it's a dumb idea. Working your way to Heaven is not as smart as you think it is. There are four reasons why we can say it is not smart to believe in a works salvation.

It contradicts the Bible (vv. 10-12)

This is fundamental. Anytime a person says, "I'm just going to try, by my own morality and my own good works, to work my way to Heaven," that person puts himself or herself in contradiction to the Word of God, which says you can't work your way to Heaven. Notice that verse nine ends with the word *blessed*. If you exercise faith, you are going to be, according to verse nine, blessed with believing Abraham. Verse 10 starts with a curse. In verse 9, you have the blessing of God and that blessing is put in juxtaposition to the curse of God. Immediately, if you are familiar with your Old Testament, that should take you back to Deuteronomy 27 and 28 where the children of Israel were on two mountains - six tribes were on Mount Gerizim and six tribes were on Mount Ebal - and the law was read to them and they said, "We'll do what the law says and be blessed and if we don't keep the law, we will be cursed." Six tribes shouted the blessings and six tribes shouted the curses, and those blessings and curses were shouted in juxtaposition one to the other.

A person might be tempted to say something like this: Even in the Old Testament, back to Deuteronomy 27 and 28, the people of God shouted all of those blessings and said they would obey and so be blessed of

God. How in the world could anybody say that the law is not the means of blessing? When the law was given, the people said, "If we do these things, we're going to be blessed." That's a good question. Didn't the law at its very inception promise blessing to the people who kept it? How then can you say that if you do what the law says you are going to be cursed?

Let's examine that thought under the microscope of Scripture. Go back to Deuteronomy 27:26. This is the first quote that Paul gives us here. It says, "Cursed *be* he that confirmeth not *all* the words of this law to do them. And all the people shall say, Amen." Isn't it true that the law promised blessing? Yes, it is true that the law promised blessing but what was the condition to receiving the blessing and not receiving the curse? The condition was you had to do all of it. So the law did promise a blessing but the only way the law could be a source of blessing was for one to keep the entire law of God perfectly.

God doesn't serve up His law cafeteria style. God's law is an indivisible unit. The Word of God is all or nothing. That being the case, if you keep every single bit of the law and yet offend in just one little bitty point, you are guilty of the whole thing. If the only way you can be blessed by keeping the law is to keep it in its entirety, how many people are going to be blessed by means of the law? The answer, of course, is none, because nobody is perfect. And because nobody is perfect, nobody can be blessed by the law because to be blessed by the law, you have to keep the entire thing and no one is capable of doing that.

It is true that the law promised blessing but it only promised blessing to those who kept it perfectly and the first quote from Deuteronomy proves this to be true. You may say: If a person is not blessed by keeping the law, then how can a person be blessed? Paul's second quote takes us to Habakkuk 2:4. If the law puts me under a curse and condemns me, how in the world am I going to be able to live? Habakkuk 2:4 answers the question. "Behold, his soul *which* is lifted up is not upright in him: but the just shall live by his faith." The first quote from Deuteronomy 27 says if I want to be justified by the law, I have to keep the whole thing. Obviously, no one is able to keep the whole thing so that means all mankind is under a curse because all mankind lacks perfection. How then am I going to be justified in the eyes of God?

The only way that I can be justified in the eyes of God is not by keeping the law; therefore, I have to be justified by another means and the Bible says that the way I am justified is by my faith. So it is not by keeping the law; it is rather by exercising faith in the revelation of God. That is how I am justified - not by rule keeping but rather by my faith. The third quotation that Paul gives is from Leviticus 18:5. The Bible says, "Ye shall therefore keep my statutes, and my judgments: which if a man do, he shall live in them: I am the LORD." Once again, the Bible is saying you can't live by the law because if you are going to live by the law, you would have to do it all perfectly.

We are seeing now that there are two ways of salvation in the Old Testament that are put into juxtaposition one to another. In both Deuteronomy and in Leviticus we are seeing that the only way the law can be a means of salvation is for one to keep that law perfectly. Obviously, no one can keep the law perfectly; therefore, the only way that I can be justified, according to the Bible, is by means of faith because I am not adequate enough to keep the entire law of God. If the Bible is making it clear that only perfect people can get to Heaven by keeping the law and it equally makes it clear that nobody is perfect, then I have to put faith in God - faith in what God can do for me - rather than what I can do for myself. It immediately becomes clear that if I am trying to work my way to Heaven, I am not in agreement with the Word of God.

Three times in this passage - by quoting Deuteronomy, by quoting Habakkuk, and by quoting Leviticus - Paul hammers the fact that trying to get to Heaven by your own good works is contrary to Biblical revelation.

How will any of us stand before God and explain to Him why we disagreed with Him about the way to get to Heaven. When you say that you can work your way to Heaven, what you are really saying is that you don't believe the Bible. The Bible says you get to Heaven by faith and not by works. So when a person says, "I think I will just work my way to Heaven," that person is simply contradicting the Bible.

It nullifies the cross (v. 13)

We have already seen that it is impossible for us to save ourselves because nobody is perfect. If the law couldn't save us, if all that it can do is curse us, how in the world are we going to save ourselves? We can't save ourselves. If we are going to be saved, who is going to do it? Obviously, somebody is going to have to save us because we are not capable of saving ourselves. The only thing that the law can do is condemn us but it can't save us. Someone has to redeem us from that curse and that someone else is Christ. The law condemned us and put us under a curse but Christ became a curse for us at the cross.

Here we are seeing that salvation is not merely justification - where God declares us to be righteous - but salvation is also redemption; it is God buying us out of a marketplace of sin. We are just as much a slave to sin as any slave on a plantation was owned by the master. Sin has our number, and Christ came to the auction block and paid the price at Calvary to get us out of sin. The only way this could be done was for someone outside the curse to do it. Slaves can't redeem slaves; free men have to redeem slaves. Since we were in bondage to sin, we couldn't pay for our salvation. I can't pay for your salvation; someone outside of the arena of sin bondage had to come and buy us out of that marketplace, and that is exactly what Jesus did. When Jesus hung on that tree, the Bible says He became a curse for us.

"For is a mighty important preposition. I went to a Christian school where everybody who went out for the basketball team made the basketball team. Consequently, I played end, guard, and tackle: I sat at the end of the bench, guarded the water bottles, and if anybody tried to get them, I would tackle them. If we were ahead by fifty points and there were three seconds left in the game, the coach would look way down at the end of the bench and he would say, "Amsbaugh, go in for Smith." I knew what *for* meant. That was the word meaning substitution - I was going in *for* Smith; I was taking Smith's place.

I am under the curse and the bondage of sin. Jesus comes in for Amsbaugh. He pays the penalty that Amsbaugh deserves to pay. I can pay for my sins in Hell for all eternity or Jesus can come and pay for those sins. Jesus stepped in and took my Hell for me when He died on that cross - He paid the price for my sin. When Jesus died on that cross, He literally suffered our curse, He literally suffered our judgment, and He literally suffered our damnation. When Jesus hung on that cross, He was damned by God for you and for me. We are under the damnation, the judgment, the condemnation, the curse, and then Jesus comes and He becomes cursed of God so that you and I will not have to be cursed by God.

This is a great offense to many Jewish people because Jewish people think the Messiah is a source of blessing and a source of triumph. They think when He comes, He will be coming as God's victor and He will have all the blessing of God upon Him. In their mind, Messiah could not actually come under the judgment of God - that was an absolutely foreign concept to the Jewish mind, and to this day, many can't absorb it.

How in the world could someone so perfect have God damn Him; how could that be true? The point is He did not deserve that damnation - rather He assumed that damnation for your sin and for mine, and the fact that He absorbed our damnation should not embarrass us - the fact that He absorbed our damnation should thrill us. We don't have to go to Hell because He paid our Hell when He hung on that cross. Apart from that, you and I are without hope. Apart from that, we have no hope.

In the moment that the law condemned us, someone stepped in and said, "I'll take that condemnation so they don't have to." Martha Snell Nicholson says it well in her poem, *My Advocate*.

> I sinned. And straightway, posthaste, Satan flew
> Before the presence of the Most High God,
> And made a railing accusation there.
> He said "This soul, this thing of clay and sod,
> Has sinned, 'Tis true that he has named Thy name,
> But I demand his death, for Thou hast said,
> 'The Soul that sinneth, it shall die.' Shall not
> Thy sentence be fulfilled? Is justice dead?
> Send now this wretched sinner to his doom.
> What other thing can a righteous ruler do?"
> And thus he did accuse me day and night,
> And every word he spoke, O God, was true!
>
> Then quickly One rose up from God's right hand,
> Before whose glory angels veiled their eyes.
> He spoke, "Each jot and tittle of the law,
> Must be fulfilled: the guilty sinner dies!
> But wait...suppose his guilt were all transferred
> To ME and that I paid his penalty!

> Behold My hands, My side, My feet! One day
> I was made sin for him, and died that he
> Might be presented faultless, at Thy throne!
> And Satan fled away. Full well he knew
> That he could not prevail against such love,
> For every word my dear Lord spoke was true!

Jesus took our penalty for all eternity so you and I would not have to take it. If it were possible to work our own way to Heaven, why would Jesus have come and done all of that? If Jesus knew by our own efforts of walking old ladies across the street, buying Girl Scout cookies, and giving pints of blood to the Red Cross we could work our way to Heaven, why in the world did He come and die on that cross? I hate to put it this way but He would have been a fool for receiving that damnation if you and I could have worked our way to Heaven.

Do you understand what you are saying when you say that you can work your way to Heaven? You are saying that the cross was unnecessary. If the cross was unnecessary, why did Jesus do it? Why would He have gone through the throes of death for every man and why did He bear the sins of every drug pusher, prostitute, and drug addict if it was totally unnecessary?

Do you understand what you are saying about Jesus' intelligence level when you say you can work your way to Heaven? You are saying that He is a fool. You understand that working your way to Heaven not only contradicts the Bible but it completely nullifies the cross and makes Jesus look like an idiot.

It excludes the Gentiles (v. 14a)

If we accept the fact that the whole world is under sin and that Jesus came to die on the cross to save the whole world, then it naturally follows that Gentiles can be saved because Jesus died for the whole word. But if salvation comes by keeping the law, then we are in a peck of trouble because the law was only given to the Jewish people - it wasn't given to Gentiles. So what you are telling people is the condition to get to Heaven is by keeping the rule book that they've never been given. How can you be held responsible for a rule book you were never given?

When I was a school administrator interviewing new students, I would always ask, "Have you read the handbook?" As a matter of fact, high school transfer students were asked to sign a statement that they have read the handbook. Do you know how frustrated people would be if they were held accountable for rules they had never seen?

When you say man is saved by keeping the law, you're basically saying that man is held responsible for a rule book that God never gave him. God gave the law to the Jews. So if salvation is through the law, the vast majority of the world is left out and God is only interested in saving the Jewish people. That would mean He is not interested in saving Gentile people. So how can you work your way to Heaven by a rule book that you have never seen? Salvation by the law cuts the vast majority of men out and obviously, that can't be right. So salvation by keeping the law is something that contradicts the Bible, nullifies the cross, and excludes the Gentiles.

It displaces the Spirit (v. 14b)

When you come to the cross and put your faith in the Lord Jesus Christ, you immediately receive the Holy Spirit. Romans 8:9 is very clear: ". . . if any man have not the Spirit of Christ, he is none of his." In other words, there is no such thing as a Christian who doesn't have the Holy Spirit. Getting the Holy Spirit is not something that happens after conversion - getting the Holy Spirit is conversion. There is no such thing as a Christian who doesn't have the Holy Spirit. Every Christian - good or bad - has the Holy Spirit living inside of him (cf. I Corinthians 6:19-20).

Why does God give us the Holy Spirit? In part, God gives us the Holy Spirit to help us live the life that we couldn't live before salvation. Before you were saved, you did good for the wrong motive and the wrong reason. No person who is living morally, even as a lost person, is doing so for the glory of God and through the agency of God. He is doing it for ulterior motives - for the praise of men - and he is not living in the graces that have been produced by the Spirit of God. Even his righteousness, the Bible says, is nothing more than filthy rags. God gives us the Spirit of God to help us live the life that we couldn't live by ourselves. That is the purpose of the Spirit.

There is only one person who lived the Christian life perfectly, and that was Christ Himself. You and I can't even come close to being like Christ if we don't have Christ because Christ is the only one who really lives like Christ. You and I, at our best moment, can't do anything in our humanity to offer good living to God, so that's why God sends His Spirit to live inside us. That Spirit inside us produces the kind of living that we need produced in our lives. If you are saying that you can work your way to Heaven, you are basically saying, "I don't need God's Spirit to live effectively." Think about how naïve that statement is.

When you believe that you can work your way to Heaven, you have not thought it through. You are saying that the Bible is wrong, that Jesus is a fool, that Gentiles are outside the plan of God, and that the Holy Spirit is totally unnecessary for effective living. Most people who think they can work their way to Heaven just haven't thought it through because if the had thought it through, they would recognize how crazy that thought really is.

You and I should not be fearful of engaging men with the gospel because we are not the ones who are thinking wrong. It is amazing all across America how intelligent people can think such crazy things. Our job is to go and turn the lights on in a dark place helping people see that the way that have been thinking is ignorant. There is nothing smarter than responding to the revelation of God in faith.

CHAPTER ELEVEN

Stop Looking for a Better Deal

Galatians 3:15-18

Sometimes when you or I are shopping for some-thing, we'll find an item at a good price, but instead of buying it right then, because we don't want anybody to accuse us of being impulsive buyers, we'll continue to look and see if we can find an even better deal.

This happened to me several years ago. We were teaching one of our daughters how to drive, and she went three feet and drove into a tree and totaled our car, and we had to get another car. In the first lot I walked onto, I saw this car and it was a good deal and I could not believe what a good deal it was. The mileage on the car was low, the car was only a year old, the asking price was great, and I said, "This is too good to be true. There is probably a better deal out there." So I went to all kinds of car lots and ended up going back and buying the very first car that I looked at. What happened in that instance was that I had a good deal but the deal was too good to be true and be-cause it was too good to be true, I decided that I would just go on and continue looking for a better offer only to discover that there was no better offer than the first one.

When the Gospel of Jesus Christ was preached to you, that was the best deal you will ever get. That was the best offer ever made concerning your future - there is no better deal out there than the Gospel of Jesus Christ. Therefore, we ought to take it.

Whenever I am leading somebody to Christ, I will frequently pull out my cell phone and say to the person, "Now suppose I offered you this cell phone as a free gift. If it really was free, what would you have to do to get it?" Immediately you can see the wheels turning in the mind of the person and he or she is thinking, "There's no such thing as a free gift." I have even had people respond to that question and say, "Work for it," because it is just in humans not to believe in free gifts. We believe there is no person out there who would absolutely give us something with no strings attached simply because they are kind.

But when it came to the cross of Calvary, that is exactly what the Lord Jesus did for you. The Lord gave you something simply because He is kind and gracious, and there is no way you can work for it, deserve it, earn it, or merit it - it is absolutely the best deal that you could possibly get. In the book of Genesis, God made a deal with Abraham and He said to Abraham, "I'm going to do all these things for you if you will simply accept it. You don't have to work for it: it is not a matter of life-long obedience or meritorious deeds. If you will simply take me at my Word, Abraham, this is what I am going to do for you, no strings attached. All you have to do, Abraham, is accept the deal and that's it."

Four hundred and thirty years passed and along came another deal. It was the law and it was offered at Sinai, and that deal was completely different. It didn't say that all you had to do was accept it. It said you have to work to keep the law of God, and you have to keep the law of God perfectly - it was a deal of absolute obedience. In the deal that God made with Abraham, everything was up to God. In the deal that God made at Sinai, everything was up to mankind. However the law is to be understood, and we won't see that until we get later on into the chapter, one thing is for certain - whatever God was offering at Sinai was not a better deal than what He offered to Abraham.

The first deal God offered in Genesis 12 certainly blew away the offer that came later in Exodus 20. The first deal was the better deal and there was no need to go looking for another deal. There are two reasons why the law was in no way, shape, or form a better deal than the offer made to Abraham. The first reason is that once God gives you a deal, you don't have to go looking for another deal because once God offers something, there is no need to alter it or tinker with it because what God offers is always good. God doesn't lack character when He makes a deal. When God offers a deal, you can say, "That has to be a good deal simply because God is the One who made it."

God is not offering little trinkets on the side of the road out of a trench coat. God is absolutely, undeniably a person of great character. So when God cuts a deal, you don't have to worry about tinkering with it to make it better. God's Word never needs to be altered.

The second reason is because when the law was given, it was never meant to supersede the deal that was given to Abraham. As a matter of fact, the law was to substantiate the deal that God made with Abraham, and we'll see that later. The law wasn't given to say, "Hey, I can really get to Heaven if I work my way there." The law was given to prove that you can't work your way to Heaven. The law was given to prove that nobody is perfect so the law, the second deal, that came along later, was not meant to be a better deal - it was meant to prove that the original deal was the best deal and God is merely giving the law not to make a way to go to Heaven but to frustrate us in our own human efforts so that we will go back to the first deal and take God at His Word. That all having been said, let's explore why the first deal is the best deal.

The Person behind the Abrahamic Covenant (vv. 15-16)

The person behind that covenant given to Abraham is none other than God Himself. This covenant was not based on Abraham's good lifestyle; it was based on God's performance. God is saying, "Abraham, you don't have to do anything." Remember that in Genesis 17, God put Abraham to sleep and God walked through the pieces of the sacrifice to prove to Abraham that He could take care of the deal while Abraham was in bed. God was telling him that this deal was up to God, not up to Abraham. All Abraham had to do was accept God, trust Him, and He'd take care of all of it. God was saying, "This deal is not based on your performance, Abraham. It is based on my performance." Now there are at least two things that we can say about the character of God.

The Nature of God's Person (v. 15)

The point of Galatians 3:15 is that once you have probated a will, you can't change it. Once a will is probated, you can't go back at a later point and change the will. The money has already been given. Once the recipients have received the money, you can't go back ten years after somebody has died and say, "Let's change the will." Once it is probated, it is done.

Even in Bible times people did this. And believe it or not, in Bible times, sometimes they would even probate a will before somebody died - this is really what is behind the story of the prodigal son. When the rebel went to his dad and said, "Dad, divide your inheritance to us," he was asking his dad to probate his will before his death. And once that will was probated, it could not be changed. Thus, when the prodigal son went off and wasted his substance on riotous living, there was no way that the older brother could get any of that money that had already gone to the younger brother. Once that will had been probated, there was no way that you could change it.

The point that is being made in this passage is that if the will of men cannot be changed, how much more can you not change the will of God? If it is customary for men to take men at their word, how much more is it customary to take God at His Word? That is the point that this passage is trying to make. Of course, normally wills are probated after somebody dies and that is true in the situation under discussion because you will notice in verse thirteen that it talks about the fact that Christ has already died. You see, the person who gave us the will has already shed His precious blood upon the cross of Calvary. He has already died and paid the price, and thus probated the will.

This is the point that the author of the book of Hebrews is going to drive home even more emphatically (cf. Hebrews 9:15). For the will to be probated, somebody had to die. Jesus did die and by His dying, His will for our lives was probated. When you go back to Genesis and see the covenant that God made with Abraham, you'll see that there was also death involved (cf. Genesis 12:7). When Abraham got this promise from God, when he received this covenant from God, one of the first things that he did was build an altar. Why would he build an altar? He built an altar to put a sacrifice on it, and the sacrifice that he placed upon that altar probated that will. Blood was shed, something died, and God's will for Abraham was probated that day right there on that altar.

Let's say that Aunt Mabel's will is probated and Aunt Mabel says, "I leave all my jewelry to Uncle Fred." When she leaves all her jewelry to Uncle Fred, you can't go back and say, "I wonder what Aunt Mabel really wanted." No, we take Aunt Mabel at her word. If she wanted Fred to have the jewelry, we let Fred have the jewelry because that was what Aunt Mabel's last will said.

We have God's last will and testament right here in the Bible. If we take Aunt Mabel's last will and testament for its word, why wouldn't we take God's last will and testament for what He says? God's person demands that when God speaks, He is not speaking with a forked tongue. If you would take the will of men, and men are known to be liars, how much more would you take the will of God when God has never lied about anything? The nature of God's person shows that the Abraham covenant is better.

The Nature of God's Promises (v. 16)

Once again think about the history. God made a promise to Abraham in Genesis 12, and He repeated that promise to Abraham again in Genesis 17. That promise that God made to Abraham embraced three things: There was a promise concerning a plot of land, there was a promise concerning Abraham's seed, and there was a promise concerning a blessing that was going to come to Abraham.

The first promise forever settles territorial issues in the Middle East. God was going to give Abraham a literal plot of property in the Middle East - He wasn't giving it to the Muslims - He was giving it to the Jews.

The second thing that He was going to do was give something to Abraham's seed and He was going to, through Abraham, give a blessing to all the nations of the earth. Paul has already mentioned in the book of Galatians that idea of blessing - that the Lord Jesus would come to planet earth, and that He would make available the gospel to all nations of the earth, and literally, through Abraham's being the progenitor of Jesus Christ and Jesus Christ giving a universal salvation to all mankind, God would use Abraham as a means of blessing the entire globe on which you and I live.

Paul's point is that the promises were not merely made to Abraham but they were made, he says, to Abraham and to Abraham's seed. Here Paul makes a hair-splitting theological point. When God made the promise to Abraham and to his seed, He did not say to Abraham and to his seeds (plural) but it was to Abraham and one descendant in particular, and Paul says that one particular descendant was the Lord Jesus Christ. The blessings that were made and promised to Abraham were not based on any genetic connection to Abraham - these were not biological promises - they were Christological promises. In other words, the promises came to us, not because we are biologically related to Abraham - they came to us because we are spiritually connected with Abraham's descendant, the Lord Jesus Christ. These promises were made not to Abraham's seeds (plural) but rather to Abraham's seed (singular), the Lord Jesus. And we get the promises, especially the promise concerning salvation, not because we are genetically related to Abraham but because we've been spiritually connected to Jesus Christ.

In other words, the promises of God are all fulfilled in Jesus and we get those promises when we get Jesus because Jesus is where the fulfillment of those promises is found. In other words, you could be a Jewish person, and there's great privilege in that, but I say this very kindly - you could be genetically related to Abraham and still split Hell wide open. The promises of God could never be yours, but if you get connected to Abraham's seed (singular), the Lord Jesus Christ, and you get Jesus, then every promise that God made to Abraham becomes yours because you're in Jesus and Jesus is the one who has received the promises.

If God gives all of His promises to Jesus and Jesus and I are joint heirs, I get everything that Jesus gets from His heavenly Father. The point that Paul is trying to make is that all the promises in Jesus are amen: they are accomplished in Him. So when I get Jesus, I receive the promises that God has made. This is vitally important. Would God lie to Jesus? Would the Heavenly Father lie to His only begotten Son? No, and so those promises that He made to Jesus are going to be fulfilled and when I get Jesus, I also receive those promises. God is going to keep His Word simply because the very nature of His person and the nature of His promises demand that God will do everything that He said He would do. I'm glad that when I got saved, it was finished and done, and the great transaction was sealed. God's person and God's promises are all that are necessary to take care of this whole thing.

The Priority of the Abrahamic Covenant (v. 17)

By stressing that the Abrahamic covenant came first, Paul is extolling here that our God is a God who keeps His promises. False Jewish teachers thought that Abraham and the patriarchs were just a prelude to when the Jewish nation really began and then later on, when God came to Egypt and saved those people out of Egyptian bondage and gave them the law, that is really when the nation of Israel started. The Jewish people thought that Abraham, Isaac, Jacob, and Joseph were the prelude and then when God called them out of Egypt, that's when the nation really began. Let's talk about that and think about that line of reasoning for a little bit. If the law is where the nation really began and that was the real covenant that God meant, what are you going to do with what He promised Abraham four hundred and thirty years before this? If the law changes everything, then God is a dishonest broker. Let me illustrate.

Once we had a missionary conference and rented a bigger hall. We hired a caterer to cook for the international banquet. We made a deal with this caterer and one of the deals was that we would supply the tablecloths so we wouldn't have to rent their tablecloths. Since we had the tablecloths, there was no need to rent tablecloths. They said, "Okay, you don't have to use our tablecloths and we will reduce the rental fee." We gave them our tablecloths and marked them, and when we showed up for the banquet, they hadn't used our tablecloths. They used their own tablecloths, and sent us the bill and charged us for tablecloth rental. I said, "We are not paying for that; we had a deal. They used their tablecloths—that's their problem. They said they were going to use ours and we made a deal." The whole catering bill was over four thousand dollars and only two hundred dollars of that was for tablecloths but I said, "We are not paying a dime of this four thousand dollars until they take that two hundred dollars off." There was a reason for that. Once they got their check, they had all the power but as long as I have the money, I have the power.

Just a couple of days ago, we got a call from the catering company wanting to know where the money was and we said, "We told you we are not paying for the tablecloths and you're not getting a dime from us until you take the tablecloths off that bill. We had a deal and you didn't keep your word." They realized we were playing hardball and they said, "Okay" and they took two hundred dollars off. I'm not letting them be a dishonest broker. We had a deal. You may think, "It's just two hundred dollars out of a four thousand dollar bill." It's the principle. Your deal is what you said and you can't change the deal at a later point. We don't let people get by with that.

Have you ever bought something and when you went to pay for it, they added all these incidental things to it and you said, "What's this? You can't throw all of these nonsense charges on top of this." Say what you mean and mean what you say. We don't let people make a deal and then later come around and make another deal. We would say that is dishonesty. We're not taking a deal if you are going to change it at a later point.

If we don't accept that with people, why would we accuse God of doing something that we wouldn't let human beings get away with? God is not going to cut a deal and then four hundred and thirty years later come by and say, "Well, I kind of changed my mind. I've got some incidentals I want to add." God doesn't do business like that. God doesn't say, "All you have to do is accept me at my Word" and then four hundred and thirty years later say, "No, you have to keep all these regulations or it's no good." God is not dealing with smoke and mirrors when He cuts a deal. If you think that the law is where it's at and that's the means of salvation, then what you are basically saying is God was a liar when He talked to Abraham four hundred and thirty years earlier.

God is not guilty of that kind of dishonest dealing. The priority of the Abrahamic covenant strikes to the very character of God. The law is not a late addition changing the rules of God. It was rather as Paul said later in this passage—a school master to show us we can't get to Heaven that way. We've got to go to Heaven the way God originally said. The law was not designed to give us a works salvation—the law was designed to prove that faith is the only way you can get there.

The Permanence of the Abrahamic Covenant (v. 18)

At this point, Paul, for the first time in the book of Galatians is going to use the word inheritance. The inheritance was to Abraham and his seed, and it was given on unconditional terms. Unconditional is vastly different from conditional. The law was conditional—the law said, "If you do this, God will bless you." God has said to Abraham, "I am going to bless you whether you do anything or not." The law says, "Do this" but grace says, "Merely accept this," so it is not conditioned by what I do—it is rather conditioned by what God does. If the law is up to me, and being saved and making it to the end is all up to me, you understand, at that point, my future is very insecure. If I get to Heaven by works, I am in a quandary.

Let's think about philanthropic things. Let's say I get to Heaven by deeds of nobility, like walking old ladies across the street, buying boxes of Girl Scout cookies, and giving pints of blood to the Red Cross. If I get to Heaven by walking old ladies across the street, how many old ladies am I supposed to walk across the street? How many old ladies does it take to get to Heaven? If I get to Heaven by buying boxes of Girl Scout cookies, how many boxes? If I get to Heaven by pints of blood that I give to the Red Cross, how many pints of blood do I have to give? Do you understand that at the very moment I decide that I am getting to Heaven by my works, I am in a tremendous amount of bondage? I don't know how much is enough.

There is great insecurity in all of that because what if I stand before God and I was supposed to have bought 12 boxes of Girl Scout cookies and I only bought 11? You understand that you are in a position of terror if it is up to you, but at the very moment that you look to the old rugged cross and Jesus says, "It is finished" and you accept it, there is rest and you cease from your dead works to serve the living God. Why? Because you are not serving Him to merit anything—you are going to Heaven by the merits of Jesus. You're serving Him today, not because you are trying to gain Heaven, but because you want to thank Him because Heaven has already been gained. There is a big difference. You are not serving God out of fear; you are serving Him out of love and devotion because He paid it all.

I don't know if you have ever been in a position where you received a bill for something you weren't expecting but there may have been a time in your life when something comes due that you weren't really expecting it. That has happened at least a couple of times in my life. I remember when our daughter Ashley was born. She had fifteen surgical procedures in the first year of her life. I graduated from school owing no man anything and a month after she was born I owed every man everything. The insurance that our church provided was okay if you were healthy and all their previous pastors had enjoyed good health, which was great. But when Ashley was born, I learned that deductibles can be very disconcerting. I didn't know what to do. So one day I called the deacons together and said, "Fellows, I don't know what to tell you other than this. My daughter is racking up medical bills left and right and I don't know any other way to say it. This insurance stinks and I've got to have some insurance that is going to take care of me and my daughter." Those deacons looked at me across the table and tears came to their eyes and they said, "Pastor, we're going to take care of you." To tell you the difference in how my heart felt going in to that meeting and how it felt coming out of that meeting would be almost impossible to do. I went into that meeting fearful, scared, and uncertain about the future and

I left that meeting greatly at ease because I had the promise of some godly men who said they were going to pay it all.

That is exactly what Jesus did for you spiritually. Do you understand the security of knowing the sin debt that's over your head and your inability to pay it and then to leave a meeting with God saying, "It's okay. I'm going to take care of everything." Do you understand the rest that comes to a soul knowing that Jesus paid it all?

I've had people often make this statement to me: "People who believe in eternal security can go off and do anything they want to do and still go to Heaven." Let's say that I told Karen, "You'd better live right, woman, and you'd better do everything exactly the way I want it done. I want my shirts done just right, I want the house cleaned just this way because if you don't live right, I'm out of here." Does that make her a better wife or a worse wife? Obviously, it makes her a worse wife. But if I say to her, "Honey, I don't care how bad the meals are, I don't care how bad the laundry is, I don't care if the house is a mess—you're stuck with me. If you run away, going with you. I'm here for the long haul." What does that make her want to do for me? It makes her want to cook what I want, do the laundry the way I like it, and clean the way I like it. Because I have given her security, she wants to do more for me.

It's funny that people understand this on a human front but they don't understand it on the divine front. I want to give everything to God because of everything that God has already given me. His security motivates me. Jesus paid it all and because He paid it all, then all to Him I owe. Because He gives me this wonderful security, I don't live in fear of Him. I live in the wonderful warmth of His security because He has given me such a priority of promise and has given me permanence that will give me an inheritance in spite of the way I live along the way. I am committed to God for the long haul because of the great blanket of fidelity and security that He has showered upon me. When I think of what God does for Jeff Amsbaugh in spite of Jeff Amsbaugh, it makes Jeff Amsbaugh want to do everything he can for that kind of God.

How about you? Isn't it great to know that God is taking care of everything? And because He is taking care of everything, tomorrow morning I'm going to get out of bed and I'm going to serve Him, not to gain Heaven—that has already been done—but to show my love for a God who has already done it all for me.

CHAPTER TWELVE

Why the Law?

Galatians 3:19-20

Throughout this whole section in Galatians 3, the apostle Paul has been hammering the fact that we are saved by faith—we are not saved by works. This is the distinguishing hallmark of Christianity. It's the thing that makes Christianity different from every other religion in the world. *Religion* is man doing something to try to merit the favor of God. *Christianity* is God doing something for man that man can't do for himself. You and I can't merit our salvation, we can't work for our salvation, and we can't deserve our salvation— nobody by their rule-keeping is going to get to Heaven.

Of course, there is a lot of confusion about this today. If you go out on visitation and you talk to people, the first thing that people say is "Well, I am trying to keep the Ten Commandments and live by the Golden Rule. I'm not intentionally trying to injure anybody. I'm trying to be a good neighbor. I'm trying to live by the side of the road and be a help to my fellow man." These are the kinds of reasons that people give for thinking they will stand before God one day and be accepted of Him. But the apostle Paul keeps hammering over and over in Galatians 3 that you and I are not saved by the rules that we keep — we are saved by exercising faith in the finished work of Christ. Salvation is by grace through faith, plus nothing and minus nothing. We are saved by grace through faith independently of works.

There are three things that Paul has hammered so far in this chapter about that. First of all, he said in verse 11 that we are not justified by the law. The law cannot justify us. You and I will not be declared righteous at the Judgment Bar of God because we have kept X amount of good rules in God's rule book. No one is justified by doing good works and no one is justified by performing the deeds of the law—the law cannot justify you.

The second thing that Paul drives home in verse 14 is that the law cannot give you the Holy Spirit. God promised us the Holy Spirit, and we receive that promise of the Holy Spirit not by keeping the laws of God but rather by exercising faith in the finished work of Christ. It was the finished work of Christ that justifies us and it was the finished work of Christ that gives us the Holy Spirit. No one gets the Holy Spirit by working enough or doing enough good deeds. You and I receive the Holy Spirit simply because we've exercised faith in the finished work of Christ.

Then in verse 18, Paul gives us a third point. We see here that the law cannot give us our inheritance. He says that you didn't get justified by works; you got justified by faith. He says that you didn't get the Holy Spirit by works. You got the Holy Spirit by faith. And he says you are not going to get your inheritance by works; you are going to get your inheritance in Heaven by faith. Notice how he puts past, present, and future all as a matter of faith, not as a matter of works. You and I got our initial salvation by faith, not by works. The Holy Spirit lives inside us every day to help us overcome the power of sin. We received Him not by the good works that we did but rather by exercising faith.

One day we are going to make it to Heaven and we are going to get our inheritance in Heaven—not because of the good works that we did but rather because we exercised faith. Faith took care of the penalty of sin, it takes care of the power of sin, and it will take care of the very removal from the possibility of sin when we get to Heaven. Our entire salvation—justification, sanctification, glorification—is a matter of a faith. It is not by the law, period. That is what Paul is saying. No aspect of salvation—past, present, or future—came about by keeping the law; it all came about by exercising faith in the finished work of Christ on Calvary's cross.

The question that we could ask ourselves is this: Why did God give the law if the law doesn't do beans about the past, the present, or the future? Why in the world would God give the law? When we ask this question—what purpose is the law? — this is much more than an academic question. Later in Paul's ministry, when he's arrested in the city of Jerusalem, he is going to be incarcerated for this very reason.

The people thought that because Paul taught justification by faith, he was completely against the law of God and hated the Law of Moses. They thought he was saying that the law didn't matter and part of the reason he got arrested was that people said he was against the law of God (cf. Acts 21:28). Paul was accused of being against the law his whole Christian life because he argued that we're not justified, we're not sanctified, and we're not glorified by the law; therefore, the argument that is placed against him is that he's against the law of God. Now only a person who teaches justification by faith would be accused of such a thing.

If you thought you were saved by walking old ladies across the street and buying Girl Scout cookies and giving pints of blood to the Red Cross, you would never be accused of being against rule-keeping. At the very moment that you are justified by faith, then the accusation could be leveled against you that you don't believe in rules and you don't believe in the laws of God. What then is the purpose law? That is the question Paul is going to answer by pointing out four things.

The Problem of Sin (v. 19a)

The law was added because of sin. There are at least two ideas imbedded in that thought. The first idea is that the law helps curb sin civically. You remember when everybody was doing what was right in their own conscience, the world ran amuck, and God looked down from Heaven and He said, "The imagination of man's heart is wicked." So God said, "I'm going to send a flood and it will wipe everybody out." There were only eight people in the whole world who found grace in the eyes of God: Noah, Mrs. Noah, Shem, Mrs. Shem, Ham, Mrs. Ham, Japheth, and Mrs. Japheth. Those eight people went into the Ark, and God wiped everybody else out. When they came out of the ark, God said, "We have to find a way to keep people from destroying themselves." So God instituted something called human government in Genesis 9 when Noah came out of the ark.

In other words, law had to be given to keep people from destroying society across the board. For example, in Genesis 9, God said, "Whoso sheddeth man's blood, by man shall his blood be shed..." Obviously, when God said that, God didn't mean if somebody kills my family member, I can take it upon myself to execute him. God was instituting human government and in instituting human government, He was saying, "I am providing agents of execution."

God gave the right to bear the sword to human government and that's why if you are employed by human government and you are the guy who gives the lethal injection or pulls the switch on the electric chair, you're not guilty of murder as far as God is concerned. Murder is taking the law into your own hands. Execution is functioning under the arm of the state. That's why soldiers who go to Iraq and Afghanistan and take people out as agents of the United States government are not guilty of murder. They are performing a government function of execution and there is a world of difference between murder and execution. The point is that laws are put into effect by human government as a means of curbing sin in society.

Because sin is everywhere doing its thing, God made rules, and penalties associated with those rules, to help keep human society in check. So there is a sense in which the law was given because of multiple transgressions to prevent sin and to put a cap on sin. God puts penalty with sin so that you and I will think twice before doing it.

Years ago, I moved from Philadelphia, Pennsylvania to Columbus, Georgia. When I was in Philadelphia, you were actually encouraged to speed. I had a pastor friend who was driving down I-95 one day with his cruise control set on the speed limit, and a cop pulled up beside him and motioned for him to roll down his window. The cop said, "If you are not going to move that car, get it off the road." When I came to Columbus, Georgia, I was used to driving that way, so the first week I was in Columbus, I got pulled over twice for speeding. The first time I got a warning and the second time I got a hundred and fifty dollar ticket. Every time I drive where I received that ticket, I set my cruise control. I set my cruise control because of the law and the penalty. Something like that is what Paul is saying here.

When our daughter Ashley was just a little girl, there was a vase on the coffee table, and she went over and started playing with it. I said, "Don't touch that vase" and she continued to touch that vase, so I took her upstairs, and I paddled her. I then brought her back downstairs. A couple of hours later, she waddled over to the coffee table and reached out to touch that same vase. You could see the wheels turning in her head. All of a sudden, she shook her head no and backed away from the coffee table. What happened? Law and penalty curbed her behavior.

Because there was a proliferation of sins, and because sins were just adding up, God established law as a way of curbing sin in a civic fashion. Law prevents sin. It is kind of funny that law not only prevents sin but there is a completely other sense in which law provokes sin (cf. Romans 5:20). There is a sense civically in which the law curbs sins, but notice there is a sense spiritually in which the law provokes sin. The law entered and when the law entered, it actually provoked more sin and it made sin abound because there was more law.

You may ask, "How in the world does the law do that?" It is because of the way we are. For example, you may be walking through the park and you see a sign that says "Do not pick the flowers" and you weren't even thinking about picking flowers until you saw that sign. Then you wonder why you can't pick flowers. Who are they to tell me that I can't pick flowers? And before you know it, you are bending over and picking flowers that you wouldn't have even thought about picking had there not been a law that said "Don't pick the flowers." In that sense, law can actually provoke sin.

There is a sense in which, legally, the law prevents sin but there is also simultaneously, because of our human nature, that the law spiritually actually provokes sin. The law does two things—legally it prevents sin but spiritually it provokes sin. Thus, the law is there really to show us in both of those instances how bad we are.

When the law comes and slaps our wrist for doing what we are doing, we say, "Why was I doing that? Why was I speeding? Why do I insist on doing things my way?" The law makes me aware that I have a problem with sin. When the law comes tells me not to do it, and I say, "I want to do it anyway," it accomplishes that same objective—it helps me see the exceeding sinfulness of sin. Our biggest problem in society is a sin problem and the law was sent to reveal it.

Society wants to redefine sin as a disease and excuse sin through victimization. Everybody is a victim. Victims say, "I couldn't help but do this because of the environment in which I was raised. I am not a perpetrator of a crime; I'm a victim of the environment I'm in." Skinner said that there are no evil people, there are only evil environments. The problem with our society is that we've gotten away from the issue of sin. Thus, the law of God comes to help us see where our problem is. Our problem is sin and the law identifies that problem.

The Promise of the Seed (v. 19b)

By using the word *till* in verse 19, Paul is showing us that the law had temporal perimeters. From its very beginning, from the very moment that God instituted the law, it had a limited duration. The law had a definite beginning at Mount Sinai and it had a definite end at Mount Calvary. The law of God started at a definite point and it ended at a definite point.

There are some denominations today like the Seventh Day Adventists who teach that only part of God's law was done away with and that the Ten Commandments are still in vogue today — that's why they keep and worship on the Sabbath. The Law of God was entirely done away with at the cross; it was fulfilled there in its entirety — it had a definite point of implementation at Mount Sinai and it had a definite point of termination at Mount Calvary. Paul is clear that the termination of the law happened when the seed came.

He has already identified for us in verse 16 who the seed is. The seed is Christ. So the law of God, the law of Moses, continued until Jesus Christ came and Jesus Christ fulfilled the law (cf. Matthew 5:17). In what way did Jesus fulfill the law? Jesus fulfilled the law in at least four ways.

First, Jesus fulfilled the law by His existence. Everything that happened in the life of Jesus happened so that Scripture might be fulfilled. His very existence fulfilled the law of God. His birth at Bethlehem was so that Scripture might be fulfilled. His birth of a virgin was so that Scripture might be fulfilled. His betrayal for thirty pieces of silver was so that Scripture might be fulfilled, and His riding into Jerusalem on the colt was so that Scripture might be fulfilled. Jesus' whole life was a fulfillment of Scripture; His very existence fulfilled Scripture.

He also fulfilled the law by His example. There is only one person who has lived in the history of mankind who has obeyed the law of God perfectly, and that is the Lord Jesus Christ. The interesting thing about it is that people often use commonality of disobedience as an excuse for disobedience. For example, how many times have you and I said, "Hey, I wasn't speeding; I was just keeping up with traffic." We are saying that everybody else is speeding; therefore, I can speed because everybody else is speeding. We are using the excuse that everybody does it.

The Holy Spirit comes and convicts us of an absolute standard of righteousness and it is Jesus Christ. Even though Jesus went back to the Father and we see Him no more, there is still an absolute standard of righteousness that you and I are made aware of. You may say, "Well, nobody keeps the law perfectly." To the contrary, I know of one person who did and His name is Jesus Christ, and by His example He fulfilled the law.

He also fulfilled it by His exhortations. You remember, for example, when Jesus gave the Sermon on the Mount, He was scraping away a lot of the traditions that had been added by the religious leaders. They had added their little tidbits about how the laws of God were to be obeyed. For example, the Sabbath was an important one. They had so many laws to help you understand exactly what was involved in breaking or not breaking Sabbath. For example, you could eat an egg that had been laid by a chicken if the chicken laid the egg on the Sabbath, but you had to kill the chicken for violating the Sabbath.

We often do the same thing today. I remember when I was a kid, we had a famous evangelist who came to our hometown and he would not have people on his platform who wore wire-rimmed glasses — that's in the Bible somewhere, I think. Sometimes we Christians have to be careful when we add our own little ideas to the Word of God. Jesus said, "You have heard that it hath been said, but I say unto you. . ." When Jesus said, "But l say unto you," He was scraping away all the traditions that had been added by people and was getting back to the pure intention of God's law, which is what we need. Jesus fulfilled the law by the way He taught, and He really helped us see the mind of God. By His exhortations He fulfilled the law.

But most importantly, and to the point of this passage, Jesus also fulfilled the law by His execution. Because I committed all of these infractions, the law said I had to die and go to Hell. Jesus, however, came and fulfilled the law on behalf of us sinners. He died in our place so we would not have to. When you and I try to do things by the law, the only thing we do is secure ourselves a hot place in Hell because we can't keep the law perfectly, and if we can't keep the law perfectly, we have to go to Hell. But if we let Jesus fulfill the law on our behalf, then we can go to Heaven because He takes our Hell so we don't have to take it.

The law is only adequate to condemn but the law is not able to save. The law can condemn us and tell us we are wrong but it gives no power to do right. Jesus can give the power not only to see the wrong, but to live effectively on a day-by-day basis. Jesus actually helps the promises of God to become effective on our part. How can we keep the law? There's only one way we can fulfill the law—not by what we do but by what He did through us— that's the only way we can fulfill the law. We see that this promised seed of God comes to fulfill the law of God on our behalf. The law was given to prove we can't do it—He alone can do it.

The Problem of Separation (v. 19c)

The third reason the law was given was to accentuate the problem of separation. In other words, the law was given to help us see how far we are from God. You remember in Exodus 19 the Bible describes the law being given at Sinai. The Bible says there was thunder and lightning and a thick cloud. God on that occasion said that no one should come close to the mountain. Any beast that touches the mountain would die. Paul interprets that fiery barrier at Mount Sinai here as the host of angels who helped to mediate the covenant. This agrees with Isaiah's vision in Isaiah 6. Isaiah saw the Lord high and lifted up but smoke filled the temple, blurring his vision so he could not completely see God. How was he going to know about God? Remember the angels shouted back and forth "Holy, holy, holy is the Lord of Hosts. The whole earth is full of His glory." Isaiah could not see God fully and live so he had to see God veiled, and the message about God was given to Him through angelic voices.

Something like that is what happened on Mount Sinai. Similarly, in Genesis 3 good angels are there for our protection. When God threw Adam and Eve out of the Garden of Eden, He put an angel there to guard the entrance. Why did He put an angel there to guard the entrance into the garden? God did not want any man to eat of the tree of life and live forever in a sinful state. You can't intrude into God's presence any way you want to—there is a method for coming into God's presence, and if you and I intrude into God's presence without being adequately prepared for that meeting, we will be smitten dead.

No man can see God and live; therefore, the giving of the law is there to show our plight, to show how our iniquities have separated us from God. The law was given to show that our problem is sin; it was given to show that our hope is in Jesus Christ. But there are some people saying that sin is not that big of an issue and Jesus is not that necessary. But if Jesus doesn't remove your sin, you're not going to be ready to meet God—you will be forever separated from God. Our God is a holy God and He is not approached lightly. There is fire and smoke and thunder and an angelic barrier to anybody who would try to get into the presence of God in an inappropriate way.

The Preciousness of Sacrifice (v. 20)

One commentator states that there are four hundred and thirty different interpretations of Galatians 3:20. Indeed, the verse does seem cryptic. Obviously, we're not on easy turf here, but it appears to me, at least in part, it is saying that at Mount Sinai there was a double mediation. You had the Jews who couldn't even come close to the mountain — they couldn't touch it — so how were they going to get the law? They had to send their mediator, Moses, and he went up on behalf of the people. God could not come down fully in His glory because if God came down fully in His glory, even Moses would have died, so God sent angels to be His emissaries.

Basically, God is saying, "I'm going to have my people get with your people." God is saying, "I'm going to send down my angels and you send up your Moses, and my angels will talk to your Moses." It was a double mediation. Sometimes when you are dealing with something and you can't talk to people directly, you hire a mediator. If you have a dispute with somebody and you hire mediators, you can't even talk to the people you are in dispute with and this is exasperating.

We are renting our house and we use a rental company to manage that for us, and one of the most exasperating things to me is I want to be involved in things but they say, "Stay out of it because you hired us to do it." I don't want to stay out of it and there is double mediation that transpires, consequently the renter tells their representative, who tells my representative, who in turn tells me. It gets frustrating after a while.

The obvious idea here is that if God is sending His people to talk with the Israeli delegation, then obviously, there is a great distance between the Jewish people and God himself. God sends somebody to talk to somebody who talks to the Jewish people. So consequently because God is sending His people to talk to their people, there is a great difference between God and the people that He is coming to do business with. God did not fully come down, and they could not go up. Thus, both sent their arbitrators to get involved in the communication.

Any time you have mediation going on, you have two estranged parties—if we are not estranged, there would be no reason for mediation. You only have a mediator if the parties are estranged from one another and, obviously, to be estranged, you have to have two parties — you can't be estranged from yourself. You don't have a mediator if only one party is involved. In the book of Genesis, when God made that promise to Abraham, and this is the contrast in the passage between Abraham and Moses, when God came to Abraham in the book of Genesis, God did not say to Abraham, "I'm going to have my people get with your people." When God came to Abraham in the book of Genesis, God showed up Himself and made a promise.

In the same way, when God showed up at Bethlehem, He didn't send an arbitrator—God came Himself in the person of the Lord Jesus Christ. He didn't say that He was going to send His angels to deal with this. When God came to deal with the sin issue, He came to Bethlehem as a baby and lived on this earth until He went to Calvary. From Bethlehem to Calvary, there were no emissaries of God accomplishing this task—it was God Himself in flesh tenting among us. He dealt with us, directly, face to face.

In the law, God kept His distance, and in the law, God used His mediators, but in the promise that we put faith in, God dealt directly with us and came directly in contact with us. We are vile, wretched, helpless, Hell-bound, hopeless sinners. When you know what we are, you understand why God would want to keep His distance. Some of us know people we want to keep our distance from. We teach our children to keep a certain distance from people who are corrupt. Though I can completely understand why God would and should keep His distance from me, He did not keep His distance from me. He came for a face-to-face encounter. He came to where I was and He came Himself. He used no mediation whatsoever other than serving as His own mediator through His Son, the Lord Jesus Christ.

When I first started taking doctoral courses at Temple Baptist Seminary, I was still a pastor in Philadelphia when I was accepted into the program. I called and said I would be flying in for my first class from Philadelphia to Chattanooga and asked if someone would come to the airport and pick me up. I had been dealing with educational institutions in a variety of fashions and I know what usually happens—they send some peon to the airport to pick you up, and some colleges hire these peons to pick people up from the airport. In many of these institutions, this is the person everybody laughs at. Because he could do nothing else, he became a driver, and I was expecting one of those guys to pick me up.

When I got off the plane at the airport, I was surprised to find standing there at the gate to meet me, Dr. Trachian, who was the president of the seminary. I don't know of another seminary on the face of the earth where the president would have come himself to pick up a new student who had been untested. I was an unknown person. I was nobody and there to greet me was the president of the seminary. I said, "Dr. Trachian, I'm so sorry. When I called and asked for a ride, I never anticipated that you would be the one who would come and get me. I'm sorry I put you out." He said, "Good to see you, Jeff. My job is to be a servant and presidents are no good if they are not servants. I came to establish a friendship with you and to pick you up. Get in the car." He grabbed my bags and he opened the trunk and threw the luggage in. The president became a servant.

Over the years, our friendship has grown and developed and he is one of the dearest friends I have in this world. If you go to my office today and look at the pictures on my wall, you will find a picture of me and Dr. Trachian there. Our friendship started that day when the president became a servant. That day there was great illustration of condescension.

I am disturbed by Bible colleges today that are training CEOs rather than servants. We don't train masters — we train servants and there needs to be an element in all of us to have the mind of the Lord Jesus Christ who made Himself of no reputation and became a servant.

There never has been a greater display of condescension than when God assumed flesh to come to where we were to pick us up. The law was given to show that our problem is sin. The law was given to show that our only hope is Christ. The law was given to show us that without Christ dealing with that sin, we would be permanently separated at a great distance from God. And the law was given to show us that God took one mighty step downward to rescue our souls. What a great thing the law did to show us how great Jesus is because what the law could not do, Jesus did and praise the Lord for that.

CHAPTER THIRTEEN

Three Functions of the Law

Galatians 3:21-25

In Galatians 3, Paul asks three big questions, and the first question is found in verse 2. How did you get the Holy Spirit? Did you get the Holy Spirit by doing good works? Is that how you got the Holy Spirit? Or did you hear the gospel and put your faith in it? Of course, anybody who is thinking straight knows the answer to that question—you got the Holy Spirit by hearing the gospel and putting your faith in it.

Then in verse 19 Paul asks the second question. What is the purpose of the law? Paul answers the question by saying that God gave the law for a specific purpose: the law comes to reveal our wickedness.

The third question that he asks is in verse 21 where he asks, "Is the law then against the promises of God?" The point is that the law seems to be put in juxtaposition against faith. You have law on one side and faith on the other side, and it appears that the law of God is against faith.

Why would God give something that would be against His very promises? He promised salvation by grace alone through faith. That is how we get saved and that is the promise of God. All we have to do is put faith in the promise of God and we're saved. If that is true, then why did God give a rule book? Doesn't the rule book seem to be fighting against that whole analogy?

Isn't the law then against faith? And if that is so, God almost seems to be dual minded. Why in the world would God give us something that was against what He established hundreds of years previously through Abraham? Why later would He give a law by Moses that seems to fight against what He promised Abraham years before?

The question immediately arises when you put law against faith: Is law then against the promises of God? Paul's response to that is in the strongest words possible: God forbid. When he uses those words "God forbid," he is using the strongest negative that was possible for him to use in the Greek language. It conveys horror and shock at the thought. The law does not contradict the promises of God—quite the opposite. The law is designed to lead you to the promises of God. The law is a road sign that points to what God is promising.

The law enters that it might fail (v. 21)

The law is not against the promises of God—the law is not even in competition with the promises of God because the law can't do what the promises of God can do. Therefore, they are not in competition with each other because the law can't do it. For example, when I go golfing with pastor friends who are good golfers, I am not in competition with them, and the simple reason is because I can't golf. I am such a failure at golfing that I am no threat to them. Well, the law of God is no threat to the promises of God because the law can't do what the promises can do. The promises can give life; the law can't give life. It's just not possible for the law of God to give life and it was never intended to do so. Doesn't the law say do this and you shall live? Isn't that what the Old Testament law said? Sure it said that but of course, you know that it can't do it.

When I was at my second church for one year, to show me how much they loved me, they bought me golfing lessons at the Great Golf Learning Center in Philadelphia. I showed up one day for my first lesson and the guy said, "Don't worry, Pastor Amsbaugh, we'll take good care of you. We'll get your game out of the nineties." I looked at him and said, "I would be happy if you got it into the nineties." They told me how to do all kinds of things to improve my golf game. I was told to bend my knees in a certain way and hold the club in a certain way. One time the instructor said, "Look at that club. You are holding it too tight. You are gripping it like a baseball bat. Just let it lie loosely in your hand and swing." I swung and the club went flying and he said, "That's a little too loose." I began to understand something — it is just not possible for me to be a good golfer. The guy said, "All you have to do is this and you'll be a great golfer." There was only one problem — I couldn't do it — it was beyond my capabilities to do it.

The law says, "Do this and you'll have life," and there's one problem — I can't do it — it's beyond my ability to do it. And because it is beyond my ability to do it, I can't have life by means of the law. No human being is capable of getting life through the law because no human being is capable of obeying the law (cf. Romans 7:10).

The law states that if I do it I can have eternal life. The only problem is that I can't do it — it is beyond me. Thus, the very thing that promised me life actually became the very instrument that killed me because I can't do it. Sometimes things that promise health actually become instruments of death. For example, it is amazing how someone can get a tumor and the doctor says, "I think if I give you all of this chemotherapy, you will live longer." I am not here to make a political statement but you understand that cancer is not caused by a lack of chemicals. In many instances, people take all kinds of chemotherapy and find the cure to be worse than the disease, and what was ordained to be more life many times can be the thing that kills them.

In the same way, the law said, "All you have to do is take this and you'll have life." I took it only to find out it isn't saving my life at all — it is just showing me how weak and sick I am. The problem is not the law per se because Paul says in Romans 7:12 that the law is good and righteous and holy. The problem is with the one who has to obey the law — the problem is with me. We must face the fact that law often increases our disobedience. The great thing about this is that it didn't catch God off guard. God didn't say, "I'm going to give the law to these people and then they will be able to get eternal life by it." Then when we couldn't keep it God didn't say, "Oh, my goodness, that's not what I expected." This didn't catch God off guard—nothing catches God off guard. So the law was never intended to give us life. God knew that it couldn't do it. God gave us the law so that we would try it and recognize what miserable failures we are and turn to somebody else to do it for us.

Let's go back to golf for a minute. When the church has a golf tournament, we play, by pastoral dictate, a four-man scramble and there is a reason for that — I can't golf. Amsbaugh is first up on the tee, and he hits the ball, which goes off the road. My friend then hits a 250-yard drive straight down the fairway. You get to take the best shot and put it down on the scorecard, and so I say, "I'll take that shot." Coming up to shot number two, I take my shot and it hits the fairway three holes over. Then someone else comes up and places a nice little chip shot on the green. By the end of the day, I am completely frustrated with my golf game. My score, however, is okay because I have become so frustrated with myself that I've taken somebody else's score.

That's exactly what the law is designed to do—you are trying your hardest to live right, but you don't have the power to live right. To do right doesn't come by you. You have to take somebody else's power and count that score on your sheet. The law entered so that it might fail. In other words, we have to recognize how big of a failure we are if we are going to turn to Christ. The problem is that many people think they are pretty good. I am amazed when I watch the six o'clock news interviewing the neighbor of a murderer. They will stick a microphone up to the neighbor's mouth and the neighbor will say, "He was a pretty good boy."

I just don't get that—good boys don't commit mass murder in the neighborhood, but that's the world in which we live. Everybody tries to excuse what they do and say that they are not too bad. God gave the law so that we would recognize what miserable failures we are. The law entered so that it might fail so that we would turn to somebody else. The law forces us to take Christ's score because we don't know how to play the game. The law is really a blessing in disguise because it teaches us what miserable failures we are so that we will turn to the only person who can help us. In that sense, it hands us the gallows but at the same time it points to the cross as a better way.

The law condemns that it might save (vv. 22-23)

The apostle Paul compares this whole situation to the imagery of a jail sentence. Scripture is the judge. The Scripture has concluded that all are under sin. He is talking about the world. All of us were sentenced by Scripture, and we were sentenced to sin who is the jailor. In this passage, Scripture is standing for God Himself because you understand that Scripture is really the expression of the mind and will of God. If you want to find out what God thinks about any matter, all you have to do is open the Bible and let the Bible tell you what God thinks about it. So the Bible here is not just a set of loosely connected documents—it is rather a cohesive expression of the will of God. When we examine the Bible as a whole, we discover the purpose of the law of God. The purpose was to conclude or to consign the whole world under sin.

You'll also notice here that we were shut up — the term means we were hemmed up on all sides; it was a word that was used frequently of a city where all the gates had been closed or of a net that had been closed up holding a bunch of fish inside of it. In other words, the law not only declares that we are guilty, but it locks us up so there is no way of escape. When you recognize that you are a miserable failure by keeping the law, you say, "I'll just try harder," but the harder you try, the deeper you get. It is like quicksand—the harder you try to get out, the more you are sinking.

Have you ever walked by a glass coffee table with a smudge? When you try to get the smudge off the coffee table with your fingers, the only thing you do is make the smudge bigger. Sometimes when we recognize our sin and the stain it makes in our lives, we try to extrapolate ourselves. But the harder we try, the more we find ourselves enslaved. The more you try to do, the more evil you find that you are. Self-made men are pitiful creations. We often say, "I'm not going to do that again," only to find that we are doing it again. The law has us in its grasp, and it consigns us under sin. The law condemns us in the cell of sin and has wrapped its iron bars around us. It is a maximum security facility and there is no way that we, by our own power, can get ourselves out of the sin in which we have been confined. We are locked up, shut down, and in maximum security.

The law is good but the Bible is telling us here that really it is an instrument of condemnation and we are beyond hope. But here is the point: The law is holding us until it can release us to Jesus by our putting faith in Him—it is holding us until Jesus comes.

When I was a little kid, the Richland Mall opened in Mansfield, Ohio, and that was a big deal for Mansfield. We had never had a mall before. Mom went out to shop at the Richland Mall and I was with her. I liked to sit underneath the clothes rack and play with the tags, and I came out from underneath the clothes rack and mom was gone. I did what any three-year-old boy would do - I started to cry. A sales clerk took me upstairs to this holding area and the next thing I heard over the intercom was, "Will the parents of Jeff Amsbaugh please come to the Lazarus office. We have found your son." I was scared to death of that girl and I did not want her grabbing me. I didn't want her taking me up there, and I was kicking and screaming as she was trying to get me up to the office but she finally got me up there and held me until my mom came. I didn't like her one little bit. She was ruining my freedom. She had incarcerated me and she was holding me until my mom showed up.

Similarly, the law holds us in its tyrannical grip until it can release us to a stronger and higher power, which is the Lord Jesus Christ. So the law is there to condemn you and hold you until you can be saved by Jesus. It is like the detention room after school. When we had detention in school, they used to bring in the mean teachers to monitor. They were there to hold you. They were there to make sure you were held in the holding tank until your parents came and picked you up. The law is like a detention supervisor — it holds you in its grip until Jesus comes to release you.

The law disciplines that it might set free (vv. 24-25)

Paul now moves from law being a jailor to law being a schoolmaster — the Greek word here is *pedagogue*. In Greek culture, when a child was born, he had several people who took care of him. First of all, there would be a slave who would be like a wet nurse who would nurse him until he was weaned — probably at about two years old. At the age of two, when that child was weaned, he was then turned over to a nanny who baby sat him from two to six. Then at the age of six, he would get a *pedagogue*, a schoolmaster, and the job of the *pedagogue* was not merely to educate him in academics but to educate him in manners. What good is it to have a bunch of facts in your head if you don't have any moral compass by which to implement those facts? So it is important that there be somebody to help you with manners. Teachers not only teach you how to count but they teach you what counts.

When Greek people thought of a *pedagogue*, they didn't think of a real soft, motherly school teacher type. You thought of somebody who tweaked your ears and cuffed your hands and whipped you and pinched you. That's what we mean by a *pedagogue* — a harsh disciplinarian.

Have you ever had a teacher you couldn't please no matter what you did? One of my elementary teachers was the meanest woman I had ever seen in my life. I've seen her take a ruler and smack a kid across the face. I've seen her grab a kid by the hair and pick him straight out of his seat. You would go to jail today for things that she did. She stood in stark contrast to the much nicer teachers in the school.

Isn't grace a wonderful thing when you've just been whacked by the long arm of the law? Some teachers believe that nobody's perfect and they are out to prove it. That's the way the law is — it says that nobody is perfect. You never can please a *pedagogue*. It's not the job of a *pedagogue* to be pleased — the job of a *pedagogue* is to show you where you are short. The whole point is to get you sick of the pedagogue so you'll turn to grace. You'll never please law. You're not good enough to please law and so you get to the place where you say, "I can't do it." You then turn to somebody else to do it for you. The law really doesn't fight against the promises of God — the law points and says the promises are that way.

When we were in the process of leaving Barbados, we packed up and went down the road toward the airport. We saw a sign that read "Construction: Road Closed." I wasn't from there and thus didn't know any other way to the airport. All I knew was that a law was staring me in the face and saying "Thou shalt not enter." I got this sad puppy-dog look on my face and looked aimlessly up to the construction crew worker. I rolled down the window and obviously he knew that I was not from around there. He came up to the window and I said, "Excuse me, sir, this van and the van behind me are full of kids from America. We've got to get to the airport to catch a plane. I don't know any other way to get to the airport. What do I do?" He said, "Leave it to me." He pointed up to the fellows in front of him and he said, "Let them through. They are going to airport." He pulled the barriers away and our vans went through. He became our bridge to get to where we needed to go.

When you and I come to the law, the law says, "Thou shalt not enter." You have no right to enter and there is no other way. If you are going to go by the law, you're not going to make it because the law says, "Don't enter." Imagine if I had just said, "I don't care what that sign says" and went full speed ahead. All fifteen of us would be in jail. So we stopped and appealed to someone who had authority. I said, "What I need from you is some grace," and he said, "I can take care of that." He made a way where there was no way.

If you try harder by your own determination, you're not going to make it through but praise God, those laws are there to help you understand who your escort is. The law points you to Jesus so that He can help get you across.

CHAPTER FOURTEEN

Your Most Important Title

Galatians 3:26-29

The other day, I was buying some plane tickets and a box popped up asking for my title. It had several choices to check. There were a couple of things in that box that immediately I knew I wasn't. For example, I knew I was not Mrs. Jeff Amsbaugh and I knew Ms. did not apply to me either. There were, however, two choices that could apply to me. There was Mr. and there was Dr., and I didn't know which one to click. I wondered which one was my most important designation.

As I was sitting there trying to decide, I was reminded of an old Andy Griffith episode where Andy and Barney went to Raleigh and Barney was signing in at the hotel and put "Barney Fife, MD." The hotel clerk said, "Oh, excuse me, Dr. Fife," and he handed him the key. Barney looked at him and said, "Dr.?" to which the clerk responds, "Yes, you signed it Barney Fife, MD." Andy asks, "MD?" and Barney says, "Yeah, Mayberry Deputy." Obviously, that was an important designation to him.

What is your most important title? What is your most important designation? I love what the Bible says in verse 26 of our passage: "For ye are all the children of God . . ." Isn't that a great designation? We are all God's kids. In this third chapter, the apostle Paul has been making a historical argument comparing Abraham to Moses, but as he comes to the end, he moves from the historical to the personal. He moves from the institutional to the individual.

Notice the little word *for* that begins verse 26. We no longer need a schoolmaster, and we no longer need a jailor who has confined us under sin, all for one simple reason—we are the children of God. And in that little statement, we find our most important designation. The most important designation is not whether I'm a Jew or a Gentile. The most important designation is not whether I am in labor or management. The most important designation is not whether I am a man or woman—the most important designation that I have in my life is to be known as a child of God.

Declaration (v. 26)

In the context, the word *all* shows us that our God is an impartial God. It doesn't matter what race we have come from. It doesn't matter what economic strata we come from. It doesn't matter of what gender we are. All of us have an opportunity to become God's children regardless of how we were born. The fact that we are children of God is because we are in Christ Jesus. Early in this passage, the Scripture has sentenced us all under sin. We have by the law been confined under sin but now Christ makes it possible for all of us to be sons. All of us were under sin but now all of us have the possibility to be sons instead of sinners.

Notice what is true of all believers. First of all, we are all sons of God. It's interesting that the title "son of God" has already been used twice in this book (Galatians 1:15-16; 2:20). We see from these passages that ultimately this title of "Son" is something that is uniquely reserved for Jesus Christ. He is the paramount and ultimate Son of God. Because we are in Christ, we have a sonship that is derived from Christ's sonship. There is no one who is as close to God the Father as God the Son. You will never find anybody in the universe closer to God the Father than His only begotten Son. When you were saved, you were placed inside of Christ Jesus, and because you are in Christ Jesus, you are positionally in the Son of God. You are as close to God positionally as Jesus Himself is. You could not be any nearer to God than you are right now by virtue of being in the Son because the Son is as close to the Father as you can get. You have become a child of God.

In the previous verses, we saw that we had a schoolmaster. We also said when a child was born, he had a wet nurse (a slave, who nursed the child), and after the child was weaned from a wet nurse, from the age of about two to six, he was a given a nanny who taught him adolescent things. Then after he moved away from the nanny, he was given a schoolmaster—someone who educated him in manners and academics, and slapped his wrist and said, "Thou shalt not." But there was a point when the child was fully adopted as a son, and when he was adopted as a son, he no longer needed a wet nurse, a nanny, or a schoolmaster—he was in every sense of the word a son, an adult son, with all of the attendant rights and privileges. We have moved beyond nurse, nanny, and schoolmaster—we are sons of God. We are adult children in the family, and we have the rights and privileges of sonship. The first thing that we see in this declaration is that we are all sons of God.

Second, we see that we are all sons of God through faith. When the Bible says we are all sons of God, we immediately see here that it is not talking about this universal fatherhood of God and universal brotherhood of man where everybody who lives on planet earth is a child of God. We all became children of God by a specific means. It was not because we were born into the human race that we became sons of God, but rather we became sons of God by virtue of the fact that we exercised faith. There is only one way that anyone gets to be God's child and that is by exercising faith in the finished work of Jesus Christ (cf. John 1:12). There are people who are God's children, and there are people who are not God's children. All of us who have become God's children have become God's children the same way: not by works of righteous but by exercising faith in the finished work of Christ. We are all God's sons through faith.

The third thing we see is that we are all God's sons in Christ Jesus. Faith is only as strong as the object in which it is rooted. Just by exercising faith doesn't get you anything if the object in which you are placing your faith is no good. Let's say that a chair is rickety, but I believe it can hold me. Obviously, if I sit in that chair it will not hold me because faith is only as strong as the object in which it is rooted. So it is no good for people to say, "I have faith" if their faith is in an inadequate object. The only faith that will take a person to Heaven is faith in Christ Jesus. It is the person who places faith in Christ that becomes the child of God. We are all sons of God through faith in Christ Jesus.

Demonstration (v. 27)

Baptism shows a decisive break with the past. Simultaneously, baptism declares a future commitment on the part of the person. This is why when a pastor baptizes somebody, he says, "Buried in the likeness of His death and raised to walk in newness of live." Baptism is always a vivid demonstration of the fact that I have broken with my past, I'm dead to that. I have, however, been raised to walk in a brand-new way of life. I have died to the old way and I have been raised to the new way. Baptism is a graphic picture that I have severed the old life and I am forever committed to the new life.

Some people have taken the word *for* in verse 27 to argue that we become sons because we have been baptized, but if that is what Paul meant to say, he has destroyed the entire context because Paul has been arguing throughout this whole chapter that rites like circumcision are completely ineffective in bringing us into a right relationship with God. No amount of keeping laws or rituals can bring us into a right relationship with God, so why would Paul spend his entire time saying rites don't matter only to get to verse 27 and say that they do matter. Why would he argue that rites like circumcision are invalid only to argue for a new rite at this point in the chapter? Would that make sense?

If you could get saved by any performance or legislation, why would Jesus have died on the cross? If you can save yourself through the ordinance of baptism, why would Jesus have gone to the cross of Calvary and there shed His precious blood? There would have been no reason for Jesus to die. Obviously, then, Paul is not saying that baptism saves. The preceding verse argues that we are not justified by baptism and we don't become children of God because we are baptized; we become children of God because we have exercised faith in Christ Jesus.

What then is the point of verse 27? In Roman culture, kids wore a garment that had a red border and by virtue of the fact that they wore a red-bordered garment, they were classified as children. When I worked at the steel plant where my dad worked, they put a little green stripe on your hard hat when you were initially hired. These new employees were called green crosses. A green cross meant you didn't know what you were doing. In other words, watch out for him; he is a menace to the steel plant. In the same way, in Roman culture, a child wore a garment that had a red border on it to show everyone he was still an adolescent and didn't know what he was doing. He was still in the state of immaturity. Watch out for him because he's still a kid.

When a child assumed the rights of adulthood, he experienced what was called the *togavarillas*. He exchanged baby clothes for an adult toga. Putting on an adult toga said, "You don't have to watch out for him; he has reached a level of maturity where he can handle himself now. He's not going to kill anybody. He has reached the level of maturity where we can treat him as if he is an adult." It was equivalent to a Jewish bar mitzvah. The child is an adult now, with all the rights and privileges pertaining thereto; he doesn't have to wear baby clothes anymore.

When we became Christians, we no longer needed a schoolmaster to say, "Thou shalt not." We didn't need somebody watching over our shoulder all the time slapping our wrists and telling us that we were blowing it. When we became saved, we became adult sons and were able to put on the garments of adulthood. Paul argues here that we have put on Jesus Christ and having put on Jesus Christ, we have branded ourselves as being mature people. In the early church, those who were baptized took their clothes off. Even today when we take people in the back to baptize them, the baptismal attendant will say, "Go into stall and take off all your clothes, shoes, socks, and underwear because everything is going to get wet. We will give you a baptismal robe to put on and then, after you're baptized, you can change back into your own clothes."

By the way, this is a strong argument for immersion. Why would you need to change your clothes to be sprinkled? In the early church, some people were baptized nude because they wanted to assume the shame of Jesus who hung naked before the world. The point that I am trying to make is that in the early church, baptism was not an afterthought. It was a frontier between two worlds. It was a denunciation of an immature way of life and the reception of a mature way of life. It was saying "I have lived like a child practicing immaturity, but now I am through with that. I don't live that way anymore. I have cast off those garments of adolescence and want everybody to know that I have done the mature thing and have embraced Jesus Christ."

Baptism in the early church was very risky business. The Bible says that people were actually baptized for the dead, meaning that when they were baptized, their neck was in the noose. In our society, we treat baptism very glibly but in the Eastern world, they didn't treat baptism that way, and they still don't today.

In India, a Hindu can pray and receive Jesus Christ as his personal Saviour and he will not be ostracized by his family. But at the very moment he goes into a baptismal tank and is immersed publicly identifying himself as a disciple of Christ, the very next day his family will print an obituary in the newspaper saying their son is dead and no longer exists.

Baptism is a decisive moment of transition in a person's life. It is where a person steps out of the closet and publicly says he has changed directions and wants the world to know he is through with that immature way of doing things. That person has died to every bit of that old life and is radically following the banner of the Lord Jesus Christ. He is radically following Jesus and denouncing all that he used to be and is putting on Christ. When you put something on, that's the first thing you see.

Many times people did not want to come to the Christian school that I administrated because of its strict dress code. We have had people admit that they have gone to other institutions because they don't want to submit to that dress standard. Clothes are important, and though people shouldn't judge other people by their cover, they do; therefore, clothes say something about who you are. Clothes are the way you advertise yourself and that's why we don't let girls wear things that are too sheer, too short, and too tight. You don't advertise what is not for sale.

Clothes are the first things that people judge us by and the Bible says that we have put on Jesus Christ. In other words, people ought to judge us first and foremost as being followers of Jesus and that is what baptism symbolizes. We are the sons of God through faith in Christ Jesus. That is our declaration, and we have demonstrated it by plunging ourselves beneath baptismal waters. That is our way of saying, "I have decisively broken with the immaturity of the past and have embraced Christ."

Realization (vv. 28-29)

Notice that verse 28 immediately follows that baptismal affirmation. When you and I were baptized, we were announcing to society that we had changed worlds. We are not the people that we used to be; we are new creations. Not only have we announced that we have been converted from the immaturity of the past, but we are also announcing simultaneously that we are part of a new community in the present and into the future. Baptism is a bridge between conversion and church life. I become saved, baptized, and added to the church—

that's the Bible order. Baptism is that door right in the middle of it where I admit that I have been converted. My past is done and I have swung the door in the new direction of the church, where I recognize that now I am a part of a community of believers that has made this same level of commitment. This community is composed of people who are serious about following Jesus and walking with Him. We are part of a new community that has different values than the world does.

Verse 28 speaks about the categories that we have transcended. There is a negative aspect to it—we are no longer Jew or Greek, we are no longer bond or free, we are no longer male or female—there is something more important to us than that. Then verse 28 speaks positively of a new reality—we are all one in Christ Jesus and that is our primary designation. Baptism is the event where that is celebrated. The word *baptizo* means "to dip or to immerse." Even at its root it comes from the word *bapto*, which means "to dip or to dye," and there really may be a reference in baptism to dying colors or changing colors.

When you and I trusted the Lord Jesus Christ as our personal Saviour, and we climbed into baptismal water and announced to the world that we were followers of Jesus Christ, we really were announcing was that we had changed allegiances. We have changed who we follow, we have changed our colors, we are followers of Christ, and that has become the most important designation of our lives. It is more important than race, it is more important than rank in society, it is more important than gender - the most important designation in our lives is the designation that we belong to Jesus.

Do you want to know what the most important title is that you can place on Jeff Amsbaugh? He is a son of God and that is the distinction that puts us on equal footing. Not everybody can say that they are the same gender; society would like to make us that way but we're not. We can't say that we are all the same race even though society is trying to change that. We can't say that we are all of the same economic status, even though governments are trying to accomplish this. But there is one thing that we can say that is true of all of us, and it is that we all have one Lord, one faith, and one baptism. This is not ecumenical togetherness; we're talking about a spiritual bond. Baptized believers are people who have changed their colors publicly, and that is more important than ethnicity, more important economical status, even more important than sexuality. The most important issue for me and my family members is that we all are children of God in Christ Jesus.

I have several male friends who, when they found out they were having a boy, said, "Now, I'm complete. I'm having a son." People who make statements like that don't understand the Bible. It would be more important for us to say, "Now, I'm complete because all of my kids, regardless of their gender, are Christians and following the Lord Jesus Christ." I don't have any influence on what gender my children are. When a man gives seed to his wife, really it is up to God at that point what the sex of that child is going to be. We can't do anything to change the race or gender of our children and we can't do a whole lot about the economic status of our children but we sure can do a lot to see that they become children of God. God forbid that you and I would be more concerned about the gender or the race of our children than the spirituality of our children. The spirituality of our children should be most important.

I am not saying that these other issues are not important. We need the divisions of race in society for culture diversity. Certain cultures are better at certain things than other people. In the same way, we need economic diversity. If everybody owned the company, there would be nobody to work for the company, and if everybody worked for the company, there would be nobody who owned a company. So we need labor and management. God knows we need men and woman, and our society is trying to change that but if everybody were the same sex, the human race would die out immediately. We need men and women to continue the race. We are not saying that these other divisions are not important, but that is not the most important classification that you have. The most important designation that you and I have is the fact that we belong to Jesus Christ.

If a person is lost, these other distinctions do not matter. When you stand before God, He is not going to ask about your race, gender, or economic status. None of that will matter when a person stands before God someday. When you look at our society, we have confusion in all of these issues. We have division in race and there is racial tension in every city in America. Our society is classified by labor division. I grew up in the home of a union worker, and I know what it is to go on strike. Our society is characterized by gender confusion. Men want to be women and women want to be men. Every bit of racial tension in this country and every bit of labor division in this country and every bit of gender confusion in this country could be solved with a proper relationship with Jesus Christ.

That's why Jesus is the most important distinction. It's not that these other distinctions aren't important, but the reason there is so much unrest in all of these other areas is because people aren't properly related to Jesus. If people got related to Jesus and changed their colors, then all this other stuff would take care of itself. Therefore, Jewish blood, free birth, or male sex is nothing if I am not saved. The only thing that matters ultimately is whether I have a personal relationship with Jesus Christ. And the great thing about it is that regardless of what race you are and regardless of what economic class you are and regardless of what gender you are, we all come to Jesus the same way: through faith.

The appeal is to everyone (Isaiah 55:1), even to people who don't have money (Revelation 22:17). In the final analysis, there is only true seed and that's the seed of Abraham. In Galatians 3, it identifies the true seed of Abraham as none other than the Lord Jesus Christ, and if you are in Christ, then you are the seed of Abraham because you are in the ultimate seed of Abraham, which is Christ. It is only in Christ that you inherit the privileges. The privileges are not inherited because of what race you are or what economic status you have or what gender you are, but the privileges are inherited because you are in Christ and that is true regardless of race, rank, or role. In our society, everybody is fighting for racial equality, proper labor recognition, and gender equality.

We need, however, people of different races, different economic statuses, and different genders to make society operate fluidly. The point is not to get everybody equal, which is impossible; the point is regardless of race, rank, or role, to allow Christ to enter our lives and to let Christ empower our giftedness. Then we understand our roles and are willing to function in them.

Don't get bent out of shape about what your title is. Your title is that you are a Christian, and if you are a Christian, you have the most important designation you can have. Being a Christian is more important than being white, black, Hispanic, or Asian. Being a Christian is more important than being male or female. Being a Christian is more important than being rich or poor. The most important thing is just to say "I am a child of God and God has empowered me to be the best me that I can possibly be. Thank you, Lord, for allowing me to be a Christian."

The problem is we get all bent out of shape because we are looking for equality in all of these other areas but really there can be no equality, and what we need to be is more concerned that Christ is flowing through us. We need to be more concerned that we have changed colors and have chosen to follow Him, and that means that all of these secondary matters pale in comparison to the fact that He is the head of my life and is ruling there. I'm telling you that being a child of God is your most important title.

CHAPTER FIFTEEN

The Thrill of Adoption

Galatians 4:1-11

In a previous ministry, I had a dear, godly friend by the name of Tom. Whenever we would open the Sunday night service for testimonies, Tom would always stand and thank the Lord for his two mothers. When he was an infant, his mother left him on the doorsteps of a constable. He also would thank the mother who adopted him and brought him into her family. Whatever else he would say in his testimony, he would start by praising his biological mother who brought him into the world and his adoptive mother who took him in.

There are many people around the world who really would like to have a baby. And sometimes because of biological trouble they are not able to do it in what we would consider the traditional way. But I want to assure you that there's no reason for any baby to be aborted because there are waiting lines all over the world of people who want to adopt children. One of the greatest things for us to know is that when we were unwanted, God adopted us. What a thrill to be a part of the family of God. Consider three things about adoption.

Life in the Orphanage (vv. 1-3)

In the ancient world, children didn't have any rights. We live in an age where we promote the rights of the child and so consequently we see many parents debating with a two-year-old as if that two-year-old is a peer. In our culture we often promote the rights of children, but in the ancient world, children didn't really have any rights. It was not until a child became an adult that he really had privileges and rights per se. It took place in various cultures at different ages.

For example, in the Jewish culture, it took place at the age of twelve when a boy would celebrate his bar mitzvah. On the first Sabbath after his twelfth birthday, a boy would enter into all the responsibilities and privileges of the covenant. At the boy's bar mitzvah, the dad would stand and pray, "Thank you, Father, for relieving me of the responsibility of this boy." And in turn the boy would pray to the Heavenly Father and say, "Thank you for giving me the privilege now to enter into the rights and responsibilities of my sonship."

In Greece, a boy was under his father's tutelage until the age of eighteen. At that time, there was a special ceremony for the boy. His hair was cut and that hair was burned to the god Apollo symbolizing that the boy was now a man.

In Rome, there was another similar thing called the *togavirilis*. In the *togavirilis*, a boy would take all his toys and would burn those toys offering them to the gods. And I think that's what the Apostle Paul was talking about in I Corinthians 13:11 when he said, ". . . when I became a man, I put away childish things." When you become a man, there's a time for you to burn your toys. Someone has said that the difference between a man and a boy is the price of his toys. Well, in Roman culture you proved you were a man by burning your toys and not playing with toys any longer.

Whatever the culture, until the child reached that time when he was fully considered to be an adult, he was still a child and not seen as an heir. More or less, he was viewed as a servant. He was under the tutelage of governors and tutors, and these governors and tutors were responsible for his education, training, and welfare. They were responsible for the day-to-day maintenance of the child. They functioned like our nannies would function today. And the child was subservient to even those slaves. He had to do what those slaves told him to do. The child could do nothing without the consent of those tutors.

But then there was a date that was set by the father. And at that particular date, the status of the child was changed. He was no longer viewed as being a slave. He was rather viewed as being a son. Up until that point, a child was essentially imprisoned; he was in bondage. Even the slaves told him what to do. But at the moment determined by the father, he emerged out of that bondage and was fully viewed as a man in his own right. Similarly, before our conversion, we were under bondage. We were under servitude. It seemed like everybody told us what to do.

I remember several years ago our youngest daughter April came up to me and said, "You know, sometimes I don't like being the youngest." And I said, "Why?" She said, "Everybody tells me what to do." In our pre-Christian days, we were at the mercy of everybody else. We were at the mercy of the world, the mercy of the flesh, and the mercy of Satan. It seemed like everybody was telling us what to do; we were at the mercy of every dictate.

Paul says here that we were under the *elements of the world*. That phrase, elements of the world, is a very interesting phrase. It was used of the alphabet, which is the building block for language. You can't write words, sentences, paragraphs, or a book until first of all you learn the alphabet. That is the entry-level building block of learning. This phrase is used in other places to refer to the mechanics of religion (cf. Galatians 4:9, Colossians 2:8). There are things that we do in religion that are basic rituals. We often perform these rituals in a mechanical way before we find Christ. If we're involved in religion before our conversion, it is often mechanical performance. It's as if we're under a tutor and a governor.

For example, when a child comes to school and is placed under the tutelage of a teacher, very seldom does he do his homework because he is madly in love with the teacher and wants to please her. To the contrary, he does his homework because he's going to get in trouble if he doesn't. And so consequently homework becomes a mechanical thing. Very few kids do homework because they want to please their teachers. Most kids do their homework because they are forced to do so with the threat of imposed penalties for non-compliance.

The same thing is true of a child who's in an orphanage. The orphan doesn't do the dishes because he is madly in love with the orphanage supervisor. It's mechanical. Similarly, the unsaved person who is involved in religion is living life in an orphanage. He is doing things mechanically but has no heart for anything. It's oppressive religion.

John Wesley was a graduate of Oxford before he was converted. He visited prisons and slums, and even came to America as a missionary to the American Indians. He gave alms, but by his own admission said that he did those things as a servant rather than a son. But one night at Aldersgate Street, he said, "My heart was strangely warmed." Do you see the difference between mechanics and warmth?

There are many people today who are doing what they're doing for God because they're scared of imposed penalties if they don't. They don't have any love or affinity for God. Out of fear of God, they mechanically go through religious rituals. But when a person becomes saved, he enters into a family. He doesn't do what he's doing to gain the favor of the Father; he does what he's doing because he loves the Father. Oh, what a privilege it is to get out of the orphanage and serve somebody not because you have to but because you want to!

Labor for an Adoption (vv. 4-5)

I have a pastor friend who has adopted two kids. One day a lady came up to his wife and said to her, "You ought to be thankful that your kids are adopted; you've never had to go through labor pains." The mom responded by saying, "The labor pains of adoption are more intense than the labor pains of biological birth." Think with me about those labor pains.

The Labor of Time (v. 4a)

The fullness of the time implies that everything had to be right before we could be adopted. The time table had to be correct. And, of course, we know that the world had to be right politically for Jesus to be born. It had to be right religiously for Jesus to be born. It had to be right culturally for Jesus to be born. And then when everything was perfect, when the timing was absolutely full, God sent His son to adopt us.

I've watched many parents labor with the time element of adoption. If there is one thing that is slower than pulpit committees, I believe it is adoption agencies. Adoption agencies are slower than molasses on Pluto. And here are potential parents who are agonizing and can't wait to have a child. It seems like every time you think you're just about there, something else comes up. A lady who gives birth knows exactly that in nine months the baby will be there. No woman has to say, "I'm two months overdue." Adoption doesn't work that way. There's an agonizing of a fullness of time. It's a labor of time.

The Labor of Law (v. 4b)

There are certain laws that have to be fulfilled for adoption to take place. So God had to meet those laws, and that's why He came. He placed Himself under the law because He had to redeem us who were under the law. Have you heard of international adoption? This was an inter-galaxy adoption. This was Heaven adopting earth. In an international adoption, there are two sets of laws that have to be met. If an American, for example, is adopting a child from China, both American and Chinese laws have to be fulfilled.

My wife Karen and I have some friends who adopted children from China. And when they adopted their children from China, they had to become immersed in Chinese culture. For all intents and purposes, they had to become Chinese. And when they adopted their daughters, they gave them American as well as Chinese names to protect both cultures. Both sets of laws had to be satisfied in the lives of those children.

It's hard to become Chinese when you're not Chinese. It's difficult to function under the laws of a completely separate society when you don't understand those laws. But if you want an international adoption, the culture of that country must be adopted. And so in order to adopt us, Christ became human. Now if you think it's hard for an American to become Chinese, think of how difficult it was for God to become man and voluntarily suffer the limitations of humanity. What a sacrifice it was on His part to fully immerse Himself in human culture and law to adopt us!

The Labor of Money (v. 5)

The word *redeem* means to buy back. It was a word that was used of purchasing slaves. Adoption is expensive. Most of us have health insurance. When we have a baby, we pay our $500 deductible, but it is nothing for someone who adopts today to pay tens of thousands of dollars. There are people who have saved aggressively for years just for the hope of having one kid.

When God wanted to adopt you, He gave the dearest and most precious thing He had. He gave His own Son. Let me tell you, it wasn't cheap. God paid it all when He bought you and me out of the marketplace of sin. There was a labor of money when He bought you and me out of the marketplace of sin. Was it worth it?

The Laughter of a Child (vv. 6-11)

For all the time that it took, all the rules that had to be satisfied, all the costs that had to be paid, praise God for the glorious results. We are God's children!

I have a friend named Preson Philips who was my favorite Bible professor. Preson's first wife died of cancer. And after his first wife died, he married a widow lady on campus. And this widow lady had a little girl named Nora. When Preson married Bunny, simultaneously he adopted Nora. And when they went down to the court for Nora to be adopted, the judge brought Nora up on the bench and let Nora take the judge's hand as the judge banged the gavel. Nora got to put her hand on the judge's hand to say, "Yes, I want Dr. Philips to be my daddy." And in that sense, once her hand was placed on the hand of that judge, she was forever, from that point forward, a Philips. Preson treated her like she was his own. He doted over her. What a thrill it is to know the laughter of a child! I want to point out to you three things about this laughter.

Laughter of the Spirit (v. 6)

It's obvious that a human father can give his human children his heart. But can an adoptive father give his very nature to his child? I would answer yes. Let me back up a little bit. I grew up in Mansfield, Ohio, seventy miles south of Cleveland. My father, who lived in Mansfield his whole life, was a big Cleveland Indians fan. When I was growing up in Mansfield, the Cleveland Indians were not a good baseball team. They were affectionately referred to as the "mistake by the lake." One year, they finished the season thirty games out of first place. We would go to the old municipal stadium in Cleveland, pay to get in, and pick our seats because the attendance was so sparse. And yet I grew up loving the Cleveland Indians. No thinking rational man would have picked the Cleveland Indians as their favorite ball club during that time. There was only one reason that I was a fan: My father gave me his heart.

When I ordered my first cup of coffee at the age of twelve, I looked up at the waitress and said, "I'll have a cup of coffee with cream." The reason that I chose coffee with just cream, of course, was that's the way my dad drank his coffee. I wanted to be like my dad.

I have watched adoptive parents bring their children to church for the first time. I have watched as they looked upon that adopted infant with tears. That child may have biologically belonged to somebody else, but that little baby will forever know the man who holds it as "dad." *Abba* is the first word a Hebrew child learns to say; it means daddy. You can tell the heart of the adopting dad is already in the heart of the adopted kid. God sent His spirit into our heart so that we can call Him *Abba*, Dad.

Laughter of Substance (v. 7)

Romans 8:17 tells us that we are joint heirs with Christ. We get the same stuff that Christ gets. How rich is Christ? If you're saved, you're a joint heir.

We had a family in a previous ministry who thought they would never be able to have a child biologically. So they adopted a son. As soon as they adopted him, the mother became pregnant with a boy. No one could tell any difference in the way those two boys were treated. They were treated exactly the same way. My aunt and uncle, who already had a biological son, adopted a little girl. The adopted daughter always celebrated two birthdays. They celebrated the birthday when she was biologically born and they also celebrated the day she became theirs. She actually celebrated more birthdays than the biological son. My aunt and uncle went overboard to prove to her that everything the son receives, you receive as well. You're part of the family, and don't you ever forget it.

Laughter of Sweat (vv. 8-11)

It's interesting that when we bring kids over to the house to visit, we don't make them do the dishes. We don't invite kids over to the house to run the vacuum cleaner or clean out the garage. They're not part of the family. The people who do the work are the people who are part of the family. Thus, because God has brought us into His family we should have a heart for getting involved in the family.

Let me illustrate. One Sunday back at our home church, we had a Mother's Day celebration and gave all of the mothers who were present flowers. We had in attendance that Sunday a little bus kid who went out the door and said, "My mother was sick today and couldn't come. Can I get a flower?" The deacon handing out the flowers said, "Sure." The boy went down the steps and put the flower under a bush. He then went to another door and said, "My mother couldn't come today, could she have a flower?" And the other deacon, said, "Sure," and gave him a flower. The kid took it and put it under the same bush and went to yet another door of the church and did the same thing. He was collecting a little bouquet of flowers. One of the deacons stood there and watched this whole thing. Finally, the deacon went up to him and said, "I have been watching what you're doing and I've got a proposition for you. I know that you've done wrong. But would it be all right with you if I treated you as if you were my own son?" The little boy looked up at him with glee and said, "Oh, that'd be great." The deacon took him downstairs and paddled him. He was letting that little boy know that he was one of the family. And if you're one of the family, you're going to be treated like one of the family. There's great security in that.

My sister-in-law and brother-in-law were dorm parents at a children's home in Indiana. There was a particular day when one of the children in the home was acting poorly. My sister-in-law was new on the job and wasn't completely familiar with all the rules of the institution. Not knowing it was against the home's policy, she paddled the wayward boy. She was reprimanded for doing so, but the boy came up afterwards and said, "Thank you for loving me enough to do that." She was treating him just like one of her own children. I'm so glad God treats me as one of the family. There's security in that.

One of the worst things an adoptive parent can do is become sentimental and think, "Oh, they've been in the orphanage so long and have been abused so often that I cannot bear to discipline them." No, the way that you respond to abuse is not by the absence of discipline; it's by correct discipline. God brings us into a good family where we can enjoy all the rights and privileges of sonship.

From time to time when I was growing up, my mom would watch other kids. And sometimes when she would baby-sit, I would watch as they watched the way our family would interact with one another. And I could almost see sadness in their eyes because their family didn't enjoy the spirit that our family had. It was almost like they wished they could be part of our family. Well, if you feel like you've been used and abused by the world, there's a family that is waiting to adopt you. This family is better than any family you've ever experienced. It is the family of God. And anybody who has ever become a part of that family, who has the rights and the privileges of that family, knows the thrill of adoption.

CHAPTER SIXTEEN

The Pastor's Greatest Hurt

Galatians 4:12-16

It's interesting that when you think about the book of Galatians, mostly you think about it as a doctrinal treatise. You think of it as one of the most highly developed theological books in the Bible. It may seem odd, therefore, when we get to these verses that the apostle Paul reveals his heart like he does few places in the Word of God. Here is this great doctrinal treatise and in the middle of it the apostle Paul allows us to see his heart. Thus, there is a direct correlation between content and concern. Every pastor ought to be characterized by good content and healthy concern. We are beginning to see that all true theology is really pastoral theology.

I think sometimes the pendulum can swing in one of two directions. Sometimes men are so concerned with solving all of the theological questions that they sometimes appear insensitive to the needs of their congregations. On the other side of the pendulum, a pastor can be so concerned about his congregation that he tries to pour balm on their hurts with self-help theories and pop psychology. The pastor must be biblically responsible but at the same time personally redemptive. There has to be a dual thread that runs through every message. The pastor has to be concerned that his content is theologically accurate but must also make sure at the same time that it is personally applicable to problems that people are wrestling with day after day. Theologically accurate and personally redemptive is the balance that the Word of God must always achieve.

When we get to this passage, it's interesting that though Paul has been making a theological argument, he is not pained because he feels he is losing an argument; he is pained because he feels that he is losing people. It is not important whether you and I win an argument but it is important that we are able to help and minister to people as they really are. The apostle Paul reveals three hurts in this passage and the first two hurts are not the greatest hurts. He will talk about two lesser hurts and then culminate with the greatest hurt that a pastor can have.

Evangelistic Pain (v. 12)

Paul has not previously issued a command in this book and the first command that he issues is this: Be like me. It sounds rather arrogant, doesn't it? When Karen and I were in Philadelphia at our first church, one of our favorite restaurants was The Black Angus Inn, and one night while we were at the restaurant, a man and a woman were having an argument. The man was very vain and was talking loud enough so the rest of the restaurant could hear him. He looked at the woman across the table and said, "What you need to be is more like me." My wife Karen and I looked across the table at each other and laughed, and said, "If he is trying to have a healthy marriage, this is not the way to do it."

The apostle Paul says, "Be like me," and the strange

thing is this is not the first time or the only time that he says this in the Bible. As a matter of fact, frequently as you go throughout the New Testament, the apostle Paul says, "Be like me" (cf. I Corinthians 4:14-16, I Corinthians 11:1, Philippians 3:17, I Thessalonians 1:6). The interesting thing is that in most instances when Paul says, "Follow me," he says it because nobody is worth following if they are not following the Lord. In this passage, it goes in a different direction altogether. He doesn't say, "Follow me" or "Be like me because I am like Christ." Rather, he says, "Be like me because I became like you." That sounds confusing.

This sounds similar to what he told King Agrippa (cf. Acts 26:28). He is saying to Agrippa, "You are a king, Agrippa, and I am a prisoner; but even though you are a king and I am a prisoner, you would be in better shape if you were like me." Why? Because Paul, even though he was in bonds, had something that Agrippa didn't have. Paul had the Lord and he said, "I would rather be a prisoner and have the Lord than be a king and not have God. I would rather you be like me." So Paul says, "Be like me" and what I think he means is, "You need to become a Christian, and the reason I want you to become a Christian is because I became like you."

In other words, the whole reason he wanted the people to become Christians had manifested itself in such honesty that he became like them. He fit into their culture and adopted their lifestyle. He ate what they ate and worked where they worked. He placed the Gospel in the proper context for the culture to understand it.

He wanted the people to become so much like him and be saved that he became like them and became virtually a Galatian (cf. I Corinthians 9:19).

Our goal is to take the people of our city and make them like us. We want them to be saved. But in order to make them like us, we've got to become like them because if we act like we are from a different part of the world, they are not going to listen to us. We have to put the gospel into the context of the environment and the culture in which people are. I'm not talking about changing the message; I'm talking about us changing the way we do things so we can enter into the lives of the people to whom we minister. Our goal is to make them like us (Christians) and in order to do that, we have to make ourselves like them and enter into their culture. When you and I try to put the gospel into the context of the cultures of different people, it can cause great growing pains.

That's what the apostle Paul is saying here and the great thing about it is the people in Galatia responded to Paul positively. They did not injure him or look upon him disdainfully when he came to Galatia. They welcomed him and received him with open arms. They embraced the Gospel warmly. In spite of all the pain he went through to adjust himself to the Galatian people, they did not injure him. If people become saved, it's worth the pain and difficulty of making the cultural adjustment. In order for the Gospel to advance, we have to adjust who we are to what they are at that moment.

Thursday night a medical doctor from Pakistan was

led to the Lord and at the same time across the city someone in the projects was being led to the Lord. I ask you could there not be two more diverse cultures than that? But the people of the church became what the people of the community are so that the people of the community could become what we are, Christians. And in both instances, we were warmly received and not rejected in spite of the fact that we know nothing about Pakistan and most of us know nothing about living in the projects. We became what they were so they could become like we are. When that happens, the evangelistic pain is worth it all. Jeff Amsbaugh wants to be the type of man that you can take to the fanciest mansion and to the worst projects. I want to fit in at both places. That's my goal because I want to become whatever I need to become for people to get what I've got.

Physical Pain (vv. 13-14)

Paul alludes to some illness that he had. When Paul first went to Galatia to preach the Gospel, he admits that he was sick. Three major ideas have been advanced as to what this malady was. Some people think he had malaria. In that region of Galatia, there was a swampy area, and it was very common for people there to get malaria. Some Bible scholars believe he contracted malaria when he went there. Other people believe he had epilepsy because in verse 14 he says they did not reject him. The word *reject* translates a Greek word that means to spit it out, and some people see this term as a veiled reference to an epileptic seizure where people foam at the mouth. Even though he was foaming at the mouth, they didn't spit him out. Some people think it was epilepsy.

I think, however, he probably had some type of eye ailment. Verse 15 references the willingness of the Galatians to pluck out their own eyes and give them to the apostle Paul. The day that Paul was saved, he was blinded by a great light. Ananias had to come to the house where Paul was staying and pray for him so he could recover his sight. Later, when Paul stood before the high priest, he could not even recognize him even though he was just a few feet away. Even in this book, the apostle Paul will validate his authorship by referencing the large letters that he is forced to use (6:11). So I think the evidence seems to suggest to us, especially in the immediate context, that the apostle Paul suffered from some type of eye disorder that was very noticeable. By Paul's own admission, God had made him weak in order that his evangelistic efforts might be strong (cf. II Corinthians 12:7).

Paul had been given many revelations from God. Knowledge, of course, tends to puff up. The more intelligent we become, the more arrogant we become. Thus, the Lord chose to humble Paul through a "thorn in the flesh." This physical ailment made Paul more dependent upon the Lord. Thus, through this weakness Paul was more effective.

I am in favor of learning techniques to perfect the art of soul-winning, but if we are wholly dependent upon our twelve-point plan, we are going to fail. We need the power of the Holy Spirit upon us. If we go in our own strength, we will be unsuccessful. But if we go recognizing our human weakness, we give God's power an opportunity to flow through us. That is what Paul is alluding to here.

Paul had a physical ailment that made him look a little weird, and the Galatians could have rejected him because of it. Instead, he says, they received him as an angel and as Christ Himself. Paul does not condemn them for this. As a matter of fact, he commends them for this. They received this ugly-looking preacher. According to secular history, Paul was short, bald, had a hook nose and slanted scaly eyes. They could have said, "Look at that ugly little preacher." But instead of spitting him out, they received him in spite of the fact that he was a physical embarrassment.

When I was in high school, I was diagnosed with a crippling disease and had to spend a good deal of time during my eleventh grade year in a wheelchair. I went to a rich, affluent school. Mom and Dad scraped like crazy to be able to put us in that Christian school, and those kids could have, because of their affluence, rejected Jeff Amsbaugh. He was an embarrassment but that school reached out to me as a crippled kid. They weren't ashamed of my aliment.

Our oldest daughter was born in need of facial reconstruction. Shortly after she was born, a lady in our church came into my office. She had been to the hospital to see Ashley and she came in and she said, "Pastor, I just saw Ashley." As I braced myself to receive negative words, she said, "I have never seen a baby with more beautiful eyes, and I've never seen a baby with a more perfectly rounded head." She was very sincere and she said, "That's one of the prettiest babies I've ever seen." I don't remember a whole lot of compliments, but I do remember that one. I needed it. That lady reached out to me and was saying that she refused to be embarrassed by this.

Our society is way too overloaded in what it thinks about glamour. We are so shallow that we judge everybody by physical appearance. If someone is ugly, we want to keep our distance because we feel they don't measure up to the standard. Paul said when he went into Galatia the Galatians didn't treat him with contempt in spite of the fact that he had a tremendous amount of physical pain.

Emotional Pain (vv. 15-16)

The Galatians welcomed Paul culturally. He wasn't from around there, and they still welcomed him. They did not despise him physically. Instead of being appalled at his eye ailment, they would have ripped out their own eyes and given them to him. Now in verse 15 there comes a great change. All of this joy and satisfaction dissipates. At a point they would have ripped out their own eyes and given them to Paul. They would have scarred and injured themselves so that he could have had a better ministry. But now he says these people despise him and treat him as an enemy. They treated him as an enemy for one simple reason—he told them the truth.

A pastor can never allow sentiment to distract him from telling people the truth. Pastors don't love people if they fail to tell them the truth. If you fail to speak the truth to someone, you don't love them — you love their love, and there is a difference. Paul could not curb his message to gain their favor. Paul wanted to be loved by his people, but the pastor is not called to be popular; he is called to be faithful. You have to preach the truth whether it is in season or not in season, whether you are warmly applauded or terribly shunned because of it.

When a pastor is hated by the very people he has tried to help, that's the most hurtful thing a pastor experiences. Sometimes pastors are warmly received by people with whom they have spent minimal time. Pastors often have silent supporters. There are others, however, whom you have put hours into. If you were to total all the time that you have spent with them trying to help them, it would be extensive. You have tried to pour the truth of God into the situation so that they will be better people, but instead of responding positively to it, they absolutely hate you because you told them the truth. The greatest pain that a pastor can experience is when people are vindictive and mean simply because they have been told truth.

A pastor can have all kinds of pain. He can have the cultural pain of trying to fit into a geographic region. He can have the physical pain of a disabled body. But none of that compares to the emotional pain of people doing you dirty because you loved them enough to tell them the truth. There are numerous hirelings who stand behind pulpits and tell people what they want to hear. A true pastor, however, advises people according to the truth of the Word of God. And none of us should hate someone because he has the courage to tell the truth. Don't count people as enemies because they tell you the truth. The truth is what will change your life.

CHAPTER SEVENTEEN

Five Questions to Ask Before I Move My Letter

Galatians 4:17-20

If the greatest pain a pastor experiences is the pain of losing people after he has invested so much in them, then, obviously, no pastor who is worth his salt loses people casually. No pastor who is worth his salt can say, "If they want to leave, let them leave." It doesn't work that way. I think many people think that because they've heard a pastor thunder from the pulpit, he is devoid of feeling and compassion, but that is not true. Pastors feel things, and they feel things very deeply; therefore, losing people after you have invested much time and effort is part of the greatest pain that a pastor experiences.

If that is true, then five questions need to be asked before anybody moves his or her letter. And these five questions are what is under discussion in the passage that is before us.

Why is this new church excited about me coming? (v. 17)

Paul here is referring to a group that is trying to win the Galatian people over. They are zealously trying to win the Galatians to their group. They are flattering them giving the Galatians all kinds of attention, but Paul is very clear that their intentions are no good. He

225

says, "They zealously affect you, *but* not well . . ." The reason they are flattering the Galatians is so they might exclude them. That may seem a little odd. Exclude them from what? In the context, they are trying to exclude the Galatians from the apostle Paul. He is saying that these people are flattering the Galatians, zealously affecting them, but their intention is bad. The intention of throwing all of this affection upon the Galatians was to exclude the Galatians from Paul. They don't want the Galatians to have anything to do with Paul any longer.

As a matter of fact, the only reason they were piling all this flattery upon the Galatians was so that the Galatians could be of benefit to their church so their numbers would go up. In other words, they were flattering the Galatians to make their group bigger. They were not concerned about the Galatians' development; they were not concerned about the Galatians' growing in the things of God. That was not the concern of this new group. This new group was not asking how they could minister to these people and help these people spiritually; that was not entering into their thinking. They were not thinking how they could affect the Galatians for good; they were thinking about how the Galatians could affect them for good. How can the Galatians build up our numbers to make our statistics better? In other words, how can they affect us?

I like numbers. I've preached to pews and to people, and I'd much rather preach to people. If it comes down to preaching to a hundred or a thousand, I'd rather preach to a thousand. If it comes down to preaching to two or five, I'd rather preach to five. I would like to be able to affect the most people as possible — I like numbers. The reason I like numbers is because I want to invest, and help develop as many people spiritually as I possibly can. The reason we are concerned about numbers is not because they pump us up and make our statistics greater. It is because the more people we have, the more we can get involved in their lives and help them spiritually develop. The point is if you are going to a place because that place is just falling all over you, that is dangerous.

If a church will tell you whatever you want to hear to get you, they will tell you whatever you want to hear to keep you; therefore, you won't grow at a church like that because they are not telling you what you need to hear. They are telling you what you want to hear. Many times there is a big difference in what we want to hear and what we need to hear. This is a fundamental philosophy of ministry: We don't use people to build our ministries; we use ministries to build our people. This is where this group completely lost it. They were trying to use the Galatians to build their ministry whereas the apostle Paul was using his ministry to build the Galatians. Thus, if a church is all excited about what you can do for them, that may be very flattering for you at the beginning but watch out! You want to be able to grow at a church. If that church will tell you anything you want to hear just to be able to land you because that's what it takes to land you, what is it going to take to be able to keep you?

Ask yourself these questions: Why is this new church excited about me coming? Are they excited because they can get involved in my family's life and help me develop, or are they just getting excited because I'm padding their numbers?

Why am I excited about this new church? (v. 18)

There is nothing wrong about being zealous, provided you're zealous for the right reason. When Paul was in town and gave them attention, Paul says, "You all were zealous for me when I was showering my attention upon you but when I had to move on to the next town and this other group started showering you with attention, then you became zealous for them. There was one point where you would have ripped out your eyes and given them to me because I was so physically infirm but now that I am out of town and you can't see me anymore; it is out of sight, out of mind." They migrated to the group down the street who flattered them and fell all over them the way the apostle Paul previously did. The only reason they were excited about this new church was because that church was excited about them.

Thousands of times over of the past twenty-one years of ministry, I've seen this scenario. People come and make an impression, and people fall all over them because they make an impression when they first come. After they are here for a time, however, we say, "These people have issues." They hid these issues for a while but we can't hide our warts forever. Who we are eventually seeps out. Then people aren't as excited about us as they used to be, and after awhile, people discover we've got some serious issues. Instead of correcting those issues, I move my letter to the next church down the street because they don't know I have issues. And because they don't know, they are going to fall all over me the same way this church fell all over me several years ago.

Instead of correcting the issues that have been brought to light and instead of getting my heart right with God, I move down the street and let the next church be as blind as the former church used to be. In short, I become the church member of the revolving letter. I move from place to place so long as people don't find out who I really am. Instead of getting that issue dealt with, I just move down the road and pray the next church doesn't find out. The only reason I am excited about them is because they are excited about me, and the only reason they are excited about me is because they haven't discovered who I really am.

If that's the way you choose a church, you are always going to have short-lived courtship. If the only reason I am excited about this church is because they are excited about me because they don't know me yet, that is not a good reason.

Is this new church prepared to work with me? (v. 19)

When Paul pointed out what was wrong with the Galatian people, he didn't do it because he hated them. When pastors point out problems in your life, it is not because they hate you. When people correct you, it is not because they dislike you. People often say, "That pastor pointed out that problem in my life, so he must not like me." The Bible, however, says that God rebukes and chastens because He loves (cf. Revelation 3:19). Paul is not pointing out their problems because he hates them—he is pointing out their problems because he loves them. He calls them in this context his precious little children.

In the context of Galatians 4, they should have been mature adults. They should have grown into maturity, but they were still acting like children. But even though they were still acting like children, they were his children. Those of you who have older children know when your adult children still act like juveniles. Sometimes you can see one of your adult children do something that looks pretty juvenile and you say, "You baby." But even when our adult kids act like little kids, they are still our kids.

Sometimes our adult children will telephone home, and the things that will come out of their mouths will sound childish. There are times when I talk to my wife and I sound like I'm five. When we are acting childish, it is difficult for others to think of us as mature, despite the fact we may be chronologically advanced.

Because the Galatians were Paul's kids—he had birthed them into the family of God—he was willing to work with them to bring them to a state of maturity. He had labored to bring them into the body of Christ and now he says that he would go into labor again if necessary to let Christ be formed in them. There is a reason that childbirth is called *labor*. A woman, when she brings a baby into the world, literally goes to the jaws of death to do so. No amount of birthing classes can adequately define what a woman experiences in labor. Imagine a woman when she goes through labor saying, "I'd like to do that again." The only thing that makes women want to go through labor again is the child who is birthed. The joy of a child overwhelms her so much that she can't remember the labor pains.

Paul says, "I would go through labor twice for you all." It is bad enough to go through labor once to bring a kid into the world but Paul is willing to do it twice. It takes hard work to bring people into the family of God. Sometimes it takes a long time to stay with somebody until the Spirit of God brings the truth of God to bear on their conscience and they are born again. For many people, it takes years of blood, sweat, tears, prayer, and anguish to bring them into the family of God. We prayed for my grandfather for eighteen years to get saved before he finally trusted the Lord Jesus Christ as his personal Saviour. When a child is born into the family of God, our work is not over. When a lady brings a baby into the world, she will never be pregnant with that baby again. But in another sense, it is just beginning. She has eighteen years of peanut butter sandwiches staring her in the face. In the same way, when we bring somebody into the family of God, we can't practice spiritual infanticide and leave that baby on its own. We have now committed ourselves to that person's spiritual development. Discipleship is imperative.

This discipleship training is no easy matter. Spiritual maturation does not come easily. Paul is asking, "Are these new people who are flattering you going to work with you?" I found out that there is a difference between flattering and fawning over a baby, and working with a baby; there is a difference between those two things.

On Sunday morning, it is nothing for me to go down to the nursery window and stand there and wave at the kids, but when that baby's diaper needs to be changed, I'm going to the auditorium. And when that baby spits up, I'm not going to be there. There are many churches that like to flatter babies but don't want to work with them. We don't prove our love for people by our willingness to flatter them— we prove our love for our people by our willingness to work with them.

Is this new church that is failing all over you and flattering you willing to go through the jaws of death to help with your spiritual development? How committed is that church to making you Christ-like? That is what Paul is asking. Unfortunately, many pastors today labor to form themselves in their congregation—they don't labor to form Christ in their congregation—and there is a difference. Is this new church prepared to work with me? That's a very important question.

Have I talked to my present pastor? (v. 20)

As Paul winds this down, he says, "I want to be near you. I wish we had an opportunity to talk." This letter, unfortunately, was being written on the eve of the Jerusalem counsel. Paul, obviously, was there on a very important doctrinal matter; it was not possible for him to be in Galatia but he wanted to be there. He was at his wit's end, and he knew that if they talked face to face, if somehow they could hear his voice, things would be different.

Isn't it amazing how things can be worked out if you can just get two people to talk? I don't know how many times in my office a married couple has come to me and both are angry to the point of divorce. I reach in my pocket, pull out some money, and say, "I want you to go to a nearby restaurant and eat. I am asking you to bring no cell phones, pagers, or communication devices. You can't have anything that will take your attention away from each other. You are going to sit there and talk, and then after you are done with lunch, you are going to take a walk and finish your conversation. When you get this talked out with each other, if you still need me, I will be here." More often than not, they never return. The only thing that needed was an opportunity to talk out their differences.

In the silence, they were ruminating. They worked themselves up into a lather, which all could have been avoided if they had just talked to each other. When you were dating before you were married, what was a bad date? A bad date was one with little or no communication. When people approach a marriage altar, however, they do so because they have opened their hearts and talked to each other. They have shared their wants, desires, and dreams with each other. Communication is the thread that knits hearts together. If communication is what put your hearts together, then what is going to keep your hearts together? Obviously, it is communication. People can always get along if they just talk.

I don't know how many times people have gotten mad about something and you tell them, "Go on and talk to them." But they'll say, "I'm not talking to him or her." Do you understand how anti-spiritual that sentiment is? Paul said, "If we could just get together and talk about this thing, I know there wouldn't be friction." How could they leave, walk off, and not even talk about it? Paul says, "You need to see my tears. You need to feel my heart and sense my pain. There is no way this breach of fellowship between the two of us can be considered ethical if there has been no talking about it." Anytime you break fellowship with somebody and you haven't talked with that person first, you are morally wrong.

Will I really respond to the Bible at the next place? (v. 21)

These people said they wanted to be under the law, but did they really understand what the law was saying? For all their talk about the law, Paul said, "You haven't really listened to the law, because if you had listened to the law, you wouldn't be doing what you are doing right now. You say that you are leaving because you want the law but if you love the law, you would listen to the law and wouldn't be doing what you are doing right now."

What is the number one reason people leave church? It may not be the number one reason, but it is the number one stated reason — I'm not being fed. Let's follow that up. Let's say you go to a new church and the pastor preaches the Word of God. Are you going to listen to it? Are you going to heed it? Are you going to practice it? When the preaching convicts your heart and the Holy Spirit brings something to mind, are you going to walk to the altar and kneel, and get that thing right with God?

The fact is that through the years, we have discovered that most people who say, "I'm not being fed" don't mean it because when they go to the next place, when the Word of God is preached, they don't listen to it. For all their talk of the love of the Word of God, they don't care about the Word of God because when the Word of God is preached, they never respond to it. The fact is people leave not because they love the Bible but because they don't want to obey the Bible. Love for the Bible is not proven by sentiment — it is proven by obedience and submission.

Am I going to this place just because they flattered me so they could inflate their numbers? Am I interested in this church simply because they haven't figured out who I am yet? Is this new church that is flattering me going to work with me when they discover my flaws? Is this church committed to that level of development in me? Have I talked to all the people who have offended me or am I just going to leave and not talk to anybody about it? When I talk about the Word of God, am I really concerned about the Word of God? These are questions that I think are worthy of consideration.

These questions are pertinent anytime we are considering a change of any kind. You and I have to make sure that when we are making a change, we are making it for the right reason. Whether we are talking about church life, family life, occupational life, or educational life, this is the way that God wants us to resolve problems. Are we willing to resolve problems in a Biblical manner? If not, we need to get our hearts right.

CHAPTER EIGHTEEN

What Kind of Mother Are You Anyway?

Galatians 4:22-31

I'd like to ask you question: What kind of mom are
you anyway? That's an important question. God in this
passage paints a picture of two vastly different kinds of
mothers and our children are largely going to be the
product of what the mother decides to be. Let's answer
that question. What kind of mom are you anyway?

The Difference of a Mother (v. 22)

The Bible tells us in this passage that Abraham had
two sons. One was Isaac, the son of promise. His very
name means laughter. He was a joy from the very moment that he was born; his parents were tickled pink to
have him. And they named him accordingly—laughter.
The other was Ishmael, who was vastly different. The
Bible says that he was a "wild man" (cf. Genesis 16:12).
These two sons, Isaac and Ishmael, were about as opposite as night and day. The Bible says concerning Ishmael
that he put his hand toward every man and every man
put his hand toward him. The other son, Isaac, was vastly different. He was submissive to the will of God, laid
his all upon the altar, and when his own father sought
to take his life, he submitted himself to that believing it
was the will of God.

What made the difference in these two boys? Certainly it was not their father for they both had the same

father, Abraham. Certainly the difference was not finances for both of these boys were adequately taken care of and both had every possible thing at their disposal. Abraham was a rich man. He could provide for his sons, and even when Ishmael was sent away, he went with a good financial package. As far as I can tell, the only difference that existed in the lives of these two boys was their mothers. God is telling us that a mother can make all the difference in the world. A mother can make or break a child.

I've often said that the number one reason I am in the ministry today is the influence of a godly mother. I'm thankful that my mother was committed to staying home. I'm thankful that I was not a latchkey kid. I'm thankful that when I came home at 3:15 every day from school, there was a mother who was willing to hear about my day. I thank God for the constant care that I received as a teenager as I went through my foot surgeries. My mother came to the hospital every morning and bathed me to save me from the embarrassment of nurses having to do that.

Every semester that I was at college, my mother would write me letters and at the end of every letter she would write I Chronicles 28:20, the verse she had claimed for my life. It was the influence of a godly mother that set the course for my life.

Oh, they talk about a woman's sphere, as if it had a limit,
But there's not a place in earth or heaven,
There's not a task to mankind given,
There's not a blessing or a woe,

There's not a whispered yes or no,
There's not a life or death or birth,
There's not a feather's weight of worth
Without a woman in it.

I get a little disturbed when a lady laments being a stay-at-home mom. I want to tell you that the noblest profession that a woman can engage in is the raising of godly children. Therefore, if someone asks, "What do you do?" and your answer is, "I'm a mom," don't ever hang your head about that. That is a great and noble profession. You have the opportunity to make legal decisions every day by deciding who's right and who's wrong. You get to minister emergency first aid every day. You get to solve the nation's problems every day. The hand that rocks the cradle is the hand that rules the world. There's a difference that a mother can make.

The Damage of a Mother (vv. 23-25)

If a mother can make a difference, then certainly it is true that she can make a difference for bad. There is damage that a mother can do. Hagar was a woman who damaged her son.

Identified with the World (v. 24b)

The very name *Hagar* reminds us of Egypt. From the very first pages of the Bible when we are introduced to this woman, she is identified with Egypt, which throughout the entire Word of God is a type of the world. She was identified with a pagan land that was accustomed to pagan practices. When we think of Hagar, we think of a bondwoman, an Egyptian. We think of a woman who is affiliated with paganism. When your name is mentioned, what images come up in people's minds? When people think of you, do they think of worldliness? Do they think of paganism? Do they think of false religious practice? What images come up in people's minds when your name is mentioned? Hagar was a bad mother because she was identified with the world.

Irritated by Her Marriage (v. 23a)

In verses 22-25 Hagar is repeatedly referenced in terms of bondage. Any woman who sees her relationship to her husband as that of bondage is not a happy woman. She doesn't have a happy life. Cursed is the woman who views her marriage as that of slavery, as that of a bondwoman.

I came across this poem several years ago, and I think it makes a point. There are two sides of looking at motherhood.

It's such a waste of time to cook;
I'm just a walking cookery book.
I make and bake the morning through,
The favorite pies and puddings too,
And then in half an hour or less,
My toil has gone to nothingness.
It's a waste of time to dust the stairs,
To clean the brass and polish the chairs,
To sweep and pick up bits of fluff

For nothing's ever clean enough.
Five minutes after I have done,
Someone is sure to romp and run,
Kick out the stair rods, flip the mat,
Slam the doors, and scare the cats.
Some sticky hand is sure to press
The brasses from their sprightliness.
I tidy up and do the dusting
But all the while my wings are rusting.
Then washing day it seems to me
Is such a waste of energy.
What use to stand before a tub
And soak and rinse and blue and rub.
Next week the same garment's stain
Will come into my hands again.
It's such a waste of time to mend
One has no sooner reached the end
Of last week's piles, need you ask it,
This week's fills up the mending basket.
The stockings, which were hale and hardy,
Returned from each picnicking party
Weak and worn and wainly show
Great gaping holes in heal and toe,
While buttons have a cantankerous way
Of disappearing every day.
Sponging off the spots and ironing creases—
Between it all I'm worn to pieces.
Woman from cradle to grave
Is nothing but a galley slave.

But here's the other way to look at it:

I've done an angel's work today.
Yes, such an honor came my way.
Real angel's work and lest you doubt it,
I'm going to tell you all about it.
Well, first I cooked; it was so nice
To plan the pies, stewed fruit, and rice.
God sent his angel once to make,
Cakes for a poor wayfarer's sake.
But just today, he honored me
And sent the task my way, you see.
And while I tidied up the place,
Gave every knob a radiant face,
Back of my mind this thought would lurk,
That I was still at angel's work.
Putting away coats and dresses
And removing all small unsightlinesses
For oh, it's such a lovesome thing,
The straightening out and freshening.
And after that I washed a few
Small wooly garments, old not new,
Things that I had rubbed and rinsed before
Probably forty times or even more
And as I hung them on the line,
I thought what God-like work was mine
To cleanse all needs, to wash out stains
Till not a single speck remains.
So later in the day 'twas sweet
To sit and rest my tired feet

Mending the clothes and planning out too
How to make old things into new.
For surely 'tis an angel's way
To put things right from day to day.
To find thin places and repair
The glad rags and the sturdy ware.
Since wear and tear must surely be
On this side of eternity.
I'm feeling very proud to say,
I've done an angel's work today.

Which way do you view your job? Are you identified by the world? Are you irritated by your marriage?

Influenced by Her Flesh (v. 23b)

While Sarah was motivated by the promises of God, Hagar was motivated by her flesh. Hagar conceived her son in an illegitimate fashion that was outside of the will of God. She had no courage to refuse the advances of Abraham. Isaac was born as the result of the promises of God, but Ishmael was born as the result of wild flesh that had gone amuck. Is it any wonder that he grew up to be what the Bible called "a wild man"? Fleshly mothers raise fleshly children. Fleshliness can manifest itself in all kinds of ways like anger, temper, or lack of control during the monthly cycle. And when you allow your flesh to take over and become a raging set of hormones, you're having a bad influence on your children.

Ignorant of True Spirituality (v. 24a)

Because Hagar was governed by the flesh, the Bible says here that she was comparable to Sinai. Sinai was that place where God gave rules and regulations, but the law was never intended to be a means of salvation. No one ever gets to Heaven by keeping a bunch of rules—no one. As a matter of fact, God gave us that big list of rules so we would become frustrated and recognize that we can't keep those rules by ourselves. The law was our schoolmaster to bring us to Christ.

Hagar was governed by the flesh. She thought that spirituality was to be found in keeping rules and regulations. If you and I are happy with our kids just keeping rules, we don't know what true spirituality is all about. If all I do is get a child to keep a bunch of rules, then all I do is make his crime more sophisticated. If, however, we parent the heart of the child, then keeping rules will be no problem. But if we think that just because our kids are keeping rules that they're right with God, you and I have missed the boat.

Spirituality by definition has to do with the spirit of a child. It has to do with his heart. Sometimes we think just because our son has short hair, has no tattoos, and hasn't come home with a nose ring that he's right with God. Nothing could be further from the truth. If we get our kids to do righteousness in the flesh, it will be just a step until they're doing unrighteousness in the flesh. We need children who are filled with the Spirit.

Institutional in Her Worship (v. 25)

If Sinai was the place where the law was given, Jerusalem was the place where the law was implemented. Jerusalem was that place where the law was formalized. Jerusalem was that place where the mechanics of worship were carried out. Our kids have to be familiar with the mechanics of religion, but it has to go further than that. We must worship God in spirit and in truth (John 4:24). Our bodies are the temples of the Holy Spirit (I Corinthians 6:19-20). When you come to church, you don't come to the sanctuary; you brought the sanctuary with you. I don't want my child to be a Christian only on Sunday. I want him to be a Christian every moment he breathes God's free air.

A person who is out of church has a bigger problem than missing church. His biggest problem is he's not walking with God on a daily basis. He does not love God with all of his heart, soul, mind, and strength. Yes, he needs to be back in church but he needs much more than that. Many times we feel just because our kids are still going to church with us that they're okay. We must, however, desire our religion to be more than institutionalized mechanics; we want our children to have a heart for God.

The Delight of the Mother (vv. 26-29)

Sarah was the opposite of Hagar. She had the right kind of motherhood. Why?

A Heavenly Perspective (v. 26)

If Hagar corresponds to the earthly Jerusalem, Sarah corresponds to the Heavenly one. In Heaven, people have a heart to serve God. When we pray the Lord's Prayer, we ask that God's will be done on earth as it is done in Heaven. How is God's will done in Heaven? It's done with heart. In Heaven when God issues a command, no one says, "Oh, I'd rather not, but I guess I will." The hearts of all in Heaven have been completely transformed. People have been glorified and serve God with total love. Oh, that we had that Heavenly perspective! It's sad that some people think serving God is bondage and say, "I guess we have to go to church today or the preacher's going to be visiting us." We should do things from a heavenly perspective.

A Happy Perspective (v. 27)

Freedom to do the will of God is largely created by atmosphere. Parents who consistently criticize the things of God should not be surprised then their children do not want to go to church. A happy heart comes from a happy perspective. Sarah's son was not a pain in the neck. He was no accident. He was in accordance with divine promise, and Sarah was delighted to have him. His very name means laughter.

When I graduated from high school, my mother put together a scrapbook for me which summarized by growing up years. And at the end of that scrapbook, my mom wrote me a letter and there were tear drops on that letter; you could see the stains from the tears. And the letter began this way, "Dear Jeffrey, no child was wanted more on the face of the earth than you were." You don't know what it means for a kid to know that he's wanted, that his mother is absolutely ecstatic to have him. For ninety years, Sarah had been praying for a boy. And finally after ninety years, that boy was born. Was there ever a boy more wanted than he was? How she must have kissed his face.

Because I was wanted, I knew that I had some responsibilities. My mom just didn't want to have a child; my mom was agonizing over a boy that she could do something with. And I felt that. I never wanted to let her down. I was shaped by that happy perspective.

A Holy Perspective (v. 28)

God didn't merely throw this child at Sarah and say, "Okay, there's your boy." When that kid came, he came with a promise. Prior to conception, Isaac was set apart for sacred use. He had a sacred purpose. Isaac came with a promise. And your child comes with a promise too. That ought to grip our hearts and shape our parenting. We must parent with this holy perspective.

A Hearty Perspective (v. 29)

Children set apart as special objects are going to be ridiculed. Whenever you have a child who has a promise attached to him, and he knows that he's something special and that God has something special for his life, immediately the other kids are going to persecute the children of promise. It always happens. But our job is to help our kids endure the persecution. A child who knows his place in the plan and purpose of God is able to withstand the ridicule. He's able to stand up because he knows that as long as God smiles upon his life, he could care less what the Ishmaels have to say about it. Our job is to help our children have tenacity.

It amazes me when a parent complains because their child has a strong will. You should desire for your child to have a strong will. When a smooth-talking Casanova comes along, I want my girls to have a strong will. The problem is not that our kids have strong wills; it's that those wills need to be channeled in the right direction. We want children with convictions and standards that have a strong will to withstand the vices of this world. Don't be angry if you have a strong-willed child; rejoice in that strong will and help your child use it to stand up against the persecution of this world. Oh, that our kids had that kind of hearty perspective.

The Decision of the Mother (vv. 30-31)

There are two decisions that a mother has to make. These two decisions will loom large in the success of the child.

Concerning the Child's Crowd (v. 30)

The kids who poke fun at good and God will never be in the inner circle with my children. I'm casting them out. When you cast kids out of the circle of acceptance, you will be vilified. But your child's holiness is more important than their happiness. I'm not going to let my kid hang out with a scorner. Cast out the scorner.

My job is to limit the bad influences on my children. You say, "You're sheltering that kid." Exactly! I am by design limiting the influences that are going to spoil the mind of my child. That's why we're very selective about where we let our kids go. That causes all kinds of problems. I'm happier when other kids come over to my house than when my kids go to other people's houses. So you want to have a sleepover. Fine, you can have it at my house. Because I know what happens in my house. I don't know what happens in your house. I've had people tell me they had character and they didn't. I'm just saying that my job is to protect. I don't want Ishmaels hanging out with my Isaac. I'm not letting that happen. I have a job to protect the crowd that my child hangs out with. That is part of my job.

Concerning Her Own Character (v. 31)

Not only does a mother have to make a decision concerning the child's crowd but she has to make a decision concerning her own character. What kind of mother are you anyway? What kind of mother will my children have? Are my children going to be children of the bondwoman or are they going to be children of the free woman? Are you going to be the kind of mother who creates the atmosphere that Christianity is drudgery and that we only serve God because we have to? Is that the atmosphere that you're creating or is there freedom in your home for your kids to serve God the way they ought to serve God? Are they free to do that?

Sometimes children respond well to preaching and develop stronger convictions than their parents. When they do, the parents get angry. I have seen people leave the church and go to other churches because they were embarrassed that their kids started getting more spiritual than they were. You don't want to be the Ishmael in the life of your own kid. You don't want to be poking fun at your kids because they have standards. I hope my kids become more spiritual than I am. Oh, that our kids would give God their whole heart.

It's very difficult to teach a kid to give God his heart if you haven't given God your heart. The very first step to be an effective parent is to have the Lord Jesus Christ in your heart, ruling and reigning in that heart. But if you're not saved yourself, I don't know how in the world you can be an effective parent. You don't have that power. So here's the first step: if you want to be a good parent, the first thing is give your heart and mind to Christ. God can and will give you the wherewithal to be a better parent.

My mother and father were saved just a couple of years before I was born. They didn't know what they were doing, but they had given God their hearts. And God began to work through their hearts. If you give God your heart, you'll be surprised at what God can do in your home. You'll be shocked. You will say, "Certainly someone else must have done that. I didn't do that." Exactly, God did that through you. You need God in your home to be a good parent. It's that simple. What kind of mother are you anyway?

CHAPTER NINETEEN

Standing at Liberty

Galatians 5:1

The book of Galatians has three major divisions. The first two chapters are the historical section of the book of Galatians. In those two chapters, the apostle Paul argues for his apostleship; he was a real apostle. There were a lot of people saying that Paul wasn't one of the original twelve and that he was not really an apostle, and he argues in the first two chapters that he is really an apostle of Jesus Christ—that was historical truth.

In the second two chapters the apostle Paul doesn't argue for his apostleship but he argues for justification by faith, and we could say that this is the doctrinal section of the book. There is only one way to be saved and that is by faith in the finished work of Jesus Christ on Calvary's cross. A lot of people try to add a little bit of works to Jesus as the proper way to get to Heaven. If you add one work to grace, you have totally destroyed grace because grace by definition is a gift. Grace stems solely from the benevolence of the giver.

The third section of Galatians is the ethical section of the book. It is here that Paul argues that people who are justified by faith should live right. We are not saved by works, but we are saved to work. When a person becomes saved, God moves into that person's life and makes a difference. A saved person should live differently after he gets saved than he lived before he got saved. Jesus invaded our humanity to make a difference. This is the point of Galatians 5-6.

It is clear how the first section relates to the second section in Galatians. If Paul were not an apostle, what difference would it make whether he argued for justification by faith or not? But because he was an apostle, God inspired him. Paul was a holy man of God who spoke as he was moved by the Holy Ghost. Thus, when Paul says that we are justified by faith alone, it is different than the average man saying it. Paul was inspired by the Spirit of God so that his writings came with divine trustworthiness. He was an inspired man of God. Paul's apostleship is very important to the doctrinal section. If he were not a known, inspired apostle, what difference would it make that he argued for justification by faith?

But how does this affect the latter portion of the book, the final two chapters? Sure, he's an apostle and that would make the fact that we are justified by faith a significant doctrine, but how does that relate to the ethical section? When we respond to the apostolic message of justification by faith, we are going to have a better life. When we really become saved by the grace of God, it is going to result in our having righteousness—both imputed righteousness logged to our account by Jesus Christ and an imparted righteousness that helps us live better on a daily basis. Justification by faith is not a morally barren doctrine.

Because we have been saved by the grace of God alone, we are now free to serve God in a way that we could not serve God before. We now have liberty to serve God. And Paul states that we should not deviate from this liberty; we should stand in it.

The Substance of Our Liberty (v. 1a)

No word is more misunderstood in the Christian vocabulary than the word liberty. What did Paul mean when he talked about Christian liberty? Sometimes to help define a word, you have to say what it doesn't mean. So let's begin by looking at what Christian liberty doesn't mean.

First, it doesn't mean political liberty. It doesn't mean that if you become saved, you will have political freedom. As a matter of fact, there are many people who become saved and will spend the rest of their lives without political freedom. Becoming a Christian does not necessarily alleviate governmental persecution. To the contrary, becoming a Christian will many times create political persecution. Just because we have freedom in Christ doesn't necessarily mean that we are going to have political freedom.

Second, it doesn't mean psychological freedom. Certainly emotional health is a desirable goal but Paul is not saying here that you will have emotional liberty if you become a Christian. If you receive Christ, you may not be able to sort through relationships, find yourself, and completely recover from whatever disjointed past you may have. There are some things in this life you may never understand. All of us wrestle to some degree every day with emotional stability. Emotional health is a desirable goal but the cross doesn't necessarily give us that in this life.

Third, and most important, Paul is not talking here about pointless liberty – that you and I are free to do whatever we want to do. Sadly, some people believe that Christian liberty means that a Christian can go out and do whatever he or she wants to do. This is the cry of many modern-day Christians. When the Bible talks about freedom, it's not talking about freedom to sin— it's talking about freedom from sin.

Before I became a Christian, I was in bondage to sin. But when I trusted Christ, I became free from the things that formerly enslaved me. This is the substance of our liberty,

The Source of Our Liberty (v. 1b)

We do not have to wonder how this emancipation comes about. If you want to be free from enslaving habits, you find that freedom in Jesus Christ. In other words, it is by virtue of our union with Jesus that we are free from these besetting sins. Human existence apart from Jesus Christ is bondage. God sent His Son into the world to deliver us from the world, the flesh, and the devil. I don't have to do what these slaveholders demand. God sent His Spirit into our hearts to awaken a new kind of life inside us that is at complete liberty. We do not have to be enslaved by the things that previously held us. As a Christian, you don't have to live that way anymore.

Because we have the Spirit of God living inside of us, we are free to live a life that we previously could not live (cf. II Corinthians 3:17). We are free to do those things that the Spirit energizes us to do. In our pre-Christian days, we were not free to love; in our pre-Christian days, we were not free to have joy; in our pre-Christian days, we were not free to have peace; and we weren't free to be patient or gentle or good. We were not free to do all that the Spirit produces, but when we trusted Christ as our Saviour, He liberated us from the domination of sin and gave us the liberty to be able to do things that were previously impossible for us to do because we were slaves.

If you don't have electricity connected to your house, you can flip the light switch all you want, but you are not going to have any light. If there is no power running to the house, it doesn't matter how often you flip the switch. Once the power is run to the house, however, it doesn't necessarily mean that the lights are going to be on—you have to flip the switch. Similarly, at the very moment we became saved, God sent the power to live effectively but we have to tap into that power by yielding to the Spirit. If you yield to the Spirit, you will live effectively. When I see a person who is not living effectively or who is not living as if the power of God is operating in his or her life, one of the two things is wrong. Either that person has never had God's power put into his or her life, or that person has the power but is not tapping into it.

Certainly, whenever a Christian is living ineffectively, it is not God's fault because God has given us all things that pertain to life and godliness. Freedom in the Bible is not freedom to do whatever I want to do; it is rather freedom to live as God intended for me to live. In the closing chapters of Galatians we are going to discover what it means to live in that freedom. But suffice it to say currently, we have spiritual freedom to live as God intended because of our union with Christ Jesus.

Our Stand in Liberty (v. 1c)

Paul has just concluded a discussion about Sarah and Hagar—two women in the Old Testament. Sarah and Hagar were two ladies who each had a son by Abraham. Hagar had a son by the name of Ishmael and Sarah had a boy by the name of Isaac. Ishmael could never please Sarah. The Bible said that he was a wild man. In other words, he was stubborn. Part of the reason he could not please Sarah was that he didn't have the nature of Sarah. Because a child bears the nature of his parents, the parents feel in tune with the child in a way that they don't feel in tune with other people's children.

It was not logical when Sarah told Abraham to have relations with Hagar and have this child that this boy would be just like hers; that was impossible. She didn't like his nature and didn't feel connected to him because he wasn't from her. He had Egypt and bondage in him, and he had the stamp of Pharaoh on him.

Isaac, on the other hand, came straight from the womb of Sarah, and because he did, he had her nature. She named him Isaac meaning laughter because it was a joy that a ninety-year-old woman could have a baby. All her life, she had wanted a boy, and now she had one of her own.

God told Abraham to look at the stars and promised to multiply his seed like those stars. Those promises almost seemed to taunt him. Abraham tried through Ishmael, and through Eleazar, his servant, to circumvent the promise of God. But God's promise held fast. Remember the question that was asked of Sarah—Is anything too hard for God? The obvious answer is nothing is too hard for God. They couldn't help but laugh because everything they wanted in their lives was found in that baby. That is where the promises of God were concentrated, where their nature was fully unionized. Isaac brought them together in a way Ishmael never could.

When we put our faith in Jesus Christ, He puts His nature within us. We actually become partakers of the divine nature and now have the capacity to please God in a way that we never could please God previously. We are His own and share His nature; we are part of Him. When we were lost, we were not God's children. We don't believe in the universal fatherhood of God and the universal brotherhood of man that says all creatures are God's children. The only way a person can become a child of God is by faith in Jesus Christ (cf. John 1:12). The only way you become a child of God and a partaker of the divine nature is to be saved, and when you are saved, God puts His Spirit in you. Only then can you please God.

When I first met God, it was because opposites attract. When I first met God, I didn't have anything in common with God. I liked Him because He was so different, but after a while I became more like Him. We have lived together and walked together, and I eventually began to think His thoughts after Him. I hope that when I speak, it is His words. When I act, it is the way He would act. This is the difference between true Christian living and legalism.

There are things in my life that I naturally don't want to do. I don't naturally want to walk in parks in Georgia with ninety-degree heat and ninety-percent humidity. Walking outside is not something I enjoy doing, but my wife loves it. But if I say today that we are going to have a new rule and I'm going to walk every day outside in blistering heat, she is still going to be one unhappy camper. She will say, "Why don't you just go home?" She will say this because my heart is not in it. I'm not doing it because I want to. The answer here is not for me to make a vow. The only way that I can enjoy walking is to become one with my wife. If I am one with my wife and in deep union with her, I'm not thinking about my desires. I am thinking about the relationship that we share, and by virtue of that relationship, I am walking with the right spirit because my nature has changed.

This is the liberty Paul is talking about here. Don't be in bondage and think about what you have to do. Get united with the Lord and discover what you get to do. Wouldn't it be great to always want to do the right thing? That happens when you live close to your God.

CHAPTER TWENTY

The Danger of Adding One Little Work

Galatians 5:2-4

When we come to this passage of Scripture, Paul has written one of his most strict sections in the entire book of Galatians. He is taking the pen out, and that quill is red hot. Paul's very introduction underscores the importance when he uses that word *behold*. He is saying, "Watch this." Then he underscores his apostolic authority when he says, "Behold, I Paul say unto you..." This is not something he heard down the street; this is coming with the full ring of apostolic authority behind it. Nobody less than the apostle Paul under the inspiration of the Holy Spirit is speaking.

And now for the first time, he really lets us know what the problem is. The problem is circumcision. For the first time in Galatians, it is specifically mentioned. The problem is that many were saying that circumcision is necessary for salvation. They are taking one little work and adding it to the atoning work of Jesus Christ. On so many issues, they and the apostle Paul would have agreed. Even though this was true, when it came to the matter of how Christ's merits were procured, there was a subtle difference. Paul said justification was by faith alone, and they said faith plus circumcision; that little addition made all the difference in the world.

When someone takes a little something and adds it to the work of Christ, whether it is baptism, circumcision, or a sacrament, and tries to make it necessary for salvation, what is the big deal about that? What is the danger of adding just one little work?

Christ's person is devalued (v. 2)

If you let yourself be circumcised to contribute something to your personal salvation—if you believe that this one little work in addition to Christ is necessary for the procuring of your own personal salvation—at that very moment Christ is of no profit to you. When you add something to Jesus, you have devalued Christ. In other words, we believe that the death, burial, and resurrection of Jesus Christ is the Gospel. If you add something to that, then Jesus and His atoning work is not one hundred percent. If I add baptism, now Jesus and his atoning work are fifty percent and baptism is fifty percent, so if Jesus is only fifty percent of what is necessary for salvation, what have I done? I have devalued Christ and gutted His value.

I am a coin collector and several years ago I needed a very important Liberty Nickel to complete my collection. Karen did some research and found a great deal on this rare Liberty Nickel that I needed. This nickel was worth well over two hundred dollars and Karen found it for fifty bucks in very fine condition—it was a good deal. For Christmas Karen bought me this nickel for fifty dollars. My brother-in-law did not understand why that was a good deal. We purchased a two hundred dollar coin for fifty dollars, and that's a good deal. In my brother-in-law's mind, however, he saw it as spending fifty dollars for five cents, and he didn't get it. He did not understand because he didn't understand how rare and precious that nickel was.

If you were to reach in your pocket today and find a Jefferson Nickel, the value would be five cents. The reason that the Jefferson nickel is worth five cents is because there are so many of them. The Liberty Nickel, however, is rare and precious. Human works are like Jefferson nickels; there is no rarity to it and hence no value. It is one out of many, but Jesus Christ is rare—there is only one like Him and because there is only one like Him, His value is great.

You cannot put a Liberty Nickel on the same level as a Jefferson Nickel. One is common, and the other is rare and extremely valuable. In the same way, Jesus Christ is not merely one of us—He is the exclusive God man who is the solitary way to Heaven. If I try to throw something else on the same level as Jesus Christ, I have devalued Jesus Christ.

If, for example, I put Mary on the same level as Jesus, Jesus will be devalued. If I put Jesus on the same level as the sacraments, I have devalued Jesus. At the very moment that I take Jesus and lower Him to somebody else's level, I have effectively gutted His value. He is of no profit.

But Jesus is not that way—He is exclusive, rare, and valuable. He is not one among the great religionists and the great moral founders. Jesus Christ is one of a kind, and if I put my circumcision or baptism on the level of Jesus Christ, I devalue Jesus.

A bottomless pit is dug (v. 3)

If you add works to salvation, where do you stop? How much work is necessary? Once human effort is added to the equation, how much human effort is necessary to procure salvation? Let's say I do seventeen acts but God wanted eighteen. If you start adding your work to the cross, you are going to be at a quandary because you don't know how much work is enough to procure salvation. If you put yourself in the equation in any way, shape, or form, you have dug yourself a pit because you don't know how much work is necessary to secure the favor of God.

When I look at the work I've done, I am always dissatisfied with it. I don't think I have ever preached a sermon that I've totally felt good about. When I'm done, I think this could have been different and that could have been different. It doesn't matter how many people say it was wonderful; I still feel that work needs to be done. My work always leaves me empty. You and I have a difficult time being satisfied with our work because we know as long as we are talking about human work, there is room for improvement.

Moreover, God's law is an indivisible unit. God does not serve His law up cafeteria style. You do not get to pick and choose which laws of God you want to keep and which laws you don't want to keep. You and I don't have an opportunity to pick which laws of God we're going to observe and which laws of God we are not going to observe.

So at the very moment we say that we are going to observe the law of God by observing circumcision, at that very moment I have just become a debtor to do the whole law of God because God doesn't serve it up cafeteria style. You must take all the law of God or none of it, but you don't have the luxury of saying, "I'll obey these laws but not these." If you have decided you are going to try to get to Heaven by legal observance, for example, circumcision, at that very moment, you've entered into the arena of law. And if you enter into the arena of law, you are morally obligated to do the entire law, not just one line item.

If I say, for example, that I want to be saved by being baptized, I can't leave it there. I have put myself into rights and rituals. Now I've got to do all rites and rituals, not just one. We have opened the door for legal observance, and if I am going to try to earn my salvation by means of the law, then I've got to do all of the law of God because God doesn't serve it up cafeteria style.

Try as you will to do all the law of God, nobody can do all the law of God; therefore, if you decided that you are going to get to Heaven by good works, you have to do them all (cf. Galatians 3:10). How many of us think we can keep them all? Obviously, none of us can keep them all. Thus, if you try to get to Heaven by adding one little work, you've dug yourself a hole that is impossible to get out of.

Christ's power is disarmed (v. 4a)

Paul gives us another reason here why we can't add

even the slightest work to grace. "Christ is become of no effect unto you, whosoever of you are justified by the law; ye are fallen from grace." If we add work to what Christ did, we are saying that Christ didn't do enough; He needs us to help Him out. We are in essence, by adding our own little work to this thing, saying Christ is not powerful enough by Himself to procure our salvation.

Some parents are nervous and cannot relax when they give their children jobs to do. We all have reasons why we get nervous, and our children can sense that. How bad is it if you and I get so nervous that we don't think God can handle something by Himself? We feel that we have to help God out with saving our souls by contributing a little baptism or circumcision.

Obviously, God has not lost one iota of power, and the blood that was good enough to save men's souls back in the first century is still good enough to save men's souls today. The blood of Christ has not lost one bit of power, but humans still feel they must help God out with salvation.

When my wife, Karen, and I changed addresses in Georgia, we had to change power companies. The second energy company was much more expensive than the first. This is despite the fact that there were power failures monthly. I told my wife that I am sick of paying three hundred dollars a month and having no power.

Years ago a lady called the vacuum company and was greatly upset. She had bought a new vacuum cleaner but it wasn't picking up anything. She was complaining to the tech guy and he said, "Ma'am, have you plugged it in?" She didn't plug it into the power source. You can work yourself up a sweat, but if you're not plugged into the power, you're not going to get the dirt out.

In the same way, people think by their own effort they can clean up their lives, but they are not plugged into the power source. Faith is the thing that flips the switch on the power of God. Human works is trying to bring success into your life by means of a different power supply. Christ's power is disarmed when we rely upon human effort.

Christ's passion is deserted (v. 4b)

Paul says in the latter part of verse 4, ". . . ye are fallen from grace." This is one of the most misunderstood verses in the entire Word of God. Many of us have talked to someone who believes that salvation can be lost, and this verse is the supposed proof text. In context, however, Paul is simply saying that when any human work is added to grace for salvation, grace is no longer necessary. Therefore, at the very moment a man adds work as a necessary prerequisite for salvation, he is abandoning grace and is no longer within the realm of grace.

Grace is the ship that is taking us to Heaven, transporting us from the shores of earth to the shores of Heaven. No one can get to Heaven unless he's on that ship. No one can get to Heaven outside of the way God transports us there. When I try to put my work into it and don't rest on the boat, I am leaning over the rail thinking about what I can do to help paddle the big ship that I am on. As I am leaning over the rail to think about how I can paddle, I lose control and fall into the water, falling from the ship of grace. If I add one work to salvation, I am no longer operating within the realm of grace; I am no longer on the ship.

When a man uses works, he abandons the boat and falls over the rail from the only vessel that can safely bring him to the shores of Heaven. It is not saying that you lose your salvation. It is saying that you have abandoned the ship and have fallen from the only means by which a person can be saved, the means of grace. If you add one little work to grace, it stops being grace. Grace ceases to be unmerited favor if I have to work for it in any way, shape, or form.

Many years ago, when I assumed my first pastorate, I was driving a very old car. We lived in fear of being stranded on the road, and we finally talked ourselves into buying an automobile. The payment was about two hundred dollars a month and that was like a million dollars to us. A fellow in the church, however, offered to make those car payments for us. I was overwhelmed by the generosity of that man. I needed transportation, but the price was beyond my ability to pay. But I had a friend who said, "I'll provide the means to get you there and pay the tab to do it." That was a gift; that was grace.

That is exactly what Jesus wants to do for you. Your good works can't get you to Heaven. You don't have the wherewithal to pay the price of transportation. But Jesus says, "I'll provide the means and pay the price." When you try to save yourself, you abandon that passion and leave all of that graciousness in the dust. You fall from grace.

You can't add one thing to what Jesus did. If you do, you devalue His person, dig yourself a hole you can't get out of, disarm His power, and desert his passion. There is no way that you or I can get to Heaven except by humbly bowing at the cross and saying, "Thank you, God, for grace." There is great danger adding the slightest little work to the grace of God.

CHAPTER TWENTY-ONE

The Right Stuff

Galatians 5:5-6

Up to this point, Galatians 5 has been predominately negative. Sometimes before you get the good news, you have to get the bad news. For example, could we even absorb the message of salvation if we didn't know first that we are sinners? You have to get the bad news for the good news to stand out in all its brilliance.

In the previous verses we have seen that some bad things are going to happen if we go back to the Law. If we go back to the law, Christ is of no value. If we add one work to grace, we have to keep the entire law, an impossible thing to do. If we go back to the law, we disarm Christ and His power becomes inoperative in our lives. Paul also states that if we try to go back to the law, we will fall away from the vehicle of grace. All kinds of negative things happen if you go back to the law.

But when we come to verse 5, Paul says two little words that raise the chapter to an entirely different level: "For we . . ." Though bad things happen to the person who goes back to the Law, I've got something better in mind for you. We can experience something different than all the negative things that are mentioned in these first four verses.

When you become saved, God moves inside of you. When people genuinely accept the Lord Jesus Christ as their personal Saviour, Christ invades their humanity.

271

And because He lives within, they can bring forth fruit. Such people will not fall from grace, disarm the power of God, create an impossible situation, or make Christ feel devalued because they have the right stuff inside and will bring forth fruit that is meet for repentance. That's what Paul is saying in this passage. Because these people have been genuinely saved, he says he knows that they can go on and do these things.

You can't disciple people who aren't born again—it's impossible. I have a famous painting of Norman Rockwell depicting a little girl holding her doll up for a doctor to examine. The doctor has his stethoscope over the doll's heart. Underneath that picture, I put this caption: "You can't doctor what ain't alive." In other words, if someone does not have an infusion of spiritual life inside, we cannot help them grow and develop in the things of God. You have to be born again to develop spiritually. Life has to be inside of you for fruit to be produced.

Years ago, my mom was going to a Sunday school picnic and she made a pie. My mom has always been known for her pies. This particular pie was perfect except for one thing—she forgot to put the sugar in it. People would take one bite of that pie and spit it out. It couldn't bless anybody because it didn't have the right ingredients in it. When you become saved, the ingredients for a fruitful and productive life are placed inside. You can't be sanctified until you are first justified. If you are justified, we can talk about sanctification.

The Process of Sanctification (v. 5d)

Faith is the thing that defines a Christian. You can't be a Christian if you've not exercised faith (cf. Romans 5:1). Faith is how we get in the family; it's how we enter the door of Christianity. Faith defines our entrance into Christianity.

Not only does faith define our entrance into Christianity, but faith also defines our work in Christianity. Faith is not merely how we get in the door—faith is how we walk down the path once we've entered through the gate of salvation. In other words, the whole Christian life—not just the start of it but the whole Christian life—is a life of faith. The Bible says that as we have received the Lord Jesus Christ, we ought to so walk in Him. How did you receive Him? You received Him by faith. How are you going to walk? You're going to walk the same way—you're going to walk by faith. The Bible says that we walk by faith and not by sight. The Bible says that the just shall live by faith. When we accept the Lord Jesus Christ as our personal Saviour, we become sanctified in our position. God has set us apart for a sacred use and purpose. I am no longer part of the world. Because that is my position, now I have to progressively live according to what I am.

For example, when we tell an adult man, "Don't act like a baby," we mean that he used to be a baby but is not a baby any longer. Thus, don't act like what you used to be—act like what you are. Similarly, we as Christians are longer part of the world—we've been set apart from the world—God has changed our position complete-ly. Because we have been set apart from the world, we must act like what we are. Don't act like what you used to be—act like what you are.

How am I going to sanctify myself and practically live out what is true of me? The Bible tells us here that we do all of this by faith. You cannot sanctify yourself any more than you can save yourself. You have to trust somebody else to make you better than you presently are. You can't save yourself and you can't sanctify yourself.

Years ago, I was working in a jail ministry, and one of the inmates asked if he could see me after class. He said, "I'm having a problem. I can't stop thinking about wom-en." I asked, "How are you trying to stop?" He said, "I keep telling myself, 'Don't think about women.'" Obvi-ously, every time he told himself to stop thinking about women, he was putting the thought of women back in his head. You cannot sanctify yourself by denunciation.

If, for example, a person walks around all day and says, "I do not want a cigarette," what does he have on his mind? Cigarettes! He trusts himself for victory. What he has to do is get into the Word of God and think God's thoughts after Him. He will then trust the Lord to deliver him from something that he could never deliver himself from. The only way that you have any hope at all of being righteous, the Bible says, is by exercising faith. We have to trust God to do for us what we cannot do for ourselves. Faith is the process of sanctification.

The Power of Sanctification (v. 5a)

The reason that we trust God to sanctify us is because He alone has the power to sanctify us; it's a power we do not possess in and of ourselves. The reason we have to exercise faith to have any hope of being righteous is because righteousness is something that comes through the Spirit. He is the dynamic that makes it all happen. You and I do not have enough power to live right; therefore, we have to trust the power of the Holy Spirit because the Holy Spirit has more power than we have to help us overcome things that we cannot overcome naturally.

When I was a young, student pastor, a lady in my church approached me with tears flowing down her cheeks. She said, "Preacher, I just can't live the Christian life." l said to her, "You're right, you can't live the Christian life. The Christian life is supernatural. If you could live it, then it would be natural. It is not a life that we live; it is a life that God lives through us." The first step to a successful Christian life is admitting we can't do it. We need a power greater than our own to do it.

My wife and I once counseled lady who had three children out of wedlock. She sat on our couch and cried. She said, "I want so bad to have victory over my illicit behavior, but just as some people can't quit chocolate, I can't quit sex." Those were her words. She said, "I just don't have the power to quit." Many times, our spirit may be willing but our flesh is weak.

The law trusts our ability, and that is the problem with legalism. It is easy to set the rule but it is a different thing to obey the rule. Every time I decide to lose weight, it never fails, someone brings donuts to the office. The power to be a successful Christian is way beyond you and me. We have to put faith in the Spirit of God.

It is the Holy Spirit's effectual working and power that gives us the grace to be able to do what we do (cf. Ephesians 3:7). Every day that you and I get up, we are in over our heads; living right is harder than the ability we naturally possess. We have to exercise faith but not just faith—faith in the Spirit of God. The process is faith but the power is from the Spirit of God in us. Without the Holy Spirit operating in our lives and our subsequent dependence upon His ability, there is no way that you and I can live the Christian life effectively. The Holy Spirit is the power of our sanctification.

The Purpose of Sanctification (v. 5b)

The purpose of sanctification is righteousness. In other words, the goal of the Christian life is doing the right thing. The purpose of getting up every morning is to live right. Many people in our society think that the number one goal of being an American is the pursuit of happiness. Your life is not to be characterized by the pursuit of happiness—your life is to be characterized by the pursuit of holiness.

The only way that we can be saved from the penalty and power of sin is by God's saving us from it, and the Gospel is the power that saves us from sin (cf. Romans 1:16). When people believe, that is the exercise of faith—that's when the power becomes operative.

It's not just faith to get in the door—it is faith to faith—it's ever-increasing stages of faith (Romans 1:17). When we accept the salvation of God by accepting the Gospel of God, we see the righteousness of God revealed. In other words, you are going to start thinking right, living right, and doing right; your life will be characterized by right living. In the Gospel, the righteousness of God reveals itself.

When it comes to righteousness, every human is completely bankrupt—we have no righteousness (Romans 3:10). When the heart exercises belief in the finished work of Jesus, that heart becomes righteous (Romans 10:9-10). It's not by trying to do righteousness but by believing that a person becomes righteous. When I put my faith in what God can do, that is when righteousness is mine.

Righteousness is not something that I work up—righteousness is a gift given to me by God when I accept the Gospel. Most of the time, when you and I think of salvation, we think only in terms of sin being removed. And it is true that God removes sin at salvation, but God does not merely take away our sin. In the place where sin used to be, God imputes His righteousness. Christ's very righteousness is logged on my account.

As a Christian, I must avail myself of that righteousness that God has put on my account so that I can live effectively day by day. The world is not right because the world is not good. Our problem is that we are a morally bankrupt, devoid-of-righteousness society. God imputes righteousness to us so that we might avail ourselves of it and allow it to be imparted in our lives. This is the goal of Christian living. The goal of the Christian life is righteousness.

The Passion of Sanctification (v. 5c)

This hope of living effectively has to become our passion. When we get up in the morning, what is our goal? The goal has to be bigger than just surviving. Righteousness has to be my passion, my hope. Tomorrow night when Jeff Amsbaugh goes to bed, if he did not live rightly, that day was a failure. If he lived the way God wanted him to live, it was a success. The passion that has to drive us every day is the hope of doing the right thing. Isn't that the reason we get saved, so that God can make a difference in our lives? This is why we use the word conversion. Conversion is a change, a transformation, a turning into something different.

The consuming passion of the Christian life is living right. You and I may not always achieve that goal, but it must be our passion. The passion is the hope of living better; it's the hope of righteousness—that's the passion.

The Purity of Sanctification (v. 6)

Sometimes we see unsaved people live more morally than Christians. Sometimes we see a person who doesn't even profess faith in Christ living on a higher plane than someone who is claiming the name of Jesus. Sometimes we are disturbed by professing Christians who apparently have no passion to live righteously. How do we explain this? A person can actually be involved in a Christian ritual for the wrong reason. Paul says that circumcision or uncircumcision is not the issue.

In the Old Testament the picture of severing the flesh and living a pure life was circumcision. In the New Testament the picture of severing the flesh and living the pure life is baptism. The unsaved do all kinds of rites and rituals that don't matter when it comes to the matter of salvation. Why does an unsaved moralist do good things? He does good things so he can brag about it. The motive is not pure.

There may be an unsaved businessman who has given all kinds of money to charity, but his motive can't be pure because it is not produced by the Spirit. He's doing it so he will get written up in the latest periodical, and so people will recognize him and say he's a wonderful man. He can't, however, be doing it for the glory of God because he doesn't have the Spirit of God inside him.

There are many people who are doing right things but doing them with wrong motives. If you are doing rituals and don't have a pure heart for God, that doesn't accomplish anything. True sanctification always stems from a pure heart, and it always has the motive of love embedded in it. Legalism is obeying the law for the law's sake; fidelity is obeying the law because you love the lawgiver. Motive is highly important and significant.

We need to get back to the place where by faith we

are depending on the Spirit of God to make the purpose and passion of our lives living right, not with an egotistical spirit, but with loving humility. All of this can only be produced if you and I recognize that it comes from a Spirit-produced, changed heart.

I'm afraid that many times our children have seen us produce pseudo holiness. They have seen us do rituals with poor attitudes and wrong spirits. Children can see through hypocrisy more than anybody else in the world. You and I have to be very careful that we are not putting up standards to conceal a lack of righteousness. Pure righteousness comes from within and has been authentically produced by God. Are you producing fake fruit or the fruit of the Spirit?

CHAPTER TWENTY-TWO

Crossing the Finish Line

Galatians 5:7-10

Sometimes, if we watch a race or a sporting event, it is difficult not to throw ourselves into it. How sad for many of us that when it comes to running the Christian race we don't even participate. We participate in races that we are not a part of, but we fail to participate in the most important race that we are a part of.

When we got to the end of verse 6, Paul is setting us up for the ethical section of the book. In the beginning section of Galatians, Paul argued that we are saved by faith apart from works. When we get to 5:6, however, Paul talks about a faith that works. We are not saved by works but we are saved to work. Just because Paul argued that justification is by faith independent of works, don't think that he is advocating that you and I be slothful Christians. We have a faith which will work itself out, and it will work itself out with the highest motive possible — love.

Before Paul gets into that, he pulls off the tarp and gives us a personal testimony. Notice how often the word *I* is used (vv. 10-11). So Paul is getting very personal in this letter. What Paul has to say to us in these verses is something that is very close to his heart.

When preachers preach, they ought to preach from the heart. Preaching is not merely head to head—preaching is heart to heart. Preachers are not supposed to impress people - they are supposed to impact people, and one of the ways we impact people is by sharing our own heart with them. There is a difference between sharing one's heart and getting something off one's chest. Paul is here revealing his heart.

The apostle Paul is driving something home to these people that is really crucial to his way of thinking. It is something very pivotal to them. He is saying, "If I have any desire for you at all, this is what I want. I don't want you to get tripped up in the race. I don't want you to fall down and get yourselves all scuffed up in this matter of winning the Christian life."

The Marathon (v. 7)

Paul compares the Christian life here to the running of a race. There are numerous athletic images in the writings of the apostle Paul. Frequently a sporting image works itself into Paul's writings. He was probably a fan of the Olympics that took place in Greece, and he was a person who wanted to see athletics preformed right.

Paul says "Ye did run well. . ." In other words, they got off to a good start. It is important to get off to a good start, to get out of the gate right. We don't want people to become saved and flounder for twenty-five years. We want people to get out of the gate right and start well. That is what the apostle Paul is saying here about the Galatians.

The image here is of an Olympic runner who gets off the starting block with vigor. Of course, this is what happened when Paul and Barnabas went into Galatia and preached the gospel. The people readily received it, digested the truth of the gospel, and responded well to it. They embraced the truth of Christianity and started down the road.

Someone, however, was apparently hindering them. While running down the racetrack, someone jumped out of the stands, came onto the racetrack, and pushed the runner down. Some intruder has come in and cut the Galatians off. Someone has been sinister and interfered with their running of the Christian race.

Paul's question could be paraphrased this way: Who got to you? Who has suddenly convinced you that this is not the right way to go? What has happened in your thinking? Some intruder has cut into the path and has prevented you from obeying the truth of the gospel. I want to know what is happening here. This is not a small thing; it is a matter of victory or defeat.

There are three things we can derive from this. First, the gospel is not merely facts to be believed; it is a life to be obeyed. Paul didn't ask, "Who did hinder you that ye no longer believe the truth?" He asked, ". . . who did hinder you that ye should not obey the truth?" The Christian life is more than a decision. Some people treat Christianity like it is a snap decision. Christianity is not merely a decision—it is the embracing of a lifestyle; it is not merely something to be believed, though it is to be believed—it is something that is to be obeyed. It is the embracing of a new lifestyle.

Second, we should never give up on people we think are done because they may not be done. We see people who are tripped up in the race. Paul believed there was still hope for people who had gotten off track. We ought to treat people more with the confidence that Paul exudes here. Don't give up on people just because you think they are done. Isn't it great to know that God hasn't given up on some people that you and I have given up on? I'm glad that when people gave up on me, God never did. I think we need to be careful not to give up on people too quickly.

Third, the Christian life is a marathon, not a fifty-yard dash. In other words, people can fall, get back up, and continue to run. The Christian life is a marathon. We are not merely going with the Lord for a short distance—we are going with the Lord for the long haul.

The Methodology (v. 8)

These preachers who were preaching that circumcision was necessary for salvation had a great influence in Galatia. What was the secret of their success? What was it that was so alluring about these false teachers? Paul answers that by using a unique word: persuasion. This is the earliest that this underlying Greek word is used. We cannot find it in any Greek literature earlier than this. There are people who used it after Paul used it, but as far as we know, historically, this is the first time that we know of in the Greek language that this particular word was used. The word carries with it the idea of taking something by storm.

Years ago there was a big hurricane that swept through Pensacola and completely devastated a house.

The house was completely swept away. Sometimes things are taken by storm. That is the way these people came into Galatia. They came in and took these people away by storm. In doing so, these fellows stood in stark contrast to the apostle Paul. Because they were physically attractive and eloquently persuasive, these people could talk some of the Galatians into turning from the Gospel. This is not the way the apostle Paul operated (cf. I Corinthians 2:1).

When you and I declare the truth of God, there is something more important than having a clever argument or a spiffy illustration. The Holy Ghost should saturate everything we do. This means I must have good theology because the Holy Spirit is not going to permeate bad theology. I have to make sure that what I am saying is biblically accurate.

Second, I have to recognize that I'm in over my head when I declare the truth of the Word of God to fallen humanity. This is why Paul came to Corinth in fear and trembling (I Corinthians 2:3). While false teachers count on their dynamic personalities, Paul counted on good theology and the anointing of the Holy Spirit. Paul reminds them that no matter how dynamic these false teachers were, this was not the method of Him that called them. In other words, this is not the method that God uses.

God does not trick people into believing a certain theological system. We want people's heads to be engaged when they become saved. We are not trying to hypnotize people into conversion—what good would that conversion be? People have to know what they believe when they accept it. We are not trying to stick it to them—people ought to know what the deal is and accept it with their eyes wide open. When people use trickery and winsome personalities, God is not in that. Our methodology must be one of clear accuracy.

The Meddling (v. 9)

In verse 8, Paul talked about their methodology and now in verse 9 he talks about the result of that methodology. He does so by quoting a proverb that comes straight from the bakery: "A little leaven leaveneth the whole lump." We might put it this way in our culture: A bad apple spoils the whole basket. If you drop a bad apple into a basket of good apples, the good apples will not make that one bad apple good, but that one bad apple will make that whole basket bad. A little bit of leaven can leaven a whole lump of bread. When these false teachers came into Galatia, they tinkered with the gospel just a little bit. They didn't overhaul the whole system—they just came and said, "Everything you believe is right, but we think you ought to add circumcision to it."

If, however, you tinker with it just a little bit and sow just a little bit of leaven into it, you mess the whole loaf of bread up. That is what Paul is saying in this passage. They had implemented what appeared to be this harmless rite of circumcision, but even a slight deviation from the Gospel of Jesus Christ is absolutely catastrophic—it can bring total ruin to an entire Christian community. Just a little poison, if it is toxic enough, can kill an entire body.

This is the warning that must be placed above every church: Perversion of the Gospel is catastrophic. The Gospel must stay absolute. Jesus alone is all you need for salvation. Jesus equals salvation, and salvation equals Jesus. Jesus is life and life is Jesus, and that is all a person needs to be right with God—no circumcision, no catechism, no confirmation, no tinkering of any kind. Don't sow any leaven into that lump whatsoever. Jesus is all a person needs to be right with God. No one can meddle with the simple truth that Jesus and His work alone is the Gospel, and God forbid that people meddle with that central truth.

The Master (v. 10)

Verses 7-9 sound pretty depressing, but when you get to verse 10, it switches. There is a complete change of mood. We have gone from the depths of pessimism to the heights of optimism in one simple statement. Why is Paul certain that these people will not change sides? Why is he absolutely certain that they will not fall flat on their faces and abandon the Christian faith? What has caused this optimism?

The apostle says, "I have confidence in you through the Lord. . ." Forty-seven times in Paul's writings he refers to people being "in Christ" or being "in the Lord." Here is the reason we hold on—we hold on because He holds on to us. Philippians 1:6 says, "Being confident of this very thing, that he which began a good work in you will perform it until the day of Jesus Christ."

Thus Paul is encouraged by these people because

they have not yet turned from the faith. Even though they may be contemplating it in a moment of weakness, they will never do it if they really belong to God. They may have wavered but they will never surrender because Paul is confident that the Master holds all true believers. Paul is also equally confident that the Master does something else—He destroys all false teachers. In the latter part of the verse he says, "... he that troubleth you shall bear his judgment, whosoever he be." This has been a thing that Paul has hammered since the very beginning of the book (cf. 1:6). People who pervert the Gospel will give an account of that devious activity on the day they stand before Christ.

God does not tolerate an inter-mingling of religions. He asks us to cast false religions aside (cf. 4:30). And what God asks us to do in time, He will do at the end of time. We must deal summarily with false religion because that's the way God wants it dealt with, and that's the way God will deal with it at the end of time. He squashes those who would seek to pervert the simple truth of the Gospel.

I am greatly disturbed that the church has tolerated so much of that which is sending people's souls to hell. God wants us to zealously protect the truth of the Gospel. We must never allow the kindness of people or certainly the economic policies of a certain candidate to allow us to get away from what is most central to all of humanity. What good is it for America to be economically solvent if one day it will be turned into hell? You and I must get back to the place where the driving force in our lives is rescuing people from the flames of hell by preaching a pure gospel that embraces the exclusiveness of Jesus Christ. We need to guard zealously this Gospel lest anybody would seek to pervert the truth.

If anyone preaches another gospel other than this, they are cutting people off, tripping them up, and hindering them from crossing the finish line. We desire all men to make it across the finish line successfully, but the only way they are going to do it is for you and I to keep the Gospel pure.

CHAPTER TWENTY-THREE

The Pain of Misunderstanding

Galatians 5:11-12

Have you ever had something come out of your mouth, and as it was being said, you wanted to take it back? The mouth is so prone to utter that which is false and to say something cutting. How often the mouth has a proclivity to say things that get us in trouble. Because we are so prone to say the wrong things, many times we find ourselves in trouble. The mouth can also get you in trouble for something that you didn't say but people thought you said. Many times in our lives we have been misunderstood.

To me, out of all the things that have happened in my life, one of the things that is most frustrating is misunderstanding. I am paid to be a communicator. Sometimes I think I am as clear as a person could possibly be, and yet somebody can take what I said and think the exact opposite of what I intended to say. Many times it seems that people are bent on misunderstanding us. It can be very exasperating when somebody portrays your words as something vastly different from what you intended. As a communicator, I hate being misunderstood. Paul in the passage before us felt that same frustration.

The Confusion (v. 11a)

Part of the confusion is that Paul's enemies were saying something about him that simply was not true. They were saying that Paul was an advocate of circumcision. These false teachers came to town and started preaching that circumcision was necessary for salvation. When they started preaching it, of course, the knee-jerk reaction would be for people to say, "That is not what Paul taught us. Paul told us that we are justified by faith alone independent of any rites, works, or rituals." The false teachers responded by saying that Paul himself was an advocate of circumcision. They were saying this so these people would accept this false doctrine that a person is somehow justified by being circumcised.

If Paul could not be misunderstood at all, this accusation would have been bogus. If Paul's words could never be twisted, then you would just blow this off right away and say that Paul would never teach anything like that. Evidently, Paul had left the door open at least a crack so that these false teachers could get their foot in the door and accuse him of something he was not guilty of. In accusing him, at the least, people in Galatia thought that maybe Paul did think circumcision was necessary for salvation.

The question we could ask ourselves is why was there confusion about what Paul taught? When you and I read his letters, it seems to us that he is clear, yet these false teachers had made something that apparently was clear into something that could be doubted. They had accused him of something, and now there was misunderstanding out there about where Paul actually stood on the nature of circumcision as it related to the conversion experience. How was there confusion over what the Apostle Paul's doctrine was?

His Tone

The apostle Paul did not preach every single sermon on the topic of circumcision. Paul said in other passages what appeared to be very mild statements about circumcision (e.g., I Corinthians 7:18). Paul essentially says that circumcision is not that big of a deal. So if you read that passage in isolation, it appears that Paul's tone about circumcision is mild.

When Paul talks about circumcision, he is not saying that it is not an important issue. He is saying that he is not going to fight this issue every single time he turns around. As far as he is concerned, once a person gets saved, whether he has been circumcised or uncircumcised is not the issue in that person's life. Because Paul didn't make it a hill on which to die, some people said he didn't have an opinion about it.

His Tactics

When people said that Paul was an advocate of circumcision, they may have referenced an event in his life. Paul had been preaching that circumcision doesn't matter with regard to salvation, and yet the first thing that he does when he takes Timothy on his missionary endeavor is circumcise him (Acts 16:3). How could he say that it was of no importance and then insist that it be done? Because of the tactic that he employed in this situation, people felt that his position had been altered.

When the apostle Paul argued about the fact that circumcision wasn't necessary, he was talking about the fact that it wasn't necessary for salvation, but when it came to reaching out to Jewish people, he became all things to all men that he might by all means save some. Circumcision is important or not important depending on what time you are talking about it. If you are talking about using it for salvation, you've got a problem, but if you are talking about it being a good testimony, then it is something totally different. Paul was simply saying that when it came to the matter of salvation, you can't make it a condition.

Because Paul said that he was against it and then engaged in that very thing with Timothy, people said, "I told you he was really in favor of circumcision all along." They misunderstood why he did what he did.

His Terms

Some people see in Galatians 5:11 a veiled reference back to Chapter 2. In Galatians 2:1-5, Paul said these false teachers came to town and were teaching that circumcision was necessary for salvation. Paul said, "We didn't give them a minute." In this passage of Scripture, there is a textual variant. In some manuscripts, the words *no not* do not occur. Thus, in some manuscripts Paul says, "We gave place to them for a minute."

The King James, which I think has the best reading, says, "We didn't give place to them for a single minute at all." The reason I think the King James is right is because it is based on the best manuscript but also simply because it fits the context better. The very fact that there is a textual variant, however, shows that sometimes you can say something as clear as it can be said and two people can leave the same meeting thinking you said different things.

Have you ever had this happen to you? You may have been clear on where you stood on a given issue, and someone said, "I think it is a little ambiguous." Two people can hear the same thing and go out with different reports about it. Have you ever played a game called telephone where you start with one person and tell them something that gets whispered down the line? By the time it gets down the line, it is nothing like what you said. Because of Paul's tone, tactics, and terms, there was confusion about where he stood on the issue of circumcision.

The Contemplation (v. 11b)

Any time you and I are misunderstood for whatever reason, we have to stop and ask ourselves: Is there any measure of truth in what these people are saying? To answer that question, the key word in verse 11 is the word *yet*—the word *yet* carries with it the idea of "still." Paul is saying, "You people have a favorable leaning toward circumcision. So if I have a favorable leaning toward circumcision, then why am I still being persecuted for being against it?" When Paul was in his pre-Christian days, he obtained letters and hauled people off to jail because they were not responding to the tradition of the fathers.

Christians believed that rites such as circumcision were unnecessary. All you needed was a personal relationship with Jesus Christ. This belief made Paul mad, so mad he solicited letters granting him permission to haul people off to jail who taught that stuff.

One day while he was going to arrest some Christians, Jesus arrested him, and when Jesus arrested him on the road to Damascus, he said, "I've been wrong." It is sobering when you have been fighting for something your whole life and then discover you were wrong. Paul had been fighting against these Christians his whole life. Then he gets this epiphany that he was wrong and does a 180 degree turn rejecting the tradition of his fathers. In that one moment of history, those things that were gain to Paul he counted as loss that he might gain the excellency of Jesus Christ. He took everything that he had been living his life for and counted it but dung that he might know Jesus and Jesus Christ alone.

Paul says, "If I'm still for circumcision and still believing the same things I did in my pre-Christian days, why are all of these Jewish people still persecuting me? If I am the type of person who really believes the things that I believed as a Pharisee, wouldn't the Pharisees love me instead of persecute me?" Paul is saying that history doesn't support what they are saying about him.

You ought to live your life in such a way that when people level false accusations against you, they don't stick—history doesn't support what people are saying about you. Years ago, a pastor friend of mine had a lady approach him and say, "I accuse you of sin." He said, "I never committed the act you are accusing me of." She said, "I know you didn't do it, but I blame you, so now you are not blameless." Blameless doesn't mean you've never been accused of anything—it means that when you are accused of something, it doesn't stick.

For example, if I were to have a Velcro target and a Teflon skillet, and you were to stand and throw Velcro balls at both items, the balls would stick to the Velcro target but they would bounce off the Teflon skillet. Blamelessness means that as far as my testimony is concerned, I am not a Velcro target—I am a Teflon skillet. When people hurl accusations at me, those accusations do not stick because I have lived my life in such a way that history does not support what people are saying about me.

When Paul was misunderstood and people were saying things about him that were not true, he earnestly and honestly looked into his life and said, "Is there any validity to what these people are saying?" There was none. You and I ought to always ask ourselves when we are accused of something if there is an ounce of truth to it, and if there is, we need to live our lives in such a way that the ounce of truth ceases to exist.

Anytime someone comes in my office and says, "Pastor, you have offended me because you have done this and this," I will immediately bring two or three people in and I will explain to them what I have been accused of and I will ask them to be unbiased and tell me if they believe there is any validity to that. The reason I do that is because if there is validity, I want to live my life so that the validity of accusation ceases immediately. You and I ought to live our lives in such a way that we honestly evaluate the situation and make sure what people are saying about us is not true. I cannot live my life so that people will never blame me about anything. I can live so that the accusations do not stick. Paul contemplated the accusation and essentially states, "I don't think these people have a leg to stand on."

The Confrontation (v. 12)

When we are accused falsely, we need to stand up. I've heard some people say that we are not to stand up for ourselves. I disagree with that. I believe your testimony is worth fighting for. Throughout this whole epistle of Galatians, the apostle Paul has been arguing for his apostolic authority, which the false teachers have been trying to undercut. Paul says, "I'm not going to have it." Verse 12 is probably one of the crudest, most forthright statements that you will ever find in the writings of the apostle Paul. He says, "I would they were even cut off which trouble you." Those words *cut off* translate the Greek word for castration. He is saying that he wished those people who were harping about circumcision were castrated. Why would Paul be so bold in his confrontation?

Logical

In north Galatia, a cult center existed for the god Cybele, who had a consort by the name of Attis. Every year the people who were involved in that cult would celebrate the death and rising of Attis, who had supposedly died and come back to life. During this ceremony, the priests who were being inducted into that cult would castrate themselves as part of the initiation process. Paul is saying with veiled reference, "You circumcisionists believe that if you cut your flesh, you are right with God. If cutting your flesh makes you right with God, why don't you cut more of your flesh?" Paul was saying that the false teachers were no different from the Cybele cult. In other words, if you believe this ritual is what makes you right with God, why don't you take the ritual even further?

Many times people have thoughts that they have not carried through to their logical end. If you take the fact that cutting one's flesh makes one right with God, does that mean the Cybelein cult is closer to God than you are because they cut more than you do?

Emotional

Some people feel that it is never right for a minister to talk like this, and they believe that a preacher should never get mad about anything. Some people would find Paul's wording here disgusting, vulgar, and unfitting of a minister of Jesus Christ. There are two things at stake here: number one, Paul's testimony is at stake. His apostleship had been denied, his ministry had been defamed, and his flock had been invaded. When someone is out to undercut your ministry, you can get angry about it. There is a time for anger, and when the ministry is being undercut, when theologians come in and try to split a church or try to hinder the work and testimony of a local congregation, somebody has to stand up and say, "Stop it."

Not only was Paul's testimony at stake, but the Gospel was at stake. If you handle people who teach this kind of stuff with kid gloves, do you know what happens? The eternal destiny of souls hangs in the balance. There are many churches that make me angry because they blur the issue of salvation. When the Gospel is being compromised, that should be something worth getting angry about. There are some issues that Christian gentlemen don't have to be gentlemanly about.

When there is a Hitler out there, you shouldn't be a Chamberlain—you should be a Truman. Harry Truman didn't always say things in the most gentlemanly way, but look what he was dealing with. There is such a thing as righteous indignation. I think there are times when you and I need to attack things that are worthy of being attacked. Paul is basically saying that he wished these fellows wouldn't reproduce.

I know some people I wish wouldn't reproduce. You may ask if I believe in population control. With some people, yes I do. I do not want to see certain people's flocks grow and I do not want to see certain people continue to invade churches, create problems, undercut the Gospel, and destroy the testimony of good men. I think it is time that some preachers get their backbones up and say, "I'm sick and tired of what you are doing. Stop it."

There is no nice way to combat evil. I don't understand these politicians or preachers who think that you can fight evil nicely. There is only one way you deal with evil—you beat it before it beats you. We think we can fight neat wars. Paul says that there is evil afoot. There are people who are destroying the flock of God and undercutting people's eternal destiny. Souls are going to Hell because of what these people are preaching, and Paul is not having it. We need to get these people to quit reproducing themselves.

Sometimes when you and I are misunderstood, this is exactly the tactic that we need to take. I've done this with my children before. I've told them, "Perhaps you didn't understand when I told you that you shouldn't do this, so I'm going to make this as clear as I can make it. Bend over." Five minutes after that spanking is done, there is no ambiguity. Why? Evil has been attacked. That foolishness that was bound in the heart of that child was driven far from him.

When evil is afoot, you have to fight it and there is no neat way to fight. Fighting at times gets ugly and messy, but when your testimony and the sake of the Gospel are at stake, you and I have to stand up and boldly confront our culture. Our society has become so concerned with toleration and political correctness that no one is allowed to get angry about anything anymore.

When Jesus goes in and cleanses the temple, we are not really sure He should have acted that way. There are some times when you and I need to confront and we need to confront boldly because that is the only thing people understand. People want to rationalize with terrorists. But there is only one thing that terrorists understand and that's terror—that's why they are terrorists. So we terrorize them more than they terrorize us and they get the message. Because of the issues that were at stake, Paul was not afraid to swing and he wasn't afraid to take these people to task. He stated it harshly by telling them he hoped they were cut off.

Have you seen something that's not right? Be like Paul and confront it before it goes any further and affects the souls of the lost that are hanging in the balance.

Becoming a Love Slave

Galatians 5:13-15

One of the fundamental differences between Christianity and every false system of religion that exists in the world is this: Religion is man predominantly trying to do something to earn the smile and favor of God. Christianity is God doing something for man that man cannot do for himself. Religion is a very works-oriented thing that says if I just do enough righteous deeds I will merit the smile of God.

Christianity recognizes fundamentally that there is no way that mankind in his fallen condition can ever earn the smile of God. All of our righteous deeds are filthy rags. There was a day for those of us who are Christians when we understood we couldn't work our way to Heaven. We invited Christ to come into our lives and do for us what we could not do for ourselves. At the very moment that you and I realized that truth and appropriated it, great liberty came our way.

It is very burdensome to be responsible for your own eternal destiny. It can be a very daunting thing if I have to earn my salvation by walking old ladies across the street, buying boxes of Girl Scout cookies, and giving pints of blood to the Red Cross. I have a tremendous weight on my shoulders if salvation is earned that way. How many old ladies am I supposed to walk across the street? How many pints of blood am I supposed to give

303

to the Red Cross? How many boxes of cookies am I supposed to buy? If salvation is earned through humanitarian effort, how much humanitarian effort is necessary for me to work my way to Heaven?

At the very moment that I became saved, God took all that responsibility off me and shouldered it Himself. Getting to Heaven is not by our work—it is rather by the work that Jesus has done for us on Calvary's cross; therefore, all the burden of trying to work our way to Heaven is relieved at the very moment we come to the cross. Has this happened in your life? Have you recognized that you cannot be good enough to earn the smile of God? Have you discovered that you need the imputed righteousness of Jesus Christ to accomplish salvation and that you cannot do it on your own?

Once we recognize that it is not by our good works, we sometimes get very angry at the system of religion that taught us differently. For example, if you were in a mainline liberal, Protestant denomination when you were saved, you may think in your mind: How dare those people tell me that I could work my way to Heaven! You are almost angered because if you had followed what those people said, you would have split Hell wide open. Therefore, you could be greatly angered at the fact that they preached that good works were the way a person gets to Heaven. If we are not careful, that pendulum can swing in the opposite direction and we can be absolutely upset whenever good works are mentioned.

For example, a fellow in my first church, who is a dear friend, was saved out of a liberal denomination. His preacher would preach on Sunday mornings about supporting the fire department, taking care of the Fraternal Order of Police, and being a nice person. The preacher said that in the end God would let you in Heaven because of your good works. When my friend finally became saved, he recognized how he had been sold a bill of goods in this false religious system. He hated preachers who preached about good works because when he heard "good works" he thought of preachers who preached that good works would get you to Heaven.

One Sunday when I was preaching about good works that Christians ought to do after they get saved, he came up to me after church and said, "Pastor, I know what you are saying is right but every time I hear a preacher mention good works, it brings me back to that old denomination. When I hear preachers talking about doing good works, anger comes up inside of me because I remember all of those liberal clergymen saying good works could merit the favor of God." I understood his point.

If we are not careful when we are saved out of a false religious system where people have held us in bondage saying we can't ever be smiled upon by God if we don't do good works, we can swing that pendulum once we get saved in the opposite direction and say, "I don't like any preaching on good works. Now that I am saved, I am liberated from that bondage of having to do this and that, and I don't want to hear it anymore." Having been saved from legalism, they swing the pendulum in the opposite direction to become absolutely libertarian in wanting no discussion about good works at all.

I am neither a legalist nor a libertarian. There is a balance that exists in the middle and that balance is what the apostle Paul is discussing in our passage.

Liberty (v. 13a)

Notice the word *for* that begins the verse connecting verse 13 to what Paul just said in verse 12. Paul has just taken a pot shot at the false teachers who were teaching that you had to be circumcised to get into Heaven. Paul said, "I have had it with you people. I want you to be castrated. You people don't need to produce any more of your kind. I want you stopped." There are two groups: the false religionists and the brothers. You are different than the false teachers who teach this nonsense of works securing salvation. You are part of the fraternal brotherhood of Christians and God has done something for you brothers—God has called you into liberty. You are not bound by doing these rites, rituals, and performances to get into Heaven. We've cut ourselves off from those people and are the people who are completely at liberty—not worrying about what we have to cut out in order to get to Heaven. We are at complete liberty to know that Jesus took care of it all.

Notice here that liberty is not something you are entitled to. Liberty is not something that we are born with rights to. It doesn't say that liberty is something that we campaign for. Liberty is something that you are called into by God. No politician can make you free. No action committee can make you free. No family heritage can make you free. Liberty is something that God calls you into.

Remember when you were a child playing outside? Perhaps your mother called you in because it was time for supper. If you were losing a ballgame 13 to 1 and your mom called you inside, you were thankful for the call because it rescued you. When you and I are in the slavery of false religion, bound by all of the moral bondage of trying to work our own salvation out, God calls us into liberty. People often sing, "Born free, as free as the wind blows." Nobody is born free—everyone is born a slave. You're born in bondage, and God says "If you want to be free, answer my call." When you give your life to Christ, you recognize the call into freedom. We are called by God out of slavery and into freedom.

Once we are called into that freedom, we have to be careful because we understand freedom sometimes to mean "moral license." Let's say, for example, that I was a Jehovah's Witness before I became saved. They told me that if I did not proselytize I would not be part of the hundred and forty-four thousand. So every Saturday, I would knock on doors and distribute Watch Tower literature because I was told if I did not do that, I could not be part of the hundred and forty-four thousand. Then Jesus saved me. I'm glad I don't have to do that anymore to be part of the hundred and forty-four thousand. But now my preacher says, "This Thursday we're having visitation and if you're not there, you're not right with God." I say to myself, "He sounds like a Jehovah's Witness." Because of what I experienced in the false cult, I have extreme views of liberty. If we understand freedom to be no obligation, no restraint, we can actually turn the grace of God into moral chaos.

License (v. 13b)

Paul says, "Be careful with that liberty. If you're not careful, you can abuse it, and it can be grossly perverted." The key word in this second part of the verse is *occasion*, and it's a military word that carries with it the idea of a springboard. Don't allow liberty to be the base of operations for your flesh. Don't allow liberty to be the beachhead from which your flesh operates.

Sometimes Paul uses the word *flesh* to refer to the arena in which we live (cf. Galatians 2:20). When I became saved, God delivered my soul, but my body has not yet been redeemed. The appetites that I had before I was saved are still there after I'm saved. For example, I still get hungry. When I was lost, I became hungry and after I was saved, I still get hungry. The appetite of the flesh is still there. When I became saved, God did not take away my sex drive. Appetites that existed in my pre-Christian days exist in my Christian days; I live in the flesh. This body with all of its appetites is still there, and the cravings that I had before I was saved are largely still the same cravings that I have after I am saved. There is no hormonal change when a person becomes saved. Life for the Christian is still lived "in the flesh." Even though I am saved and raised to walk in newness of life, it is still in a body that has appetites.

Sometimes Paul uses the word *flesh* to refer to that arena of appetites in which we live, but Paul also uses the word in an ethical sense because when you and I have appetites, many times those appetites are wrong. Thus, Paul sometimes uses the word *flesh* of our fallen nature. We live in a body that has appetites, and many times those appetites can be a beachhead from which you and I do wrong activity. We live in the flesh but we can't live according to the flesh. In other words, I still have appetites, but I have to control my appetites. I cannot allow my appetites to control me.

God doesn't take your appetites away when you become saved, but in your pre-Christian days your appetites tell you what to do. Once you become a Christian, you have to tell your appetites what to do. You still live in an arena of appetites when you're saved—God doesn't take them away. Those doughnuts on the counter still say, "Come here and eat me." You don't automatically stop liking donuts just because you are a child of God—it doesn't work that way. The guy who is saved still craves fattening food like the guy who is lost. Those appetites still exist when we become saved but now we have the power not to allow our appetites to control us. Rather, because we have a regenerated soul, we can now control those appetites. We don't have to allow this liberty that we have in Christ to be a beachhead out of which our fleshly appetites dictate the way we go.

Paul is saying that you have liberty now as a Christian and are not in moral bondage of working your way to heaven. But you can't allow that liberty that God has given you to allow your flesh to have no moral restraint. As a Christian, even though ethics don't get you in with

God, you can't go around saying that you are going to ban ethics. You cannot allow your liberty in Christ to be a license to do whatever you want to do. You can never turn liberty into a license to sin. If you do, you are morally wrong.

Love (vv. 13c-15)

I have liberty. I don't have to do all these things to become right with God, but I can't turn liberty into a license to do whatever I want to do. So where is the balance? I have liberty yet I don't have a license, so what do I have? I have love. The alternative to license is to love one another. In other words, Paul says that I am to make myself a servant to everybody that I come in contact with. If my appetites are controlling me, who am I thinking about? I'm thinking about myself. Here is what I would like to do.

Living the Christian life for the satisfaction of self is not what the Christian life is about. You have liberty but liberty is not a license—rather liberty is to be regulated by love for other people. Christian liberty is the liberty to love people and serve people even when they are not loveable or candidates for service. It is interesting that Paul links liberty with slavery. He says if you want to use your liberty right, become a slave. He says, ". . . by love serve one another." The word *serve* is the word for slavery, and so Paul is saying that love makes us slaves to one another. True freedom is only found when I have put myself in slavery to somebody else.

The Christian life is a paradox. If you are concerned

about yourself and being free, you will be a slave to something. If you want to be free to smoke, you are going to be a slave to nicotine. If you want to be free to drink, you're going to be a slave to alcohol. Anytime you want to take an absolute approach to freedom, you are going to end up in slavery.

Absolute abuse of freedom always leads to slavery, but if you lay down your life in service for other people, you are going to find freedom. Serving other people does not restrict your freedom—it initiates it.

In your pre-Christian days, when you were part of the legalistic movement, you served God because some religious people were telling you to and you thought that would get you right with God. You were serving the law for the law's sake. When you became a Christian, you started serving God not for the law's sake, but because you love the lawgiver. When you serve the law for the law's sake, it is legalism. When you serve the law because you love the lawgiver, it is fidelity.

This is why Paul says the law is fulfilled in this one statement, ". . . Thou shalt love thy neighbor as thyself." If the law is just a law and that is all it is, it is a tyrant. When God is working in my heart, however, the law is not an element of frustration. I'm not keeping the law because I have to. The law is fulfilled in me not because I've got to keep it to be right with God but because God has transformed my heart and I like ministering to people.

If a kid loves his teacher, the teacher doesn't have to put a list of rules on the blackboard. We don't pick out the five best kids in school and say, "Here's the handbook. Take this home and memorize it." Good kids don't need a rule book. We only have rule books for bad kids—not for good kids. If kids' hearts are with us, we don't need a rule book for them. Every day is fine with a kid whose heart is in love with his authorities. But if a child's heart is far removed from us, then he needs a rule book.

That is what this passage is saying—law is fulfilled if you get your love right. If you get the love in your heart right, you are going to be fulfilling the law. Because you love that neighbor as much as yourself, you are going to reach out to that person and minister to his or her needs without someone telling you to do it. You are going to do it because it is part of who you are. When the law becomes fulfilled in my life, no one has to stand over my head and watch what I'm doing. I am fulfilling the law because I love people.

When, however, people do right things for wrong reasons, all kinds of frictions exist. The Bible says that when you and I engage in law for the wrong reasons—not because we love people but because of ego—we're going to bite and devour one another.

Legalism is a fleshly attitude. Legalism is not what you do—it is why you do what you do. Legalism is a fleshly attitude that does right things for wrong reasons. When you obey the law for the law's sake, it is legalism. When you keep the law because you love the lawgiver, it is fidelity.

We have two extremes. The first extreme is the belief that doing works gains the favor of God. God likes me because I've kept all these rules. The second extreme is the belief that people can do whatever they want because God is not interested in rules. Therefore, I will use my liberty as a beachhead to do whatever I want to. Both extremes are wrong.

In the middle of these two extremes stands the man who regulates his life by love rather than pride. I am going to regulate my life so that I can effectively minister to others. I have made these alterations in my life so my flesh doesn't have a beachhead from which to operate. When my life is so regulated because of my desire to be the best testimony and benefit that I can be to someone else, that's when I become a love slave. My desire is to help others. How can I help you? How can I help you see the heart of Christ today? How can my hands be the hands of Christ in your life today? How can my feet be the feet of Christ today? What's the best way for me to show you the love of Jesus?

When the flesh is not regulated by love, we bite, devour, and consume. You and I have to be in the place where we become the slaves of love to the people around us. When we do, we manifest Christ to a lost world.

CHAPTER TWENTY-FIVE

Walking in the Spirit

Galatians 5:16-18

In the verses above our passage, the apostle Paul has been talking about Christians who do right things with wrong motives. When we do right things with wrong motives, we bite and devour one another. Sometimes our flesh can get in the way and friction becomes inevitable. There is a remedy for biting and devouring one another; it is walking in the Spirit. Notice that Paul says, "*This* I say then. . ." which is another way of saying, "Here's my advice. If I could say something to you, here is what I would say. Here is the resource for victorious Christian living." When you feel like you just have to allow your flesh to have its way, and you have to bite and devour someone, there is a way that you can rescue yourself from that and live in a victorious manner above the "dog eat dog" world.

Paul says, ". . . Walk in the Spirit, and ye shall not fulfil the lust of the flesh." Here is the way that you and I can have victory. It is not a matter of personality development. It's not a matter of ability. It's not a matter of how many degrees we have. It doesn't work that way. It is not a matter of going to a new seminar or even getting psychotherapy. None of that is where the answer lies. When it comes to biting and devouring one another, you and I have to learn how to walk in the Spirit, and if we walk in the Spirit, we will not see our flesh reacting the way our flesh is so prone to react to people when they do things that annoy us.

The Life of the Spirit (v. 16)

You receive the Holy Spirit at the very moment you become saved (cf. Galatians 3:1-3). Galatians 3:2 made this specifically clear. We did not receive the Holy Spirit by keeping any rules but rather by placing faith in the Gospel. We received the Holy Spirit by hearing the Gospel message and responding to it in simple child-like faith.

At the very moment that you respond in simple child-like faith to the Gospel message, you receive the Holy Spirit of God. There is no such thing as a Christian who does not have the Holy Spirit. Receiving the Holy Spirit is not something that happens after conversion; receiving the Holy Spirit is conversion. It's not something that happens in a post-conversion experience; it's something that happens at the very moment that you and I put our trust in Jesus Christ. There is no such thing as a Christian who doesn't have the Holy Spirit (cf. Romans 8:9).

Now that we have the Spirit as Bible believing Christians, we need to walk in the Spirit. What does walking in the Spirit mean?

The first thing that I would say is involved in walking in the Spirit is dynamic interaction. My wife likes to walk. Virtually every day that the sun rises on planet earth, she goes for a walk. Amy, our daughter, likes to walk as well, and many times when Karen goes for a walk, Amy goes with her. Sometimes, as the dad, I will stand at the back door and watch them take off into the neighborhood on their walk, and as they are walking, their hands are going and they are talking to each other as they are walking. There is lively, dynamic interaction between them.

When we are going in the same direction with somebody, it presupposes that there is going to be lively, dynamic interaction with that person. Every day that the sun rises on planet earth, you and I ought to have lively, dynamic interaction with the Spirit of God. There ought to be a communication that exists between us and Heaven. We are not just mutually on the road together—we are to interact with one another in a lively and dynamic way as we go through life. We are walking in the Spirit.

Not only does it mean that we are walking with dynamic action, but I think to walk with somebody you also have to be going in the same direction. When my wife Karen first received her driver's license, she made a wrong turn and was going the wrong way down a one-way street. As she was going the wrong way, everyone was waving at her trying to get her to stop. Her sister, who was in the car, said, "My, this is a friendly street." She didn't realize that the people were not being cordial; they were trying to stop her because she was going in the wrong direction.

I think sometimes in our Christian lives, we are so oblivious to the things of God that we think God is very happy and pleased with us when actually God is trying to tell us that we are walking in the wrong direction. God is not being cordial; He is being cautious. For me to walk in the Spirit, the Spirit and I have to be going in the same direction. Some people are innovative in their theology, and they will say, "Why don't you just catch up?" I couldn't catch up if I doubled my speed because we are not going in the same direction. You and I have to be headed in the same direction as God.

This is why I think it is completely bogus for us to poll our neighborhood and find out how we should have church on Sunday morning. I'm not trying to walk in agreement with the neighborhood—I'm trying to walk in agreement with God. God and I are the ones who are supposed to be going in the same direction with each other. Going in the same direction, of course, seems to suggest that we have the same purpose the Spirit has and that we want to arrive at the same destination and achieve the same goals.

You not only have to have dynamic interaction with God and be headed in the same direction with God, but you must also want to arrive at the same destination as God. You must walk in the Spirit. Notice here that it says if we walk in the Spirit, we're not going to be sidelined by our fleshly appetites. Walking in the Spirit means even more than walking with the Spirit. The life of the Spirit and my life are so intertwined that we walk together—it's not two separate entities occupying two separate spaces walking down the road together. We're not side by side; we are rather heart in heart. I'm not merely with the Spirit, though I am with Him; I am in the Spirit and the Spirit is in me—we are intertwined with each other and tied together in heart. We are occupying the same space and our cohesive oneness is intact. There is no residue of the Spirit left over—He is in me and I am in Him. My life and His life are one and the same, and I feel His pulse as I walk with Him.

When Karen and I were engaged to be married, we walked into a drugstore to buy something. While we were there, a girl walked into that drug store, and she was scantily clad. Immediately, when that girl walked into that store, I turned my eyes and riveted them on Karen. I did not move my gaze off Karen the entire time we were in that drugstore. When we walked out of that drug store, Karen looked at me and said, "I love you." There was a cohesive oneness that existed between us, and because that cohesive oneness existed between us, there was no fleshly thing that could lure me away from her; she and I were one.

That is the way we ought to be with regard to the Spirit. My life and the Spirit's life ought to be so intertwined that there is nothing out there that can lure me off track in my Christian life. I am so into God that I cannot be altered from what I am doing in my daily life. Just as Karen and I were one, and I could not be distracted, I cannot be distracted by all the lustful things that exist in the world. My mind will not be sidetracked away from that which God has for my life. I will not be fulfilling lustful appetites because my life has been completely intertwined with the life of the Spirit. I am walking in Him and He is walking in me.

The Lusts against the Spirit (v. 17)

There is something that is fighting against this Spirit life that I have. The Spirit came into me and fused His life into me, and that life that now courses through my veins is the life of the Spirit of God. I am to walk in that arena and conduct myself within that Spirit life that He has given me. But there is something that is seeking to pull me away from that spiritual life. There is something that is fighting against the Spirit of God having His way in my life. What is fighting against that spirituality, that life of the Spirit that needs to exist in me, is the lust of the flesh. And this battle is all-out war.

The Spirit and the flesh are contrary to each other. You understand what it means to be contrary to something else, don't you? The very first week that I ministered in Columbus, Georgia, a man came to me after church and asked, "Auburn or Alabama?" I said, "I don't know," and he said, "Preacher, you have to decide. There's no neutrality on that issue." No one who understands college football could say, "I like Alabama and Auburn." These are contrary one to the other. You cannot say, "I like my flesh and I like my Spirit too." These entities are diametrically opposed to each other. There is a competition out there. This competition started the very moment you became saved.

From the very moment you became saved and spiritual life came to dwell within you, you have a fleshly life and a spiritual life, and these two lives are pictured in Isaac and Ishmael (Galatians 4:29). They've been butting heads from the very moment of birth. From the very moment that you were spiritually birthed into God's family, a war was declared. When God put His Spirit inside your body of flesh, a war began. The spiritual life that God infused in you declared war on your fleshly bad habits. That war is going to continue until you go to Heaven.

Until we complete life on planet earth, we're going to be tempted to do things in the energy of our flesh rather than by the spiritual power that God has given us (cf. Galatians 3:3). We're going to try to mature ourselves by our own fleshly means rather than by God's means. From the very moment of spiritual birth to the time of physical death, there will be a war that exists between the flesh and the Spirit.

If any preacher stands up and tells you he doesn't feel any war going on, I wonder about him. On a moment-by-moment basis, there is a war going on inside of us—the flesh against the Spirit. If that war starts at spiritual birth and doesn't quit until physical death, then every day there is going to be a dog fight that goes on inside of me. This is the point of Romans 7. What I want to do, I don't do, and what I don't want to do, that's the thing that I find myself doing. There is a war going on inside of us as our flesh fights against our Spirit and our Spirit against our flesh. These two contrary things exist inside of us.

This fight didn't take place before you were saved—your lust just did what it wanted to and there was no Spirit fighting against it. Once you became saved, however, the Spirit of God moved inside you, and the things that you could do and not be bothered about, now you are bothered about doing them. Some people come to me and say, "Pastor, I'm bothered by my habits. I don't think I'm saved." That's proof you are saved because it is evidence that the Spirit is warring against the flesh. Before you were saved, you could do whatever you wanted to, but now that you've been born again by the Spirit of God and the Spirit has come inside of you to fight your flesh, you can't do what you want to do anymore without conviction. The Spirit of God has declared war against your flesh.

You can never overcome your flesh unless you have the Spirit inside of you to do it. The flesh is weak, and you need a superpower to overcome it. You need the Spirit of God to come into you and wage war against your flesh. In previous administrations in America, there were nations that militarily were weak and they had to call upon us to assist them. You remember when President Reagan was in office, Grenada called and asked for our assistance, and we went and helped them. When Bush was in office, Kuwait called and asked for our help when they were invaded by Iraq, and we went over there.

You and I, spiritually speaking, are nothing more than a Grenada or a Kuwait. We don't have enough power to whip that which is fighting against us, so we need to call on the help of a superpower and that superpower is God. When the Spirit of God comes into the life of your flesh, He can help whip that thing that is fighting against your soul. Aren't you glad that when you face something tomorrow, the Spirit of God is able to come to your rescue?

The Leading of the Spirit (v. 18)

In verse 18, when it talks about the leading of the Spirit, it is not talking about somebody leading somebody by the hand. That's not the way God leads us—He doesn't lead us by compulsion, by pulling our hands and dragging us down the aisle. God leads us by creating within us the right impulses to do things. The Bible says that when you are led by the Spirit, it's not a matter of law. The Spirit is not over you saying you have to do this and you have to do that. That is not the way the Spirit of God leads us.

Law often creates natural rebellion in us. If you are walking through the park and you see a sign that says "Do Not Pick the Flowers," you wonder why you can't pick flowers. Who are they to tell me I can't pick the flowers? And before you know it, you are picking flowers, and the only reason you are picking flowers is because there was a law that said "Do Not Pick the Flowers." Law doesn't usually produce right conduct in us. There is something in us that rebels when somebody tells us we have to do something. That is the way human nature is. That is not the way God leads us. He would create rebellion in us if He did that. What the Spirit does is come inside us and give us the desire to do the right things.

Because our human nature is so weak, the law could

never say, "You all do the right thing," and we would do it. As a matter of fact, many times when the law says, "You all do right," we say, "Over my dead body." God says, "Okay," and He kills our body of flesh and puts His Spirit inside of us to give us the drive to do right. God doesn't change you from the outside in—He changes you from the inside out—He leads you from within, not from without. When you are led by the Spirit, that is when the rule book becomes obsolete, you begin to do supernaturally the things a Christian does because God has altered your heart. God never leads His people by legislation from without.

If we have God's heart, rules become obsolete. The rule book is made for the disobedient and the rebellious. If, however, we are following God, there may be some things in our lives that we don't understand why God wants us to do them, but we don't want to be at odds with God, so we do those things. We love God so much that we just don't want to be at odds with Him even if we don't understand the reason for what He asks us to do. We want His heart and we want oneness with Him.

Years ago, one of my friends was saved out of Students for a Democratic Society in New York City. That was a left-wing, hippy, flower child group. Immediately after conversion, my friend enrolled at Tennessee Temple University, which at that time was an ultra-conservative school.

At that time, Tennessee Temple had a rule that a student could not have a mustache unless he had possessed it for ten consecutive years prior to enrollment, which means if you were starting as a high school graduate, you would have to have had your mustache since you were eight. My friend, believe it or not, had had a mustache for ten years, and so according to the rulebook, he was allowed to keep it.

Fellow students, however, constantly referenced my friend's mustache. Finally, because it became such an item of controversy, the vice president asked him to shave it. My friend protested that he was within the letter of the law. The vice president said, "I know, but you've become such a distraction on campus that I want you to shave it if you want to stay." My friend was upset. He was following the rule book and still being punished. He said, "I don't understand this at all." He packed his bags and prepared to go home.

Before leaving the dormitory for the bus station, he took his bags into the lobby restroom and looked in the mirror. He said the Holy Spirit spoke to his heart and asked him, "Are you willing to leave the will of God for facial hair?" He said he reached into his bag, took out his razor, shaved his mustache, and stayed in school for one reason: the Spirit had led him there.

It could be something as small as a mustache, but some of us have allowed something as small as facial hair to drive us from the will of God. It happens all the time. The key thing in our lives is not whether we have facial hair or don't have facial hair—that's an arbitrary rule. What's most important is that I have the heartbeat of God and that I'm in the place where God wants me to be. That is the most important thing for any child of God. I must be willing to do whatever is necessary to be in tune with the heart of my Heavenly Father.

If you are in step with the Spirit, you're not going to fulfill lustful desires. Being in step with God—walking in the Spirit—is the most important thing in your life. How's your walk?

CHAPTER TWENTY-SIX

Works of the Flesh or Fruit of the Spirit?

Galatians 5:19a

When I'm done sharing what I'm going to share with you in this chapter, you may say, "Duh, that's obvious," but I want to tell you that what I'm going to share with you, I wish someone had shared with me when I was about twelve years old. It would have saved a whole lot of problems for me in my teenage years. It was not until I was late into high school and early into college that the truth I am going to share with you became operative in my life. When it did, it revolutionized everything about Christian living for me.

Sometimes in our lives, I think we believe that victory is just a matter of choice. If someone is a pothead, we say, "Stop doing drugs. Just say no." If someone is a drunkard, we say, "Just stop drinking alcohol." If someone is smoking or involved in some type of vice or deviant sexual behavior, we may simply say to them, "Why don't you just stop it?" Several months ago, someone presented me with a video clip of Bob Newhart where this lady comes into his Chicago office for advice. She is compulsive, and he says, "What is your problem?" She says, "I have this fear of being buried alive in a box." He says, "I'm going to give you some simple words that will help you." She asks, "Should l write them down?" He says, "There is no need to write them down. It's only two words and most people feel that they can remember them." She says, "Okay, I'm ready. What are they?" He shouts, "Stop it!" She says, "Stop it?" And he says, "Yes, just stop it." She says, "You don't understand, my mother..." He interrupts, "No, we don't go there." She starts giving all types of excuses, and he responds, "No, don't go there." She says, "So I should just stop it?" He says, "That's right; stop it." She blurts, "Well, I think this counseling is going too fast. I'm completely disturbed about how fast this counseling is going." He says, "Okay, I'm going to give you nine words and these you might want to write down. Stop it or I'll bury you alive in a box!"

Unfortunately, sometimes in our lives just being told to stop something is not enough. There are things in my life I wish I could stop, but I'm too weak to stop them. Have you ever had a particular habit or flaw in your life that keeps besetting you? Someone may say to you, "Why don't you just stop it?" Deep down in your heart, there is nothing that you would like better than to stop it. The Spirit is willing but the flesh is so incredibly weak. Even if we were to stop it, we may stop it in a fleshly way so that now we are arrogant about the changes that we have made in our lives. Our self-righteousness is just as repugnant in the nostrils of God as the unrighteousness that we used to practice because its done in such a haughty way.

In the passage that is before us, Paul talks about the works of the flesh. There are four noticeable things that I want you to see about these works of the flesh.

A Matter of Conniving

Paul talks about the works of the flesh, but when he talks about what the Spirit produces, he refers to that not as the works of the Spirit but rather as the *fruit* of the Spirit. There is a difference between work and fruit. When we think of work, we think of something that is devised, manufactured, or connived. Work is something that we make with our hands; it is something that we have connived, devised, or manufactured.

In the Bible there are two significant accounts of people who tried to produce religious things with their own hands. One is the Tower of Babel in Genesis 11. When men connived their own religion, God did not say, "Wow, what a wonderful project." God came down and destroyed it. You also remember when Moses was on the mount receiving the commandments of God, the children of Israel connived their own religion and gave their gold earrings to Aaron who melted them into a golden calf. Regardless of how Aaron tried to disavow himself of it and say that the calf popped out of the oven, it was clearly obvious that it was the work of man's hands—it was something that man had manufactured, and because it was something that man had manufactured, it received the judgment of God.

When we think of work, we think of something that we think up and produce. It is all about self-effort and self-actualization. It is all about what we do. You'll notice here that when Paul moves to his list of Christian virtues later in the passage, he changes words. He moves from the realm of technology to the world of nature and talks about fruit. When we think of fruit, we don't think of steel plants and automotive industries. When we think of fruit, we think of things like apples, oranges, and peaches. It does take work to produce fruit, there's no doubt about that. Someone has to plant the seed, someone has to water the seed, someone has to fertilize and cultivate the plant, but whenever you talk about fruit, there's an element that's beyond human control.

There are things that man cannot control when it comes to the matter of producing fruit. For example, we have no control over the weather and we have no control over insects. We can spray all kinds of pesticides but how the insect population manifests itself is something that we have no control over. Though much effort goes into it, in the final analysis when fruit occurs, it is a gift of God. Though there is some human work put into it, all of our human work cannot make a tree produce fruit.

Several years ago, Lane Packing in Peach County, Georgia, had a terrible crop of peaches because there was a drought. My wife and I made our annual pilgrimage to get our tasty peaches, and they weren't very good. The people at Lane Packing were apologizing for the peaches. Obviously, the people at Lane know what they are doing. They grow peaches for a living. But for all of their technology and ability, if God doesn't give what only God can give, the peach will not grow on the tree.

In the same way, you and I have to recognize that what is produced in our lives is largely a gift from God— that is why it is called fruit. For example, in Psalm 127 the Bible says that the fruit of the womb is God's reward. Now a husband and wife, obviously, must have relations for children to come, but unless God touches that marital act, no baby will come out of it. Fruit production is dependent on God. For all of the human effort that goes into it, unless God steps in and places His hand upon it, no fruit will be produced in the womb.

Thus, if these traits are to exist in the Christian life, they are not something that we connive, or manufacture; they are not something that we produce in frenzy by sweating and saying, "I will be good." Try as you will, patience, love, and joy cannot be manufactured by grit—it is not merely a decision that a person makes—it is a sovereign gift from God. The Bible says that every good gift and every perfect gift is from above, and comes down from the father of lights (James 1:17).

You understand that work is something that I do with my hands, but fruit is something that is produced from within as life courses through me. As the life of God courses through me, God produces in my life those things that He desires to be there. What God produces is fruit and what I produce is works. When I'm talking about Christian virtues, it is not something that I produce—it is not a matter of conniving. However, the works of the flesh are a matter of conniving.

A Matter of Chaos

We also see a different way in which these lists are structured. The first is plural—works. The second list is singular—fruit. It is not the fruits of the Spirit; it is not the work of the flesh. It is the works, plural, of the flesh and the fruit, singular, of the Spirit. The first list contains all kinds of wicked obsessions, vices, and no-good deeds. The second list, however, is very well organized, and it comes across as a cohesive whole when we read it. The fruit of the Spirit is an orderly arrangement, whereas the works of the flesh are frenzied.

When my wife Karen and I were in college, we had a variety of jobs. When I completed our first joint tax return, we placed all our W-2s together. For all of those works that we had performed, there was a variety of tax that was assessed because of the variety of works that had been done.

In the same way, when you and I do the works of the flesh, we're going to find ourselves highly taxed, and we're going to find ourselves very exhausted. But when fruit is produced, the tree is not worked into a frenzy. Fruit production is just the natural byproduct of life coursing through the tree. It is not a frenzied activity.

Have you ever met people who looked tired all the time? Some people look like a fractured, fragmented mess. Fruit is not like that—it is a cohesive whole. For example, an apple has a stem, a core, and seeds, but we don't usually think of an apple in terms of its individual components—we just say it's an apple. We don't think of an apple as stem, seeds, and pulp—we think of all of that stuff together as an apple. In the same way, God doesn't want our lives to be fragmented and frenzied compartmentalization. Fearing God and keeping His commandments produces wholeness (cf. Ecclesiastes

12:13). In other words, God wants to end your fractured, fragmented, piecemeal life, and God wants to give you wholeness. God wants to give you a cohesiveness that you do not presently have.

Jesus said that if your eye is single, then your whole body will be full of light (Matthew 6:22). God doesn't want you to be like the cowboy who got on his horse and rode off in all directions. God wants you to be a person who has tunnel vision and seeks the kingdom of God. As you seek the kingdom of God, everything else has a way of being added to you because your life is not the frenzied, fractured life that it used to be. It is not works (plural); it is fruit (singular).

A Matter of Conglomeration

You'll notice here that when these works of the flesh are listed, the list is not exhaustive. Notice the postscript: "... and such like ..." (v. 22) In other words, when these vices are listed, the author hasn't given an exhaustive list. Paul is saying that he could go on forever and name all kinds of evils in which people become engaged. He is saying that he can't list all the perversions, excesses, and obsessions that can dominate a person's life. There is no end to the vicious cycle that is recorded for us in verses 19-21. In fact, there is only one person who can end your depravity, and that is God Himself. Sin is so plural and so intermingled that there is no way that you and I can work our way out of it.

One night I was on visitation and stumbled upon a house. In this house was a woman who had been separated from her husband for over 20 years. She was now living with a man with whom she had been intimate for over ten years. Through that state of infidelity, they had produced a child who was about two years old. That night I had the privilege of leading both the woman and her boyfriend to Christ.

Upon her conversion, the woman asks me what she is to do. I'm trying as a pastor to straighten their lives out - what would you tell them to do? Should she go back to her husband and be reconciled to him? If she goes back to her husband, what will happen to that two-year-old? What do I say? I didn't know what to do. Today, I still don't know what to do. By the time we get to many people, their sin has become so intermingled and twisted that there is really nothing that you and I can do to completely unravel the mess.

I know of a woman who went through a gender transformation and became a man. After this procedure, the person trusted Christ. Here is a woman who became a man and then became saved. The church where this person attended was having a men's retreat, and the person did not know whether to attend or not. What would you do if you were the pastor? I would say, "There is a nice church down the street. I would like to recommend it to you." We live in a society where the works of the flesh have been so dominate that we encounter multiple messes. Sin is always a conglomerate mess, while righteousness is always a cohesive whole.

A Matter of Contrast

The great philosophers created lists of virtues and vices. But when we move to the apostle Paul, we see that he stands in stark contrast to philosophers. To Paul, the flesh and the Spirit were not merely lists—the flesh and the Spirit were opposing powers that were locked in conflict. This is the great struggle of the ages: the flesh wars against the Spirit and the Spirit against the flesh, and these are contrary, the one to the other (5:17). What we see in these lists is not merely a matter of choice or preference. What we see in these lists is the difference between victory and defeat—the difference between life and death.

There is such a thing as evil and Jesus Christ will one day come to planet earth and conquer evil. But the struggle between good and bad is not something that merely exists out there in the world—it is something that exists inside every child of God. There is a battle ground going on inside of you.

There is a struggle going on inside of us. The flesh and the Spirit are no more at peace than the Middle East is at peace. Inside of us there is a great contrast, and we have fleshly appetites that are part of Adam's curse. The Spirit of God is at war against the flesh and the flesh is at war against the Spirit of God. That battleground is real and it exists inside the child of God. How am I going to win this victory? Most of my life I've been trying to live the Christian life, and every time I have tried, I failed because it was a matter of work. It was a matter of conniving, and that conniving always resulted in chaos and a conglomerated mess.

What we need to do is quit trying and start trusting. When we yield to the Spirit and the Spirit begins to flow through us, then we find ourselves producing Christian virtue, fruit. When we depend on God, Christian virtue is inevitably generated. After all, it's the fruit "of the Spirit."

Too many times people are living the Christian life by true grit rather than by dependence upon the Spirit of God. You cannot save yourself from the penalty of sin—you have to trust God to do that. Similarly, you cannot save yourself from the power of sin—you have to depend on God to do in and through you what you cannot do for yourself.

Every time someone thinks that through works he can have victory in an area, he finds that's not true. It's not true in any area of our lives where flesh gets involved. You are not strong enough to will yourself to victory. Without Jesus, we can do nothing (John 15:5).

Living the Christian life is beyond us. That's why we are so defeated. Victory is not self-manufactured. Such connived attempts result in a catastrophic and conglomerate mess, and contrast with everything that God's wants to do in our lives. Only when you and I depend upon God and allow His life to flow through us will we have that harmonic, cohesive wholeness that God desires us to have.

We need to quit trying to produce works and ask God to produce fruit in us by His Spirit. Are you going to be a person who is characterized by the works of the flesh or the fruit of the Spirit? These are the only two choices you have, and the one you choose will make all the difference in the world in your life. Choose wisely.

CHAPTER TWENTY-SEVEN

The Bed Undefiled

Galatians 5:19b

There is a big difference between work and fruit. Work is something that we generate; it is something we plan and muster up, whereas fruit is the natural byproduct of the life that is coursing through us. Sin is something that people muster up, and it is something that they connive to do, whereas the fruit of the Spirit is the virtue that God seeks to produce in our lives—it is the natural byproduct of being yielded to Him and allowing His Spirit to flow through us.

We see in this passage a great contrast between the works of the flesh and the fruit of the Spirit. It is interesting that when Paul begins to talk about the works of the flesh in this passage, the first four things that he discusses are things that have to do with sexuality, and that is very common for the apostle Paul to do. For example, in I Corinthians 6 when he lists vices, the first things in that list are sexual sins. The same thing is true in Ephesians 5:5 when he begins to list vices; the first things on the list are sexual vices. Again in I Thessalonians 4 when the apostle Paul begins to talk about things that ought not be in the Christian life, he talks about us having a life of sanctification, and the first thing that he tells us that we need to have right in our lives is our sexual conduct.

It is interesting that in Mark 7, when Jesus is discussing things that are evil and come out of the heart and defile a man, before Jesus ever gets to murder or thievery or anything like that, He begins to talk first of all about adulteries, fornications, and things of that nature. The question that we could ask ourselves is why in the New Testament is there this emphasis on sexual immorality? Why does it seem in the New Testament that if nothing else gets right in our moral life, our sexual life ought to be something that is morally pleasing to God? Why is that true?

The Bible puts sexual sin in a category all by itself (I Corinthians 6:18). It says all the other sins people commit are sins that are committed on the outside of the body but when a man commits some type of sexual sin, there is a stigma that sticks to him. For example, very seldom in the ministry will a pastor lose his church over lying, not to say that he shouldn't lose his church over lying, but that does not carry with it the same stigma that adultery carries with it. There is nothing that more graphically depicts us as being selfish and as being in direct rebellion to God like sexual sin does, and the tragic thing is that what is true in the world across the board has in recent years filtered its way even into the church house.

Many of us have seen leaders in the church fall into a state of adultery and have to resign the ministry because of it. We have witnessed youth leaders actively involved in fornication and the fact of the matter is in recent years, we have seen the church become incredibly dirty. Things that used to not be mentioned in public are now being committed in broad daylight, and they are being committed by people who claim the name of Jesus Christ. The time has come for the church to address it, the time has come for us to stand behind our pulpits and say, "Ladies and gentlemen, these things ought not to be done."

It seems whenever a pastor begins to address sexual matters like this, sometimes the opposition will come in and people will say, "I don't think these things ought to be addressed. I don't think this is the time or the place for these matters to be discussed." If the church is going to abandon discussing public morality, who is going to do it? We have made our sexual appetites our God, and there are some things that the preacher ought to stand behind the sacred desk and clearly, with a thundering voice, say, "We have reached a point where our society is going to incur the judgment of God if it does not turn back from the sexual deviancy that it is currently committing."

When I published my book on the evils of pornography, a fellow who was serving as one of the proofreaders was making it very difficult for me to make the deadline. Finally, when I spoke to him about his failure to meet the deadline, he said, "Pastor, I'm just a little schoolgirl. I don't believe in reading stuff like this." I was talking to someone else about it and he said, "That proofreader had better get his head out of the sand because somebody has to say something about it - it has become an epidemic problem in our society."

The preacher has to say something about these matters and the Bible does not shy away from these matters. As a matter of fact, when the Bible begins to discuss vices that exist in our society, it puts sexual sins at the very top of the list.

The Dereliction of Duty

Adultery refers to the violation of marriage. In I Corinthians 7:4 the Bible says that the wife does not belong to herself—she belongs to the husband, and the husband doesn't belong to himself—he belongs to the wife. The reason that man and wife are the exclusive property of each other is because they have entered into a bond with each other through the vows of matrimony. This exclusiveness that exists in marriage is something that we have vowed and covenanted to do. At a marriage altar, a man stands there before God and witnesses, and he vows to keep himself only to his wife and to cleave unto her only so long as they both shall live.

That is why in the book of Hosea, unfaithfulness to God is referred to as adultery. When we became saved, we entered into a covenant with God. We said that we would have no other gods before Him, and we vowed to keep ourselves only to Him as long as we would live. We have entered into an agreement with God and, therefore, when we go pursuing other deities, we have violated our word and turned our back on what we said we would do. We are to love God exclusively and are to let nothing get in the way of that exclusive love.

In the same way, when a man and a woman go to the marriage altar and commit themselves to each other, they are to live exclusively for each other. There is no other woman that ought to mean more to me than my wife. There is no other man that ought to mean more to my wife than I do. There is an exclusiveness that exists in marriage. I drink coffee the way it ought to be consumed—black. My wife is quite the opposite—she believes in latte and cappuccino, and when Karen pours all of that sugar and cream into a little bit of coffee, I ask, "Why are you adulterating your coffee?" What am I saying when I say that? I am saying that she is putting into coffee things that ought not to be there. Coffee is supposed to be strong and hot; it is not supposed to be lukewarm, tepid, and sugary. If you want that, go to Dairy Queen—you are adulterating that coffee.

Just as that is true of a cup of coffee, it is infinitely truer of a marriage. My job as a marriage partner is to prohibit things from getting into my marriage that will weaken it, make it tepid, and make it less than the strong entity that God intended it to be. That's why in the Bible, when people are divorced and remarried, the Bible refers to that divorce and remarriage as adultery because things have entered into a marriage to destroy it and make it weaker and break it down. Jesus even says if a man looks on a woman and lusts after her in his heart, he has committed adultery because he has allowed something to seep into his marriage that ought not to be there. What he has allowed to seep into his marriage has made his marriage weak and tepid, and has turned his marriage from the hot, strong entity that it used to be.

The very day that I stood at the marriage altar and promised certain things to my wife, at that very moment, I was posted as a sentinel to guard the exclusive union that God had created that day. I must be on guard every single day that nothing gets into my life that makes null and void the agreement I made with my wife when I stood before her at that sacred altar and pledged myself to her as long as we both shall live. Anybody who allows things to get into a marriage—to water it down, to make it less strong, to make it less hot than it used to be—that person is guilty before God of being a derelict in his duty of keeping his marriage as strong and as hot as it can be.

The Perpetuation of Bondage

The second word that is mentioned here is the word fornication. It's interesting that in the Greek language, the word *pornea* initially referred to prostitution. It actually came from a root word that meant to sell people into slavery. Thus, the nuance that provides the idea of fornication is the idea of bondage or slavery. Just as a prostitute was owned by another, when someone commits sexual sin, that person becomes in bondage to the sin he or she commits. Jesus said that whoever commits sin becomes the slave of sin, and if that is true in no other area, it is true in the area of sexual immorality.

The sexual liberation society has done nothing to liberate men—it has only put men in deeper bondage and deeper slavery. Several years ago, when I was a pastor in Philadelphia, a lady came to us for counseling. This lady had three children out of wedlock and sat in our living room with tears flowing down her cheeks. She said, "Pastor, there is nothing that I would rather have in the entire world than victory over this particular vice but it has me wrapped in its tentacles. I don't know how to get out of it. Pastor, I am in bondage."

The very term from which we get our term *pornography* is this Greek word *pornea*, here translated fornication. Pornography is a binding addiction. Many years ago, a man looked up my name in the phone book and came to visit me for counseling. He had been visiting a pornography shop down the street on a consistent basis. He said, "I know that when I go there, I am going to see things that are going to nauseate me, but I continue to go. When I leave, I actually stand outside of that shop and vomit because of what I witnessed. But the sad thing is that the next week, I'll go right back again. Pastor, I'm a slave and I don't know how to get out of my bondage."

Our society is trying to teach us that there is great liberation in being sexually loose, but the Bible knows nothing of that. Sexual liberation does not produce liberation—it produces slavery and bondage with a tyrannical grip from which people will find it very difficult to extrapolate themselves.

The Contamination of Filth

The third word that he lists in this passage is the word *uncleanness*. Even today in the medical industry, we refer to cleansing a wound. Many years ago, when I was going through my foot reconstructive surgeries, I had casts on both legs. Halfway through my rehabilitation, I developed a very intense pain in one foot and asked my mom to take me to the doctor. He said the pain I was experiencing was very unusual. He cut a window into that cast and when he opened that cast, he discovered that one of the incisions he had made during the surgery had not healed properly. The wound was still open and there were all kinds of infection inside that wound. He looked at my mother and said, "Hold him." Mom held me and he reached into that open wound with a sterile gauze and began to scrape that infection out. I thought I was going to go through the roof.

The outside of that cast was so white, but underneath there was all kinds of contamination. Something like that is what the Bible says happens when a person has sexual immorality. A man may dress up in a business suit and may cut his hair right. A lady may look pristine, but God looks deeper than the surface. God sees the spiritual infection that lies beneath the surface that is eating away at the very heart of our soul.

A while back, I was cutting the grass at my house and was mowing underneath a tree with a riding lawnmower. I pushed the limbs back so that I could get underneath the tree, but the branches slipped out of my hand and came back across my face, cutting my face and arms. Immediately, I shut off the mower and went inside. I was sweaty and dirty, and could not afford to let that dirt and grass clippings get into that wound. That wound had to be immediately cleansed so that no infection would set in.

The longer you and I fail to deal with sexual issues, the more infected our souls become. Praise God, the Bible says that God is faithful to forgive our sins if we confess them (I John 1:9). What a great thrill it is to be clean rather than unclean! Unfortunately, in our society today, so many people are dirty that cleanliness is not considered a high standard. We have girls who live dirty and still wear white to the wedding altar. Sometimes they are even in a maternity wedding dress. A lack of purity has become not that big of a deal in our society.

Because I am a perfectionist, I don't like people pointing out flaws in me, and sometimes when we are eating spaghetti, I might get a little bit on my cheek. My wife will say to me, "You've got spaghetti on your cheek." Instead of saying, "Thank you" and wiping it off, I get mad at her for pointing out my dirt.

Something like that has happened in our society. People have become so accustomed to being dirty that instead of thanking a church for pointing out imperfection and trying to correct it, people would rather walk around town dirty. Dirt doesn't bother us like it used to and our society is unclean.

The Proliferation of Parties

The last word that is used in this verse is the word is *lasciviousness*. This word refers to a lack of shame over deviant behavior. We live in a society that does not blush over sin any longer (cf. Jeremiah 6:15). We live in a society where there is a total lack of restraint, a total lack of decency. We have such a loose disregard for standards of purity that we actually schedule parties to announce that we are going to live a deviant lifestyle.

At our political conventions, people will stand up and champion homosexual behavior. Sodomy is still sin—it does not show the broadmindedness of America to champion deviant behavior. It rather reveals our depravity.

People actually put wicked activity on the calendar and schedule it. You can hear people chat on planes about the deviancy that they are planning to do. You can see students on college campuses put announcements on their online bulletin boards announcing that at such and such a time, we will get together for an orgy. Our society has gone amuck so much so that very few people are falling into sin anymore—they are walking into it with their eyes wide open.

We as Christians cannot allow the world to squeeze us into that mold. We cannot allow our standards to be jaundiced by the spirit of our age. Somebody has to stand up and say, "This is unacceptable behavior." If you are married, you ought to do everything in your power to protect the sanctity of that marriage. If you are unmarried, you need to abstain from any behavior that would bring you to a state of bondage and slavery. You ought to live your life in such a self-respecting way that you can look into the mirror and see a clean person on the inside and out, and you ought not delude yourself into thinking that you can be proud and unashamed of such an abominable lifestyle.

Not too long ago, I was at a wedding reception and sitting across the table from me, was a homosexual who was bragging about the fact that he was. I thought about how far our society has come. Even when I was a child, people who embraced sexual deviancy did not brag about it at receptions—they hid it because they knew there was a moral code of acceptable lifestyle that existed within our society. Some of us have been so diluted by our own television sets that our minds have been totally reconditioned to think moral purity is not a huge issue.

According to God's laundry list, this is a big deal, and you and I, no matter how much we are encouraged to be quiet about it and no matter how much people in the church say they don't want this type of thing discussed, somebody has got to say that our society is falling into Hell.

If you have a marriage today, protect it. If you have freedom today, protect it. If you are clean today, protect it. If you have no party scheduled to pervert yourself, let it stay that way. Our society needs to get back to some good, old-fashioned purity. Keep the bed before and after your marriage undefiled.

CHAPTER TWENTY-EIGHT

Keep Yourself from Idols

Galatians 5:20a

In this passage, Paul is talking about the works of the flesh versus the fruit of the Spirit. As he talked about the first works of the flesh, he talked about things that were sexual in nature. Now the apostle Paul moves from immorality to idolatry. When you and I think of idolatry, many times we think about bowing down to some hunk of wood or stone and our minds may take us to some section of Africa where we would see witch doctors bowing before carved images. It may take us to an Eastern country where idolatry is practiced with gold statues and molten graven images.

Idolatry is more complicated than that—you do not necessarily have to have a hunk of wood or stone, or a graven image of gold or silver to be guilty of the sin of idolatry. In America we practice idolatry. Idolatry is not confined to the tribal sections of Africa and it is not confined to the Eastern religions of Buddhist and Hindu temples. Idolatry is practiced right in our midst.

Idolatry

Idolatry is the worship of a fabricated god. I use the word *fabricated* because there is only one God, and anything else that purports to be God is a fabricated god—it is a god of one's imagination—it is not the true, real God (Deuteronomy 6:4, I Corinthians 8:4). In the book of Isaiah, the prophet made a play on words. The Old Testament name for God is *Elohim* but when Isaiah referred to idols, he would use the Hebrew word *elilim* which means "nothing." When he would talk about an idol, he would call that fabricated deity to which people were bowing "a hunk of nothing." When we are talking about idolatry, we are talking about the worship of a fabricated deity.

Its Association With Sex

When Paul mentions idolatry, he puts it right on the heels of four sexual sins: adultery, fornication, uncleanness, and lasciviousness. On the heels of these four sexual vices comes the term idolatry. From the ancient fertility cult of Baal until the time of the apostle Paul, sexual deviancy has always been associated with false religions and the worship of false deities.

Idolatry is often accompanied by shameful, sinful, and sensual displays. America worships at this shrine and America is guilty of worshiping the goddess of fertility. We may not find anybody who is enrolled in the first church of Baal or on the rolls of the Aphrodite temple, but nevertheless, every day our society bows before a box that is concerned with presenting nothing more than sexual, sensual, illicit images. Idolatry is very much connected with our illicit sexual appetites. These images that we see on film and television are real. America has made a god out of sexual appetites that is no less real than the Baal religions that existed in the Old Testament or the goddess Aphrodite that existed in the New Testament. There is an association of idolatry with illicit sexuality.

Its Assertion of Selfishness

Whenever someone engages in illicit sexual activity, that person is making the creature more important than the Creator. In Romans 1:23, for example, Paul talks about idolatry—people who worship birds, four-footed beasts, and creeping things. This is not man made in the image of God; this is God made in the image of man—it's idolatry. Then in Verse 25, he talks about the fact that people actually worship and serve creatures more than the Creator. They believe that their fabricated deities are worth more than God Himself. They believe that their way is better than God's way. It is nothing more than selfishness, the professing of self to be wise (vs. 22).

Witchcraft

Why put witchcraft right on the heels of idolatry? Though it is true that an idol is nothing and it is really a fabricated deity, you understand that there is something behind an idol. The idol itself is not really a god but there is a force that exists behind the idol (cf. I Corinthians 10:20). What is behind the idol is the devil. I Corinthians 10:14 tells us to flee idolatry because even though an idol is nothing, there is something behind that idol which purports to be God and what is behind it is demonic activity.

When we engage in idolatry, though we are not really worshiping a true god, we are bowing down to satanic forces. Idolatry leads us straight into the world of the occult. It is very important that you and I don't get involved in things that have cultic associations with them. I'm still amazed at the number of Christians who play with a Ouija board, play Dungeons and Dragons, or get involved in all kinds of cultic video games, and read their horoscopes. We don't have to read our horoscopes or see how the stars are lined up to know what the will of God is for our lives. We should not be giving place to the devil by getting involved in witchcraft.

Its Association with Pharmaceuticals

The word that is translated *witchcraft* here is the Greek word *pharmacon* and it means "drugs." The word is the Greek term from which we get our word *pharmacy*. There has always been a connection between Eastern religion, African witchcraft, and drug use. If you are not that old, you remember the flower children in the sixties and how much of their occult practices involved drug use. You had music that was bowing down at the shrine of Satan connected with drug use.

The association between the occult world and pharmaceuticals is why drug use is very serious. Drug use tries to do the same thing that Eastern religion does—it tries to blow your mind and put it in neutral. When your mind is neutral through medication, you are opening it up to the infiltration of Satan's trafficking, and we have to be careful about that. When the Bible talks about meditation, it never talks about putting your mind in neutral or getting into a trance and trying to short circuit your head. When the Bible talks about meditation, it is talking about putting God's Word in, not taking all thoughts out. This is what many pharmaceuticals do. Drugs blow your mind.

Its Advancement into Psychology

It used to be that when we used legitimate drugs, we used them for a physical problem that had been clearly diagnosed. For example, I have pain, and I don't want to be in pain; therefore, pain medication is prescribed for me. Or I may have sinus trouble and so I get a decongestant so it will relieve the sinus pressure in my head. I have a known medical problem, and the drug is there to deal with the problem that presently exists—that's the way we understood drugs for years.

In recent years, drug use in America has become much more preventive than corrective. I don't have heart disease, but the doctor has told me that I have high cholesterol and the doctor says it could lead to heart disease. But I don't have it, so the doctor, as a preventive measure, prescribes me medicine to prevent a disease from happening when the disease doesn't even exist yet. Why is that an issue? A subtle change has taken place in the way we use drugs. Now I can afford to have deficient character because I can pop a pill. I don't have to avoid bacon and ham—all I have to do is take this medicine, and this medicine will actually help me continue with my deficient glutinous behavior. Medicine now has taken the place of what the Spirit is supposed to do in our lives.

This trend has even advanced into character modification with regard to adults and adolescents. I'm depressed. The fruit of the Spirit is joy and peace, but instead of being yielded to the Spirit and allowing the Spirit to produce joy and peace, I just go to the pharmacy and they give me a prescription to help me with my discouragement. I could get started on Ritalin. Basically, I don't have to be a parent and modify the behavioral deficiencies of my child. All I have to do is compound a prescription to modify my child's behavior because he supposedly has ADHD. Pharmaceuticals are used for relatively new purposes. We have actually entered into the realm of psychology so that now I can be deficient in my character whether it is rebellion, depression, or glutinous behavior. I can now back out of any character development through the influence of the Spirit of God. I don't have to be yielded to the Spirit and allow Him to produce fruit. I can just pop a pill to take care of what I am unwilling to do with self-control.

Its Allurement to People

Not too long ago, a friend of mine went to the doctor. When the doctor came in, he sat down and pulled out his pad and said, "What do you want?" The doctor had not even diagnosed the problem. He had not even pulled out the stethoscope or drawn any blood. He just said, "What do you want?" and ripped out a prescription pad. The doctor was prepared to write down a prescription without even knowing what the person's sickness was. Why has our society gone this far? They have gone this far because it is easier to compound a prescription than it is to exercise character. It is much easier for me to go get medicine than it is for me to modify my eating habits. It is easier for me to get a prescription than it is for me to be involved in the life of my child and discipline him constantly.

People ask me all the time how my kids turned out okay. My kids had just as much of the devil in them as your kids did, but we decided from the beginning that we were going to be parents. People think if kids turn out right that those kids never gave their parents any trouble. We think that some people have it easy and some people have it difficult, and for those of us who have it difficult, we just go get a prescription. There is only one way to parent and that is through hard work, prayer, being yielded to the Holy Spirit, and being involved in the life of the child. It is hard work but it is necessary.

The pharmaceutical industry has taken dependency upon the Holy Spirit out of everything in life. We simply fulfill the lust of our flesh and take a pill to deal with it, and no character modification becomes necessary at all in our living. This is not new—it is as old as the Bible. In Ephesians 5:18, Paul gives two options to modify behavior. You can modify your behavior by taking a drug or by being yielded to the Spirit of God. You have a choice between being yielded to God's presence in your life or modifying your behavior with artificial stimulation, and the choice is yours. You can be filled with the spirits and the substances, or you can be filled with the sweet Spirit of God—the choice is yours.

The allurement that popping pills has to people is they would rather pay money than yield to the Spirit of God. Elvis Presley said shortly before he died that he would pay one million dollars for a single day of peace. God keeps in perfect peace the mind that is stayed upon Him. Here was a man who was willing to take a million dollars and pay for something God gives away for free. But there was a difference. The difference was it took effort on his part to yield to the Holy Spirit and he did not want that price tag. He considered paying a million dollars easier than submitting to God—our society is in that same boat today.

I am not saying that anybody who takes a Bayer aspirin is outside the will of God. But in our society, we have taken areas of character deficiency and have tried to compensate those character deficiencies by purchasing pharmaceuticals and the Bible calls that witchcraft, which is using the pharmaceuticals for what only God can and should do in the life of a person.

If you are using artificial means to produce character traits that only God should be producing, you are guilty of idolatry and witchcraft. God wants us to be yielded to Him and He wants no artificial stimulants to take the place of what only His Spirit can do in our lives. Isn't God worthy of that?

What is governing your life? What is controlling your mood? What is your temperament? Is everything in your life governed by the latest purchase or by a capsule? If it is, you are not yielded to God and you are guilty of idolatry and witchcraft. The Bible commands us to be yielded to and filled with the Holy Spirit of God.

CHAPTER TWENTY-NINE

The Wrath of Man

Galatians 5:20b-21a

My parents, separately, not knowing that the other was coming, came to me on the day I was married and gave me two separate pieces of advice, which were actually the same piece of advice. My mother came to me and said, "Son, you had better be careful. You are not an easy man to live with." Out of all the things that you would expect your mother to say on your wedding day, that is not one of them. She was shooting straight with me and letting me know that I had the propensity to make my home a very dangerous place. My dad, not knowing that my mom had come to me, also came to me on my wedding day and said, "Son, if you ever lay a hand on Karen, I will come to wherever you are, and I will beat the ever-living tar out of you."

These are not the traditional warm, fuzzy sentiments that you would expect a person to be receiving on his wedding day. But for the twenty-two years before that day, my parents had been working on honing my character and developing me, and they knew some areas still needed work. I reflect on their wedding advice and recognize how pertinent that advice was to the man who was about to take Karen Aspray as his wife.

In the beginning years of our marriage, I was not a very good husband. When Karen would do things that I didn't feel ought to be done, I would explode. I learned very quickly that the wrath of man doesn't work the righteousness of God. One day when Karen did something (I don't even remember what it was), I took her shoulders and shook her. I said, "You will not do this, do you understand me?" As I was venting, a deacon of my church walked into the back door and saw me shaking my wife. It was extremely awkward, and I knew at that moment I had a problem.

My wife looked at me and said three words: "Not soon angry." I knew what those words were part of the requirements for a pastor, and what my wife was simply telling me was, "You're not qualified. The way you are treating me is not right. You're not qualified to be a pastor because of the way you vent of your anger. You are not even a good person." I was an angry young man. The man that I am today, praise God, is vastly different from the man who existed years ago, and I thank God for that. Anger is a common problem.

Much of what we call righteous indignation is nothing of the sort. When we are driving down the street and someone cuts us off in traffic, and we lay on the horn and pop a blood vessel, that's not righteous indignation. That is fleshly wrath. In our passage, the Bible talks about several things that you and I need to work on when it comes to not allowing our life to be fleshly. Many times when we hear the word *fleshly* we think of sexual sins and certainly that is involved in it, but you understand that there are many times that our flesh becomes volatile, especially when things don't go exactly the way we feel they ought to. We often believe that people ought to always do things the way we want them done, and we explode when they do not.

I want to explore the wrath of man from the eight characteristics that the Bible gives us in this passage. And I want you to ask yourself if you are an angry young person.

Posturing

The first word in our list is the word *hatred*. Some translations render this word as quarrels, but I think that is too weak. Sometimes the King James renders this word *enmity*. For example, in Romans 8:7, the Bible says that the carnal mind is at enmity with God. Imbedded in this word *hatred* is the idea that someone else has been assessed as being my enemy. In other words, hatred is something that postures somebody on the opposite side of us—we are in opposing camps one to the other.

Once you've branded someone as your enemy, that person can do nothing right in your eyes. Even the good they do will be evil spoken of on your part. The Bible says in Corinthians that love is something that endures all things, believes all things, and hopes all things; therefore, when we love somebody, we put up with their idiosyncrasies and endure them. If we were given a choice about whether they did right or wrong, we would believe in them and say they must have done the right thing. And even if they didn't do the right thing, we have hope that they will change. That's what love does.

Hatred does the exact opposite. It does not put up

with anything; it does not endure the slightest infraction. Rather, it disbelieves a person if given a choice about whether that person did the right thing or the wrong thing. We automatically assume they've done the wrong thing, and we have made the assessment that they will never change. When someone becomes a person that we hate, we actually perceive them as being our enemy and even when they are trying to do something good, we have already made up our mind that person is out to get us. They are doing something bad and even their good we misconstrue as a backhanded way of getting at us. We posture them in continual enmity because we hate them. They are the enemy.

Pettiness

The word *variance* is a word that speaks of strife and discord. It carries with it the idea of wrangling and ill will, and it is a continuous temper that is motivated by rivalry and pride. The main idea here is that of petty bickering. In other words, once I have determined that someone is my enemy, I will look at everything they do, even the little things, and will get upset with those little things. I will be petty in my assessment of that person and will criticize their life. Even the slightest thing they do, I will pick at it because I have become petty. The things that they used to do rolled off my back like water on a duck's back, but now those things do not roll off and every little thing sticks, jabs, and stabs me. I have become very petty in the way that I assess that person. I explode at the littlest things they do.

When Richard Nixon gave his farewell address to the White House staff, this in one of the closing paragraphs of his speech, "Never be petty. Always remember that others may hate you but those who hate you don't win unless you hate them because then you destroy yourself." How true that is. Richard Nixon ought to know—he had his critics and enemies, and though he had to give up the White House in defeat because of some of the ways that he obstructed justice, Richard Nixon was saying, "I'm not going to let my critics ruin the rest of my life even though I have to leave the White House. I am not going to let this thing eat me alive. The only way my enemies will win is if I hate them back—that is a sure way to self-destruction."

You and I have a variety of battles to fight in life, and we have to pick the hills that we die on. If we are fighting every little petty issue that comes up in life, we are going to self-destruct. Posturing someone as the enemy always leads to petty assessments of things that are going on in their life.

Possessiveness

The third word mentioned is *emulations*. It translates a Greek term from which we get our word *zeal*. Many times it has a negative connotation of jealousy. A jealous person is someone who wants what other people have. For example, if a kid in the nursery is playing with a toy and another kid becomes jealous of that toy, he will toddle over and hit the other kid in the head to get the toy the kid is playing with. Jealousy desires to possess what is in the possession of another. When we talk about jealousy, stuff is not the only thing that people are jealous of.

In a vast majority of instances, people are jealous over position and popularity. A good example of this in the Bible was Joseph. Joseph was in thick with his father in a way that the other eleven boys were not, and the boys were jealous of Joseph not so much because he had a coat of many colors but because he had access to the father that they did not have. Because Joseph had position with the father and popularity with the father, they became jealous of him and that is why they sold him into slavery.

You and I must accept that some people are going to have some things that we will never get. It may be a possession we never get, a position we never achieve, or a popularity level we never reach. The Pharisees, because of jealousy, turned Jesus over to Pilate. The Bible even says that Pilate knew that for envy they had delivered Jesus to him. Jesus had popularity with the people and position with the people that the Pharisees did not have and never would have. They were not as attractive as Jesus was and so they delivered Him up for envy because they desired to have His position and popularity. You have to be careful that does not describe you.

Someone once asked a famous orchestra leader what is the toughest position to play in the orchestra and he said, "Second fiddle." When I became station manager at WVMC in Mansfield, Ohio, I had as my program director a fellow by the name of Jim Stanley. Jim was much better at radio than I would ever be. He went on to work for the Moody Broadcasting Network. Jim Stanley had a golden voice and understood every aspect of Christian radio.

Yet when it came time to pick station manager, they picked me and Jim had to play second fiddle when he knew much more about radio than I did. Jim had the potential to make my life miserable but he didn't. He played second fiddle well. There are some people who can never play second fiddle because they are characterized by possessiveness.

Passion

Paul's fourth word is *wrath*. Wrath refers to fits of rage and to tantrums. When I was not even a year old, my mother went to change my diaper, but I did not want my diaper changed. I laid in the floor and waved my arms and kicked my legs, and my mother turned me over and stung my bottom. That was the last time I pitched a tantrum when she went to change my diaper.

There are adults who have never quit throwing tantrums. They are prone to outbursts of anger, and their hostile feelings are directed at other people. It is uncontrollable verbal violence. Many times, there is something in us that tells us to go ahead and say something even though it is hurtful. We think we have to say it or die. My experience through the years is that on such occasions, you would be better served to die than to say it.

You and I cannot excuse these outbursts as "my Irish temper" or by saying, "That's just the way I am."

Or, "That's the way we solved problems in our house growing up." You and I cannot explode. Believe it or not, there are some people who know how to push your buttons to make you explode so they can ruin your testimony. Sometimes I have had to stop a conversation and say, "We have to end this now because if it goes any further, I'm going to say something that I'm going to regret." You would be better served to solve the issue later than to deal with it now and end your testimony.

You can shoot that verbal dagger, but it is going to leave a scar. And that scar will take a long time to heal. Sometimes we blame these violent outbursts on Matthew 18 where the Bible tells us to go to our brother if we are offended. Matthew 18 is talking about the fact of going, not the method of going, and when you go to your brother with a violent fit of rage, don't blame that on Matthew 18. You are to go with the right spirit and attitude when you go to someone.

Politics

The word *strife* actually comes from a Greek word for politics and was used initially of somebody who was seeking office. It was used in the Greek language of someone who was seeking self-promotion instead of letting facts stand for themselves. We slant facts so we can win the argument. You cannot slant facts to bring people over to your side and go canvassing for votes to bring people into a fight that they were not initially a part of. Many times in our life we share information with people and cloak it in religious piety when it is nothing more than gossip, nothing more than maligning someone's character.

When I entered a previous ministry, there was an elderly woman who loved my predecessor. But when I came to the church, she struggled. My predecessor's temperament was so different. Thus, it was an adjustment for her. So she polled the church to see what they thought about my preaching. Not one time did she come to me and say, "Pastor, I would like to talk to you about your preaching." She rather went around the church and tried to get everybody in the church to say something negative about me. That was an unnecessary developing of strife by going around and spreading malice among the congregation.

Parties

The next word is a term that refers to parties. It's the word *seditions*, which is used only one other time by the apostle Paul (Romans 16:17) where it is translated *divisions*. The word *sedition* was a political term that referred to a political party. For example, we have the Republican Party or the Democratic Party. The word references an attitude that thinks my way is right and all other people's ways are wrong. It is like in Corinth where they said, "I am of Paul" or "I am of Apollos," or "I am of Christ." They had developed their own political action committees within the church of Corinth.

Our church ought never have sub-churches within the church. I've been at some places where they have Christian schools and the Christian school teachers are in a clique. When you go to that church, the Christian school teachers are always in a corner by themselves, and when other people walk by, the conversation always stops and they look at you like, "What are you doing here?"

When Pastor Henderson was my associate pastor, he and I went to a Georgia Association of Christian Schools meeting. They appointed me to be on the advisory council, and the position was just a résumé bullet—there is no authority in the position—you don't even meet. It's just to say, "I was on the advisory council of the Georgia Association of Christian Schools." At one meeting, they announced that they were going to have a meeting of the executive committee. The executive committee is only about three or four people who make the decisions. The advisory council doesn't make the decisions; they don't even talk to the executive committee. Pastor Henderson nudged me because he misunderstood the announcement, and he said, "That's you, you need to go." So I went and sat down, and they all kind of looked at me like, "What is he doing here?" The more I sat there, the more I was being looked at and finally I said, "This is the advisory council, right?" They said, "No, it's the executive committee." So I left. I don't know if you've ever been in a situation where you knew you didn't belong and people were looking at you like you were really out of place.

We as church members ought not look at anybody in this church and think, "How dare they be in our group." We have no political parties in the church. We have only one affiliation and it is the Lord Jesus Christ.

Pride

Notice the word *heresies*. The root word means "to choose." In other words, we draw a line in the sand and make people choose. If I were to put a footnote in my Bible, I would circle this word and out in the margin, I would put "My mom's family." My mom's family functions like this. If one of her brothers is fighting with one of her sisters, they come to my mother and say, "You have to choose. Which side are you on?" Many people draw lines in the sand and say that you can't talk to this certain person if I'm not talking to that person. If that is you, quit it.

When I worked at Northeast Baptist School of Theology, Fred Schindler was the president and Bruce Miller was the executive vice president. I love both of those fellows like brothers. They, however, reached an impasse and Dr. Schindler relieved Bruce Miller of his responsibilities. Someone asked me where I stood in that debate and here is what I said, "Fred Schindler is my friend and Bruce is my friend, and I'm for my friends." Because two brothers are in disagreement doesn't mean that I have to choose one or the other. That is not the way Christian living ought to be. We often have friends who are at odds with one another, but we shouldn't ever allow our friends to give us ultimatums and say, "If you are a friend of his, you can't be a friend of mine."

Plurality

The last word, *envy*, is very close to the word zealous that we looked at earlier, but the difference is that this word is plural, whereas the first word was singular. In other words, this is referring to many expressions. There are all kinds of ways that you and I are tempted to express envy. The Bible says in James 4:5 that the spirit that lives in us lusts to envy. In other words, you and I always have a tendency to want our own way, and the only way that we can overcome that tendency is by God's grace. The spirit that dwells in us lusts to envy, but He gives more grace. Aren't you glad that God's grace can help you overcome anger? No matter how it is going to manifest itself, God's grace can help you overcome anger no matter what way it seems to seep into your system.

Why do you and I get angry? Many times we get angry because things are beyond our control and we want to control things. Maybe it is the wife who is doing something that we don't think she ought to be doing, or maybe it is someone at work who is doing something and we try to control that person either by force or verbal abuse. The whole method that we are using to bring that person into line shows that we are out of control. How can we help people be self-controlled when we ourselves are uncontrolled? It is like a teacher who grabs a kid by the hair and pulls him out of the classroom, gets in his face outside the classroom, and yells at him to get control of himself. The teacher is about ready to have a nervous breakdown trying to get someone else under control, and the whole time she is modeling a lack of control.

When we try to control other people in an uncontrolled fashion, we take fire and pour gasoline on it because the wrath of man never works the righteousness of God. You can never get people to do right by anger. The only way that you and I can get people to do the right thing is by being in control when we talk to them.

The control only comes when we allow the grace of God to become operative in our lives. You cannot will yourself out of anger—you only make the anger worse. You have to allow God's grace to conquer the anger. We need more than caged anger, because at any moment the door could fly open and anger can jump out. Anger needs to be killed, and only God's grace can do that.

CHAPTER THIRTY

It's My Party

Galatians 5:21b

Since I've been an adult, God has given me the opportunity to travel to a lot of places around the world. Some of these places have been in remote jungles, and some have been in major cities, and it has been a privilege to go to the mission field and preach the gospel. But you understand that I wasn't a traveling person until I became an adult. I was born on a Tuesday and came home from the hospital on a Thursday. I lived in the same house until I went away to Bible college.

Because that was true, just going away from home was a big deal, so the very first time I went away to church camp, I got homesick and couldn't wait for Saturday morning to come so I could go home. When I left the camp and went back home, my parents were having a yard sale. They were busy. So when the van dropped me off, I wandered into the backyard and mom and dad were busy selling their stuff and taking care of people at the yard sale. No one noticed that I had arrived home. I thought they didn't even miss me. I'd been gone for five whole days. I remember sitting by the garage crying because they didn't miss me.

I had come home, but the homecoming wasn't anything like I anticipated it would be, and it was devastating to me. Have ever gone to a party where you anticipated that the party was going to go a certain way and it didn't go the way you anticipated? In our world, a lot of people have parties trying to find satisfaction, but these parties leave them completely empty and distraught. Isn't it funny that happy hour seldom makes anybody happy?

The old song said, "It's my party and I'll cry if I want to." I think a lot of people do that. They have another party thinking that one more party will be the answer to their problems. They think they will be able to get over it by immediately having one more party only to discover that after they have that party, they are just as depressed as they used to be. Notice three things about these parties.

A Bucket of Blood

You'll notice the first sin that he mentions in this list is murder. It's interesting that right above this, there is a laundry list of sins of animosity. In verse 20 he talks about hatred, variance, emulations, wrath, strife, seditions, heresies, and envyings—all of these are sins of animosity. It makes sense that after he concludes these sins of animosity, the very next thing that he would put on the laundry list of the works of the flesh is murder. Murder is the inevitable result of hatred. Indeed, Jesus said if a man hates somebody in his heart, he is guilty of murder. Hatred is the beginning stage of the devaluation of life. Life has lost its preciousness in our society.

C. Everett Koop, in his book *Whatever Happened to the Human Race*, argues that once we legalized abortion, it would have the domino effect of devaluing life across the board, and that has happened in our society.

Most people don't understand the Roe vs Wade decision in 1973 that legalized abortion. Justice Blackmun really did not argue that a woman had a right to choose. He rather argued that a baby in the womb prior to the third trimester is not really a person in the full sense of the word. So the reason that a woman had a right to terminate a pregnancy in the first six months was because it was not until the seventh month that you could really say that what was inside her womb was a person. In short, a fetus prior to the third trimester has no value.

We not only see devaluation at life's conception but we also see it at life's conclusion. Many elderly people are shoved into nursing homes and completely forgotten. All the babies we have aborted were the babies who would have grown up to take care of us in our elderly years. The babies that we've aborted will not be there to take care of us in our old age, and the elderly generation will be aborted itself by a generation that was not allowed to live. If there is baby discrimination and if there is elderly discrimination, then you can bet between those two extremes, life across the board will also be devalued, and that is exactly what has happened.

Michael Vick, the football player, went to prison for dog abuse. I'm not in favor of abusing dogs, but if Michael Vick had a mistress who he paid to have an abortion, he would have never went to jail. Our society has determined that human life is so devalued that it is worth less than animal life.

People now go to parties, and bullets fly because someone walked off with a girl that I wanted. I take a person's life for stealing my girlfriend. Or a boy is wearing a pair of tennis shoes that I want to have, so I kill him for his tennis shoes. Or a drug deal goes south and immediately bullets are flying and the whole transaction ends with a bucket of blood. There are places in our own town where the military will not allow the soldiers to go because blood flows too readily.

So much murder exists in our society today that murder doesn't even faze us the way it used to. Human life has been so devalued in our society that people dying is not a big deal to us anymore. If you were to go to New York City and turn on WABC, they would not even give the murder stories in their news — they would just give the number of people murdered. People have been reduced to human statistics.

On the authority of God's Word, dogs were not made in the image of God and cats were not made in the image of God. Man was made in the image of God. Because man is made in the image of God, his life is to be valued and protected, and the taking of innocent life is something that our society must stand before God and one day give an account for — murder is sin.

A Bottle of Beer

Not only does Paul talk about murders, but he also talks about drunkenness. How often in our society is fatality associated with alcohol? Alcohol blurs mental judgment (Proverbs 31:4). We should not have people in leadership who are drinking alcoholic beverages, and part of the reason is that alcohol pickles your brain. You cannot make clear judgment when your life has been affected by alcohol.

Beverage alcohol is still ethanol, and when you take alcohol into your system, it is not digested the way other foods are. It goes straight into the blood stream two or three minutes after it is swallowed. The first beer always affects your judgment with regard to the second beer, and the second beer blurs your judgment with regard to the third beer. Alcohol changes your brain cells; it impairs your coordination and dulls your senses. Alcohol depresses the central nervous system just like barbiturates do.

Alcohol is not a stimulant; it is a depressant, a toxin, and a poison. There is no way that anybody can hold a beer in his hand and ask God to bless that to the nourishment of his body. Industries advertise that alcohol assists with relaxation, fellowship, and even sexuality, but the Bible says wine mocks and deceives.

You may say, "Preacher, I don't think you ought to be talking about that. It's nobody's business what I drink." My friend, it's everybody's business what you drink.

> It's nobody's business what I drink
> I care not what my neighbor's think
> Or how many laws they choose to pass
> I'll tell the world I'll have my glass.

> Here's one man's freedom cannot be curbed
> My right to drink is undisturbed.
> So he drank in spite of law and man
> Then got into his old tin can

Stepped on the gas and let it go
Down the highway to and fro
He took the curves at fifty miles
With blurring eyes and drunken smiles.

Not long till a car he tried to pass
There was a crash, a scream, and breaking glass
The other car was upside down
About two miles from the nearest town.

The man was clear but his wife was caught
And he needed the help of that drunken sot
Who sat in a maudlin drunken daze
And heard the scream and saw the blaze

But was too far gone to save a life
By helping the car from off the wife.
The car was burned and the mother died
While a husband wept and a baby cried

And a drunk sat by and still some think
It's nobody's business what they drink.

It's everybody's business what you drink. The truth is that people who argue for social drinking in moderation have never grown up in the home of an alcoholic. The Amsbaugh family knows what alcohol is and what it can do. My grandfather was an alcoholic, and my dad was an alcoholic until the day he met Jesus Christ as his personal Saviour.

I still remember as a little boy sitting in a service one day when an old-fashioned evangelist came to our town. He said, "There is not a bone in my body that does not hate alcohol and what it does to the American family." Even as a little boy, I can still remember sitting there in the pew hearing my dad say, "Amen, preacher, I hate it too." I can remember the impact of my father's agreement with that evangelist. My dad knew what it was like to grow up in the home of a drunk. He knew what it was to be the father of a household that was characterized by alcohol. Do you think that you could get my dad to argue that alcohol is okay in moderation? He would argue that is like saying that strychnine is okay in moderation. Anybody's life that has been affected by the curse of alcohol knows that the safest course of action for any home is total abstinence.

Someone may ask, "Preacher, why are you against it?" I would support the liquor traffic if it weren't for a few things, such as children abused, decency refused, wrong excused, Satan amused, lives misused, and minds confused. If it weren't for that, I would support the liquor traffic. If it weren't for dishonesty, brutality, infidelity, immaturity, impurity, immorality, and non-spirituality, I would support the liquor traffic. If it weren't for truth compromised, good ostracized, evil exercised, God criticized, children terrorized, homes jeopardized, and wrong legalized, I would support the liquor traffic. If it weren't for the drunken sot, the hungry tot, the devil's knot, the mind's rot, the widows' lot, the damning spot, and the final plot, I would support the liquor traffic.

Alcohol is doing a lot to kill the homes of America, and we are paying to keep an industry in existence that is destroying hundreds of American homes every year. You and I know we can spend our money more wisely than that. A bottle of beer has a high price tag attached to it.

When I was a little boy, one of my friends went to a convenience store and bought a liter of Coca-Cola. The clerk put it in a brown bag and my friend brought it back to my house. My friend asked if I would like a drink, and without even thinking, I said, "Sure." I put that brown paper bag up to my lips and started taking a drink. My mom was at the kitchen window, and she yelled, "Jeff, take that bag away from your mouth." I said, "It's Coke." She said, "I know it's Coke, and you know it's Coke; but the neighborhood doesn't know it's Coke. Take it out of the bag." For years, I couldn't even drink IBC root beer because it came in a bottle that resembled beer.

That type of holy hatred ought to be in our system for alcohol and what it is doing to the American family. Many people have asked, "Do you believe Jesus can still turn water into wine?" I don't know if He's still doing that today, but I know today He is still turning beer into furniture.

A Barrage of Balloons

I think the reason that we have such a cheap view of life, and the reason we live from bottle to bottle is we have conditioned ourselves to think that life ought to be one party after another. No doubt you've seen the bumper sticker that says, "Life's a Beach." In other words, we think life ought to be a continual vacation that is devoid of responsibility. If you want to live your life totally devoid of responsibility, you prove you are acting like a child. Adults accept responsibility; children shun it. Just as balloons lose their air and become limp at the end of the party, so is the life of the carouser. He starts off the party as a bag of hot air and ends up as nothing more than a limp, cheap substitute. Perhaps you've seen the Snickers commercials where they are advertising Snickers as a feast. One guy comes out in a toga and says, "Sound the feasting horn." The guy comes out with a horn and accidentally knocks the Snickers out of his hand and he says, "The feast is ruined."

That's our society. The happy hour never quite delivers happiness, does it? It says in this passage that this is something we just don't get. Paul states, "I've told you before as I've told you in time past." This is like a mother saying, "How many times have I told you?" When a mother says that, she is not asking for a figure. She is saying, "You're not getting this." That is essentially what Paul is saying here. There is a world where happiness can be found, and it is not in establishments where there is a bucket of blood, a bottle of beer, and a barrage of balloons. That is not where you and I find happiness.

The place where happiness is found is in the kingdom of God. What is the kingdom of God? The kingdom of God is the area, the sphere, the jurisdiction where God is calling the shots. He is the authority. When God is in us and is controlling our spirit, and calling the shots, life will be characterized by love, joy, peace, longsuffering, gentleness, goodness, faithfulness, meekness, and temperance. Where God rules and reigns, where God calls the shots, where the authority of God is felt and realized, life is lived the way it ought to be lived. No one has to call for police backup in the kingdom of God. No one has to call for legal intervention because the party has turned south. There is no bucket of blood, no bottle of beer, and no barrage of balloons in the place where God's will is felt and actualized in all its fullness.

You and I do not find happiness by exterminating that which gets on our nerves. We don't find satisfaction by intoxicating ourselves beyond feeling, and we do not find ourselves by entertaining ourselves to death. We find happiness in the kingdom of God. How do you get into the kingdom of God? The question is very simply answered by Jesus in John 3:3 where He states, "Except a man be born again, he cannot see the kingdom of God." In other words, the only way that you and I can get in the door where Jesus is felt, where His authority is actualized, where his rule, reign, power, and omnipotence is felt is by being born again.

We were born into a world of condemnation and death. We practice all kinds of artificial stimulants to make ourselves fulfilled and happy, but that kind of life doesn't satisfy and fulfill. It doesn't bring the level of happiness that we thought it was going to bring. But when we come to the old rugged cross and ask Jesus to come into our lives, the old life with all of its misery is killed, and God creates a new us to take the place of the old us. This is the new birth.

You are never going to find satisfaction and happiness until you get into the kingdom of God, and you get into the kingdom of God by virtue of the new birth. If meaning to life is found in another bucket of blood, another bottle of beer, and another barrage of balloons, you are not even close to the kingdom of God. You can't inherit the kingdom of God if that is your measure and standard of happiness. True meaning and satisfaction is only found when you and I surrender to the rule and reign of God, and allow Him to be the controlling interest of our lives. When you and I give our lives to God, we find a whole new life of satisfaction that can never be found by virtue of these works of the flesh.

Are you going to try to find your satisfaction by scheduling another party? If you do, you are going to be just like nine-year-old Jeff Amsbaugh—you are going to be sitting against the side of the garage crying because that party never turns out the way it is supposed to turn out. When you give your life to God and let God become the controlling interest of your life, that is when your life starts to have meaning.

In a beer commercial, a guy has an open bottle of beer and invites a girl to sit in the car. They ride off together and we're told that life doesn't get any better than that. You never see that guy vomiting in a latrine or standing over a fiery car or anything like that. You never see the way the story ends, but when you come to God and submit to His authority, and accept His plan and purpose for your life, His kingdom becomes actualized in your person, and the story ends well. The last chapter is written with joy because this is the standard by which you and I find ultimate satisfaction.

What kind of party do you want? If you go to the party of the world, you'll cry. If you choose the party of God, your life will always end in great success. Which party are you going to?

CHAPTER THIRTY-ONE

The Greatest of These

Galatians 5:22a

After Paul has spent time talking about seventeen ugly manifestations of the flesh, he now moves on to talk about nine graces of the Spirit. As Paul talks about these nine graces of the Spirit, he begins to move from that which is ugly, disorderly, chaotic, random, and compulsive to that which is balanced, harmonious, symmetrical, and productive.

I've noticed that my teenage girls have used the word *random* in recent years. They'll say, "He's so random." I think they mean his life is chaotic and compulsive; there's no cohesiveness or balance in his life. When a life is characterized by the works of the flesh, it is so random—it has no cohesiveness around which it can operate.

At the very moment that you and I submit ourselves to the Spirit of God and allow His influence to be felt in our lives, our lives become much more beautiful, productive, symmetrical, balanced, and harmonious. What a wonderful thing it is to have your life characterized by love, joy, peace, longsuffering, gentleness, goodness, faith, meekness, and temperance! These are excellent qualities.

The first three of these qualities talk about our relationship to God. There's love—we ought to have a love for God. There's joy— we ought to enjoy the Christian life. There's peace—nothing exists between us and God. Then there are things that describe our relationship to other people: patience, gentleness, and goodness. Finally, there are ways we treat ourselves: faithfulness, meekness, and self-control. We ought to live right in relation to God, to others, and to ourselves, and all of this is possible when you and I are submitted to the Spirit of God and allow His influence to flow through our lives. In the Bible, these graces are called fruit.

In the Old Testament, Israel was compared to a vineyard and God went to that vineyard and sought fruit. He wanted Israel to be productive, but in many instances she was not. The Bible says that the blessed man will be like a tree that will bring forth his fruit in his season. In other words, God doesn't want our lives to be a barren wasteland that lacks productivity. God, on the other hand, wants our lives to be fruitful, green, and productive, bearing those things that are beautiful and tasteful for people to come in contact with. Once again we draw attention to the fact that the Bible does not refer here to the fruits (plural) of the Spirit but rather to the fruit (singular) of the Spirit. Just as you would bite into an apple and find seeds, skin, and pulp, but call all of it "apple," so these nine graces are all the singular, cohesive fruit that is produced in the Christian's life. We are the trees of God, and the Spirit inside us is the sap that produces the graces which are here referred to as the fruit of the Spirit.

The very first aspect of fruit that is mentioned in this passage is love. Obviously, this is significant. Of course, we know in another passage of Scripture that the apostle Paul listed other graces and then said, "The greatest of these is love." The greatest thing that you and I can do with our lives as Christians is to love God and others.

The Superiority of Love

It is interesting that the Greek word *agape* is not used in many secular writings, but it is used frequently in biblical Greek. Seventy-five times the noun is used in the New Testament by the apostle Paul. Thirty-four times the apostle Paul uses the word *agapao*, which is a distinctively Christian term. The secular world does not know a lot about love, but God's people ought to know much about it. It is right that love would be the first thing that adorns the list of Christian graces. Paul might very well have said, "The fruit of the Spirit is love" and put a period at the end of the word *love*. Everything else that follows flows from love. If you and I do not have love, we are not going to be able to produce any of the other graces in the Christian life. Love is not merely the first among equals. Love is the source and fountain from which all of the other graces in the Christian life flow. Love is the thing that predominantly brands us as being children of God (cf. John 13:35).

We tend to think that the external appearance is the thing that distinctively brands us as Christians. But Mormons cut their hair okay, and other cults may dress appropriately. People know we are Christians predominantly by the love that we manifest. The Bible says that God is love. Thus, there is nothing that brands us as being godly more then love. Love is superior because of its effect.

Nothing more clearly reveals that you are from God, that you've been born of God, and that you have the nature of God, than love does (cf. I John 4:7-8). Love is the thing that impacts the world with the fact that you have God inside you. God is love and that is what people think about when they think about God. People predominantly think of God as being an entity of love. When you and I manifest love, we are the agents that carry God to a lost world. People say, "He's been with God" when we love them.

We would tend in our minds to think something else. For example, I put much time into preaching, and I think that what I do behind the pulpit every Sunday is mighty important, but this pulpit doesn't impact people with God as much as my loving people impacts them with God. I think we've all heard sermons that were sound, accurate, and had great detail but we didn't sense that the preacher loved us. Thus, he didn't impact us. His message didn't affect our heart because we didn't sense that there was any love for the people to whom he was ministering.

My beloved predecessor, Walter Lee Hodges, was not a great man in the pulpit and was never invited to speak at any major conventions, but he knew how to love on people. Many people have told me that Brother Hodges would come up and put his arms around you and say, "I love you." There is nothing like love to impact the human heart.

There are all kinds of preachers around this nation who will never be able to speak at major conventions, but they are building solid works in major cities; and the reason they are doing so is they have learned the secret—nothing impacts people like the love of God flowing from my heart to your heart.

Love is also superior because of its endurance. When you love people, you are practicing for eternity. We are going to love people throughout eternity in Heaven. The Bible says that charity never stops (I Corinthians 13:8). In other words, there never will be a point when we will be done loving. The Corinthians were arguing about what gifts were the best, but Paul says their arguing is misplaced. The gift they have is not as important as how they exercise that gift. The most important thing is that you minister your gift with love. When we get to Heaven, spiritual gifts will have ceased but there will always be a need for love in Heaven.

When God created the universe, he declared it to be very good. But God declared one thing to be not good. God said that it was not good for man to be alone. God looked down into a paradise and said in that paradise there was something that was not good. If man is alone, he has nobody to love. So God created a woman out of man's rib, and God only gave one primary command to man with regard to that woman. Love your wife the way Christ loves His church.

Even paradise itself cannot be paradise unless there is an opportunity to exhibit and receive love. Love prepares your heart for Heaven. If you want to practice heavenly attributes, attitudes, and actions now, all you have to do is start loving on people because that is what we are going to do for all eternity. Love can do in the life of people what nothing else can do in the life of people. You can't just say something to a person and everything is going to be all right. You can't give someone a tidbit of knowledge and make everything okay. There are some things that can only be done with love. There is nothing that takes the place of love in a person's life. Love is superior.

The Source of Love

There is only one reason that you and I can love other people and that is because God first loved us (cf. I John 4:19). God is the source of love. People are responders, and if you want people to love you, then you have to love on them. If a man wants friends, he has to show himself friendly. People aren't going to love on you if you don't love on them first. Husbands, for example, want their wives to love them and admire them, but women only admire men who love on them. You can't command people to love you; you have to love people into loving you.

If I am being mean and ugly, I can't expect my wife to love me. I have to love her when she is mean and ugly, and that in turn causes her to respond to me. Love is not blind. Love knows exactly what people's faults are and loves them in spite of those faults, indeed loves them out of those faults (cf. Romans 5:8). My job as a husband is to know the shortcomings of my wife and to love her out of those shortcomings. You and I would not be able to love that way if the love of God was not first infused into us because it is the love of God that we use to love other people. His love becomes shed abroad in our hearts to reach other people. He is the source and fountain of that kind of love.

In Galatians 2:20, Paul talks about living the dying life. What does it mean to be dead to something? The other day, I blocked out time to watch Ohio State play a football game. But because ABC had coverage rights to that game, it was blocked out of Dish Network, and the Ohio State game was not aired. I was upset because I had blocked this time out to watch the football game. I wanted to see Ohio State beat Perdue, but the program was not available in our coverage area. I was fit to be tied. But my wife Karen was not upset at all because she is dead to football. It means nothing to her.

All this world's temptations ought to mean nothing to us because we are dead to them. Why are we dead to it? We are dead to it because somebody loved us and gave Himself for us, and because He loved us and gave Himself for us, we want to give our lives in total service to Him; therefore, this world's attraction pales in comparison. That day when Adam took the forbidden fruit and damned his soul to Hell, if I had been God, I would have said, "Well, I gave him a chance. I wash my hands of him." God didn't do that. God came down to the garden seeking and saving that which was unlovable.

He went to another garden, the Garden of Gethsemane, and there He thought about what He was about to do and how He would be separated from His Father in that eternal moment upon the cross. But He was willing to take all of my Hell for all eternity because He loved me. Praise God for the source of love! We can love today because somebody loved us.

The Sobriety of Love

What difference does it make whether I love people or not? Some pop artist sang, "What's love but a second-hand emotion?" It is significant that you and I love people, and it will make a difference. If we do not love people, two very serious things will happen. First, the worship of the church is disrupted. An example of this existed in Corinth. Corinth was a very talented church. They came behind in no spiritual gift. In other words, every gift of the Spirit that could be manifested was manifested at that church. The church at Corinth was full of talent, both natural and supernatural, and yet they didn't love one another. And because they didn't love one another, their gifts degenerated into disruptive competition.

Any time you have talent without love, you disrupt cohesiveness. Parents, for example, who have natural talent are often some of the most untalented people at parenting. Junior comes home with his medal from the fifty-yard dash and dad talks about his days in the army. Every time a kid does something good, we use that as a springboard to brag on ourselves. We should brag on the accomplishments of others. That is why talented people sometimes make untalented parents. When you and I are so concerned about our own talent and ability that others are ignored, then worship gets disrupted and cohesiveness gets destroyed.

Second, when we fail to love, the witness of the church is diminished. We've already seen that the world will know we are Christians by our love. Let's say, for example, my home is in disarray and is characterized by strife, division, anger, and frustration. And let's say that I visited a church on Sunday and discovered that there was a bunch of bickering and fighting going on in the church. Why would I leave my home of strife and come to a church of strife? I'm looking for an answer to strife. Let's say I'm having trouble at work and I can't get along with people, and I want to learn how to have better relationships at work. How am I going to enter a church house that is characterized by division and learn how to do that? There is nothing that helps people be impacted with Christ more than love, and there is nothing that turns people away from a church more than Christians who fight all the time.

I have a brother-in-law who was very much into church when he was a little boy. When he was a little boy, he professed Christ as his Saviour and was called to preach. He memorized verses and was on fire for God until one Sunday. He saw two deacons that he admired fighting in the church parking lot. He loved those men and admired them until that day. The day he saw those two godly leaders in the church fighting, something happened in his little mind and he has never been the same since. I don't believe that he is going to be able to stand before God and use that as an excuse for living his life independently of God, but I do believe that by the same token, those two deacons will stand accountable to God for the way they destroyed what a little kid thought about Christianity by their lack of love for one another.

A pastor in my hometown was in trouble with the church where he was pastor, and the church asked him to resign. He said, "I will not resign." The church body took him to court to get rid of him, and a secular judge looked at their constitution and determined that the pastor indeed did have to leave. This was front page news in our hometown paper. The pastor went across town and started a new Baptist church which he named *Free for All Baptist Church*. He meant, of course, that the church was free for all people, but after they had just spend the last few months fighting, many wondered. I wonder how many Baptist churches could be characterized as the free-for-all Baptist church? When you and I do not take the matter of love seriously, we become a joke in the eyes of a lost world.

Years ago when Jackie Robinson broke the color barrier in major league baseball, he obviously was heavily booed when he went to stadiums across America. On one occasion when Robinson made an error and was booed by the fans, a fellow teammate, a white man by the name of Pee Wee Reese, went over and put his arm around Jackie Robinson, motioning for the crowd to be silent. Jackie Robinson said, "That arm around my shoulder that day is what saved my career."

How many careers have you saved? When there has

been somebody out there that somebody was chewing up and spitting out, have you decided that you would take your stand with that person and put your arm around that person and try to help that person? I think that we as Christians are very selfish. I think that some of us have been saved for years and yet sit around and moan about the way we are treated. We are not supposed to sit around and wait for people to take their stand for us; we're supposed to take our stand with other people. God didn't sit up in Heaven and say, "I can't believe those humans are treating me like this." At the very moment they were spitting on Him and calling Him names, He reached out and put His arms around them and loved them. As children of God, that is the way we ought to be. There is someone out there who needs the love of God.

My wife was walking through the neighborhood the other day and as she did, she passed one of our neighbors and found out that his mother was very close to death. He said to Karen, "I know that your husband is a pastor. Could you have your husband go up and see my mom? She has some concerns about her eternal destiny." Karen told me his story and I went to the hospital to talk to the woman and I plan on going back and having more conversations with her. I was in the home of my neighbor to report to him about what our first meeting was like and what I anticipated our second meeting was going to be like and he said, "I'm sorry I bothered you. I was just kind of emotional that day and I know I shouldn't have bothered you with that kind of stuff."

How sad it is that Christians have lived their lives in such a way that the world thinks it can't bother us with its problems. That is why we are here. If there were no problems, there would be no need for us to be here. The greatest thing that you can do with your life is to invest it in the lives of people. In the upper room the night before Jesus was about to go to the garden, He was going to wash His disciples' feet. John makes a very interesting statement when he talks about that event. He says that His disciples remembered that Jesus loved them unto the end. I wonder how many people will be able to say of us that we loved them until the end. The greatest thing that you can do with your life is to love on somebody.

CHAPTER THIRTY-TWO

Rejoice Evermore

Galatians 5:22b

In his book, *Surprised by Joy*, C. S. Lewis says, "Joy bursts in on our lives when we go about doing the good at hand and not trying to manipulate things and times to achieve joy." I think most Americans spend their time trying to manipulate events, things, and times to achieve joy. Do you know that you cannot manipulate joy into being? Joy bursts into our lives when we do, as C. S. Lewis says, "the things at hand." The fruit of the Spirit is joy. As you and I engage ourselves in loving one another, the inevitable result is joy in our hearts. Joy is not to be found when other people love us; joy is to be found when we love other people. It is love, then joy. Joy is a fruit of the Spirit that is produced as you and I engage in love.

The great Christian psychologist Henry Brandt used to say that whenever someone came to his office contemplating suicide, the first thing he did was assign them a task to do for someone else. If you are concerned for other people, you're not thinking about yourself and all that is wrong. When you reach out in service and love other people, that is when joy bursts into your life. If you try to manipulate events and times to achieve joy, you will never find it. You and I can find joy in our lives when we engage in practical love to other people.

The Source of Joy Is God

The source of joy is God. It is important for us to notice that joy is a fruit of the Spirit. Therefore, joy is not something that we manufacture in our lives. Joy is not something that you and I work up. Joy is something that is given to us as a gift from God. Anytime that you and I try to manufacture joy in our own lives by our own effort, we get nothing more than wax fruit. Wax fruit is not very satisfying. For example, if I were to manipulate a compliment out of my wife, that compliment would ring hollow; it won't satisfy me because whatever joy she is trying to send my way, I have manipulated it.

When you and I manipulate events and times to achieve joy, it will be like wax fruit; it will not produce the nourishment that we need. We will never have true joy in our lives until we recognize who gives joy, and the source of joy is God. That's why numerous times in the Bible it says, "Rejoice in the Lord." The Bible says that you and I ought to turn to God as the true source of joy. This is true for several reasons.

First of all, it is true because of the weakness of the flesh (Philippians 3:1). Paul places rejoicing in God in direct opposition to having confidence in the flesh. In other words, if you and I put confidence in the flesh, we will always be disappointed because the flesh will always let us down, but if we put our confidence in God, we will never be disappointed because God never lets anybody down.

Several weeks ago, our youth pastor was asked to babysit some dogs in a fancy house with a huge television. He was babysitting the night that his favorite team, Georgia, was playing Alabama. He was so excited. He had the whole night planned to watch the game on TV with surround sound and high definition. There was only one thing that he couldn't control that whole night—the flesh of the Georgia Bulldogs. In one quarter Alabama was eating them for lunch. What happened in that situation? He had everything except one: you can't control the way people perform. You can't control how people come out of the locker room and how they play the game of life. You can control all the events except the flesh and many times that just cannot be controlled. You understand how many times the flesh leaves us disappointed, and how you and I put our confidence in men to provide happiness for us and that happiness isn't there because flesh always lets us down. We have to put our trust in God because of the weakness of the flesh.

Second, we have to find our joy in God because of the worries of the future. Not only are we unable to control people, but you and I are also unable to control events (Philippians 4:1-7). We are to rejoice in the Lord. We know we can't rejoice in people because Euodias and Syntyche; they will always let us down. When we put our confidence in people like that, they could be fighting with one another, and they will not help us be happy. We might have to be the person who gets in the middle of that and solve their difficulties.

We can't wait for other people to make us happy; we have to go make them happy.

We cannot control people, and we cannot control events. We cannot worry about tomorrow. We are to be careful about nothing—that is, don't be anxious about anything. If we are conditioning our joy on events, sorrow will always ensue because events never turn out exactly the way we hoped they would. When our first child was born with a birth defect, because of her disabilities, all the things that we had planned to do we were unable to do. The things we planned to do were replaced with fifteen surgical procedures. It doesn't matter how carefully you plan for the events of life—you're going to find that those events will be laced with elements of imperfection. You and I have to derive our joy from God because if we are deriving our joy from other people and from events of life, we will be disappointed. The source of joy has to be God.

The Supply of Joy Is the Gospel

The word here translated *joy* is the Greek word *chara*, and it is closely connected to the Greek word that is translated grace, *charis*. Obviously there is a close connection between the two — you and I derive joy by means of grace. The Gospel is the vehicle that brings the grace of God to us, and grace makes joy our own.

For example, I think of the Judean shepherds out on the Bethlehem hillside the night Jesus was born. They were weak in social class and strata. They were third-shift shepherds and not even allowed to testify in a court of law because they were considered riffraff. They were at the bottom of the ladder; they obviously had worries about the future.

An angel, however, appears in the sky and tells them not to fear because they are being brought tidings of great joy. That night those shepherds needed strength for the day and bright hope for tomorrow. And that is exactly what the gospel provided them – joy.

The gospel is our supply of joy. Why is this true? First, it is true because it provides companionship. Every one of my girls has come to me at some point during their junior high or early high school years and said, "Daddy, I'm lonely." I know why my kids are lonely — nobody wants to hang out with the preacher's kids because if you hang out with the preacher's kids, you're going to get told on. So consequently there is just a certain element of loneliness that they experience in life. What my girls have articulated to me I don't think escapes people who are not living in the parsonage. I think all of us at times in our lives have felt friendless. The gospel brings that kind of friendship to us.

Romans 5:10-11 tells us that we were enemies of God, but the gospel reconciled us to God. Now we actually joy in God because we have received the atonement. We have become one with God through Jesus. Therefore, wherever I go in this world and whatever I am engaged in, I have an intimate friend who walks with me, a friend who says to me, "Lo, I am with you always, even unto the end of the world."

Several years ago I read a story about some mission-aries who were captured and put in a cell where they were forbidden to talk to one another. If they talked to one another, they would receive the death penalty. Not able to talk to one another, those missionaries felt very lonely, isolated, and ostracized until one of the missionaries decided to write something on the ground with a straw. He spelled out the word Emanuel. When he wrote the word *Emanuel* in the dirt, his other mis-sionary friends beamed with joy. Why? Emanuel means "God with us."

Regardless of what prison house you are in, if you are a child of God, you have been reconciled to God. You are one with God and have Emanuel with you. If God is your best friend, you don't have to improve on your social network. What better friend in the world can you have than God? What more influential friend could you have than God? God is a dear friend that sticks closer than a brother, and the gospel is the thing that brings us that companionship.

The gospel also brings joy because it provides con-fidence. In Romans 1:16, my life verse, the apostle Paul tells us that we do not have to be ashamed of the Gos-pel because it is the power of God that brings salvation. That word *ashamed* doesn't so much carry with it the idea of embarrassment as it does the fact that the gos-pel never disappoints us. The gospel never lets us down. The gospel is a guaranteed hope, and the gospel does exactly what it promises it will do. No one who has truly tried the gospel has found that it failed to deliver—the gospel always works every single time it is implemented. This is important because one of the things that robs of joy is fear. People are paralyzed by fear. We allow circumstances to rob us of joy. Fear is a paralyzing thing that robs people of joy.

II Corinthians 1:24 states that if you want to help people's joy, give them something to believe in. Our job as Christians is to go out and preach the gospel of Jesus Christ in order to give people something in which they can place their faith. When we give people something they can legitimately believe in, we provide joy.

The Strength of Joy Is Guaranteed

Aristotle defined joy as "living between the excess of pleasure and pain." In other words, Aristotle defined joy as being middle class. If you get excess pleasures, they'll let you down. If you get an excess of pain, that will let you down. Try to live somewhere in the middle and you'll be joyful. By definition, then, joy depends upon circumstances. Even our word *happiness* comes from the root from which we get our word *happenings*. Christian joy is much deeper than that. Christian joy is not conditioned by my circumstances—it happens in spite of my circumstances because it is a gift of God, a fruit of the Spirit. I am guaranteed a supply of joy, regardless of what is going on in my life.

If you were to ask the average American how he is going to get his joy back, he will start listing all the things that are going to make him happy. In so doing, he is looking at the wrong administration. The kingdom of God is not meat and drink (Romans 14:17). In other words, joy is not conditioned upon what is sitting on the table in front of me; it's not conditioned on how much you have to eat or drink. God does not give us joy by making all of our circumstances on the outside right. God supplies us with joy by giving us internal qualities from within. He gives us righteousness that we did not have, peace that we did not have, and joy that we never experienced before.

People all around us are thinking about killing themselves because of the economy. Politicians think that if they can give us things, this will produce happiness. But God's administration is vastly different from that. God doesn't provide external stuff and hope that will give us internal happiness. God fortifies our standard of living not from without but from within, and the joy that God infuses into us actually becomes our source of strength. It is guaranteed. No human politician can supply or guarantee that, but there is an administration that can supply and guarantee it. The administration that can do it is the kingdom of God.

Years ago, I read about a pastor who was leading a worship service in a leper colony on the Island of Tobago. There was a leper woman who had her back to the pulpit the whole service. Finally, toward the end of the service, the pastor asked if anybody had a song they would like to sing. This woman turned to the pulpit and raised her hand. The pastor said that when she turned to the pulpit, he saw the most hideous face he had ever seen in his life — a face that had been eaten away with leprosy. He said all the fingers on that woman's hands were gone as she raised her stub to request her song. He called on the woman and asked what she would like to sing, and she said I would like to sing "Count Your Many Blessings." When the pastor told that story, one of his friends said, "I bet you'll never sing that song again." He said, "I'll sing it, but I'll never sing it the same way." I don't care what is eating you away, you are guaranteed joy on the inside because of the kingdom of God—an internal administration produces it.

Anybody can sing on good days, but God wants to hear you sing when no one else believes you can. There is a God in Heaven who has dispensed His gospel to us from the third Heaven and has guaranteed us joy in spite of what is going on in this wicked world in which we live. In the world we will have tribulation according to the Bible, but be of good cheer: Jesus has overcome the world. The joy of the Lord is our strength.

CHAPTER THIRTY-THREE

Peace I Leave With You

Galatians 5:22c

Just this week I went to the Web site for The Association of Baptists for World Evangelism (ABWE) and logged on to view the memorial service of one of my favorite preachers, Wendell Kempton. As I looked at his memorial service, I was reminded of some of the messages that he had preached in the past that had impacted my life. In one of the messages, Dr. Kempton made the statement that if he could pick any term to describe the world in which you and I live, he would choose the term *ungodly*. He said if there was a second term he could choose, he would pick the term *uptight*. Our society is uptight because it is ungodly.

Elvis Presley said shortly before he died that he would pay a million dollars for a single day of peace. Peace is such a precious commodity in our society, and yet it seems to elude many people. Many Americans find themselves in uncertain times and wonder if there is such a thing as peace. And if it is available, how in the world do we find it? What a precious thing it is for you and I to know that the fruit of the Spirit is peace. Jesus said, "Peace I leave with you."

The Positiveness of Peace

Just in case you are wondering, *positiveness* is not a word, but I have invented it for this occasion because it is something that I want you to think with me about. Peace is an infusion of something positive into your life. Even in the Old Testament, when Jewish people would greet one another, they would say "Shalom" or "Peace." They were not saying, "May all your troubles be eradicated." Or, "May all your strife cease to exist." In the Jewish mindset, peace was not getting rid of something negative; rather it was the infusion of something positive from God so that you could be "Fiddler on the Roof." In spite of all the adversity that Jewish people have faced from their persecutors, they could still find peace in the midst of the storm.

The storm does not have to be eradicated for the child of God to find peace. Peace is not getting rid of all your negatives—peace is rather the infusion of something positive from God that helps you deal with the adversity that you face on a daily basis. The fact that Philippians 4:6-7 states in a context of peace, "Be careful for nothing," would seem to suggest to us that there are things out there that are going to make us anxious. Yet in spite of the fact that we are tempted to be anxious, we are to make our requests known to God so that His peace can fill our hearts. It's a peace that doesn't make sense. Your trials have not been eradicated—you are still tempted to be anxious. And yet there is peace.

If all your trials were eradicated, peace would make sense, but the fact that you can have a peace that doesn't make sense shows that you can have peace even when things aren't going your way. This peace will keep and guard your mind. We are actually in a circumstance where we could lose our minds, but that is not going to happen because the peace of God is arrived. Peace, therefore, is not merely the eradication of all strife, violence, or negative influences in our lives—that is not what provides peace. It is not necessarily the eradication of the storms of life that produces peace. Rather, in spite of all the negatives that are going on, God infuses a positive quality of peace to help us deal with all the calamities that are going on around us. Peace is not the eradication of negatives; it is the infusion of something positive from God—there is a positiveness of peace.

The Possibility of Peace

We may be tempted to think that if these storms are not going to go away, then it is impossible for us to have peace. Peace is possible in the midst of chaos because chaos is not what provides or subtracts from peace. Peace comes from God; He is the one that gives it. The Bible says that the fruit of the Spirit is peace—it comes from God. Peace with regard to God needs to be thought of in two ways.

First of all, think about the peace with God. Romans 5:1 talks about having peace with God. You and I were alienated from God because of our sin, but by virtue of what Jesus did on the cross, we have now been made one with God and are no longer alienated from Him. And because we are no longer alienated from Him, we have peace.

I think the most intimate relationship on earth is the relationship between a husband and his wife. Let's say that before I go to work tomorrow morning, I do something really stupid. Let's say I am really grouchy on Monday morning and I chew my wife Karen out for no apparent reason. She is in tears, but I have to be at church on time to give devotions for the staff meeting. So I leave her in tears and rush off to work. Let's say that when I go to work, everything at work is going well and everybody on staff is doing what they are supposed to be doing. There is great harmony among the staff. Even if things are going perfectly well at work, they are not going well for me because in the back of my mind, there is this thought that I am not right with my wife. In the most intimate relationship of life, ostracism has taken place, and that ostracism from my wife affects everything else that goes on during the day. It is like a cloud that hangs over my head.

If that is true on a human level, how much more is that true of what exists between a man and his God. The most important relationship of life is not even the relationship that we have with our spouse—it is the relationship that we have with God. If our relationship with God is not right, it will affect every other relationship and event in life. No matter what you are involved in or how successful you may be, looming in the back of your mind is the fact that you don't have peace with God. You will never have harmony and wholeness in your life until first of all the friction that exists between you and God has been nullified through the cross of the Lord Jesus. For us to have the possibility of peace in our lives, we have to be united with God through a salvation experience—we have to have peace with God.

Second, as a consequence of having peace with God, we can have the peace of God (Philippians 4:6-7). Everything can be alright with everything else because regardless of how bad those things may be, I am okay where it matters most. Let's go back to the illustration of the husband and wife. Let's say that tomorrow morning I get out of bed and just the opposite happens. Let's say that Karen and I are having a good time and are laughing together. I go off to work and everything at work goes bad. I don't care because of the joy that awaits me at home. Not only can the primary relationship overshadow all the good if it is bad, but if it is good, it can also overshadow all the bad. I don't care what my staff thinks about me as long as my wife is in love with me.

In the same way, when you and I have peace with God, it overshadows everything else that happens in life. Because we have peace with God, we can have the peace of God. If God is in your corner, who cares if others are against us? If God is for you, who can be against you? Regardless of what happens in life, God is with me in the midst of the fire. I am so fixated on God that I have the possibility of peace. Not only is peace a positive infusion, but it is a possible infusion because it comes from none other than God Himself. Thus, it supersedes everything else that happens in life.

The Principles of Peace

If God keeps us in perfect peace because our minds are stayed upon Him, then the question could be asked: How do we keep ourselves fixated on God? How do

I stay my mind on God, and what specifically am I to think about God so that I can have peace in my heart? To answer that question, let's go to Matthew 6:31. Jesus is speaking about the eradication of worry and tells us several things that we should know about God to eliminate worry. Here are some things that we know to be true about God, some things that we can concentrate on, some things that we can concentrate on about God, and in so doing know peace.

God Has Saved My Soul

Worry is something that characterizes an unsaved society. When a man goes off to work in the morning and kisses his wife goodbye, he heads off into the dog-eat-dog world. He does so with no personal relationship with God. How does he survive? He doesn't. He worries about everything. He worries about the election and the economy. That is the way the Gentile world conducts itself. When God saved me, God saved me out of that heathen world and I am no longer a part of that society. God has lifted me out of that arena.

If God freely gave us His Son, shall He not also freely give us all things? (Romans 8:32) God has already proven to me that He is going to take care of me. He has already saved me from the worst calamity that's ever happened in the world. God sent His precious Son to die upon the cross to pay the price so that I wouldn't have to go to a devil's Hell, and no matter what happens in my life, I am headed to Heaven. The last chapter of my life is going to end well. Thus, when all is going bad in the world, it is well with my soul—I am headed to Heaven. God is on the throne and He has saved my soul. I know God is going to take care of me because He saved my soul, and if He took care of my biggest problem, certainly He can take care of all my lesser problems.

God Knows All Things

Worry basically denies the omniscience of God. We're not certain that God knows how to handle our situation. We're not sure that God knows about it, and if He knows about it, we're not sure He knows how to handle it. Certainly you and I know that God knows everything. We would not deny that in a theoretical sense. We would give that advice to other people. If a friend is going through a trial, we would say to him, "God knows about your situation." But when it happens to us, we are not so sure. When we worry, we are really saying, "I don't believe God really knows about my situation." I have to fixate on God and remember that God knows all things. There is not anything that is going on in my life that has escaped the knowledge of God. My God knows everything, and He knows everything about everything. God is an omniscient God.

God Rewards Kingdom Seekers

When we don't seek the kingdom, we increase worry. Remember in the Garden of Eden that Adam ate fruit that he wasn't supposed to eat. What happened? He failed to seek the kingdom and live according to

God's rules. So when God went looking for Adam, he was hiding. God said to Adam, "Why are you hiding?" Adam said, "I ate of the fruit and I knew that I was naked." Adam thinks his big problem now is that he needs a new set of clothes. Adam's big problem was not a new set of clothes. God kills a lamb, sheds blood, and as a result of Adam's receiving the blood sacrifice, he is clothed by God.

Adam's problem wasn't that he needed clothes - it was that he didn't seek the kingdom. When he started seeking the kingdom again, God gave him the clothes. When you and I seek the kingdom, all the other stuff gets added to us. But if we seek the other stuff, God will always make it elusive because God doesn't want us to seek other stuff—He wants us to seek the kingdom. In our society today, a fellow will take every paycheck, load up on beer, buy two cartons of cigarettes, a bunch of lottery tickets, godless movie theater tickets, and then blame the politicians because he doesn't have any money. He doesn't need a stimulus package—he needs to seek the kingdom of God. If he seeks the kingdom of God, it's amazing how much all of this other stuff will find a way of working itself out because God rewards kingdom seekers.

Faith believes that God rewards those who diligently seek Him. I don't have to worry about stuff. I just seek the kingdom, and when I seek the kingdom, God adds all of that other stuff to me. God rewards kingdom seekers.

God Limits Trials

God never puts on us more than we can bear. You have enough on your plate today without borrowing trouble from tomorrow. God limits your trials. He is not going to put on you more than you can handle. So don't play the "What if?" game with yourself. What if this happens and what if that happens? Sufficient unto the day is the evil thereof. In other words, there is enough trouble today without borrowing it from tomorrow. God is against us borrowing trouble.

The Bible says, "As thy days are so shall thy strength be." God always gives me enough strength for today. Thus, I don't have to worry about tomorrow because I'm not there yet. Mark Twain said, "I'm an old man and have known many worries, few of which have ever materialized." You and I often worry about stuff that never happens. Therefore, when I concentrate on God, I know God has promised to limit my trials and not put on me any more than I can bear.

When I recognize that all of these things are true about God, then I can come to God and fix my mind and thoughts on Him. I can cast my cares on Him because I know that He does indeed care about me. I can let my requests be made known unto God, and as I roll that burden off on God, He will in turn send back His peace that will guard my mind. If I follow these principles and remember who He is, I will be more inclined to throw those cares on Him and say, "God, you handle this. I'm going to bed."

The Pursuit of Peace

Because peace is such a precious commodity, you and I ought to pursue it (Romans 14:19). What are you pursuing? What are you following after? The Bible says that you and I ought to follow after the things that make for peace. I have some members in my family who would rather walk five miles barefooted to start an argument than to stand still and have peace. You've meet people, I'm sure, who make it their goal in life to push your buttons and start an argument. If peace is such a precious commodity, then you and I ought to make the pursuit of things that make for peace a goal of our lives. We ought to even have it on our "to-do" list every day.

Some of us have used Romans 12:18 as an exception clause. The Bible says that we should live at peace if it is possible, and with that person it is just not possible. God, however, did not put that verse in the Bible for an exception. He put it there to show you and me the extremes to which we ought to go to try to have peace with one another. If there is any way possible for you and me to have peace with people, we ought to try to have peace with people. It ought to grieve us when it is not possible to have peace with people.

When you and I try to destroy a person's peace, it is unbiblical. You and I ought to be pursuing the things that make for peace. The Bible places the responsibility for the pursuit of peace on our shoulders. The Bible says, "Blessed are the peacemakers." It is not compromise to live at peace with people. You and I to the best of our ability ought to try to get along with people and it ought to grieve us when we can't.

You and I shouldn't be people who always try to open up a can of worms that has already been closed. You and I ought to be pursuing the things that make for peace. God blesses people who are peacemakers. You and I as Christians can be the disseminators of peace to a world that is completely uptight. By God's grace, let's do just that.

CHAPTER THIRTY-FOUR

The Patience of Job

Galatians 5:22d

A while back, I read a story about a young man who had surrendered to be a missionary to India. He applied to a particular mission board and the director of that mission board asked the fellow to come for an interview to see whether he would recommend the fellow to the board as a missionary candidate. The director set the appointment for 6 am on this particular date. The fellow lived a good two or three hours away from the mission board so that meant if he was going to make a 6 am appointment, he had to get up very early in the morning.

The fellow was on time but was left waiting until mid-morning before the director invited him in for the interview. The executive said, "I'm glad to see that you are here. Come on in. I have several questions that I would like to ask you to ascertain whether you are fit to be a missionary or not. The first question is, do you know how to spell?" The missionary candidate said, "Yes, I think I know how to spell." The executive said, "Spell the word cat." The missionary said, "C-A-T, cat." The executive said, "Very good. Spell the word dog." The missionary candidate spelled the word correctly. The executive said, "I guess your spelling is okay." The executive then asked, "How are you with mathematics?" "Average, I guess," the candidate answered. The executive said, "Answer this question. What is two times

421

two?" The missionary candidate said, "Four." The executive said, "Good! It looks like your mathematics are okay." The executive said, "Okay, that will be all," and he dismissed the fellow. He went to the board and said, "I think this fellow will be a fine missionary because he can put up with obstinate people."

I think that you and I fail in ministry because we don't have the ability to put up with obstinate people. We have objectives for our careers or ministries, and then people get in the way of where we want to go. Many times we feel that sheep get in the way of our ministry and we fail to recognize that the sheep blocking the road are our ministry. God wants us to have patience in dealing with people. We often pray, "God, take these sheep out of the way." But if God took the sheep out of the way, we wouldn't have a ministry.

An Explanation of Patience

Etymologically

The word used here for patience is the term long-suffering. The same etymology exists in the Greek language. The word Greek is term is *makrothumia*. You may have heard of a micromanager. A micromanager is somebody who manages the small individual parts but a macro-manager is looking at the larger picture. The word *macro* means "large" and the word *thumia* is the word for temper. Someone who is longsuffering is someone who is large tempered. In other words, it is not a person who has a short fuse—it is the opposite of being short-fused—it is being long tempered. It is someone who does not explode quickly.

The Bible doesn't say that we are to be no tempered; the Bible says that we are to be long tempered. There are some things that you and I ought to get mad about from time to time. There are things that are worthy of our indignation, but before our indignation settles on something, a period of time needs to elapse. We ought not to come to a position of hatred quickly. We ought to be large tempered—somebody who is not quick to explode.

Exegetically

As you and I begin to practice exegesis of the Scripture, we begin to discover that this is exactly what the Bible has to say about being longsuffering. You and I are supposed to have a temper but we are not supposed to use it quickly. In no way does the longsuffering of God mean that God is going to acquit the guilty (Exodus 34:6). The Bible is very clear that God does not acquit the guilty—God will visit judgment upon people who violate His commandments. There is such a thing as the judgment of God. Even though there is such a thing as the judgment of God, that judgment is long in coming because God is gracious, merciful, longsuffering, and plenteous in goodness. So the idea is that even though one day God will judge, that judgment is long in coming because God is a longsuffering God.

Clearly, there is such a thing as the vengeance of God and judgment of God but that judgment of God is being reserved because God is slow to anger (Nahum 1:2-3). Once again we have the idea that God has a temper, God has anger, but that anger is long in manifesting itself. The judgment of God is sure—the worlds are being reserved for the judgment of ungodly men (II Peter 3:7-9). We wonder why God is delaying it so long if He is a God of judgment. God is not bound by time the way that you and I are bound by time. One day with God is as a thousand years and a thousand years is as one day. The reason that God has tarried His coming so long, and has not returned and put vengeance and judgment upon this earth is because God is a longsuffering God.

God has judgment, but that judgment is long in coming. God is longsuffering to us, not willing that any should perish but that all should come to repentance. Once again we are seeing the idea that the judgment of God is sure but at the same time, the judgment of God is slow. That is what we mean by longsuffering—it is being long tempered. It doesn't mean that we habitually and indefinitely put up with sin—there is a point where sin needs to be dealt with but you and I need to have protracted periods of patience in dealing with those things. God's anger is sure but at the same time God's anger is slow, and that is what we mean by the word *makrothumia*—long tempered. God puts up with stuff longer than most people do.

An Example of Patience

We have already seen by the three passages we have read from the Bible that the greatest example of patience is God. There is no greater case study that a person could give if they want to find out what patience is all about than looking at God himself. When we go to the synoptic gospels—Matthew, Mark, and Luke—we see that there are only two times that the word longsuffering is used and in both of those instances, the word longsuffering is used in a parable with reference to God. In looking at both of those parables, I think you and I can understand something about the nature of God with regard to patience.

With Regard to Reconciliation

In Matthew 18:23 we have a story about a man who owes his lord a whole bunch of money. He goes to the lord, and asks to be forgiven of the debt. He says if the lord is patient with him, he will pay it off. If you calculate the sum, he could have spent a lifetime and not have eradicated this debt—it would have taken complete patience to forgive a debt of this magnitude. The guy said, "Don't worry about it. I forgive you everything," and he wrote on the bill, "Paid in full."

The servant who had just been forgiven all that debt went out from this experience of wonderful compassion and found somebody who owed him a very small amount. He grabbed that person who owed him a small debt by the throat and said, "Pay me what you owe." The debtor said, "Please be patient with me and I'll pay this money back to you." The man said, "No way" and had the guy thrown into the debtor prison. When his lord heard about it, he said, "How could this be? I forgave you all that debt and you won't forgive somebody a small pittance."

In all this, you and I should see ourselves in our relationship to God. You and I had a tremendous sin debt that we owed God, and we said, "God, will you forgive me all this debt that I owe you?" God, just because you asked Him, forgave you. God forgave you because He wanted to have a relationship with you. God did not want the debt that was between you and Him to stand in the way of your having a meaningful relationship with one another. God said, "Because I want to hang out with you, I'm going to forgive your debt." Then as forgiven Christians, we go out to somebody who has committed this small infraction against us and grab them by the throat and say, "I'm going to let you have it, buddy." Wait a minute. Aren't you glad that God doesn't deal with us the way we deal with other people? If God forgave us all of that debt, shouldn't we be willing to forgive other people?

You've heard people say, "I don't get mad; I get even." Or, "I can forgive, but I can't forget." Those types of statements reveal that we don't really want a relationship with people. If we want a relationship with people, we should be able to put things behind us and go down the road and move on. God does that with us. He wants to be reconciled with us in spite of all the infractions that we have committed against Him. God wants a relationship with us. He is so longsuffering that He puts up with us so He can have a relationship with us.

With Regard to Requests

The second parable is found in Luke 18:1. In this story, the judge said he didn't really care about this woman and he really didn't care about God. But if he doesn't listen to this woman, she is going to nag him to death. He says he doesn't care about the situation but the only way he is going to get any peace and quiet is to give in to this woman and let her have her way. So just to get her off his back, he capitulates. Sometimes in leadership, we are very pragmatic in this way. We may not care what happens, but the squeaky wheel gets the oil. This woman keeps nagging, and the judge says, "Okay, have your way." Jesus asks if we heard what the unjust judge said. God puts up with us asking Him for stuff—He's patient. Sometimes in our Christian lives we may think that God wearies of us asking Him for things. God is very patient and has never gotten tired of your asking Him for anything.

Sometimes you and I get weary of the requests made of us, but I'm glad that God doesn't get weary of the requests we bring to His throne on a daily basis. If I were God, I would say, "Jeff Amsbaugh only comes to me when he wants something." But I'm thankful that God always has a listening ear when I need something. God is so interested in reconciliation and so interested in hearing my requests that He makes longsuffering a permanent part of His character.

The Extent of Patience

I understand that I need to be patient, but how patient is patient? How long do I have to put up with these people? All Christians need to be patient but especially ministers (II Timothy 4:2). Anyone in the ministry needs patience to be effective. Three specific areas are highlighted.

In Developing Convictions

That word *reprove* is the same word that is used of the Holy Spirit in John 16:8. In other words, the Holy Spirit convicts us about sin that is wrong, about righteousness that we ought to be engaged in, and about the consequences of doing wrong and not doing right. The Holy Spirit produces conviction in our lives, and that is the job of the preacher too. The preacher's job is to help people develop convictions in our lives.

Spiritual convictions do not happen overnight. It takes a while for people to develop spiritual fiber. The light of the Ring Nebula in the Lyra constellation first reached earth in the year 1054. They say that ring is still exploding at a rate of growth of seventy million miles a day. If you were to look at that ring tomorrow in a telescope, it will look exactly like it looks today. The point is that it is growing and it is growing fast, but from our perspective, it doesn't look like it is growing at all.

I know some Christians who are growing at a faster pace than really they should be, but yet to me it appears like they are not making any movement whatsoever.

A lot of people are growing faster than we think. We should not take somebody who has been saved for two weeks and expect that person to have the spiritual convictions of somebody who has been saved for twenty years. It takes a while for people to develop convictions.

If we want people to have convictions in their lives, we have to have patience with them in the development of those convictions. How many of you have more convictions now than you did ten years ago? We ought to have them but it takes time.

In Developing Confession

Paul not only says we must reprove, but rebuke with longsuffering. The word rebuke obviously refers to sin. Sometimes it takes a long time for people to say that they are sorry about something. Church discipline is a necessary thing but it needs to be taken slowly. We go to a person individually, and then give that person time to respond. If the person doesn't respond, we go to him with two or three witnesses, and then give him time to respond. If he doesn't respond, then the whole church goes, and then we give the person time to respond. It is only after all of that has failed that we treat that person as a heathen man and a publican. Matthew 18, therefore, tells us to implement church discipline but seems to suggest to us that there is a time period involved.

I read a Jewish parable not too long ago about an elderly idolater who came to the tent of Abraham. Abraham asked him if he worshiped the true and living God. The fellow said no, he worshiped the sun, the moon, and the stars. Abraham picked him up by his robe and threw him out of the tent. God came to Abraham and said, "Did you see that man who came to your tent today?" Abraham said, "I did." God asked, "What did you do with him, Abraham?" Abraham said, "I threw him out of the tent." God said, "Why would you do a thing like that?" Abraham said, "He said he was an idolater who worshipped the sun, the moon, and the stars. What did you want me to do with him?" God said, "Abraham, I have been putting up with him for eighty years. Couldn't you put up with him for one day?" How true that is.

I was told of a man who went to a yard sale and bought an aquarium. It was a little dirty when he bought it, so he went home and cleaned that tank until it was immaculate. Then he bought some fish and put them in the tank, and every fish that he put in that tank died. Finally, he went to the pet store and said, "I don't understand it. I bought this dirty tank, cleaned it up, and now all my fish are dying. What's the problem?" The pet store owner said, "It's the soap. You cleaned it so well that the soap you used is killing the fish."

I think sometimes that you and I get so aggressive in trying to clean people up that we kill them in the process. We lose influence because we want someone to be clean immediately. I'm not saying that people shouldn't confess their sins, but confession takes patience.

In Developing Comfort

The word *exhorting* carries with it the idea of encouragement. Sometimes it takes hurting people a long time to get over stuff. When I came to a hurting church, several people came to my office and asked, "Pastor, what are you going to do with these disgruntled people?" My answer was that I wasn't going to do anything with them because sometimes it takes awhile to get over stuff. Sometimes we need to let people alone for a while, and in the silence big problems become small. They may not get over it tomorrow, but they are going to get over it if we give them time.

I read a story about a fellow who was on a motorboat and was riding it full throttle. He hit a wave and was thrown off his boat. He plummeted beneath the waters. He didn't even know where the surface of the water was so he just waited for his life vest to move him toward the surface. Once he saw which way the life vest was carrying him, he began to swim toward the surface. If that fellow had not waited for that vest to begin lifting him and had just tired to swim, he may actually have been swimming deeper into the water rather than closer to the surface.

Some people have been hurt so badly, they don't know which way is up. Do you know how we deal with people who don't know which way is up? We wait for them to experience buoyancy and then when the buoyancy comes in their lives, we help them rise to the surface. But sometimes, you can't help somebody rise to the surface until first he knows which end is up. Many people in life are hurting and are in over their heads. You and I need to wait awhile. Frequently, as a pastor, I get calls from people who want me to straighten other people out. It's amazing to me that people always want mercy when it's in regard to them but they always want judgment when it's in regard to someone else. God is a patient God. God's anger is sure but His anger is slow.

For example, we walk into a restaurant and there is rock music playing. I don't like music that gives me indigestion any more than you do, but if the very first thing that we do is go up to the counter and say, "Bless God, I'm an independent, fundamental, Bible-believing Christian. You have to do something about that music if I'm going to eat here." I don't think that does a lot to endear that person to the Christian cause—they'll look at you like you are crazy. I am against rock music just as much as anybody, but I think sometimes you and I ought to exude patience with a world that acts like the world. Many times people cannot hear our position because they've been too adversely affected by our disposition.

God is asking us to be patient with people. The world acts worldly. You cannot go out into the world and aggressively clean the fish tank—you may actually kill the fish you are trying to nurture. If the first thing that people see is us flying off the handle, then we have not demonstrated to those people the fruit of the Spirit, and the fruit of the Spirit is what impacts people's lives. If we look like we have no anger management whatsoever, even if it is for a righteous cause, we hurt the cause of Christ. We have to learn to put up with the world acting like the world so that the first thing the world sees is not our rules but our heart, and that our heart desires a relationship with them through the mercy and forgiveness of God.

There was one particular day in school that I knew I deserved a spanking. I was third chair trumpet, and there was a guy who was second chair trumpet who constantly harassed me. One day when we went into the band room to put our instruments away, he made a comment about my sister. I didn't hear it all; I just heard him say something negative about my sister, and I tore into him like a windmill. We were all over each other in the band room fighting.

In came the band director, and he put a hand on both of us and separated us. He said, "I don't even know how to deal with you two anymore. Go to the principal's office." I remember walking up to the principal's office not worrying about what he was going to do but worried about what Dad was going to do after I got home. We sat down in the principal's office, and I knew that if he paddled me, mom and dad were going to paddle me even worse when I came home.

The principal sat down with us and said, "Fellows, the handbook says that I should paddle both of you, but I really don't believe that is the answer today. We have to find some way for you two boys to be able to get along with each other. And to be honest with you, I have exhausted my patience, but I think patience is what I need to exhibit more of, so we are going to work on this situation." He put his hand on both of us and prayed. That brought more conviction to my heart than any paddling could have done. His patience that day led me to repentance.

That same attitude that our principal showed to me that day is the same attitude that you and I ought to exhibit to the world. It is true that some of us don't have that type of patience, but God said if He could put up with someone for eighty years, we could put up with them for one day. When people see our patience toward their incorrigible activity, it only makes their incorrigible activity seem all the more repulsive. This is how you and I by patience win the hearts of people. Do you have patience?

CHAPTER THIRTY-FIVE

Be Ye Kind

Galatians 5:22e

A famous class at Tennessee Temple was *Courtship and Marriage*, which was taught by my favorite professor, Preson Phillips. I would go so far as to say that his class was such a great class that if you went to Tennessee Temple and did not take that class, you could not really say that you graduated from Tennessee Temple. Every time that Preson was lecturing on courtship and marriage, when the bell would ring, he would begin to pray by, "Father, help us to be gentle men and gentle women of God." What a great prayer! God's people ought to be characterized by gentleness.

It's interesting that in the vast majority of instances, this word translated *gentle* is translated *kindness* or *kind* more than it is translated any other way. God's people ought to be people who are characterized by gentleness. We ought to make it our goal in life to be considerate of other people.

In his book *I Was Wrong*, Jim Bakker talks about when he was released from prison. Shortly after he was released, he had dinner with Billy and Ruth Graham. While he was at their house eating supper with them, he pulled out his wallet to show them a picture. When he pulled out his wallet, it was obvious that it was torn and beat up. Ruth Graham said to him, "Jim, is that all you have for a wallet?" He said to her, "While I was in prison, basically everything was taken from me. This is all I have to function as a wallet." She said, "Just a minute," and excused herself from the table and went to the bedroom. When she came back, she said, "People are always giving Billy wallets that he never uses. We would like for you to have this." And she gave him a beautiful wallet, which he said he continues to use to this day. He said that one act of kindness made a tremendous difference in his life.

I'm not here to argue about the theology of Jim Bakker or of Billy Graham. The point of the illustration is that you and I can make a tremendous difference in some person's life if we are concerned with being considerate, kind, and compassionate to that person. It is amazing what a little act of kindness can do.

The Balance of Kindness

By kindness we do not mean that we should overlook sin. As a matter of fact, kindness balances our holiness. In Romans 11:22, the word translated *goodness* is the same word that is translated *gentleness* in Galatians 5:22. The Bible tells us that we should behold the gentleness and the severity of God. God is a very kind God but that fact in no way negates the fact that God is also severe. Both of these things—the severity of God and the gentleness of God—are things that we need to hold in balance when we think of the God we serve.

Several years ago, I saw an interview where someone in the media was talking with Ronald Reagan's son, Ronnie, and in that interview, Ronnie was describing his dad. He said, "My dad is a big teddy bear, but if you were to ever punch my daddy, you would discover inside of that teddy bear a steel column. And if you hit that teddy bear hard enough, you will discover that steel column." The fact that we are gentle in no way means that we are minimizing sin. It means we are attacking sin with the right spirit, and we are attacking sin with a kindness toward the people who are practicing it.

When Stephen was preaching in the book of Acts, the Bible says the people who heard him that day could not resist the wisdom or the spirit with which he spoke. That is the way people ought to be with you and me. Even as we are condemning certain activities because we believe these activities to be morally wrong, no one should be able to look at us and say, "His spirit is bad." You and I need to attack sin with a certain amount of Christian gentility so that no one we are attacking can say, "I don't like his attitude." We need to go at sin with kindness toward the people who are trapped in it.

When we exhibit kindness, it must not be theatrical kindness—it must be authentic kindness. For example, you can actually be kind in a backhanded sort of way to stab people. Let's say I forgot to take out the trash and I went to Karen and said, "Karen, I'm sorry I forgot to take out the trash." And she said with veiled gentility, "I never thought that you would forget to take out the trash." You understand that if she says it that way, she is veiling a knife with a sheath of gentility. That is not what we are talking about when we are talking about kindness. Kindness is given to show a heart of concern, not to conceal a heart of malice.

We are severe in our understanding of the damage of sin but even as we attack that severe sin, we recognize that we have to do it out of a genuine concern for people and manifest that attack in kindness and gentleness toward those we are trying to restore. This is the balance of kindness.

The Benefit of Kindness

When you and I determine in our hearts that we are going to be kind to other people, there are two immediate benefits that follow our kindness.

We reveal the heart of our Saviour

It is hard for us to think about kindness without thinking about Jesus and how kind He was. The Bible says in Ephesians 4:32, "And be ye kind one to another, tenderhearted, forgiving one another, even as God for Christ's sake hath forgiven you." Christ had a tender heart that was always willing to forgive. When you and I are kind to other people, we reveal the heart of God.

I think about this aspect when I think of Jesus coming down from The Sermon on the Mount. At the end of Matthew 7, when Jesus came down from the mountain, the people were marveling that Jesus had such great authority. As Chapter 8 opens with Jesus coming down from that great mountain-top teaching experience, Jesus is approached by a leper, and Jesus reaches out and touches that leper and heals him. I wonder how often that leper cried, "Unclean, unclean, unclean," and didn't give anybody an opportunity to even get close to him lest they contract his malady. He had to tell other people to stay away from him, but Jesus was not afraid to touch lepers.

I wonder how many of us have touched a leper in the last week. I wonder how many of us have actually reached out to be kind to somebody to let them know the kindness of the hand of God.

> I prayed and said, "Master, I know a man.
> He needs you, so please take hold of his hand.
> Stretch forth Thy finger and touch him today."
> I prayed, then I listened and I heard Him say,
> "You are the finger of God, don't you see?
> You know somebody who is in need.
> Point them to Calvary; show them the way.
> You are the finger of God today."

Many times when we see somebody who is down and out, we pass by on the other side of the road in our Christian piety and don't want to get involved in the situation. When we fail to reach out and touch someone who is down on his luck, we do more to harm the cause of Christ than anything else. Kindness shows the heart of God.

When our daughter Ashley was born with all of her difficulties, Karen and I were distraught. I remember after her surgical accident I was standing in my office and a deacon of my church came in. I do not remember much of what he and his wife said that day, but I do remember both of them giving my wife Karen and me a hug. That hug was more therapeutic to me than any word could have been. There ought to be a love, a deep, holy affection that you and I have for one another, a love that reaches out and embraces people in their hour of need. There ought to be a physical kindness that exists in the body of Christ.

I read not too long ago about a father and son who were playing catch in the yard. The boy asked his dad if there was such a thing as God. The father said he didn't know—he had never been to church and he hadn't thought much about it. So they decided to put a message inside a helium balloon and let it go, and the message said, "God, if you are really out there, send somebody to us to let us know what Christianity is all about." It wasn't long after they sent the message that the guy and his son were out and they saw a sign on the side of the road that said, "Free car wash." They pulled in to get a free car wash. They asked where the bucket for donations was and were told they weren't taking any donations— they were just washing cars for free to show people the love of God. The guy said, "Are you one of those Christians who believes the Bible and believes in God?" The guy at the car wash said, "That's exactly the kind of Christians we are." Through that experience the boy and his father accepted Jesus Christ as their personal Saviour.

You and I help give God a face and a name in our community when we are concerned with showing kindness toward people and treating people the way we would want to be treated. When you and I are kind, we reveal the heart of God.

We announce the message of salvation

My favorite Bible teacher Preson Phillips used to say that if you walk up to somebody and punch him in the face, stomp on his toes, kick his shins and then quote John 3:16, you haven't given that person the gospel. The only way you and I can help people see the message of salvation is if we deliver the fixed body of truth in the envelope of kindness (cf. Romans 2:4).

When my mom and dad, as down and out people, showed up at a Sunday school picnic, totally removed from the things of God, the kindness of those people made my mom and dad want to go to church the next day. The preacher preached a gospel message that morning and through that gospel message, my parents received Jesus as their Saviour.

No one gets saved without a fixed body of truth—you can't lead people to the Lord just by smiling at them. We have to understand, however, that very few people receive that fixed body of truth if it is not delivered with kindness, concern, and gentleness. My mom and dad could not have been saved without the message being preached, but they would have been in no position to receive that message had there not been a church that exhibited kindness toward them. The kindness that flows from you is what aids your evangelistic efforts and makes that fixed body of truth worthy of an audience.

I don't understand this debate that takes place about whether we believe in confrontational soul-winning or life-style evangelism. Your testimony is a lip and a life, a walk and a talk. Kindness and the preaching of the gospel always go together. You and I have to show a heart of kindness because as we show a heart of kindness, we reveal the heart of our Saviour and announce the message of salvation.

The Beauty of Kindness

When I got up this morning, I had to choose what to put on. I have thirteen different suit combinations—that's my uniform. Usually, I wear a suit and then move it to the back of the line. Today, I had a sport coat and pants combination next in line, but I didn't feel like wearing that today. Thus, I chose not to take what was next in line. I made a conscious decision of what I was going to wear today. The Bible says that just as we choose to adorn ourselves with certain articles of clothing, we must choose as Christians to put on kindness (Colossians 3:12). In other words, kindness ought to be one of the first things that people see when they come in contact with us.

Kindness creates an impression

We've often heard it said that clothes make the man. A couple of months ago, I was at the gym swimming. The suit that I was going to put on was hanging beside my locker, and a fellow looked at me and said, "Can I ask you a question? What do you do for a living?" I said, "I'm a preacher." He said, "I thought you were a banker or something like that." When he looked at the suit, he thought just by the clothes I wore that I was involved in some professional business. His words to me were, "I like your suits." The way that I dress had made an impression upon him because of the clothes that I had chosen to wear.

Several weeks ago we had a new student who interviewed for enrollment at Grace Christian School. The student was a little boy, and he had hair that looked like my mom's old kitchen mop. He came in and sat down for the interview. I said to him, "Before you enroll in school, you are going to have to get a haircut." He asked, "How short?" I said, "Like mine," and his eyes bugged out of his head. He said, "Sir, can I ask you a question?" I said, "Yes," and he asked, "Why?" I said, "Your mom is a health care professional. I can tell by the way she is dressed today. I've assumed certain things to be true about your mother already. I've assumed that by the way she has adorned herself for work that she is a competent, caring, compassionate nurse. It may be that your mom graduated last in her nursing class, I don't know, but by the way your mom has carried herself and adorned herself, I've assumed certain things to be true of her. When you graduate from Grace Christian School, you are going to have to go out and interview for a job, and when you go out and interview for a job, you're going to have to look like you have your act together. We shouldn't judge a book by its cover, but the fact of the matter is we do."

Clothes and attire, to some degree—whether it is right, wrong, or indifferent—create a certain impression. The initial impression that people have of us is often the lasting impression that they have. You and I as Christians ought to adorn ourselves with kindness. In other words, the first impression—and hopefully the lasting impression—that you and I leave with people is an impression of kindness. If the first thing that people know about us is our meanness, we're not going to make an impression with people. I didn't marry Karen because she is so solemn. Kindness is what makes a lasting impression on people.

The Bible says adorn yourself with kindness because that is the thing that people are going to see first, and they are not going to be able to understand the skeleton of Christianity until first of all they see that the skeleton is wrapped and adorned with the clothing of kindness.

Kindness conceals our iniquities

Clothing not only creates an impression but clothing also conceals shame. From the earliest days in the Garden of Eden when Adam knew that he was naked and ashamed of it, God made a coat for a covering. People often talk about a revealing garment. God never made clothes for revealing—God made clothes for concealing. Some ladies create an impression of iniquity because clothes are worn to accentuate things that the Bible says ought to be concealed. Clothes cover a lot of things that ought not be revealed.

When I was a pastor at my first church, Karen had to go out and get some groceries, and I was sitting around in our apartment without a shirt on. About three or four seconds after Karen left, the doorbell rang and I thought Karen had forgotten something and was coming back. Thus, I just went to the door and opened it. When I opened the door, there stood a lady from our church and there stood me without a shirt on. She started laughing. Time will not permit me to tell you all the reasons she was laughing, but I will tell you that she saw me in a way that I didn't want to be seen by one of my church members. I did not want one of my church members to see me without my shirt on. I felt so ashamed because she had a visual image of her pastor that I didn't want her to have.

The Bible says that kindness is like a covering—it is one of the things that helps cover the faults that you have. When you are a mean, austere person, people tend to hang you at high noon quicker than if you are a kind person. Kindness helps people deal with your idiosyncrasies and iniquities better.

For example, growing up at my home church they had a rule that divorced people could not teach Sunday school. Our pastor was a part-time pastor because the church was so small, and he was a social worker. In the process of doing his social work, he discovered that one of our Sunday school teachers was actually divorced and no one knew it. He went back to the board and explained the situation to them. He didn't give any names; he just said, "I discovered that one of our Sunday school teachers is divorced, and I want to know what you think needs to be done." The board was ready to hang her. Then somebody asked, "Pastor, who is it?" And when the pastor revealed the name, the board changed their tune because this lady was one of the kindest, sweetest ladies in the church. Five minutes earlier they were ready to hang whoever it was until they discovered it was one of the kindest people they had ever met. Those guys who wanted to crucify her said, "Maybe we have been a little rash in this thing."

What happened? When you are a kind person, people tend to take it easy on you. If you live by the sword, you are going to die by the sword. Kindness is a thing that helps people accept even your idiosyncrasies and sometimes even your iniquities because you reap what you sow. If you are a kind person, people are going to treat you with kindness. If you are a mean, harsh, and critical person, people are going to treat you that way. When those board members discovered who the teacher was, the dogs were called off because that teacher lived a life of kindness.

The Bible says that love covers a multitude of sins, and that is not only talking about your covering other people's sins—it is also talking about other people covering yours. When you are a loving person, people won't judge you as harshly and critically as they will if you are a mean person. When we have a mean-spirited child at our school, I'm looking for a reason to kick him out. If his spirit is like a cancer that is affecting our institution, I'm looking for a reason. When people are harsh and austere, we want to deal with them with harshness and austerity, but when people are exhibiting kindness, we want to deal with them in a kind fashion.

Christ came to exhibit kindness. Many times when people call me, they want me to deal with people in a way that they wouldn't want to be dealt with themselves. We always want the other guy who is wrong to be nailed to the wall and nailed to the wall quickly. If those shoes were swapped, would you want people to treat you that way or would you want to be treated in a gentle way? Many times in the body of Christ, people cannot hear our position because they are so put off by our disposition.

When I first went to Christian school in the third grade, the first teacher I had was Mrs. Robinson. Mrs. Robinson was one of the kindness teachers I ever met in my life. When Mrs. Robinson had to paddle a kid, she would have to go into the restroom first and cry, and get herself together. She was such a sweet lady. She personified what it means to be a Christian teacher.

God's people ought to be characterized by kindness. God is looking for gentle people, and the prayer that I would offer is the prayer of my former Bible teacher: "Father, help us to be gentle men and gentle women of God."

CHAPTER THIRTY-SIX

Why Callest Thou Me Good?

Galatians 5:22f

Maybe you've read that the Humanist Association has taken out a $40,000 ad campaign that is going to be displayed on the side of Washington, DC, buses and that ad campaign says: "Why believe in God? Just be good for goodness' sake." Can you imagine that? Probably if someone wanted to put a Bible verse on the side of a bus, the bus system would reject that ad campaign. But if you want to say, "Why believe in God? Just be good for goodness sake," they'll take your money.

People believe you can be good without reference to God. They believe that you can just be good for goodness' sake, but the Bible is very clear in our passage that goodness is a fruit of the Spirit; therefore, it is impossible for you and me to be good without first of all understanding our relationship with God, for God is the one who gives goodness to us and helps us be good.

The Absoluteness of Goodness

In the absolute sense of the word, there is only one person in the universe who can rightly be said to be good, and that is God Himself (cf. Matthew 19:17). The Bible is very clear that in the absolute sense of the word, there is only one being who is good and that being is God. Immediately, we may recoil at that statement and say, "I know of good people." But when you and I use the word *good*, we are using the word as a relative term in reference to other people. We know of some bad people and we know people who live better than those bad people, and because they are better than bad people, we call them good people. They are relatively better than those around them and hence we tag them as being good.

The Bible says that when you and I compare ourselves to one another, we are not wise. If the only quality of being good is to live better than my neighbor, you understand how much we have watered down goodness. We tend to think of ourselves as being good because we are better than our next-door neighbor and usually we pick that next-door neighbor who lives like the devil and say, "I'm better than that, and because I'm better than that, I'm a good individual."

I do recognize that among men there are varying degrees of corruption. For example, if we were to walk on a battlefield today and see corpses lying there, those corpses would have varying degrees of corruption but all of those corpses are dead. There are not varying degrees of death—there are varying degrees of corruption but not of death. In the same way, it is true that certain human beings stink worse than others. It is true that some humans have more corruption than others but as far as being bankrupt of enough goodness to get to Heaven, we all fall into the same category because the standard of goodness that God has set is an absolute standard of goodness, a standard of goodness that equates to His own.

When you and I look at how good God is, we fall infinitely short of that and the Bible declares that as far as absolute goodness is concerned, not watered-down goodness, there is only one being who is absolutely good and that is God Himself.

The Absence of Goodness

Because absolute goodness is the standard, we all fail short of it and are all absent of absolute goodness— we don't possess that quality. For example, the Bible says in Romans 3:10, ". . . There is none righteous . . ." There is not a single person who can say, "I am perfect and absolutely good." It takes only the slightest infraction to spoil the gene pool. All you and I have to do is have the slightest contaminant within us and it makes us unfit for the kingdom of God. None of us can claim absolute righteous.

Many years ago, I heard a story about this priest in the Roman Catholic church who wanted to convince this protestant woman that Roman Catholicism was the right religion and he thought if he could perform a miracle before her eyes, she would convert to Roman Catholicism. So he asked her if he could come over and perform the rite of transubstantiation, which in Roman Catholicism is where the priest says the blessing over the bread and purportedly turns it into the body of Christ. The priest said, "If I can perform the miracle of transubstantiation before you, would you convert?" The lady asked, "Can I bake the bread?" The priest agreed.

The priest went over to her house, the lady had baked the bread, and he went through the rite of supposedly transubstantiating the bread into the actual body of Christ. The woman said, "Before you partake of this bread, is it really the body of Christ now?" He confirmed that it was, and she said, "I just want you to know that I've laced it with arsenic, but since you have preformed this miracle, that won't matter. Go ahead and eat it." The priest didn't eat it; he ran out of the house. No matter how many good incantations or formulas we may recite in church, no religious activity can eradicate the taint of our sin any more than that incantation over that bread can change it into not being laced with arsenic.

The apostle Paul said in Romans 7:18, "For I know that in me . . . dwelleth no good thing. . ." I am morally bankrupt as far as the absolute goodness of God is concerned. Because God's standard of goodness is absolute, I am absent of absolute goodness—I do not possess it in my heart. Because I am no good, I cannot perform good, and that is why the Bible says in Romans 3:12, ". . . there is none that doeth good, no, not one." Because I have an absence of goodness in my fountain, I cannot produce goodness with my hands. Because my heart is bad, my hands cannot perform goodness. It is not merely the fact that I cannot be good—it is that I cannot produce good. I cannot do good things because as far as God is concerned, I am morally bankrupt.

You are going to produce what you are (James 3:11). We often get this confused. We are not sinners because we sin—we sin because we are sinners. At our core, our heart is no good—that is the way we were born—we were born bankrupt of righteousness and because we were born bankrupt of that absolute standard of goodness, we cannot produce goodness. Everything that you and I do with our hands is tainted with unbelief; therefore, we cannot do good because we are not good.

Let's say that I am sitting in my chair and my daughter comes into the house after making mud pies. And let's say that she decides that she wants to give her daddy a glass of water. She goes into the kitchen, and without even bothering to wash her hands, she reaches up and grabs a glass as mud sticks to the side of that glass. She then sticks it under the faucet, fills it with water, and then puts her fingers over the lip of that glass as a big clump of mud slides down into the glass polluting the water. She then brings that glass to me and says, "Daddy, here's a glass of water for you." I can appreciate her noble intentions, but I cannot drink that water because it is tainted with mud.

In the same way, when an unregenerate man tries to do good acts for a holy God, those good acts are tainted with unbelief—they are tainted with the fact that we have rejected God's Son, the Lord Jesus Christ, who died on the cross to save us from our sins. And because our acts are tainted with unbelief, though God can appreciate the noble intentions that we may have, God cannot accept that gift because it is tainted with unbelief. You and I cannot do good because in our hearts, we are not good. Because the standard is absolute, goodness is something that is absent in all our lives.

The Arrival of Goodness

If the standard is perfection and I cannot live up to that standard, how in the world can I get this goodness in my life? Because I am not good, I cannot produce good; therefore, what is needed in me and in you is a change of heart. I need to do more than just modify my actions. I need my heart, my nature, to be completely changed and altered.

You can't change your fruit until you change your root (Matthew 7:17). There are many people who believe that if they modify this or that, maybe God will accept them in Heaven. If, however, you want to produce good fruit, you have to become a good tree because an evil tree cannot produce good fruit. We cannot be doing righteous things until first of all we are made righteous, and the only way we can be made righteous is for God to give us a gift of righteousness and impute to our account a righteousness that is better than our own.

The Pharisees were very meticulous rule-keepers, but Jesus said that you and I need a better righteousness than meticulous rule keeping (Matthew 5:20). We need to be changed in our hearts to be right with God. We need to be made right at heart to do good. When I stand before God, I am going to need a better goodness than my own. Self-righteousness will not hold water at the judgment bar of God because the standard of God is absolute.

You and I do not have absolute goodness, and if we are going to get absolute goodness, it is going to have to be given to us as a free gift by the mercy and the grace of the Lord Jesus Christ. Out of this goodness of heart, we will then be able to do good. I think this explains the dichotomy that many people see between Jesus's teachings and Paul's teachings. Paul is teaching in the New Testament about goodness as a gift that is given to us. We put our faith and trust in what Jesus did on the cross, and at the very moment God puts goodness on our account. Jesus states if you want to go to Heaven, you have to do good, and it almost looks like Jesus is saying that you merit Heaven by doing good. But that is not what He means at all. Jesus is not saying that if you do these good things, you will merit Heaven. Jesus is saying the only way a person can do any good things is for him first of all to be changed at heart through the miracle of regeneration.

Everything that you and I do in an unregenerate state that we think is good is not good at all in the eyes of God because it is tainted with unbelief. That is why the Bible says that all of our righteousness is nothing more than filthy rags. Every good work that you have done is an offense to God who sent His only Son, the Lord Jesus Christ, to die in your place. If you think you can work your way to Heaven, then you are saying that what Jesus did on the cross is of no account, and that is an offense to a holy God.

There is an absolute standard of goodness. We are absent of it, and the only way we can get it is for it to be bestowed as a gift through the mercy and grace of the Lord Jesus Christ who died for us on Calvary's cross. It is not that doing good merits us Heaven; rather, those who do authentic good reveal that they have had a heart change through the miracle of the new birth. The arrival of goodness comes when we receive it as a free gift from the Lord Jesus Christ.

The Accomplishment of Goodness

Once my heart has been changed by accepting what Jesus did on the cross, and once my heart has been fundamentally altered through that miracle of regeneration, the Bible says that the Spirit of God lives inside me. Because the Spirit of God lives inside me, He is able to produce the goodness in me that I could not produce on my own. The goodness that I produce now is a fruit of the Spirit. God makes my heart new, changes me, and alters me, and now the good that I do is nothing more than the inevitable result of the Spirit of God living inside me and producing that goodness that otherwise I could not produce.

I see that the standard is absolute, and that I am devoid of it. I put my faith in Jesus and what He did on the cross, and when I do, goodness arrives in me and is able to help me now achieve goodness. What is the goodness that God wants to be achieved in my life? Micah 6:8 gives the Bible's definition of goodness.

Goodness is based on revelation

Goodness is based on what God has shown us in His word and what the Lord requires of us. Goodness is based on God's requirements—not our speculation. We live in a society today where people are calling evil things good and good things evil. We don't get to determine what is good and bad—God determines that.

We do not have the right in our society to determine by popular vote what is the moral thing or the immoral thing to do. We don't have that luxury. What is good is what the Lord requires of us. What is good is what God has shown us in His Word. Goodness is always based on divine revelation—it is never based on human speculation.

Goodness always does right

In our society many times good is determined based on the expediency of the moment. For example, let's say that somebody in our family dies and we don't want to break that news to one of our relatives so when they ask, "Has so-and-so died?" we say, "He hasn't died," and we have our fingers crossed behind our backs. In that moment, because we think in our mind that it is the kindest thing to do, we think it is justified in that moment to lie. The Bible does not allow that. If something is right, it is right, and if something is wrong, it is wrong. It is always right to do the right thing. According to the Bible, goodness always does right. It is never good to do the wrong thing. Sometimes in our minds, we concoct reasons why it is okay to lie or why it is okay to steal or why it is okay to cheat because we feel there is a better good out there. Goodness is what the Lord requires, and the Lord requires us always to do the right thing regardless of how inconvenient it may be.

Goodness is not ruthless

We stress doing the right thing, and when someone does the wrong thing, we stress the right thing to them. When they confess the wrong and do the right, we immediately embrace them. Good people never like to rub people's noses in stuff—good people always love mercy. At the very moment that a person confesses sin, no matter how bad that sin may be, we forgive because we love mercy. No person can think he is good if he is ruthless, domineering, and unforgiving. Quite the opposite is true—good people are always merciful people.

Goodness is respectful

Goodness walks humbly with our God. When I talk about performing righteous acts, it should never be so that people will think good of me. I never say, "I got a haircut the other day and my haircut looks so much better than those hippies over there." If you are doing good so that you can brag about yourself, you don't understand goodness. The Bible says that men shall see our good works and glorify our Father which is in Heaven. Every good that you and I do should be so that people can see how wonderful our God is and the difference that He can make in a life—it is never so people can see how wonderful we are. We must walk humbly with our God.

Many years ago, one of my relatives visited us at a church where I was pastor, and we were going to a men's retreat. One of the fellows who normally drove our church van drove the van and as pastor, I usually rode shotgun in the van and everybody else rode in the back of the van. I didn't even think about it because we always rode that way so the driver got in the van, I climbed in, and everybody else got in the back. When we were ready to leave the conference, my visiting relative jumped in that shotgun seat that I normally sat in and everybody else was in the van, which meant I had to climb over the tire well and get to the back of the van. The deacon who always drove for me looked at me as if to say, "What is he doing? He's got your seat. That's the seat for the pastor," and I said, "Let it go. It's not that big of a deal. I can sit in the back."

Many times in our lives, I think we are content to ride in the front seat and make God drift somewhere in the back when it's God's world. Many times we do good so people will look at us. We want to be in that seat up front that has notoriety. God is saying, "Wait a minute. If it's all about you, that's not goodness." Pride is a sin; it's not an asset.

We need to show respect to other people because we want people to see God in all His glory and majesty. When it is about us and our petty agendas, God gets lost in the process and we don't understand what goodness is all about. I think this is the difference between a lost person who does moral acts and a saved person who does moral acts for the right motive. Even when a lost man does good stuff, he does good stuff because it is all about him, but those who are saved do good things because it is all about God. We ought to want God to look very favorable in the eyes of people who are not yet affiliated with His party.

We see that we have no goodness because the standard is absolute, but when we come to the cross and we accept the goodness of God, then absolute goodness is put on our account. When that absolute goodness is put on our account, we are able to do the right thing with the right motive. We are able to do goodness that is based on revelation, goodness that always does the right thing, goodness that is not ruthless but merciful, and goodness that wants every fellow human being to be respected and to have God as the pre-eminent thing in their lives. This is the goodness that God, by His sweet Spirit, wants to produce in your life and mine, and by our submission to His Spirit, may that goodness be achieved.

CHAPTER THIRTY-SEVEN

Keep the Faith

Galatians 5:22g

In the Bible, the word *faith* is used in three significant ways, and I want to examine them as we think about the keeping the faith.

Objective Truth

Sometimes the word *faith* refers to the articles of faith, which is that objective body of truth in which you and I place our trust. God does not let us put our trust in something that is nebulous. God has given us a fixed body of truth, articles of faith in which our faith can be placed; it is objective truth. There are several things I would like you to think about with regard to this objective truth.

Objective truth is settled

In Jude 3, the term *faith* refers to the articles of faith—that fixed body of truth in which you and I place our trust. In other words, it's talking about the Bible when it talks about the faith that has been delivered to the saints. Several things can be said about this fixed body of truth.

First, it is complete. The Bible is not a fluid document that changes and alters itself over a period of time. For example, in our society there are Supreme Court justices who look at our Constitution as if it is a fluid document, and they change it and alter it to societal whims. They think they don't have to worry about what the original intent of our Founding Fathers was—they adjust it from period to period, generation to generation.

The same thing that people do with our Constitution, people try to do with the Bible—they try to make God say something different than what He originally penned in Scripture. Our Bible is not a fluid document that alters with time—our Bible is an enduring document that is timeless and is always applicable to man's situation wherever he finds himself. It is timeless truth that has been once for all delivered to the saints.

Not only is this body of truth settled because it has been fixed, but it is also settled because you'll notice that it was once for all delivered to the saints, not once for all delivered to the scholars. In liberal seminaries all across America, they are voting now about what verses belong in the Bible and what verses don't belong in the Bible. Sadly to say, in some fundamental colleges, they are offering classes on textural criticism where people determine what verses they think belong in the Bible and what verses don't belong in the Bible.

It is not up to the scholars to vote what verses go in the Bible and what verses don't go into the Bible. The Bible has been once for all delivered to the saints and God bears witness with our spirit that the truth of God is indeed the truth of God. We have a fixed body of truth that is not subject to seminary alteration and not subject to social alteration—we have a fixed body of truth that has been once for all delivered to the saints. God's Word is settled and therefore, when I click on my television and see the Mormon Church offering another testament of Jesus Christ, I have to say, "I have the entire testament I need right here. It has been once for all delivered." There is nothing else you can add to the Bible to improve it or to make it better. It is a fixed body of settled truth.

Objective truth is spoken

In Galatians 1:23, Paul gives his testimony and says that he used to try to destroy the faith, but now those articles of faith that he previously tried to destroy, he preaches. The articles of faith are worthy of preaching.

Like Paul, I can now preach the very truth that I desperately tried to obliterate before. Part of the reason that it is important that God preserve His Word is so that you and I will have something today to be able to stand up and preach to a society that is on its way to Hell. In many circles today, even in our camp, there are some people who'd take a bullet for this Bible, but they don't use it when they preach it. If God took the time to preserve His Word, then you and I ought to take the time to preach His Word.

We have a faith that is settled and because we have a faith that is settled, we can also have a faith that is spoken. There is objective truth that is fixed and this objective truth needs to be distributed.

Subjective Trust

Because there is a fixed body of truth, there is something in which you and I can place our belief. It does no good for God to preserve this fixed body of truth if you and I are not going to put our trust and dependency upon it. If the Bible is indeed settled, then you and I can say with every fiber of our being, "Because God said it, I believe it. I put my trust and my faith in it."

I was reading not too long ago about this guy who wanted to photograph a parachutist so he asked if he could go up with these parachutists and jump out with them. As they were parachuting to the earth, he could take pictures of them as they were descending. This guy got in the plane and jumped out with the rest of the parachutists. In so doing, he made sure he had his camera around his neck and was taking pictures, and when he went to pull his ripcord, he discovered that he hadn't put his parachute on. Consequently, he plummeted to his death. He was so concerned about taking his camera that he forgot his parachute.

There are many people who want to see what is happening around them but they forget the thing that's going to help them get safely where they are headed. Having faith in a camera is not a good thing if you are twenty thousand feet up in the air—you need to have faith in a good parachute. We have to put our trust in a significant object if we are going to make it to our final destination.

Faith is only as strong as the object in which it is rooted. I could have an old chair that has three broken legs and could sit down in that chair and have all the faith in the world that the chair will hold me. But if I sit in that chair, I'm going to hit the ground no matter how much faith I have in that chair because faith is only as strong as the object in which it is rooted. Therefore, if you and I are going to make it to Heaven, we need to have faith in the right object, and the right object is the precious, imperishable, and practical Word of God.

God has taken the time to preserve His Bible so that you and I might put our faith in it. In so doing, we will reach our final destination safely. We have a book that is worthy of our trust. We have a fixed body of truth in which we can place our trust.

Subjective trust brings salvation

Romans 5:1 tells us that we are justified by faith. Over and over again, the Bible hammers the fact that you and I are saved by faith (cf. Ephesians 2:8-9). The Bible is very clear that when you and I put our trust in the Word of God, we are saved, not by our works but rather by trusting Christ's work and what He did upon Calvary's cross.

Many years ago, I read about a Boeing engineer who was partly responsible for designing the Boeing 707. The designer was sitting on a different plane discussing with a passenger who was sitting next to him the advantages of the Boeing 707. He told the passenger that he was the engineer and that the Boeing 707 was a great plane that would really help people get from Point A to Point B. He listed all the positives of the 707 that he had helped design. Finally, the passenger looked at him and said, "Have you ever ridden in one?" The man said, "Not yet. I want to wait until it is around for a little while."

We ought to do more than just talk about Christianity—we ought to commit our life to it. There is a difference in talking about something and putting your trust in it. There is only one way that you and I will safely be able to take the journey to Heaven and that is through faith in the Gospel. When you and I commit ourselves to the Gospel, and put our trust in it, at that very moment, we experience salvation.

Subjective trust brings serenity

When we trust in God and put our faith in God, it does more than punch the ticket for Heaven—it also brings peace to a troubled mind (Isaiah 26:3). I'm glad that whatever happens in this world, I'm going to be okay because I know how the final chapter of my life is going to be written. Our great salvation brings with it attendant serenity. I'm so thankful that God gives me peace of mind. Because God is competent, God always does what He says. Thus, I have no doubts about where I'm going when I die. I know where I'm headed, and I have peace about my future. I know that regardless of what the stock market does, I'm living in a mansion someday. I know regardless of what the economy does, I'm going to walk on streets of gold. I know that whoever else in my family may be taken in death, if they know the Lord Jesus Christ, we are all going to get together again around the throne of God. The salvation of God will give you peace of mind.

Several years ago, our church was trying to buy a bus, and we gave our bid to someone who promised us he would place that bid. That person didn't keep his promise, and because he didn't keep his promise, we lost the bid on that bus. I'm glad that when I give my soul to God, He'll keep that which I've committed unto Him. My middle daughter, Amy, is getting ready to go to college and she is nervous about new things (she gets that from her dad). She doesn't even like to call her admissions advisor on the phone to find out what classes she needs—she gets nervous about new things. Sometimes I feel sorry for her and I'll say, "I'll take care of this part," and I notice that when I say that, she relaxes.

There are many things in life that I just don't know about, but I rest in the fact that my heavenly Father is going to take care of that for me. When I put my trust in the Lord, it gives me great serenity because my Father has never dropped the ball yet. He has always accomplished everything that He said He would do. Subjective trust brings great serenity and peace of mind.

Subjective trust brings service

Faith does not eradicate service; it inspires it (Matthew 21:21). The big question in my life is not what can I do—I already know the answer to that—not much. The question in my life is, How much can I believe God? God can do things in my life that are impossible for me to do. I can't move a mountain by myself, but when I trust in God and don't doubt, His power is my enablement. When I commit my life to God, it allows me to do things that would have been impossible had there been no God. The Bible says that all things are possible to the person who believes.

Jesus said you will be able to do more than He did if you believe in Him (John 14:12). Jesus's ministry was confined to the foothills of Judea and the Holy Land. Look at where Christianity has expanded today through the influence of His church, which has lived after Him. When we believe God, He makes all things possible for us. If you really believe in God, it will inspire your service and make you want to attempt things that you never attempted before.

By nature, I am a very timid person. When I was growing up, I was scared of my own shadow. I was one of those ninety-pound weaklings who hid behind his mother's skirt. When I told people that I was called to preach, they would look at me with a blank look on their faces. My natural abilities did not inspire much confidence.

I am told that the antelope-like impala can jump thirty feet wide and ten feet high but when they put an impala in a zoo, they keep him confined by a three-foot wall. What good is a three-foot wall if you can jump ten feet high and thirty feet wide? Despite their ability, impalas won't jump if they can't see where their feet are going to land.

I know many Christians who are like impalas—they don't jump unless they can see where their feet are going to land. God is looking for some people who will jump, who will trust Him for where their feet are going to land. When you really believe that God is going to help you land safely, then you will attempt great things for Him. God gives us the ability to walk where we may not be able to see our steps, but we don't have to see how it is all going to end if we trust Him. He has always been good on our behalf and will make sure it will happen the way it ought to happen.

Descriptive Tenacity

Many times when the Bible uses the word *faith*, it is using that word to mean "faithfulness." This is the primary meaning in Galatians 5:22. Think about the word *faithful*; it means "full of faith." A faithful person is really a person who is full of faith, and if you are full of faith, you will be a faithful person. Faith provides tenacity in three great areas.

Faith provides tenacious labor

Because God is a faithful God, He does what He says He is going to do (I Thessalonians 5:24). Being faithful means you do what you say you are going to do. God does not give His Word and then renege on His promise. When God calls you do to a task and says He will be with you, He'll be with you and He doesn't quit in midstream. God does everything that He says He will do; His labor goes to the end.

God requires that deacons not be double-tongued. In other words, they ought to say what they mean and mean what they say. Everything that you say you are going to do, you ought to do it. You should not say you are going to do something and then quit. If you are faithful, you are going to carry the job through to its completion.

While I was growing up in the Amsbaugh home, there was a rule that if we started a game, we had to finish it. And if we ever quit a game before its completion, we received a paddling. We ought to carry things through to completion. Your word ought to be your bond, and if you say you are going to do something, you ought to do it. If you and I are faithful people, we're going to have tenacious labor that stays with something until the end.

Faith produces a tenacious lip

The primary responsibility of a steward, the Bible says, is faithfulness (I Corinthians 4:1-2). I've heard preachers preach on that for years and it's true, but don't divorce this verse from the verse before it. In the context, it is predominately talking about stewardship of the mystery of God. In other words, you and I ought to be faithful in giving out the Word of God. God has committed His Book to us, and if God has taken the time to commit His Book to us, what good is that Book if it is just sitting on the coffee table collecting dust? God wants us to give His Word out, so you and I need to be faithful to get it out.

It's interesting that whenever a preacher preaches on soul-winning, we hit the altar. The Bible says that we ought to be sowing seeds but most of us sow seeds in handfuls. A preacher comes and preaches a message on soul-winning and we take a big handful of seed and throw it down, and we're good for five or six months until he preaches another sermon on soul-winning and then we throw another handful of seed. We are characterized by handfuls of seed rather than by systematically, every day, handing out the Word of God as we go through life. God doesn't want us to go to Heaven with handfuls of seed placed five months apart. God wants us to go to Heaven having faithfully disseminated His Word day after day. We ought to have a faithful lip in telling other people about Jesus Christ.

Faith produces a tenacious life

Revelation 2:10 implies that you should keep living tenaciously until you die. I didn't stand at the marriage altar and look into Karen's eyes with all the love I could muster and say, "Until adversity do us part." No, I said, "Until death do us part." Faith of our fathers, holy faith, we will be true to thee 'til death.

Isn't it amazing how easily people quit? We live in a very faithless society. I am reminded of that fellow who was rescued off a desert island. He was living there by himself and when he was rescued, his rescuers found three huts on the island. Someone asked him what the first hut was for and he said, "That's where I live." Someone else asked, "What's the second hut for?" He said, "That's where I go to church." The rescuers asked, "What about the third hut?" He said, "That's where I used to go to church." God is looking for faithful men.

Not too long ago, Karen and I were doing some counseling with a woman who had been divorced, and with tears rolling down her cheeks she said, "My husband was unfaithful to me." She said, "It would have been easier for me if he had died instead of being unfaithful." If someone dies, we could chalk it up to the sovereignty of God because the Lord made that decision, but when human beings are unfaithful to us, it hurts us because it is a choice.

If human beings can be grieved by unfaithfulness, think of how much God is grieved when you and I are unfaithful to Him. God has never been unfaithful to us. God went to the very jaws of death to protect our lives, and that kind of God deserves our faithfulness. Because God has given us objective truth, He has given us something we can place our subjective trust in. And because we place our subjective trust in it for the long haul, we have tenaciously described ourselves as people of faith who will stay with God forever. We prove all of this by our labor, our lip, and our life. Is faith part of the fruit of the Spirit in your life?

CHAPTER THIRTY-EIGHT

The Meek Shall Inherit the Earth

Galatians 5:23a

Meekness is not a word we use frequently to describe other people. We would not usually say, "He is so meek." What does meekness mean?

The Definition of Meekness

It approaches in humility

Matthew 21:5 speaks of Jesus coming into the city of Jerusalem, but this is not the way you would anticipate a king to come. He came meekly. He came on a donkey, and it was a borrowed donkey. When Jesus came, He approached us in the most unassuming manner.

I've noticed recently in college football games that when teams come out to the center of the field, it is almost important to start a fight before the game even starts. They gather around the logo of whatever team they are playing, and everybody has to establish their swagger—that's not meekness. Jesus did not come with swagger; He came in a most unassuming manner.

When I think of this, I think of my father-in-law. For many years, he bought used cars because of other financial commitments that he had such as keeping his kids in a Christian school. He bought this old station wagon that had a hole in the muffler, and when he would drop the kids off at school, everybody knew it because the car

473

was so loud. One day, Dad was taking Mom Aspray to the store to get some things and she went into the store and Dad just sat out in the car to read a book. He was slouched down in the car and two old ladies came out of the supermarket and did not see Dad Aspray sitting in his car. These two ladies began to talk and one said, "Look at that hunk of junk. Who in the world would drive a car like that?"

That is the way Jesus came into the city of Jerusalem. He didn't come with swagger—He came on a borrowed donkey. He approached us in humility.

It asks in humility

When Jesus asks us to shoulder a burden, He says that His yoke is easy and His burden is light (Matthew 11:29). Jesus never tries to weigh us down with His importance, even though He is the most important person on the face of the earth. The commands of God are not grievous ones. In other words, Jesus asks in a gentle way. If you constantly try to throw your weight around to make people feel how important you are, and you give commands rather than suggestions, you are not a meek person. A meek person does not go around demanding or weighing people down with how important they are. A meek person has a burden that is light and a yoke that is easy. A meek person not only approaches in humility but also asks in humility.

It abides in humility

Meekness is not mere theatrics for the moment (II Corinthians 10:1). Sometimes you can be gentle by way of manipulation and take a gentle approach. It is like the girl in high school who bats her eyelashes at the guy and says, "I'm sorry. I just can't get my locker open. Can you help me?" You understand that is not what the Bible is talking about. Meekness is not something that is done for the theatrics of the moment. Meekness is something that is done continually while we are in the presence of somebody else. While we are among them, we are continually gentle people who take the back seat to others. Meekness maintains itself in an abiding fashion during a protracted period of time, and it is willing to take the back seat. Meekness is a permanent quality of conduct.

The Development of Meekness

In developing meekness, an important question is necessary. To whom am I to display meekness?

To All Individuals

There are some people it is easy to be gentle and submissive to but there are other people we'd prefer not to be gentle with. The Bible says that we are not just to be meek to a select group of people or to people we find it easy to be meek to—we are to show meekness to all men (Titus 3:2). Meekness needs to be exhibited to the alcoholic as well as to the affluent. Meekness doesn't fluctuate in degree based on people because the Bible says here that we are to exhibit meekness to all men.

Some of us have a meekness barometer whereby certain people get a big dose of meekness and other people get a little dose of meekness, but the Bible says we ought not to be that way. Not only should we be indiscriminate about whom we give it to, but everybody ought to get the adult dosage—we ought to give meekness to all man. That means as much as we can be submissive to people, we ought to do it and it doesn't matter who the individual is.

To the Ignorant

It's easy to some degree to be meek to people who are living right. If people are living right and doing the right thing, we find it easy to get along with those people and that's a good thing. But the world is full of people who are the opposite. The world is full of people who are doing stupid, ignorant things to hurt their own futures. When we find people who are deliberately hurting their own lives, it's easy for us to say, "I'm going to give that fellow a piece of my mind." The Bible, however, says this is not the response that you and I should have. If we are true servants of the Lord, we don't argue with people—we go in a spirit of meekness (II Timothy 2:24-25).

I was visiting someone who visited the church, and the visitor said that my preaching was dead. The reason this person thought that was he was coming from a church where the pastor got as red-faced as the choir robes when he preached. If every Sunday the preacher is as red-faced as the choir robes, then something is wrong with that preacher because the Bible says we are not supposed to get in the pulpit and split a spleen. Sure, we need to get something off our heart, but there is a difference in getting something off your heart and getting something off your chest. We are not using our pulpits to help us vent; we are using our pulpits to minister to the souls of people.

If you and I think we can get to the place where we are absolutely right by being mean-spirited, angry, and venomous, then we don't understand the spirit that God's people ought to have. There are many ignorant people in this world and to be honest with you, I'm as tempted as any preacher in the world to let ignorant people have it. I think we have an overdose of ignorance in our world, and I think we need to start boycotting it to some degree. Even though there are a bunch of ignorant people out there, that doesn't mean that these ignorant people don't deserve the right approach from the child of God. The Bible says that our spirit toward those people ought to be meek.

At Insistence

Before we had cell phones, Karen and I seldom went in different directions in the mall because we don't like looking around for twenty years to find each other. Now, however, we simply call each other's cell phone and say, "What store are you in?" Karen called me yesterday. I was visiting with my father and she was doing her bus route. She called and asked, "Where are you?" She was at McDonald's eating and I was at the Burger King right behind it. Imagine if we didn't have cell phones how hard it would be to find people.

The Bible says that one thing you ought to be diligently seeking after is meekness (I Timothy 6:11). You may think to yourself that there are people you just can't be meek to. How in the world do you put up with people like that? Here's how—you put meekness on your to-do list. Nobody is meek by accident. Some people say, "He is meek—that's just the way he is." No, that's not just the way he is. All of us know people we'd rather not be nice to. Meekness is something we have to make a covenant with ourselves to do. We have to decide we are going to yield to the Holy Spirit and allow the Holy Spirit to produce meekness in our lives. We are going to zealously seek after it.

All of us have certain people who just rub us the wrong way. When that person comes up to you, what are you supposed to do? You are supposed to say, "Lord, help me deal with this person in meekness." I am insisting that my life will be characterized by meekness. I have put it on my to-do list, and it is something that I will follow after and seek.

The Derivatives of Meekness

If you and I determine that our lives will be characterized by meekness, certain things will automatically follow. Notice the derivatives of meekness.

The Scripture is received

No one has to teach us how to be filthy—we've got that down. No one has to teach us how to be naughty—we're overflowing with that. We have to lay aside filthiness and naughtiness, and we've got to get back to receiving the Word of God by meekness (James 1:21). You and I are so prone to think that nobody can tell us what to do. That is not a meek spirit—a meek spirit is open to instruction and counsel from other people.

If you and I listen to nobody else, we ought to listen to God. God doesn't drop into our living room and say, "Here is what I want you to do." He speaks to us through His Word—He gave us a manual by which we are to live our daily lives. The Bible is key to Christian living. If I have meekness, I'm going to do what the Book says regardless of whether I understand it or not.

You cannot approach your life by saying, "Here is what I want to do. Let me go find a Bible verse that will help support that." You and I don't impose our wills on the Bible—we must allow the Bible to impose its will on us. If you and I have already determined in our minds what we want to do and then run to find a verse to justify it, we're going to be in trouble. Meekness says, "God, I'm going to come transparently to your Word and ask you to speak to my heart." If I do what the Bible says to do, I reveal that I am a meek person.

Our spirit is regulated

Paul contrasts the spirit of meekness with coming

to a person with a rod (I Corinthians 4:21). In other words, when you are going to straighten somebody out, it would help if you had the right spirit when you did it. If you come to somebody with a big rod ready to blast, you don't have meekness. Meekness regulates the spirit, handling a situation with the proper decorum that is fitting for a child of God. It regulates austerity—it doesn't make harsh or abrasive statements.

Most of the time people don't reject what we say but the way we say it. If you went to someone with a gentle spirit, you would be surprised at what you could get done. Most of us need to have a meek spirit that regulates the way we handle people. If you go to somebody and you are ready to explode, you need meekness because meekness is something that regulates your spirit and causes you to approach even the most volatile situation calmly.

The sinner is restored

Paul lists meekness as a fruit of the Spirit and then immediately he gives us one area where meekness really helps (Galatians 6:1). The Bible is clear that one of the key ways to get sinners restored is a spirit of meekness. When someone is doing wrong things, what is the number one gripe they have about the church? The church has a holier-than-thou attitude, and it does a whole lot of damage. The Bible says to restore someone in a spirit of meekness. The goal is restoration—not to win an argument. Repeatedly, in the steps of confrontation in Matthew 18, the goal to gain a brother is stated. Throughout the whole process, the goal is to gain a brother and it is only after everything else has failed that we treat someone like a heathen. Most of us, when we confront people, don't want restoration—we want to vent, and we go after people saying whatever we want, however we want, and then say, "I feel better now."

Such conversations may be meaningful to you, but they are not meaningful to the hearer. The goal is restoration, and if you and I don't have meekness, the sinner is not going to be restored. Your spirit will drive people further into error if you use the wrong spirit.

The seeker is rewarded

If I meekly submit to God's plan of salvation, I will inherit the kingdom of God and I will be part of His millennial reign (Matthew 5:5). If I submit to His plan of salvation, I'll rule and reign with Him on planet earth. In way of application, if you are a meek person, the whole world gets opened to you. If you go up to someone and demand something right away, there is immediate rejection. If someone says, "You must do this," a negative response is inevitable simply because the must was used. That is the way human nature is. If you use a meek spirit, it is amazing what doors will open to you. It is amazing what you can do if you are cordial and get along with people.

When my wife Karen gave our daughter April her first driving lesson, it started five feet from a tree and ended with April driving straight into that tree. April has done nothing in her life moderately—she is wide open, full throttle. Thus, her first driving lesson ended with her totaling my car. I was at the office when it happened. Karen called the office started the conversation by saying, "Jeff, just divorce me right now." I said, "What are you talking about?" She said, "Jeff, it's over. I know you are going to be so upset with me about what I've done. I should have had more sense than to let this happen. I didn't do it right and Jeff, if I was you, I would disown me right now." I said, "Honey, it doesn't matter. Whatever it is, it will be okay." She said, "No, Jeff, I don't think it is going to be okay. April hit the tree with the car." Oh, is that all?

By taking a meek approach, Karen got the world. Most people don't understand that when you have a meek spirit, the whole world gets opened to you. It is the meek who inherit the earth—it is the insubordinate that get closed doors. When you take a back seat and lower yourself and give somebody else the position of authority and power, it is amazing what is opened to you. Are you in a confining situation? If you are a meek person, you'll be surprised what is opened to you.

Joseph, for example, was a very meek person. No matter what cistern he was put into, he submitted. He submitted to Potiphar and became ruler in his house. Joseph submitted in prison and became a chief interpreter of dreams. He submitted to Pharaoh and became second in command. All this happened because the meek inherit the earth. The problem with many of us is we absolutely refuse to be meek. We put our foot down and dig our heels in, and we end up living a life of loneliness. Meek people have doors of opportunity available to them that are absolutely phenomenal because the meek are the ones who are rewarded. When you seek meekness you will be surprised at what God offers you.

Meekness causes a whole world of new opportunities to be available to you. Why don't you just kneel before God and say, "God, I want to be meek. Teach me your Word, regulate my spirit, and help me to restore sinners instead of alienating them. Lord, give me the world by means of submission to your will and your way. Lord, help me to be meek." Blessed are the meek: for they shall inherit the earth.

CHAPTER THIRTY-NINE

The Temperance Society

Galatians 5:23b

The Meaning of Self-Control

When we use the word *temperance* in modern English, most of the time we think of it in regard to alcohol. In our society today, we see that alcohol is certainly an area where people need to exercise restraint. The number of alcoholics in America is growing by leaps and bounds, and certainly people need to have temperance when it comes to what they drink. While it is true that temperance is essential to what we drink, that is just the tip of the iceberg. Temperance applies to basically every area of life.

With Regard to Ethics

In Acts 24:25 we see Paul witnessing to a government official by the name of Felix. Paul reasons with Felix concerning three areas. He reasons with Felix concerning righteousness, which is doing the right thing and engaging in the proper ethical conduct. He also reasons with Felix concerning judgment, which is the penalty that you and I get for not doing the right thing. When we fail to do the right thing, judgment comes down upon us. What comes between righteousness and judgment is our word *temperance*. In other words, you and I many times know the right thing to do, but if we are going to do the right thing to avoid judgment, we have to practice self-control.

Self-control is the thing that helps us do the right thing so we can avoid the judgment of God. Most of us, for example, know that the Surgeon General has issued a warning against smoking. Most people know that tobacco is very harmful to the body, and we are aware of what's the right thing to do. Very few people think it is the right thing to keep smoking. We know the right thing to do and we know that there is judgment if we don't do the right thing. We know the judgment could be emphysema, lung cancer, or a variety of other diseases if we don't stop. What is going to help us implement the right and avoid the judgment? It is self control. We have to have control to quit.

The same thing is true of alcohol. Most people know that alcohol is harmful to their body and they are aware of the dangers associated with it. Certainly there have been many campaigns and organizations such as Alcoholics Anonymous that have been formed to help us understand that there are dangers with alcohol. Yet many people who know full well what the dangers are suffer the judgment and the ill effect of alcohol today. Why? Because they are missing the essential ingredient of self-control. Temperance is that thing that helps us implement the right and avoid the judgment. You and I have to always understand self-control with regard to ethics—it is the power to do the right thing and thus avoid the judgment of God.

With Regard to Education

Self-control follows immediately on the heels of knowledge (II Peter 1:6). We can't exercise self-control if we don't know the facts about a situation.

Several years ago, I was having severe chest pains in my lower shoulder. I was under the clear impression that I was having heart trouble. I went to the doctor to see if he could discover anything, and he said we needed to run a stress test. So they put me on a treadmill and discovered that my heart was in good shape. The doctor said what I was suffering from was a bad case of acid reflux. The doctor said I needed to cutback on drinking coffee. He said if I cut back on drinking coffee, the acid reflux problem would go away.

I could not exercise self-control with regard to coffee until I knew the facts of the test. It never dawned on me that it was coffee, and it wasn't until I went to the doctor and discovered the true facts of the situation that I could exercise the self-control to lay off the coffee and now be pain free. I could not evaluate that pain until first of all I knew the facts about what was causing that pain. Then, once I was aware of what the facts were, I could exercise the self-control to avoid those circumstances.

In the same way, there are many people today who are having problems in their marriages, at work, or with extended family members, and their lives are characterized by pain—it could be physical pain, emotional pain, or social pain. They don't know why they are experiencing these high levels of pain in their hearts and in their psyche, and then they go to the Word of God and they see why. There is a principle they are violating. Maybe they've not been living right as a husband or not living right as a son, and once they get the facts of what is causing the pain, then they need to exercise the self-control to alleviate that pain. They can't exercise the control to alleviate that pain until first of all they get a proper diagnosis according to the facts of the Word of God.

You and I cannot do right and avoid judgment until first of all we get into the Word of God and know what the truth is of the situation. Most people's ethics are formed by speculation of what people are saying at work or what the community at large is saying, but those are quack doctors. You and I have to get to the Word of God, find out what the truth of the matter is, and once we find out the truth of the matter, then we can exercise self-control to do the right thing and avoid the judgment that comes with doing the wrong thing.

The Manifestation of Self-Control

There are four major areas of life where you and I need to exercise self-control, and these are areas that are constantly under attack by Satan and our own flesh. These are areas where we really need to work hard to be controlled individuals.

In Our Marriages

I Corinthians 7:9 doesn't mean that if you don't marry, you are going to go to Hell. This verse means to burn with desire, and the word *contain* is the same word that is translated *temperance* in Galatians 5:23. If you can't exercise self-control, you need to marry because God wants us to always be self-controlled with regard to sexual appetites. In other words, marriage is one of those areas where Satan is always going to try to get us to lose control, and there will always be a temptation in this regard.

A man may be having a hard day at work. He comes home from work and begins to unload on his wife telling her all the problems that are happening at work. She says, "I think you ought to go back there and do this and that." The man begins to think that not only does his workplace not respect him but his own wife doesn't even respect him. She doesn't think he has the brains God gave a gerbil. So now he is not only discouraged at work but he is also discouraged at home and feels completely underappreciated.

He begins to reason something like this in his mind: I don't need this. I don't need this job, I don't need this wife, and I don't need all this hassle. And the temptation suddenly begins to form in his thinking that he just needs to go off with reckless abandonment and find himself. You understand that this man is undisciplined in his thinking. He is not self-controlled in his thinking, especially with regard to his marriage.

Every single day, thinking has to be harnessed in order to have a good marriage. Your wife doesn't hate you as much as you think. Many times in life we begin to think that we don't need the pressures of home life, and there is always that subtle temptation to marital infidelity. You and I have to be contained in that area. Marriage and self-control always go together.

You have to harness your emotions no matter how much your spouse is putting you down, and no matter how much friction may be in the home. You have to constantly work at harnessing emotions and keeping them under control. In your marriage, God wants you to be temperate.

With Our Money

Another area of our life where we tend to be unharnessed is finances. After all, we work hard and play by the rules. We begin to think that we deserve certain things. I deserve a bigger house, a newer car, and nicer clothes, and before long, if we continue that line of thinking, we are people who are totally devoid of any fiscal restraint. We use credit cards to purchase everything, and before long, we are actually using credit cards to pay off credit cards.

Sometimes in debt counseling you will even talk to people who have over $30,000 in credit card debt, and they don't even know what they purchased with it. They can't point to anything that they can hold in their hands and say, "This is what I purchased by going into debt." Spending can very easily get out of control.

There is no need to amass a bunch of debt to buy toys that kids aren't going to play with anyway. Many times when a kid unwraps a present at Christmas, he leaves the toy sitting there and plays with the box, and boxes come relatively cheap. God's people need to be characterized by a certain amount of fiscal restraint.

In Our Ministries

In I Corinthians 9:25-27, Paul speaks of self-control with regard to ministry. Any time you are involved in ministry, the devil is going to try to make you feel underappreciated. It may be a nursery worker who has just stayed for two hours in the nursery with your kid who is a spoiled brat and when you go to pick up that kid, instead of blessing that nursery worker for her patience, you chew her out for feeding him too many Cheerios or whatever, and the nursery work goes home and says, "Nobody appreciates me." It may be a bus worker who leaves early on Sunday morning and gets home late on Sunday afternoon, and we criticize him because he did not fill the bus up with gas when he was done. He leaves and goes home, and says, "Nobody appreciates me."

Anytime you are involved in ministry, the feeling is going to be there that no one cares about what you do and no one appreciates what you do. Once that mindset of under appreciation filters into your ministry, you are a very vulnerable person at that point. When I went to my first church, my predecessor had been fired, and he had been fired largely because the board was getting all over him about things he could improve. He got to the place in his life where he said, "Nobody appreciates me." So instead of going to the office, he played golf in the morning and watched cartoons in the afternoon. The board essentially said, "We are not paying him to play golf and watch cartoons." So they fired him.

Why was he playing golf and watching cartoons? He was doing so because there was a feeling of under appreciation in the ministry, and anytime you and I allow that attack of Satan to come into our lives, at that point, emotionally, we become very vulnerable in ministry and are open to attack. Ministry is always an area where you have to be self-controlled.

In Our Meals

In our society today, we often find comfort in food. When we are hurting and feel like no one appreciates us, one of the first things that we do is go to the refrigerator. Food becomes a source of comfort to a hurting soul. Many Americans today are absolutely destroying their bodies by comforting themselves with all kinds of junk food. You handle defeat with emotional stability; you do not handle defeat with a bag of Cheetos. There has to be a certain amount of restraint in America with regard to food.

Many people that I have counseled with enormous credit card debt have come to this place of economic disaster by financing food. They have used their credit cards to afford themselves the luxury of eating out in restaurants.

We often don't have money to do the necessary things of life because we spent money on eating out. This is affecting our health care system because we are developing more heart problems all because we are eating terrible as a way of comforting ourselves. There has to be a certain level of self-control where we recognize that the way we are eating in our society is not healthy.

The Mark of Self-Control

If you and I understand self-control and practice it, we are going to leave an important mark on society. There is nothing that creates an impact like a self-controlled person. A self-controlled person is a person who makes a tremendous, significant impact on our society.

Hitting the Target

Undisciplined people always miss their target (cf. I Corinthians 9:26). For example, I get upset at work. My emotions are amuck and I'm all upset about what happened at work. As I walk in the door at home, my wife says, "Don't forget to take off your shoes." I say, "Why are you always hollering at me about my shoes? The floor can be mopped again!" I start yelling at my wife. What's the problem? I'm missing my target. I'm not even mad at her, but because my emotions are unharnessed and I don't exercise self-control, I'm hurting her verbally. She, however, is not even the target. I am upset at somebody else, but because I'm uncontrolled, I get angry at other people.

Years ago, my dad's best friend, Dave Graybeal, was on vacation with his family. He took his wife's mother along on the vacation with his two kids and his wife. His wife was in the front seat with him in the car, and in the back seat were his two kids with his mother-in-law in the middle. The kids were acting up in the back seat, and Dave said, "I want it quiet." They were not quiet; they kept acting up. He said, "The next one to act up is going to get it." They kept on acting up, and Dave reached over the back seat and said, "I said, quiet!" He then proceeded to slap one of the kids. When they arrived at the motel, his mother-in-law said, "Dave, when you reached over the back seat and thought you hit one of the kids, you missed the kid and hit me." The kids got real quiet because they thought if dad would hit Grammy, he certainly would do worse to me. Dave had let his kids get him so upset that he missed the target.

Any time you are uncontrolled, you are going miss the target. You will often attack the wrong people, people who have nothing to do with your irritation. Uncontrolled people always miss the target. If you are controlled, you will hit the target.

Honoring Our Testimony

When you don't keep your body under subjection, you lose your testimony. When you and I go half cooked, and speak and act without self-control, we lose our testimony. In one moment of uncontrolled action, a testimony can be ruined. It takes a lifetime to build a testimony but only five seconds of being uncontrolled to lose it.

Every day that stretches before us, there is too much to lose. I have to get into the Word of God and educate myself about what is the ethical thing to do. Then in every area of life, such as my marriage, my money, my ministry, and my meals, I have to be a self-controlled individual because it is only then that I will have a testimony that will honor God and be able to make an impact in our society as I hit the target that God intended me to hit with my life.

There were all kinds of guys I went to school with in seminary who are much more talented than this preacher, and today they are selling cars and insurance. There is nothing wrong with selling cars and insurance, unless God called you to preach and you lost your ministry because you were uncontrolled— then there is something wrong with it. All over our cities, there are people who have become castaways for service because they decided that five seconds of pleasure was worth an entire testimony that had been built up for God. That is totally inappropriate thinking. You and I need to be part of the temperance society.

CHAPTER FORTY

Dead Men Walking

Galatians 5:24-26

This whole section has dealt with vices from which you and I should abstain, and virtues that you and I should emulate. We are to put off the works of the flesh, and we are to adorn ourselves with the fruit of the Spirit. This is the constant struggle that you and I have in our Christian lives. We will never, this side of Glory, ever get to the place where the Spirit will not war against the flesh and the flesh against the Spirit. We will never get to the place in this life where we can say, "I am so thankful that I don't have to battle sin anymore. I am so thankful that my flesh is not giving me any more trouble." Sorry to disappoint you, but this side of Heaven that is not going to happen.

When I first became a pastor in Pennsylvania, I made an appointment to talk to a pastor who believed that he had gotten to the place in his Christian life where his sin nature had been eradicated. I scheduled an appointment with this preacher and said, "I've heard that you believe you can actually get to the place where flesh and Spirit don't battle anymore." He said, "That's right." I asked, "How long has it been since you have sinned?" He looked at me with all the sincerity he could muster and said, "I haven't sinned in twenty-five years." I looked back at him and said, "Sir, that is amazing." He said, "It is amazing what the grace of God can do." He believed that his sin nature had been completely eradicated and that he had reached a state of sanctification where his flesh no longer battled his spirit.

The flesh, however, does battle the Spirit consistently. You and I might be tempted to become discouraged and say, "If this is a battle that I'm going to face the rest of my life, advancement in the Christian life must be impossible. It's always going to be three steps forward and two steps back. My entire Christian life is going to be small steps, and I'm not going to ever know victory the way I want to know it in my Christian life."

It is that exact point that the apostle Paul is addressing here in these three verses. There is a way that you can move forward. You can move forward aggressively in your Christian life by walking as a dead man.

The Principle of Crucifixion (v. 24)

The vast majority of time that you see the word *crucifixion* or *crucify* in the New Testament, it is referring to the crucifixion of Jesus. There are only four instances in the New Testament where the word *crucifixion* is not applied to Jesus. By looking at the three other instances where this occurs, we might have an idea of what Paul means in verse 24 when he tells you and me to crucify ourselves.

The first is found in Romans 6:6. Paul states that when Jesus died, there was someone who died with Him, and the person who died with Him was the old you. That old you that used to exist before you met Jesus was crucified with Jesus so much so that it was a co-death.

The second reference is Galatians 2:20. Here again we see the idea that the man you were prior to meeting Christ is dead—he doesn't exist anymore. That pre-Christian person has been crucified with the Lord Jesus Christ and no longer exists.

The third reference is Galatians 6:14. Here it is saying that when we died with Jesus, we were dead to something. We were dead to the world, and the world simultaneously became dead to us so much so that when we became Christians, the world did not hold the same attraction to us that it previously held.

I have an uncle who gets on everybody's nerves—he seeks to destroy unity within our family. The only way members of our family can get along with one another is to pretend that my uncle doesn't exist. People in the family refer to him as "the dead man." If we ever see him in town, we will say to one another, "Hey, I saw the dead man today." In other words, as far as we are concerned, we buried him a long time ago. As far as the family is concerned, my uncle is still walking the earth, but even though he is walking the earth, he's a dead man.

Something like that is what happens when we become saved. Our life becomes crucified with Christ so much so that we are dead to the world. Sure, the sights, the sounds, and the attractions of the world still exist, but as far as a child of God is concerned, we died to that at the very moment we received Jesus Christ as our personal Saviour. We have died to it and it has died to us. We have decided that we are not going to spend time with each other anymore. For all practical purposes, the world doesn't exist. In each of those instances, the very word *crucifixion* is used as a graphic term for death. At salvation, a dramatic death occurred, and our flesh was crucified to this world. The world does not hold the attraction, the allurement, and the enticement to us that it previously held. We have died to it. But if that is all true, then why is there still a battle?

Years ago my grandpa decided that he was tired of store-bought chicken. He said the chicken you buy at the supermarket tastes terrible. Thus, he said he wanted fresh chicken, a chicken that he could kill himself and eat. We went to a farm and bought several chickens and took them to his house, which was in a subdivision of a middle-class neighborhood. Grandpa relived his days in West Virginia. He took those chickens, and I watched him ring their necks. For the first time in my life, I understood the expression "he's running around like a chicken with his head cutoff." The chicken was dead, but he was still flopping and running around. That's the way you and I should look at this world.

When we accepted the Lord Jesus Christ as our personal Saviour, God rung the neck of this world, and the world, for all intents and purposes, was dealt a death blow at Calvary. But that world that was effectively killed on our behalf at Calvary is still very much flopping around the barnyard of this earth like a chicken with its head cutoff. Though this flesh was dealt a death blow at Calvary, it's still flopping around on this earth, even though eventually it will be inert.

What was killed at Calvary, you and I have to reckon to be killed every day. When you became saved, your flesh became crucified with Christ. Nevertheless, crucifixion in this verse is not something that God did to you, but something you must do to yourself. That would seem to suggest to us that we are the agents of our own crucifixion. Even though the old life was dealt a death blow at Calvary, there is still something practically that you and I must do every single day that stretches before us. At Calvary our flesh was dealt a death blow, and now you and I have to practically reckon to be true what we know to be true.

Crucifixion was not a sudden death. Crucifixion was a slow, painful, gradual, and agonizing death. We have to fix our bodies to the cross until they are completely and totally reckoned dead. There is no quick fix to a spiritual life. There is no Miracle-Gro for Christianity. There is nothing that you can sprinkle on yourself to make you a super Christian. Life doesn't work like that.

The blow that was dealt to our flesh at Calvary has to be constantly and continually affirmed in our life day after day. We have been crucified, and we must continue to stay on the cross and not take ourselves off it. We have been crucified, and we continually crucify ourselves and die daily to the world and its lusts and affections.

Recently, Ohio State played Penn State in a football game. Everybody who knows me well knows that I am an avid Ohio State fan. So I carved out a section of time from eight to eleven to watch what I thought was going to be Ohio State beating Penn State. The first half was nip and tuck—it was three to three at halftime. I was very nervous and looked over at my wife Karen and said, "You know what is going to happen in this football game, don't you? It is going to come down to one critical mistake, and whoever makes that critical mistake is going to lose the football game." About ten minutes after that, Karen said, "I'm going to bed." My muscles were as tense as they could possibly be, and she was sleeping like a little baby. What's the difference between me and Karen during an Ohio State football game? The difference is she is dead to football. Football does not move Karen. It is not part of the world in which she operates. I have tried to explain to her how to get a first down about twenty times and she still doesn't get it. Football is not part of the world in which she lives. As far as my wife is concerned, there is no such thing as football.

When you are dead to something, the allurement of it doesn't entice you. When you are dead to something, no one can tempt you with it. You and I as Christians have to be dead to this world with all of its lusts and affections. The world does not faze us anymore because we have died and are dying daily to all of that.

The Principle of Conformity (v. 25)

The fact that you have put your old life to death in no way should suggest to you that your Christian life is passive. You are dead in your flesh, but you are alive in your spirit. Since we have a new spiritual life that has been infused in us by God, we now have to walk in accordance with that spiritual life.

The word *walk* is a military term that means "to keep in step with." How many of you have ever watched a military march? A marching soldier can't be aware of what is around him—he must focus on staying in line. He can't say, "Isn't that a lovely tree over there?" He can't walk off and do whatever he wants to do—he has to stay in line. To stay in line and walk in line, you have to be oblivious to all of the allurements and attractions that are on every side. You are focused on staying in step with your company commander.

In the same way, we need to stay in line with God. This term was used metaphorically in the Greek language of following somebody's principles. In other words, God has told us how we are to conduct our lives and we have made up our minds that we are going to follow God's principles. We are not going to deviate from God's principles. We are staying in step with God. The fact that our flesh was killed in no way should suggest to us that the Christian life is completely passive and inactive. Quite the opposite is true. Because we are dead to the world around us, we are actively following the Lord. We are actively in step with Him. We have aligned ourselves with God and are not deviating from that path. We have conformed our lives to His principles.

My daughter Amy is an elementary school teacher. Often she will tell her class to stay in line when they are moving from one room to another. The class, however, is prone to wander. So Amy bought a jump rope and had each one of her students hold on to that rope as they moved from place to place. This helped the class to stay in line.

In our Christian lives, you and I are prone to wander and do things our own way. But we have to stay in line with our leader and conform to Him. The Christian life is not merely one of crucifixion. We are dead to the old life in order that we might follow God. We have died to the world so we might live unto Him.

This is the very thing that we demonstrate in baptism. We are buried in the likeness of His death and raised to walk in newness of life (Romans 6:4). We don't have the old life of digressing into every little cesspool that attracts our attention. We have died to all of that so that our lives might be alive to the single purpose of following the Lord and doing exactly what He says. We have died in order to conform our lives to Him and what He wants for our lives.

The Principle of Conceit (v. 26)

There are many people who divorce verse 26 from the verses above it. Many commentators that I've read start their new chapter with verse 26 allowing it to stand alone. It should be obvious, however, that the verses belong together. We are to keep in step with the Spirit. The reason people don't keep in step with the Spirit is because they are conceited. For example, in Isaiah 53:6 states, "All we like sheep have gone astray; we have turned every one to his own way; . . ." Why have we gone astray? We have turned to our own way.

Years ago, I was watching a broadcasted concert of Frank Sinatra performed at Madison Square Garden. At the conclusion of this concert Frank Sinatra said, "Now,

I'm going to sing the American anthem but you don't have to stand." I thought he was going to sing "The Star Spangled Banner" but instead he sang "I Did It My Way." Largely that is the national anthem of America because people want to do things their own way.

People naturally recoil at the thought of conformity because they are full of conceit. Following the Spirit is the very antithesis of vainglory. You and I have to be consumed with the glory of God. When you and I think that it has to be our way, that is vainglory. Of course, the problem with pride is that it not only affects us but it affects other people. How we treat other people is going to largely depend upon what we think about ourselves. If we are full of conceit, pride, and vain glory, then we are going to do two things to people.

The first thing we are going to do to people is provoke them. Pride always leads to provocation because if it is all about you, then you don't care how anybody else feels. The Christian is always aware of who is around him and the feelings of those people. Christians always take into account the feelings of others when making a decision. A Christian doesn't think about only what is in his best interest—he is not consumed with the empty glory of self. A Christian is concerned about what's happening on the bigger scale of life because if he is only concerned about himself, he is going to provoke somebody.

Pride provokes people and it also leads to envying people. A proud person thinks that he deserves what other people have. Proud people are always envious of what other people possess. It's like the elder son in the story of the prodigal son. Prideful people are always constantly looking at what they have been deprived of rather than what they can do for other people. Pride is always an envious thing.

The devil knows this. It was the very first temptation that the devil offered Jesus. He said, "If you are the Son of God, turn these stones into bread." In the preceding verses, Jesus had just been baptized and a voice thundered from Heaven, "You are my beloved Son in whom I am well pleased." The devil enters right after that heavenly proclamation and says, "If you really are His Son, don't you think you would have more to eat than this?" The devil always wants us to think that we've been deprived. If you go around saying, "They never did this or that for me" and are constantly envious of what other people have, you reveal that you are a proud individual and that life is supposed to cater to your every whim.

Instead of bestowing what is necessary upon others, you want other people to boast about you. You think life is there to serve you rather than you being there to serve life. How un-Christian that is. While we are arguing over who is the greatest, Christ picks up a towel and begins to wash our feet because Jesus is not envious. If you and I have Christ's Spirit, we are not envious either. We don't keep our feelings on our shirt-sleeves—we have crucified ourselves to that and are able to step in line with what the Spirit wants for our lives. When we step in line with what the Spirit wants for our lives, that is the direct opposite of the self-conceit that is constantly provoking other people and wanting the affection that other people have been given.

Recently I was visiting someone who is in a drug rehab program and was speaking very strongly to that person about how he is injuring his family members. I said, "Your actions have caused hurt to your parents and to your siblings. Don't you understand what you are doing to the people around you with the way you are behaving?" He seemed completely unmoved by that argument. Do you know why he was unmoved by it? He's proud and wants to do what he wants to do. That conceit leads him into not following the Spirit but into being susceptible to every cesspool of this world. He has not crucified himself and because he has not crucified himself, he's not able to conform to the Spirit's wealth for his life because he is consumed with conceit and pride.

Carnality and willfulness do not only reveal themselves in drug addiction, but they also reveal themselves in envying other people, walking around with a haughty spirit, and provoking other people on a constant basis by having an inflated perception of who you are. That is the ultimate un-Christian spirit. When Christ walked this earth, He was not in it for what He could get out of it—He was in it for what He could give to it. If you only live for what other people can do for you rather than what you can do for them, you are into total opposition to the Spirit of Christ who came and laid His life down so that other people could be saved.

You and I need to get our feelings off our shirt-sleeves and quit letting lust and ill will motivate us in our Christian lives. We must crucify our affections and step in line with the Spirit of God. In order to step in line with the Spirit of God, our lives cannot be about ourselves. Our lives cannot be lives of conceit. That makes for miserable company.

You and I must practice the principle of crucifixion—conformity with no conceit—if we are to know happiness and promote happiness within the body of Christ. We have to be dead men walking. When we practice being dead to self, we serve others and become more like Christ.

CHAPTER FORTY-ONE

Setting Bones in the Body of Christ

Galatians 6:1-3

I don't know what it is, but it seems like throughout my whole life, I have had a problem with broken bones. When I was in third grade, my mom dropped us off at the Christian school, and as I was getting out of the car, I closed the door on my index finger and broke it in two places. It was almost severed. They had to rush me to the emergency room. I was thankful that it was only broken in the top and middle knuckle, but not at the base. That is, until I got into junior high and played baseball, and received a fast ball on that knuckle and broke it too.

Many of you are aware that I had a rare genetic disease when I was in high school and the doctors, as part of the rehabilitation, had to basically break my ankle bones and fuse them back together. Then, just a couple of years ago, I was walking down the road and a big truck came by with oversized mirrors, and one of those mirrors hit my left arm at about fifty miles per hour and completely shattered that arm. I had to be rushed to the emergency room and now my left arm is held together by a plate with screws.

And, of course, there were all the struggles we had with our daughter Ashley when she was born with a dislocated hip. Numerous surgeries were required to place that hip back in joint. So it seems like bones and disjointedness have been a part of our family through the years.

Paul states that there are many people in the body of Christ who are out of joint (cf. Ephesians 4:16). For the body of Christ to work properly, every Christian has to be in his or her place supplying to the body what he or she is supposed to supply. When Ashley's hip was dislocated, her entire leg dragged behind her. She could not put any weight on her leg because her leg was completely out of joint.

We would watch her crawl around the living room and one leg would work very strong and powerful, and the other leg would just dangle behind the rest of her body. I remember when her surgeries were finally completed and successful, we watched our daughter ride a bicycle for the first time. I stood on the steps of our house and cried as I watched her leg in full operation. There was a long period of time when we thought she would never have the use of that leg.

My job as a pastor is to help set disjointed people into their proper place in the body of Christ. Our job is to set joints in the body of Christ so that people can supply to the body exactly what they ought to supply. In Galatians 6 the word translated *restore* means "to put in order." It means "to restore to its former condition." In the New Testament, this word is used of mending fishing nets. In secular Greek, the word was in the medical world of setting a fracture or a dislocated bone. I want you to go into the emergency room with Dr. Amsbaugh and I want us to set some bones in the body of Christ.

Be Competent

Throughout Chapter 5, Paul has been contrasting the works of the flesh with the fruit of the Spirit. If you are fleshly, you are going to produce bad works, but if you're spiritual, you are going to bear good fruit. Before I help other people, Paul says the first thing I need to do is consider myself.

Part of the way I consider myself is to ascertain if my life is a spiritual life. Obviously, if I am sitting back and saying, "I'm spiritual," I don't think that is the idea he has here. What he is saying is to analyze your life and look at these laundry lists of works of the flesh and fruit of the Spirit, and honestly ask yourself if your life is more characterized by the works of the flesh or by the fruit of the Spirit. It is not until my life is characterized by the fruit of the Spirit that I should seek to restore somebody else. In other words, before I work on anybody else's spirituality, I need to work on my own spirituality first.

Jesus articulated the same idea in the Sermon on the Mount (Matthew 7:3-5). Jesus is not saying that we should never deal with other people, but rather if we are going to deal with other people, we need to deal with ourselves first. To help us with this, Jesus gives a humorous story of a man who has a pole sticking out of his head. Imagine this guy walking down the sidewalk with this telephone pole sticking out of his head. He goes up to someone else and says, "Excuse me, I believe you have a piece of lint on your coat." Jesus says that we need to remove the telephone pole before we assist with the lint. If a person has a telephone pole in his head, he can't see clearly to deal with other people's problems.

Sin always blurs perspective. Because sin blurs perspective, you and I have to deal with our own sins first before we even begin to think about dealing with other people's sins. Jesus is not saying that you and I should never judge other people. As a matter of fact, in other passages Jesus said, "Judge righteous judgment." The apostle Paul in the book of I Corinthians said, "I have judged already concerning this guy in Corinth who has committed fornication." You and I have to pass moral judgment. However, before you and I make moral judgments on the lives of other people, we must first make moral judgment concerning our own lives. We cannot see properly to deal with the sin of others until first we deal with our own sin. We are in no position to help other people until first we have established a spiritual competency level in our own lives.

When Ashley was born with her dislocated hip, we were immediately referred to an orthopedic doctor in the town where she was born. This doctor put Ashley in a series of harnesses only to discover that none of those harnesses were adequate in getting her hip back in joint. He said, "This is beyond me. I need you to go to Children's Hospital in Philadelphia." This doctor was very kind, but Ashley's problem was beyond his level of competence.

At Children's Hospital we were introduced to another very kind doctor. He tried several surgeries to correct Ashley's hip. He too failed and with tears admitted to us that this was beyond his level of expertise. We were then referred to the head of orthopedics who was the most competent orthopedic surgeon in the entire city of Philadelphia. He fixed our daughter's hip. Of all three doctors, he had the least bedside manner—he was very arrogant. The other two guys were kind, but he was competent. If you have to choose between compassion and competence, by all means choose competence. It does no good for doctors to cry over your problem if they can't help you.

Often, if someone has a wayward child, he will run to someone else who also has a wayward child to seek advice. This is done because the parent is seeking compassion. People like that may understand, but they don't know how to solve the problem because if they knew how to solve it, they wouldn't have a wayward child. Christians always run to compassionate people rather than to competent people to get their bones set. The problem is if you want to go to somebody to find out how to help your wayward child, why don't you go to somebody who doesn't have a wayward child? If you want to find how to do the job right, go to somebody who has already done the job well.

When I went to have my reconstructive surgery on my feet, there were two orthopedic doctors in my hometown. Friedreich's ataxia was a very rare disease. So we wanted to find out who had experience in doing this type of orthopedic surgery. One doctor had never done a surgery like that before, and the other had performed that type of surgery once before. We picked the guy who had already done one surgery. He did not have much experience, but at least he had a little. I wanted to have a doctor who had already been into an ankle like mine and had been successful at it.

When you and I go to set bones in the body of Christ, predominately we are not to look for compassionate people, though that is important—we are to look for competent people. We are to look for people who know what they are doing. If we are going to restore people, you and I need to have a certain level of competence. In many instances people engage in things for which they have no competency, and if you and I are not able to handle a situation, we need to refer that person to somebody who is capable and competent in that situation.

Be Compassionate

Just because you are competent doesn't mean you can be arrogant. This entire passage is laced with compassion. Notice that there are three significant times that Paul says, "Brethren." When you and I go to treat people in the body of Christ, we ought to treat them like kin because they are family. When you need to have something dealt with, you don't want to feel like you are just a number. When you go to a doctor, you don't want him to say, "Welcome, Number 43-503. How are you?" I want to be more than a number with my doctor.

I have a doctor in town and I have his cell phone number. When I call him, he does many things for me because he is more than just my doctor—he's my friend.

My doctor is from India but he treats me like a brother. He's not even a Christian, but he treats me more like a brother than some Christians do. When you have a kid you are taking to the doctor, it is different than when you are taking someone else's kid to the doctor. Any parent recognizes that if you are taking somebody else's kid to the doctor, you'll sit in the waiting room while they are in the back, but if it is your kid, you are hovering over the examining table and asking a bunch of questions. I remember when those doctors used to do pelvic rotations on Ashley's legs to try to get that bone back in place, we watched carefully because Ashley was bone of our bone and flesh of our flesh. When we go to help people, we ought to recognize that they are not just files or case studies—they are people and more important, they are people who are related to us by virtue of the blood of Christ.

The second word that is important is *overtaken*. That seems to imply that this fellow was a victim of sin— he was overtaken by it. This word in the passive voice, as it is here, carries with it the element of surprise—he was surprised by sin. The person who has committed the sin must never see himself as a victim. If the person who has committed the sin sees himself as a victim, it will hinder repentance because he sees it as not his fault— it is somebody else's fault and he couldn't help himself. From the vantage point of the fallen, they can never see themselves as victims—it will annul repentance. But from the vantage point of the restorer, we see that person as a victim so it will temper the way we restore them. We must put ourselves in the position of that person and say, "There but for the grace of God go I." Consider thyself.

Not only must you treat this person as kin and as a victim, but you have to treat him the way you would treat yourself. How would you treat yourself if you were the doctor? How would you treat yourself if you were the dentist? My wife hates the dentist. She wants to go to a dentist who treats her like he is sitting in the chair. You ought to give other people the same kind of treatment that you would want if you were falling into sin.

The key word in all of this is the word *meekness*. We have to be gentle throughout the entire process of setting someone right in the body of Christ. We have to have, as it were, good bedside manner. When the doctor first diagnosed me with Friedreich's ataxia, it didn't really hit me at first what he was saying. Hours later, after the news began to sink in, a nurse walked by and heard me crying. She came into the room. I don't even remember her name. She began to give words of comfort to me. I didn't know that nurse, and I didn't know how competent she was, but that nameless nurse cared about me, and the fact that she cared about me meant a lot to me. If we're going to set people right, we've got to be competent, but we also have to be compassionate.

Be Credible

Out of all the broken bones that my family has experienced, the one that frustrates me the most is Ashley's severed finger. She was in the hospital to get her hip fixed. Three surgeries had failed already, and finally we had a successful surgery and were going home. A nurse, in haste to get us out of the hospital, broke a cardinal rule of nursing —you never cut what you can't see— trying to take the IV out of Ashley's hand. That day she cut into the tape to remove the IV and cut Ashley's pinky off. We talked to dozens of nurses over the years about that event and virtually every nurse has said the same thing—she broke a cardinal rule of nursing—you never cut what you can't see. I have asked myself a thousand times why she broke that rule. I've played that event a thousand times in my mind wondering if something could have been done different.

The Bible says in this passage that you and I are to fulfill the law of Christ—we are not to break the rules of God—we are to keep the rules of God and fulfill the rules of God. We are to bear one another's burdens. The term *burden* refers to a heavy weight or stone, and *bearing* refers to carrying something for a long distance. It is like when Jesus said, "If someone compels you to go a mile, go with him twain." Are you and I fulfilling the law? Are we carrying the load for someone else, or do we feel on any given occasion that it is okay for us to break the rules of Christianity and give up on people?

The night that Ashley's finger was severed we were about ready to go home from the hospital. A phone call was immediately placed to Ashley's facial reconstructive doctor, who was one of the most competent cardiovascular surgeons in the country. He rushed to the hospital, and we knew if anybody could have saved her finger, he was the man who could have saved it. For seven hours that night, he did everything in his power to save Ashley's severed pinkie. Every hour he would send somebody out of the surgery room to where we were waiting to describe what they were doing. That night that doctor took our burden and made it his own. Another facial reconstructive doctor told us, "If my daughter were lying where your daughter is lying, I would want that doctor because if he can't do it, no one will be able to do it."

At the very moment someone chose to break a law of nursing, someone else decided to fulfill the very law of Christ by taking our burdens and making those burdens his own. This is how we become credible Christians. How can we claim the name Christ if we won't fulfill the very essence of Christianity by taking other people's burdens and shouldering those burdens as if they were our own?

Be Consistent

Some people think spirituality is a stagnant quality. In other words, they think this is my church, I sit in the same pew with my children all in a row, and by the demeanor and the way I carry myself, I prove that I am a very spiritual person. I sit here in this pew and look very good, and I hope that my demeanor and my presence communicates to other people that I am spiritual. The Bible says if you think you are spiritual and you're not doing anything to help restore people, you are deceived.

Spiritual people don't sit and do nothing. Spiritual people are involved in restoration ministries—that's what spiritual people do. Spiritual people work on church buses and hug under-privileged kids. Spiritual people get involved in addiction ministries and help people get off drugs. Spiritual people get involved in junior church and help in the nursery. If you think that spirituality is looking pious and sitting in a pew without doing anything, you are deceived about what spirituality is. Spirituality is not a stagnant condition—it is service.

That night when I was walking down the road and the car hit me, Karen said, "Should I call the ambulance?" I said, "No, I don't want to wait for the ambulance to get here. You can drive me now and get me to the hospital quicker than if I wait for an ambulance. Let's get in the car and go." I thought that was the intelligent choice, but because I wasn't brought in on an ambulance, they didn't think there was anything wrong with me. If I had been brought in an ambulance, they would have taken me in the back door and I would have gotten immediate attention. But because my wife drove me, I had to wait.

My arm was shattered, and it was hanging there in intense pain. Finally, I got to the window and I said, "I'm going into shock. I need some help." A lady who we knew and worked in the emergency room just happened to see me at the window. She said, "Pastor, can I help you?" I said, "You sure can," and she said, "Come on back." She got me back immediately. She got me in touch with the technician who put me on the table and took an X-ray of my arm. The technician looked at the X-ray and said, "Oh, my goodness, if we knew you were hurt this bad, we would have gotten you back much sooner." I had been sitting in the waiting room needing my bone restored while health care professionals walked by and didn't do anything.

We have churches like that. As Christian professionals, we are walking right past the wounded. If you think you are spiritual without involvement, you are deceived. What good is competence, compassion, and credibility if we don't consistently help people? What good is being a well-credentialed bone-setter if he does not set bones?

When our middle daughter Amy was born, she was born with a lazy eye and was referred to one of the most competent eye doctors in all of Philadelphia. This doctor not only did eye surgeries, but he taught others how to do eye surgeries. Because he was competent, he always had interns around him learning how to do eye surgeries. Every time we would take Amy in for her appointment, three or four students were present. One day, we had a nine o'clock appointment and didn't get taken back to the exam room until about noon. One of the nurses came in and said, "Doctor, what would you like for lunch?" One of the interns said, "I'll go get lunch," and the doctor said, "That's why we have secretaries. Learn the medicine." What good is a doctor who doesn't know how to doctor?

When we moved to Georgia from Philadelphia, we asked Amy's eye doctor for a referral. He recommended a very competent eye surgeon in Atlanta. Every time we visited the Atlanta physician, he would say, "You ought to thank the Lord for that doctor in Philadelphia. You had the best surgeon." Our Philadelphia doctor had more than just a piece of parchment on his wall—he helped people. He was a surgeon in the ultimate sense of that word.

The story was told of a man who walked into a movie theater only to find a man lying across his seat. The man is in obvious pain. The guy says, "Hey, fellow, you've got my seat." The fellow in pain continues to moan, and the ticket holder says, "You're in my seat. What's the matter with you?" The fellow still lays there and continues to moan. The guy with the tickets says, "Where did you come from?" And the fellow says, "The balcony."

Someone may be in your pew next Sunday who has just had a terrible fall. Don't say, "Hey, buddy, you're in my pew." He is in too much pain to worry about what seat he's in. He needs help, not condemnation. You and I need to be there to help people who have fallen from the balcony instead of saying, "Hey, buddy, you've got my seat." You and I must be competent, compassionate, credible, and consistent in helping people who are hurting.

CHAPTER FORTY-TWO

How Helping You Helps Me

Galatians 6:4-5

I read a story about a state trooper who was a K9 expert. He received an award because he had trained his dog to sniff out bombs, and he and his dog were good at it. When the trooper got the award, he got a lot of publicity about the great job that he had done. The pressure of the notoriety, however, led the trooper to make bombs himself. He would then hide the bombs he had made and then have his dog go find them. He thought the more bombs that he could discover, the more notoriety he would receive. After a while the police thought there couldn't be this many bombs in the area, and he was sniffed out. When he was captured, he said that all the notoriety had gone to his head and that he was only trying to project more of his image on the community. As long as he was serving others, his image was improving, but at the very moment he started to be self-serving and promoting his own image, he hurt himself. When you help somebody, you help yourself, but when you help yourself, you hurt yourself.

When video cassettes were first developed, there were two systems: VHS and Beta. VHS cassettes were developed by a company named JVC, and JVC decided that its discovery was too good to keep to itself. So the company made it available to the market at large. The Beta format was developed by Sony, and Sony decided its information was so good it must be kept secret. So Sony didn't share it with the rest of the market. Because VHS technology was shared with the rest of the market, everybody else started using VHS, and it became 90% of the video cassette market, which meant that Sony and its Beta technology was being used by a minimal number of people. Because Sony had hoarded its information, Sony only captured 10% of the market and was pushed out of the video cassette industry. When JVC decided to share its information, the company actually helped itself by making the market of VHS cassettes even larger.

When you and I are concerned with helping other people, the result is we usually end up helping ourselves. However, when you and I are consumed with only helping ourselves and keeping everything for ourselves, at that very moment, we hurt ourselves and injure ourselves. Jesus put it this way: if you sacrifice your life, you will save it, but if you try to save your life, you'll lose it. Every single time that you and I try to help other people, there will be something for us. We will be helped when we help others, but if we decide that we are not going to help other people and that we have to watch out for number one, we are going to injure ourselves in that process.

Every single time that I decide I want to help you I help me by helping you. That's what is under discussion in Galatians 6:4-5. When I decide that I am going to lay down my life in service for other people, there will be three immediate things that will come back my way.

It Proves My Spirituality

Throughout chapter 5, there has been a contrast between the works of the flesh and the fruit of the Spirit. Flesh is obviously the height of self-centeredness. When I am a fleshly person, I am only thinking about me. At the root of fleshliness is the idea of self-centeredness. Contrast that with the fruit of the Spirit where the key to the fruit of the Spirit is selflessness. The fruit of the Spirit is living for other people and providing love, joy, peace, patience, and gentleness for them. Fleshliness is self-centeredness and spirit living is selflessness. When I deny myself and reach out to other people, one of the first things that happens is I prove my spirituality— I prove that I am a person who is controlled, filled, and dominated by the Holy Spirit because Holy Spirit living always reaches out to other people.

The word here that is translated *prove* is a word that was used in the Greek language of trying silver or gold to reveal its purity. Helping other people is what proves my spiritual value to the world. I've proven that I am of value to planet earth when I reach out and serve other people. Some say, "He's so heavenly minded that he's no earthly good." But this statement could never be a true statement. Anyone who is heavenly minded will be earthly good, and if you are of no earthly good, you're not spiritually minded because spiritually minded people always prove their spirituality by reaching out and ministering to other people.

As we saw earlier in this chapter, spirituality is not

stagnant (6:1). If you are spiritual, you are going to reach out and try to restore people who are overtaken in a fault. Spirituality is not a stagnant quality where you sit and do nothing. Spirituality always reaches out in ministry and service; if you're not involved in any ministry or service for other people, you are not a spiritual person. Spiritual people always try to reach out and restore people who have fallen; they get involved in the lives of the downtrodden and reach out to the people who are hurting and try to have some type of restoration ministry. Spiritual people always reach out in service to other people. Spirituality is not a stagnant quality—it is a dynamic quality that always reaches out in ministry.

The word *prove* automatically suggests to us that there is some standard under discussion. There is some criterion whereby someone's purity and spirituality can be gauged. There has to be some standard by which we can say that spirituality has proven itself real. That standard by which spirituality is measured is given to us in verse 2. When you and I reach out and begin to get involved in the lives of other people, that is when we prove that we have met the criterion of what the Bible is talking about when it talks about spirituality. All of this talk about bearing burdens, fulfilling the law of Christ, achieving spirituality, and reaching this standard of spiritual maturation leads us to the statement found in verse 4. We prove our spirituality when our efforts are used to aid and assist other people who are overwhelmed with the burdens of life. When you and I see somebody who is burdened and weighed down with the cares and stresses of this world, and we decide we need to do something for that person and reach out and help that person in some way, that is when we prove we are spiritual.

Many years ago I read a story about a cop who was working in the city of Los Angeles and came upon a car that was illegally parked. The officer wrote a citation for illegal parking and put that citation on the dash of that car. The cop didn't even recognize that there was a fellow sitting in the front seat. He couldn't have missed the fellow because the fellow had been sitting there rather stiff for forty-five minutes before the cop put that citation there. The fellow in the car was stiff because he had been shot through the head. He was sitting in the seat dead as a doornail, and the cop reached through the window and put a citation on the dash for his being illegally parked. Our problem is that we are trying to cite people who are spiritually dead.

These people don't need citations—they need miracles. They are dead in trespasses and sins, and they need somebody to come in and shoulder the responsibility for their spiritually dead condition. The world has already been condemned and has received its death sentence by virtue of the fact that it believes not. We do not need to indict the world—the world has already been indicted—we need to reach out and help somebody get to the doctor.

When I was at my first church, we had a children's ministry on Wednesday nights, and we would take the church buses out to pick up kids for that ministry. Our church was located at a major intersection. And a guy coming home from work had his car break down right in front of our church. So he pulled into our church parking lot to try to get his car repaired. Just as he was looking under his hood, our bus was pulling out to go pick up kids for Wednesday night church service. Our bus driver at that time pulled the bus alongside this guy's broken down car, and the bus driver said, "Hey, buddy, don't get any oil on the parking lot" and then drove off. The likelihood of us getting that guy in a church service is zero because we didn't evidence any spirituality that day.

Whether oil is on the parking lot or not has nothing to do with spirituality. Helping someone who is in distress has everything to do with spirituality. Sometimes I think that you and I are more worried about stains on the carpet or oil on the parking lot than we are about people who are dying and on their way to Hell. We need to understand that if we are not reaching out in some practical way and helping people who are in distress, we are not spiritual people. One of the first ways that I can prove to the world that I really mean what I say about spirituality is by practically helping people. If I as a Christian am indicting the world but not helping the world, I come across as very unspiritual. When we help people, it helps us because it makes us look spiritual when we reach out and minister to others.

It Provides Me Satisfaction

The second point that Paul makes is that when you

and I help other people, we feel good about ourselves. When you and I sit around and wait for other people to serve us, we become mean-spirited. The reason we get mean-spirited is because the world is not going to serve us or minister to our needs the way we think the world should minister to our needs. Consequently, when I sit around and think about what the world should be doing for me, I'm going to end up being a cranky person, but when I reach out and give my life in service to other people, that's when I am going to be fulfilled.

We often get confused in our thinking. We think if people meet all our needs, then we are going to be happy. But if that is the way you think, you will always be a miserable person. Satisfaction in life only comes when you reach out and quit thinking about yourself. Anytime you and I feel like life has dealt us a major blow, and we just can't go on, and life is not worth living, we need to reach out and help other people.

The Christian psychologist Henry Brandt said that anytime someone came to his office and was contemplating suicide, he would give them an assignment where they were to go out and serve other people. Why? Suicide is a selfish thing where people are willing to end it all because people aren't ministering to their needs. It is not about people ministering to your needs; it's about you ministering to other people's needs. If I am always thinking about what the world owes me, I'm going to be bitter. If I think about what I can do for other people, I'm going to find satisfaction and fulfillment.

I read a story not too long ago that I think illustrates

this point. A little boy came into the living room where his grandfather was sitting and offered his grandfather a peach. The grandfather took the peach from the little boy and bit into it, and as soon as the grandfather bit into the peach, the little grandson just started crying. The grandfather said, "What's the matter? I thought you gave me the peach." The little grandson said, "No, I just wanted you to get the worm out." When you try to bite and devour, you will always have a weird feeling in your stomach, but when you reach out and serve other people, and minister to their needs, you will feel much better. Reaching out in service is the ultimate in satisfaction.

Endurance of the cross was done for the joy that was set before Jesus (Hebrews 12:2). When Jesus laid down His life for other people, He received joy in doing so. You wouldn't think by going to a cross you would receive joy, but Jesus received joy by laying His life down. We're out to emulate the practice of Jesus by laying our lives down in service and sacrifice for other people, and when this is done, joy will come our way.

We can't worry about what sinners ought to be doing for us. If we do, we are going to be weary and faint in our minds. What is clear is that when it is all about us, we get weary, but when we do the opposite and lay our life down in service for other people, that's when we find the ultimate joy, satisfaction, and fulfillment of life. Helping other people helps me by providing me with personal satisfaction that cannot be found by any other means.

It Promotes My Stability

Nothing says that I am a mature person like shouldering the responsibility of other people. The height of immaturity is wanting somebody to shoulder my burden, but the height of maturity is for me to reach out and shoulder the burdens of other people. When we bear the burdens of other people, we are literally making their burden ours and shouldering that which another person had been shouldering. That is the greatest display of maturity. If it was someone else's responsibility, but they dropped the ball or were overwhelmed by it, or it was getting them down, and I take care of it for him, that is maturity.

Immaturity is just the opposite. It is plowing through other people because they are in the way. Adolescence is a difficult time of life because often it is a child's spirit in an adult body. One of the things that we attempt to teach adolescents is how to be mature. Mature people are conscious of their surroundings. Immature people only think about themselves.

When you bring a baby home from the hospital, that baby needs the whole world to cater to him and his needs. A baby cannot feed himself or change himself. When we first brought our children home from the hospital, we recognized how much they demanded. It was hectic. I understand that in the life of a baby this schedule has to be maintained, but this is not a schedule you want to keep the rest of your life.

Part of teaching a child how to grow up is to teach

him or her how to do things for himself and to be responsible. When my children are 15, I'm not going to sit at the table and hold a spoon and say, "Here comes an airplane." The world will not cater to you. You must be conscious of what is going on around you, and you will not sit there at the breakfast table while everyone is waiting in the car for you because you are oblivious to what is going on in the rest of the world. You are going to learn how to do these things by yourself without getting a play-by-play manual every five minutes.

You cannot allow a child to think that the entire world revolves around him—that child has to learn that there are certain things that he must shoulder responsibility for. The world cannot be catering to him every time he cries or pitches a fit.

When my cousin Anita was growing up, it became clear that she was mentally retarded. Anita has the mind of six-year-old child even though she is middle-aged. When my grandmother died, her inheritance was divided among her descendants, and Anita received one twenty-seventh of the inheritance. Dad, who was the executor of the will, went to the home where Anita lived and asked what Anita would like to have. They said she had always talked about a bicycle. Dad went out and bought a twenty-six inch bicycle with training wheels and delivered it. Anita was thrilled. When she came out and saw the bicycle, she hugged my dad. She got on that bike and rode it up the driveway. Then she would get off and hug my dad again. As we watched Anita, we cried because there is nothing wrong with a six-year-old acting like a six-year old, but there is something terribly wrong when a fifty-year-old acts like a six-year-old.

We have to teach people how to be mature. If you come to church and sit there and say, "I wonder if anybody is going to shake my hand today," you are immature. There is nothing wrong with a baby Christian acting like a baby, but if you have been saved for any period of time and you are still acting childish, you need to grow up. Mature Christians always assume the responsibility to reach out and minister to others. But if you wait around for people to come to you, then you suffer from spiritual retardation. This is the way a baby acts. When you shoulder responsibility, you are mature, but when you abandon and abdicate responsibility, you reveal that you are an immature person.

When I wait for people to help me assume responsibility for the issues of life, then I reveal that I am still a kid at heart. The Bible says that when I help other people, I reveal something about myself. I reveal to them that I am a mature person because that is what mature people do. Needs seen are assignments given. By God's grace may you and I bear one another's burdens and in so doing prove something to be true about ourselves. When we help others, we help ourselves.

CHAPTER FORTY-THREE

How to Pay the Preacher

Galatians 6:6

One of the most controversial subjects in any church is how much to pay the preacher. If you asked the preacher, he would probably say a little bit more than he is presently making. If you asked the average person in the pew, he or she would probably say a little bit less than what he is currently making. Obviously, when you are talking about how much to pay the pastor, it becomes a very controversial subject. One thing I promised God, not only on this subject but on any other subject, was when I come to a verse in the Bible, I'm not going to neglect it because it's in the Bible.

There are two extremes when it comes to this regard. I had a deacon say to me one time, "I really believe that it is the job of the church board to keep the pastor as poor and humble as possible because that way he can relate to the poor people in the congregation. If you pay a pastor too much money, he obviously will not be able to relate to the poor people of the congregation so I really believe the pastor ought to make less than anybody else in the church." I'm glad he was not able to sway the rest of the board to his point of view but that was his assessment and he honestly communicated that to me.

At the other extreme, I remember when I first moved to Georgia, the church was doing everything in its power to make our transition there as easy as possible, and Karen and I had always lived in parsonages and had not built up any equity in spite of the fact that we had been in the ministry for a good number of years. When we went there, the church graciously gave us an interest-free loan of ten thousand dollars so we could make a down payment on a house. We began to look for a house and felt that God led us to one, and we put a bid on that house and it was accepted. The church gave us the down payment and we went to settlement.

It was weird because I was committing to thirty years of payments—that seemed to be a long time. I saw the stack of papers on the table and you could tell that I was a little apprehensive about the whole process because I had never signed for anything for that long. One of the ladies at the table said to me, "You look uncomfortable. Is there anything we can do to make you more comfortable?" I said "I don't really know if there is. I just know that as a pastor, you are always apprehensive when you go to spend this amount of money. What are people going to think about me spending this amount of money?" She laughed at me and said, "Honey, I've helped one pastor in this town buy two houses for three hundred thousand dollars each." If one pastor owns two houses that are worth three hundred thousand dollars, I think that is the opposite extreme.

I think there are the extremes of, "Let's make our pastor the poorest man in the church," and "Let's let our pastor build two houses worth three hundred thousand dollars each." There ought to be a happy medium in between, don't you think? I think if we follow the principles of the Word of God, we will be able to find that balance. Obviously, this has been a controversial subject for years, so we are not going to settle everything in this lesson. But I think there are three principles from this verse that will help us as we consider this topic.

The Responsibility of the Pastor

When God ordained employment, he did so that man could obtain bread. God has created certain cravings in us, and he has provided a legitimate means for those cravings to be fulfilled. For example, God created the craving of sex and that is a legitimate craving that God put in mankind. Because God made that craving, He created a legitimate way for that craving to be fulfilled and the legitimate way for that craving to be fulfilled is marriage. If sex takes place outside of marriage, it is wrong. If sex takes place inside of marriage, it is a very beautiful thing. God creates the craving and then God creates a way by which that craving can be fulfilled.

God has created another craving inside of us and that craving is hunger. There is a legitimate means whereby this craving can be fulfilled and it is called employment. The Bible says that if a man does not work, he should not eat. So God created a legitimate craving for food to be adequately fulfilled in our lives by working. God created employment as a means for a man to win bread. The main reason that man gets a job is so he can eat. Obviously, if a man chooses to marry and that marriage produces children, this only compounds the situation. A man not only has to provide enough food for himself to eat but he also has to provide enough food for his wife and children. The reason that a man sweats in his brow is so he might get bread for himself, for his wife, and for his children.

The Bible says if a man does not provide for his house, he has denied the faith and he is worse than an infidel. Therefore, it is a very noble thing to go to work and to earn bread for your family to eat. There are all kinds of other reasons that a man may go to work. Most men choose work that they enjoy doing. For example, a guy may choose to be a doctor because he is fascinated with anatomy and physiology. A man may choose to be a dentist because he likes an attractive smile. A man may choose to be a banker because he is good with numbers and finance. There are many other reasons people choose the particular job they choose, but whatever job a man may choose to do, the man's main job is to earn enough money to put food on the table for his family.

My dad was a steel worker for over thirty years. My dad did not work at the steel plant for all those years because he had a fascination with steel production. My dad did not work there because he was excited about edge trimming coils of steel. Some people criticized my father and said, "Why do you always try to bid the job that pays the most?" My dad always answered, "I have to be at that place from 8 to 4. So while I'm there from 8 to 4, I'm going to get the most money I can to benefit my family. It doesn't make sense to bid the lowest job. Why not bid the highest job that you can to maximize your potential and earn as much for your family as you possibly can?"

My dad did not go to the steel plant because he had an infatuation with steel any more than any other man who goes to his job goes there predominately because he has an infatuation with the career that he is involved in. Predominately, whenever you are talking about a secular profession, the main thing that drives that man into that profession is he has a desire to eat, and employment is the best way to earn money to do that. That holds true in basically every secular profession, but when you and I get to the ministry, we find the exception.

When a man goes to a secular profession, the biggest thing that drives him into that secular profession is the earning of money but the Bible says that when a man goes into the ministry, he cannot be greedy of filthy lucre (I Timothy 3:2). Earning as much money as possible is not the main thing that drives a man into the ministry. Money is not the force that motivates him—in fact, quite the opposite is true. Anybody in the ministry who is worth his salt is motivated to do what he does by the souls of men.

You cannot put a price tag upon the souls of men. When God calls a man to preach and separates him from fishing for fish to fishing for men, God has called him to catch something more than a source of revenue—God has called him to catch souls that will spend eternity in either Heaven or Hell. The job of the preacher predominately is to use the Word of God to rescue men from the flames of the damned and transport them into the portals of Heaven, and making money is simply a peripheral issue to the big thing at hand—saving souls for all eternity. This is the fundamental difference between secular professions and ministries. When a man goes into the ministry, he devotes himself to the Word of God more than he devotes himself to pay.

I've been pastor of several churches, and some have paid me well and some have not. But every single ministry that I have ever taken, I have never asked how much I was going to make before I took the job. I want to know the will of God, and if I am in the will of God, He will provide. I don't want money to be a factor in deciding where I go to preach the Word of God. I am not after a paycheck—I am after the souls of men and that is vitally important.

A pastor cannot be worried about other people's paychecks. In Acts 6, for example, we read of widows in the church who were being deprived of benevolence, and the pastors were getting involved in helping these widows get enough food on their tables. This business so distracted the pastors that they were taking time away from their study of the Word and prayer. Thus, deacons were appointed so that they could take care of those needs and the pastors would not become involved in this business. The deacons were to take care of that so the pastors could predominately give themselves to the ministry of the Word. Feeding people is not why a pastor opens his door every day. A pastor doesn't open his door to feed his family or anybody else's family—he predominately goes to the office every single day to get into the Word of God and to use that Word of God to get as many souls fit for Heaven as possible. That's why a pastor must totally and completely devote himself to the ministry of the Word of God and prayer. You understand how necessary this is in light of the benefit that it produces.

We are not here to present clever arguments or fancy tricks or gimmicks to get people saved or even to give food baskets (I Corinthians 1:21). Predominately what saves people is the foolishness of preaching. Preaching is the most important thing that our nation needs. Our nation needs preachers of the gospel of Jesus Christ—that's the big thing needed in our society.

A pastor must devote himself to that and not be concerned with all the other peripheral issues—he must be consumed by how important that task is. Preaching is the thing that saves people from Hell. The Bible makes it clear that it's useless to feed a body or clothe a body only for that body to end up in Hell someday. What good is it for someone to go to Hell immaculately dressed or adequately fed? It is better to go to Heaven sick than to go to Hell healthy (Matthew 5:29-30). Our big job as a church is not putting food on people's tables. The big reason that we open our doors every day is so that the souls of men might be rescued from the flames of Hell.

That being the case, preachers can't be predominately concerned with retirement funds, fancy homes, or any other perks of the ministry—they must always be focused and enamored with the souls of men—that is the big driving purpose of a pastor's life. A pastor is to be a teacher of the Word of God.

The Relationship of the Pastor

The pastor who communicates the Word of God has a relationship with the people who receive that Word. The word *communicate* carries with it the idea of sharing or partnership. In other words, there is a bond that exists between the man who communicates the Bible and the people who receive the Word. Whenever God's Word is communicated and the transmitter is doing his job of disseminating it and the receiver is doing his job of absorbing it, at the very moment there is a spiritual bond that exists.

People who have benefited from the Word of God always have affinity toward the preacher who disseminated it. They feel a deep appreciation for that man because they have been helped spiritually by him. He has communicated to them the deepest truth that can possibly be communicated and has given them the very gospel of God, which is able to help them through the difficulties of life and help them understand what to do in difficult days. There is nothing that can help a person like dissemination of the Scripture; therefore, when a man of God stands up and hands out the Word of God and a person takes that Word of God and applies it to their situation, he feels love for and a bond with the man who has communicated that Word to him.

When people feel that bond, they want to give something back to him and the most practical way that can be done in this context is with money (cf. I Corinthians 9:11). The word carnal means material things—

it is talking about money. If someone benefits you spiritually, the reaction of that spiritual benefit is financial compensation. In other words, release from spiritual hell deserves and merits financial remuneration—that's the point the Bible is making here. What type of price tag can you put on spiritual help?

For example, I have a spiritual bond with my wife—my wife and I are spiritually one. Because Karen is such a spiritual help to me, I want to give money to her. If she wants a new dress, she's got it. If she wants her hair done, it's done. If she wants to make a long distance phone call to her relatives, no questions asked. If I have it in my power to do it, I will because of her value to me. I am going to take care of her the best way I can because of the benefit that she gives me. Karen's bond with me is much more than a sterile principle. Yes, as a husband, I recognize my moral responsibility to take care of my wife. But I don't have to read a Bible verse that commands me to take care of her. Because of the oneness that exists between us the money I earn is more hers than it is mine.

That same type of idea of repaying the support is the principle that Paul uses here by using the word *communicate*. If people feel the pastor is helping people spiritually through the Word of God, and if people understand the value of that help, they won't have to be commanded to take care of the preacher. It's not a sterile principle to pay the pastor—it's a passion. The same way that I feel passionate to take care of my wife because she has met my spiritual needs is the same way a congregation ought to feel toward their pastor. If a pastor is taking care of people spiritually, then the natural thing is for us to take care of that pastor. There is a bond that necessitates giving.

We should never oppress a hireling in their wages (Matthew 10:10). A worker is worthy of getting paid. When we go out to eat, we should not want a waitress to say that we under-tipped her. If people are doing the job, we ought to pay them for the job. People are worthy of their hire. The point that is being made here is that if you value a common laborer who is placing food on your table, how much more would you value the person disseminating the Word of God and helping your spiritual development? The pastor should be valued and it should be proven that he is valued with cash. We have a relationship with our pastors.

The Recommendation to the Pastor

Let's say these first two steps have been followed. The pastor knows his responsibility—he can't be enamored with money. He gives out the Word and the people of God respond to it with financial remuneration. What is the recommendation to the pastor in light of that? If the pastor knows his responsibility and he is rewarded for fulfilling that responsibility, he must keep something in mind. If he is rewarded sizably for being a pastor, he still has to teach the right things.

In other words, there is a seduction that comes with money. Money can cause people to do weird things. As a pastor, I have never ceased to be amazed at how good, sane, logical, spiritual people act like absolute hellions when a will is read. When money is under discussion, people go crazy. As soon as someone dies, even before the body is in the ground, people are fighting over the money left behind. If you and I aren't careful, money can change us. A love of money is the root of all kinds of evil. If the pastor, then, gets too comfortable in his job, he can become a hireling.

I remember when I received my first cell phone from the church where I ministered. Karen and I were going to the hospital to make a visit. I got out of the car and said, "Karen, do I have my cell phone?" She looked at me and said, "Do you have your Bible?" Money can change you and cause you to look at things that aren't really important and leave behind things that really are.

If I become too enamored with money, then I cease to give from the pulpit what people need every Sunday. I begin to tell people what they want to hear rather than what they need to hear. There is a sense in which I am accountable to people who pay my salary, but that is not where my ultimate accountability lies. My ultimate accountability lies with the Lord, and if I accommodate my message in any way because of the people who pay my salary, one day I will stand accountable before God for making that concession. A pastor's ultimate accountability is to the Lord who called him. A pastor must recognize his calling, and no amount of money should change that.

When I first started preaching in the chapel ministry of Highland Park, Dr. Jennings asked me one question. "Did God call you to preach?" To be honest with you, I didn't anticipate that question, but it was the only question he asked me. If it is true that God has called me to preach, then that answers everything else.

I'll tell you what the Hillview Baptist Chapel paid me for being their pastor—nothing. That church couldn't afford to pay me anything and that was fine. Occasionally, an old lady in the church would take us to lunch. I can assure you there was no pressure at that chapel. I could preach whatever I wanted to because what were they going to do - dock my salary? But I have to preach today with no encumbrance just like I did then. That's why I never want to see tithing records. I never wanted to be tempted to alter the message based on the financial repercussions of the sermon.

A pastor's responsibility is to teach the Word, and the people's responsibility is to give the pastor what he needs. A pastor can't let what the church is giving him affect him in any way, shape, or form. He has to preach the same thing he's always been preaching unencumbered by whatever the paycheck is. When the pastor knows his responsibility, the people respond to that responsibility financially, and the pastor doesn't let any of that go to his head, you have a good church. That's the circle that the apostle Paul creates in this verse to help us understand the relationship that the people and the pastor ought to have when it comes to the matter of paying the preacher.

CHAPTER FORTY-FOUR

Laws of Sowing and Reaping

Galatians 6:7-8

Since the very beginning of time when God created planet earth, He put certain laws into effect. For example, there is the law of gravity. If you jump off a building, you're not going to go up—you are going to go down. A lot of people have tried to see if the law of gravity is bendable, but it's not. God has put certain laws like that into effect.

One of the laws that God has put into effect is the law of sowing and reaping. It's simple when looking at this law from an agricultural standpoint. You put seed into the ground and you get a crop—that seems pretty simple. We seem to understand that whatsoever a man sows, he reaps. If he sows green beans, he's going to reap green beans. If a man sows peas, he reaps peas. We understand that as long as we're sticking with agriculture, but it's strange that when we move out of the realm of agriculture and apply it to other areas of life, people suddenly think that this law doesn't work or they try to get around it. The Bible is very clear that whatever you and I put into life, that is what we are going to get out of life.

To drive this point home, Paul gives us at the very beginning two very short, staccato statements: "Be not deceived" and "God is not mocked." The word *mock* actually comes from a root that means "to turn your nose up at something."

My wife and I have the exact opposite taste in eating. If she would like it, I probably wouldn't, and if I would like it, she wouldn't. For example, we went to lunch and my wife ordered a pecan waffle. I'm not going to eat a pecan waffle for lunch—that is the exact opposite of my taste—I got a piece of prime rib, medium with a little bit of blood. Just as I turned my nose up at her waffle, she turned up her nose at the prime rib. That curling of the nose at a repulsive thought is this word *mock*. Don't turn up your nose at God—when God declares something to be true, don't turn your nose up at God about it.

This comes from Ezekiel 8:17. In this passage, they couldn't curl their noses as high as they wanted to in the face of God. So they took a stick and upped their noses at God manually even a little bit more just because they couldn't get their noses as high as they wanted. God responds that if you turn your nose up at God, He will turn His nose up at you. It is a foolish thing for you and me to mock God because if we mock God, He will hold us in derision. What goes around, comes around. What you give to God is what you are going to get back. Don't be deceived about that and don't try to mock God.

The second thing that Paul says here in this short staccato statement is that if you try to mock God, you're a self-deceived person and the reason you are a self-deceived person is because you fail to understand this principle that what goes around, comes around. You think that you can turn your nose up at God and there not be any repercussion about it whatsoever. You are self-deceived to think that you can turn your nose up at God and there not be any ramifications about that—you are a deluded individual to think that way.

This word *deceived* is used in several key passages in the New Testament. The first is I Corinthians 6:9. This passage states that if you think you can live like the devil and claim inheritance in the kingdom of God, you are deceived—it doesn't happen.

A similar passage is I Corinthians 15:33. The verse tells us that you cannot hang out with the world and think it isn't going to affect your life. Who you hang out with will shape you. If you think you can hang out with the people of Hell and come out smelling like the scent of Heaven, you are a deceived person.

Over and over again the Bible says there are certain laws of God that we cannot violate without there being repercussions, and if we try to violate those laws and try to mock God, we are going to find out that it doesn't happen. We are deceived if we think we can violate the laws of God without repercussion. This brings us to the principles of sowing and reaping. This is an area of life where you and I so often delude ourselves and try to throw our noses up at God. We think that we can live in violation of these principles and there not be any repercussions. We think we can sow something into this life and reap something totally different—it doesn't work that way. Whatsoever a man sows, that is exactly what he is going to reap. What are the laws of sowing and reaping?

You Reap What You Sow

This is an irrefutable law of nature. If you put corn into the ground, you are going to reap corn. You cannot put corn into the ground and get grapes. It works this way with every crop. If you plant wheat in the ground, you get wheat; if you plant barley, you get barley; if you plant oats, you get oats; if you put beans into the ground, you are going to get beans; if you put radishes into the ground, you are going to get radishes; and if you put cucumbers into the ground, you are going to get cucumbers. Do you see a pattern developing here? Whatever you sow, that is exactly the thing that you are going to reap.

We completely understand this with agriculture and we think a person would be a complete moron to put corn in the ground and then cry because he didn't get wheat. But we don't get it when we get out of the realm of agriculture. We think we can sow one thing and reap another.

My Grandpa Massey quit going to school at the age of sixteen because he needed to help his family put food on the table to survive during the Great Depression. Grandpa Massey went to work in the coal mines of West Virginia simply to help his family survive. He recognized that his education was not nearly as important as giving to his family, and from that very moment, Grandpa set a precedent for the rest of his life. Grandpa was a giver. He gave to his sister so she could go to college when he himself did not even graduate from high school. When my sister and I were in school, every semester we were in school, Grandpa Massey paid for our books. When my dad was on strike at the steel plant, my grandpa made some Christian school payments for us so that we could have a nice Christmas.

At the end of Grandpa's life, he got four checks—he got a Social Security check, a check for black lung, a United Mine Workers retirement check, and a United Steel Workers check. Grandpa did well in retirement. Why did money come Grandpa's way? Grandpa sowed money; therefore, he reaped money. Even when I was in the early years of being a pastor, he would say, "Looks like those tires are getting a little thin, Amsbaugh. I think I need to buy you some tires." Grandpa never came around me when he didn't buy something for me.

One of Grandpa's daughters, Joyce, is a good giver—she sacrificially gives to people she doesn't even know. Because Joyce has sown money, Joyce reaps money—she is just like her dad. If you put in money, you get money. If you put in corn, you get corn. If you put in barley, you get barley—whatever you put in is what you get back. Whatsoever a man sows, that is the thing that he reaps.

What you want out of life is what you have to put into life, and we think the opposite. You're not going to get something from somebody unless you are giving something to somebody. You reap exactly the thing that you sow—nothing more, nothing less. You get back what you are putting into life.

You Reap after You Sow

Notice in these verses how sowing comes first. The Bible doesn't say, "Whatsoever a man reaps that shall he also sow." The Bible says, "... whatsoever a man soweth, that shall he also reap." In other words, to get a crop, you've got to sow some seed. When a man prays for a garden, God expects him to say amen with a hoe. You are going to get what you put in and you've got to put in first before you get something out of it. You cannot go to a field that is uncultivated and unsown, and say, "Lord, if it please Thee, reach down thy mighty hand and supply green beans. Amen." That's not going to happen.

You didn't put any green beans in the ground—you're trying to refute the law. If you want to reap something, you have to sow it, and it is not until you sow it that you are going to reap it.

I am amazed, especially when it comes to money, how generous people can be with money they don't have. They'll say, "Lord, if I win the lottery, I will be glad to give 10 percent of it to Thee." They're trying to refute the law of sowing and reaping. The law doesn't say if you reap, you get to sow—the law says if you sow, you get to reap. People are awful generous with what they don't have. I love the story about the preacher who went out to see Farmer Brown and asked, "Farmer Brown, if you had six cows, would you give God three?" Farmer Brown said, "I sure would." The preacher said, "If you had four cows, would you give God two?" Farmer Brown said, "You know it, preacher. If I had four cows,

I would give God two." The preacher said, "If you had two cows, would you give God one?" Farmer Brown said, "Preacher, that's not fair. You know I only have two cows." It's amazing how generous we can be with what we don't have.

How many times have you and I prayed, "Lord, give us money so we can give to thee"? We're messing with the law of sowing and reaping. The law doesn't say, "Whatsoever a man reaps, that shall he also sow." If you want it out of life, you have to put it into life. We understand that in agriculture, but we don't understand it in other areas. Many times we say, "Now, Lord, if you will do this and this, then I will give." God says, "No, it doesn't work like that. You have to take those little seeds that you have in your hand put those things in the ground. And until you put them in the ground, I'm not giving you a crop." You have to sow it if you want to reap it. You reap after you sow. That's the way the law works.

You Reap More than You Sow

You sow to the flesh and then out of your flesh, you reap more than you sow—corruption. If you sow to the Spirit, then out of the Spirit, you reap more than you sow—life everlasting. What you put into the ground is less than what you get out of it. You always reap more than you sow.

A man sows a kernel of corn into the ground and a stalk of corn grows out of that. I'm told that one single ear of corn has seven hundred and fifty kernels on it. A man sows one kernel and he gets a stalk, and that stalk probably has at least two ears of corn on it so he reaps at least one thousand, five hundred kernels per kernel planted. If I give up one kernel, and I get fifteen hundred back, that's a good deal. I have reaped more than I have sown. You always get more than what you put in.

A family in our home church had a farm. They didn't cultivate all of it, so they gave us a few rows so we could plant whatever we wanted. Mom and Dad would always say, "Okay, get in the car. We are going to plant the Blue Lake beans." What Mom had in her hands was a little package of seeds with a rubber band tied around it, and it could fit in the glove compartment. We went out there and raked up the dirt and tilled the ground and made the rows. Then we took that little package of seeds and started laying those seeds in the ground. That was in the spring. In the fall, we had to go and pick those beans. I guarantee you that what we picked did not fit in the glove compartment. We got bushel baskets to transport those beans home. We started with just a handful of seeds and ended up with a trunk full of beans.

God always works that way. In His economy, if you sow a handful, He will give you a basket full. That's what the Bible means when it says if you sow to the wind you are going to reap the whirlwind. I suppose a whirlwind is bigger than a wind. Whatever you sow, you are going to reap more of it.

I've heard people say, "Preacher, people are so mean to me and I don't understand it. I'm not the kindest person on the face of the earth, but people are really mean to me and I don't understand it." I understand it—you reap more than you sow. What you put into life, you are going to get more of it back. What you tolerate in moderation, other people heap upon you in excess. It is an irrefutable law of nature that what you put in the ground, you get more back out of it. Thus, if you are treating people moderately mean, don't be surprised if somebody slaps you upside the head. You reap more than you sow.

You Reap in Proportion to What You Sow

In another passage, the Bible says that if you sow sparingly, you will reap sparingly. The Bible also says that if you sow bountifully, you will reap bountifully (cf. II Corinthians 9:6). Reaping always stems from the proportion that you sow. If sowing one seed gives me a stalk of corn, guess what would happen if I sowed four seeds? I'm going to reap in proportion to what I sow. The more I sow, the more I'm going to reap. Praise God, there is no cap with the Lord. The more you keep putting in, the more you're going to keep getting out.

This is the opposite of the one-arm bandit. People go to Biloxi, Las Vegas, or Atlantic City and put money in a machine and pull the arm, and four lemons come up. The more you put in, the less you get back, but God doesn't work that way. When you throw what you have into God's kingdom, God gives you more back than you put in. God gives to you in proportion to what you give to Him.

Several years we had a major in the army who attended our church. One day he called me and said, "Pastor, I've got a question for you. Should I tithe on the net or the gross?" I don't want to just give people an answer because they'll say, "Pastor said this." I want them to think it through. I said to him, "Major, what do you want? Do you want net blessings or do you want gross blessings?" He said, "I guess gross is the way to go then, huh?" I said, "I want you to think it through, but yeah that's the way to go because you are stifling what God can do for you if you only tithe off a limited figure." He said, "Okay, thank you, sir," and he hung up.

Sometimes people ask me if I believe in tithing, and as simple as that question is, it is a difficult thing for me to answer. I believe that tithing is a great place to start, but I think it's a terrible place to finish. If you've been saved for twenty-five years and you are stuck on ten percent, your gauge is broke. If someone comes to me and asks where to start, I'll tell them to start at ten percent because that's what they did under the law, and under grace we should do no less than what they did under the law. But for the rest of your life, if you're pinching your pennies and stopping at ten percent, then you've capped what God can do in your life. You are sowing sparingly instead of bountifully.

We have to be careful that we don't stop our children when they want to give. When some of us were in our twenties and thirties, we had a very entrepreneurial spirit. Now that we are older and facing retirement, we are apprehensive to give like we used to. Fears often come with old age. Don't transfer those fears to your children when it comes to giving. You will stand accountable to God for doing that to your kid.

There are many old people who get mad at their kids for giving at the level that they gave at forty years ago. You and I need to be developing within our children the desire to take risks and to trust God when it comes to the matter of giving. We must be very careful that we do not squash that risk factor in our children when they start giving because what they do with their money is going to impact the blessings of God upon their lives.

These laws are so simple that any person who has the least bit of farming experience in the world will say, "Yeah, I can see that. You reap what you sow, after you sow, more than you sow, and in proportion to what you sow." These laws are irrefutable and they work. These laws work with peas, beans, barley, wheat, and oats, and they also work in nontangible things. Contextually, if we sow fleshly character traits, that's what we are going to reap. And if we sow to the Spirit, that's what we are going to get.

You and I have to recognize that regardless of whether we are talking about character or corn, these laws hold true and they are irrefutable. They do not alter and they do not change. If you and I think that we can ignore these laws, we stick our noses up at God and become deceived people. These principles work because God said so, and God is no liar. Don't try to outthink God on this. These laws will work in your life if you apply them.

CHAPTER FORTY-FIVE

Don't Quit

Galatians 6:9-10

Dr. Lee Roberson frequently told us Bible students, "Don't Quit!" Dr. Roberson used to always say, "Quitters never win, and winners never quit." I remember one day, Dr. Roberson came to chapel and he was very worked up. He had just left a counseling session with one of the preacher boys who told Dr. Roberson he was burned out and was going home. Dr. Roberson, who was in his seventies at the time, said, "Excuse me. I've never been burned out. I've traveled all across this country preaching in various cities all over the nation and I've never been burned out. Here's a little boy not even shaving yet telling me he is burned out and he is going home." Always in life I think there is a great temptation to quit.

There are various reasons why we get discouraged, but the Apostle Paul's admonition to us is very clear: Don't quit. No matter how discouraged you are, don't give up. This is Paul's final admonition to you and me—this is the last word. He essentially says, "If I could say one last thing before I wrap this thing up, here is what I want to say to you: Don't quit."

The Task of the Christian

The task of the Christian is to do well. What is doing well? In our society the word *well* has become a very static quality. We ask people how they are doing and they say, "I'm doing well." They mean that they are devoid of any illness—nothing bad is happening. Because The Christian in that sense should be doing more than well—a Christian should be doing good. I know that is not proper grammar, but when people ask me how I'm doing, I never say, "I'm doing well" because I want to be doing more than well—I want to be doing good.

Most people's religion is a religion of "nots." As long as they are not doing the taboo things, they feel their religion is okay. Because I don't do all of these unacceptable things, I'm an okay Christian. God does not want the Christian life merely to be the absence of vice. There are not only sins of commission in the Christian life, but there are also sins of omission. If you are merely abstaining from a bunch of vice and living in a vacuum, your life is not pleasing to God. God wants us to be doing some positive things for His honor and glory. God wants us to be permeating our society by doing good.

As a Christian, everywhere you go, you ought to be doing good. The task of the Christian is not merely to walk around this world and abstain from all the pollution that is out there—your job is to contribute something positive to a society that is on its way to a devil's Hell. God has put us on planet earth to do good—that is the task of the Christian.

The Temptation of the Christian

The temptation of the Christian is to grow weary in doing good. The word *weary* is the normal word for fainting—it carries with it the idea of becoming weak in the struggle, of capitulating to the problem, of living under the circumstances.

There are several reasons why you and I can become weary. First, we can become weary because of the opposition of other people. Do you ever get tired of people opposing you? Don't you just want to tell your critics to shut up? Not only do we have the opposition of others, but we have the misunderstanding of motives. Sometimes people misunderstand why we do what we do. You're serving the Lord and someone says, "I know why you're serving God—you just want recognition." No, you just want to honor your Saviour. Sometimes your motives are misjudged by other people and they think they know exactly why you are doing ministry and they don't have a clue as to why you are doing it.

When Charles Spurgeon was living in England and preaching there, he and his wife had some laying hens and the hens always produced more eggs than Dr. and Mrs. Spurgeon needed, so they sold the remainder of the eggs that they didn't need. People many times criticized the Spurgeons for selling those eggs. They said, "The Metropolitan Tabernacle is paying you enough money. How dare you sell those eggs! You ought to be giving those eggs away. If you had any charitable heart at all, you would give those eggs away." The Spurgeons never responded to that criticism. It was only after they died that people found out that the money they got from selling those eggs was given away to dozens of widows in the city of London. They didn't keep a dime of it.

People had misjudged their motives.

We can also get weary because no one appreciates our efforts. Sometimes when we do a lot nobody seems to recognize it. We begin to think that it just doesn't pay to do right. We get sick of doing right because nobody notices. For all these reasons and more, we are tired and want to quit—we want to faint.

My daughter Amy is a fainter. We've had her checked by doctors, but if she doesn't eat a certain amount of food, she passes out. We often had to pack her some bananas and crackers so she could get a little snack along the way because if she didn't get that snack, she would faint. You and I have to be constantly fortified and nurtured with the Word of God because if we are not receiving daily nutrition, we are going to faint in the battle.

There's a constant struggle in life to fight depression. God frequently told Joshua to be strong and of a good courage. How often discouragement comes our way! Depression is rampant. Finances, relationships, and schedules can make us weary in doing the good thing, and we can very easily get into a discouraged state of mind. Our task is to do good, but the temptation is that in the midst of doing good we can become weary.

The Truth for the Christian

The truth for the Christian is found in the latter part of verse 9. If you faint, you don't reap, but if you stay strong, payday is coming. There is a harvest for those who don't get weary in well-doing. The analogy, of course, is taken from agriculture. The farmer has to do a lot of labor before he can sink his teeth into the harvest. He has to cultivate the soil, plant the seed, pull the weeds, water the plants, and fertilize. The only way the farmer is going to reap a harvest is if he doesn't quit before the harvest. He has to stay with it through that long, protracted period of time because if he quits prematurely, he is not going to reap a harvest. The same is true of the child of God. The harvest always comes to the child of God who refuses to quit.

When I was little, my dad would always take me to see the Cleveland Indians play baseball. One summer when we were there, the Indians were playing the Yankees, and it is just written in the codes and bylaws of Indians baseball that if you like the Indians, you hate the Yankees. During this particular game, the Yankees were killing us, and finally, about the seventh inning, Dad said, "Come on, let's go." We walked out to the car and started home. Dad turned on the radio to see how the game was going. To our surprise, the Indians had loaded the bases. As we were traveling down the interstate, an Indian hit a grand slam that gave the Cleveland Indians the victory in that game. We left in the seventh inning and missed seeing the victory.

I think there are many Christians who don't see victory because they pull out too early. Victory is always on the horizon for the child of God if he doesn't quit or get weary in well-doing. There are all kinds of people who went to Bible college with the idea of serving the Lord. Bible college towns are full of people who went off to Bible college and had every intention of one day sewing the Lord. And some dean gave them a rule that put their nose out of joint, and they gave up and got weary in well-doing. Now, they are just a resident of that city, not doing anything for God because they got weary in well-doing. God had wonderful things planned for their lives but they got weary.

The problem is they've forgotten when the harvest is. The harvest doesn't always happen immediately—it comes to those who absolutely refuse to get weary in well-doing. The promise of God is very clear: in due season we shall reap if we faint not.

I heard a story many years ago about this farmer who lived in Iowa. In the same town was another farmer who was an atheist. A tornado came to town and totally destroyed the crops of Christian farmer, yet totally bypassed the crops of the atheist. The atheist ranted in the paper of that Iowa town, "I don't believe in God and look at the bumper harvest that I have. Look at this Christian who loves and serves God—he has nothing to show for it." The Christian replied to that scalding rebuke with one line of rebuttal in the paper, "God does not settle all His accounts in the month of October." God will always reward in His time the people who do not get weary in well-doing. That is the truth for the Christian.

The Timing for the Christian

Two Greek words in verse 10 are translated with the solitary English word *therefore*. The Greek phrase conveys the concept of truly grasping something. Really get it. Because there is a harvest that can be reaped out there, you and I must act now. The word *opportunity* refers to a fixed, distinct period of time. Paul is not referring to occasional opportunities arising. He is rather saying that we have a specific period of time to act. He is saying that now is the opportunity for you and I to do something with our seed.

If you wait to plant, cultivate, fertilize, and water, you are not going to get a harvest. The harvest comes to people who seize the opportunity and do what they must do now because if they don't do it now, it's not going to get done. While you are living here on earth, you have an opportunity to do something. This is the day when service is rendered. We must work while it is day, for the night is coming when no man can work. You cannot wait for tomorrow because tomorrow may never come.

Service for God is always placed in the immediate. You only have this hour. You are not guaranteed tomorrow, and you don't know what tomorrow holds. Thus, now is the time.

The Tenderness of the Christian

The good that we do, we must do now, and he makes it clear that we must do it to all men. There ought not to be a single person outside the reach of our goodness. I am to do good, not just to people who have reached a certain socio economic strata. I'm to do good, the Bible says, unto all men—especially those who are of the household of faith. When Paul uses that word *household*, he uses a family term. You can have love for everybody, but there is something about people who are your kin that makes you feel even more for them.

My daughter, April, knows how much I love The Andy Griffith Show and she bought me the entire third season on DVD. There is only one person who likes Andy Griffith more than me, and it's her. I was teasing her a little bit and said, "I know why you bought this present for me. It's so you can watch it." Right away my wife piped up and said, "No, that is not the reason she did it. She did it because she loves you and is concerned about you. How dare you question her motives!" That's mommy sticking up for her children! Karen is always sticking up for the girls—it's a mother thing. Family takes up for family— that's what families do.

I once had a deacon whose brother came under discussion, and he defended his brother. Someone said, "You are just defending him because he's your brother." I said, "Of course, he is defending him because he is his brother. If a brother doesn't defend a brother, who is going to defend the brother?" Obviously, if we are going to do good to anybody, we are going to do good for our kinfolk.

May I say to you that there is a family that is thicker than blood and it is the family of faith? I'm so glad for the household of faith. If Christians don't stick up for Christians, who is going to stick up for Christians? The Apostle John says that a sure sign a person has been saved is that he has love for the brothers. There is just something about being in the family of God that makes you want to be around family.

Sunday is my favorite day of the week because I get to hang out with my family. Every Sunday is a family re-union. I like the song that says, "I'm so glad I'm a part of the family of God."

One time when I was a little kid about four years old, Dad brought me into the Grace Bible Church where we were attending in Ohio, and there was a seventy-year-old man named Brother Keifer. Everybody just revered Brother Keifer—he had a great testimony, and everybody would just stop by and say, "Good evening, Brother Keifer." So as a four-year-old boy, I looked up at that seventy-year-old man and said, "Evening, Brother Keifer." Everyone around me started laughing. Here was a four-year-old calling a seventy-year-old man "brother."

The song continues, "You'll notice we say brother and sister 'round here. It's because we're a family and these folks are so dear. When one has heartache, we all shed a tear, and rejoice in each victory in this family so dear." Because there is that family bond, we have to do good now because the time will come when that opportunity is going to vanish.

As a pastor, I have conducted many funerals. One of the most agonizing things about a funeral is to see an adult child come up to the casket of an elderly parent and shed tears because they knew they should have done something to make things right and they didn't do it. They knew that there was a wedge between them and their parent, and one day sooner or later down the road, they were going to get it resolved. They had every intention of one day doing good for their mom or dad but that opportunity, just like a vapor, vanished away. And now they stand over a casket shedding tears onto a cold corpse because the opportunity has faded and there is no opportunity to do good in the household.

If you are weary and you quit now, think about how weary you are going to be when the opportunity to have done good in the household vanished without you doing good.

> Have you knelt beside the rubble of an aching, broken heart,
> When the things you gave your life to fell apart?
> You're not the first to be acquainted with sorrow, grief, or pain,
> But the Master promised sunshine after rain.
> Hold on my child, joy comes in the morning.
> Weeping only lasts for the night;
> Hold on my child, joy comes in the morning,
> The darkest hour means dawn is just in sight.

CHAPTER FORTY-SIX

Be Sure to Read the Large Print

Galatians 6:11-13

Paul starts off this passage of Scripture by drawing attention to the large letters that he is using. He's not referring to the length of the epistle; he's referring to the size of the letters that he is using in this epistle. In other words, he is drawing attention to the fact that he is using his own hand. In our society, people are always quick to tell us to look at the fine print. Paul here is saying the opposite; he is telling them to look at the big print and see what it's all about.

Let's put this statement into context. In verse 10, Paul says that we ought to do good to all men. So whatever he is talking about by drawing attention to these large letters, he is talking about Christians doing good. Then in verses 12 through 15 he talks about the false teachers and how bad their false doctrine is. Thus, Christians ought to be doing good, and the teaching of the false teachers was really bad. Merging those two thoughts he says, "Look at these large letters that I'm using."

Paul wrote with large letters for a variety of reasons. I personally believe that Paul's thorn in the flesh was bad eyesight. You remember at the time of his conversion when he was on the road to Damascus to go arrest some Christians, Jesus made Himself known to Paul with a great light. This light produced temporary blindness. Paul makes mention of the residual effect of that blindness in Galatians 4:15, referring to his noticeably bad eyes. It wasn't just that he had an eye problem; he had a physically noticeable eye problem.

In Bible times, people used large-letter public notices to make something stand out. It is similar to us sending an email in all caps. We are stressing the content of what is being said.

That seems to explain the idea, especially in light of verse 12, that the false teachers desired to make a fair show of the flesh. Paul was not trying to impress people with his scholarship like these false teachers were. They were people who always said things with eloquence in order to fool people with a fair show of the flesh. Paul is not so concerned with making an impression as he is with stressing the content of what he is saying.

Because Paul's eyesight was so poor, he normally dictated his letters to a secretary. In this letter, however, Paul took pen in hand and wrote the entire letter with his own hand so that they would know how important it was. We could really say that the book of Galatians was the first large-print edition of the Bible because this book was written entirely with large letters so that the people who were receiving it would know that it came from Paul. In so doing, they would grasp the importance of the content. The Galatians needed to see these facts in large print. What does this large print show about Paul? And what does teach us?

It Stresses the Fact that We Are Not Proud

The false teachers were motivated by pride. They

wanted to make a good showing of the flesh. They were not concerned with an inward righteousness; they were concerned with an outward impression.

A lot of Christians are like that today. They aren't concerned with inward righteousness; they're concerned with outward impression. One of the dangers of having a hyper-conservative ministry is that people assume outward standards insure a right relationship with God. But an outward impression never produces an inward righteousness. The Bible is very clear that you and I should be predominately concerned with inward righteousness, not outward impression. In other words, righteousness always comes from the inside out, never from the outside in. The heart must be right with God.

If, for example, I am merely giving so people will see it, I'm not rewarded for that kind of giving (Matthew 6:1). If I am merely praying so people can see it, I'm not rewarded for that kind of praying. If I'm merely fasting so people can see it, I'm not rewarded for that kind of fasting. God is not concerned with my making an outward show of the flesh to impress someone. I ought to be doing what I'm doing because my heart loves God, not because I want to impress my neighbors.

Jesus told a parable in Luke 18 about two people who went up to the temple to pray - one was a Publican and the other was a Pharisee. The Pharisee bragged on himself loud enough in the temple so everyone would hear him. The publican wouldn't even lift up his eyes to Heaven, but the Bible says he beat upon his chest and said, "God, be merciful to me a sinner." Jesus said that the publican was the one who went down to house justified. It was the one who was humble rather than the one who was trying to make a big impression. No act that is filled with religious conceit pleases God. The Bible says in Isaiah 64:6 that all of our righteousness is nothing more than filthy rags. Any work that you and I do that claims to gain the smile of God is bogus.

God doesn't love Jeff Amsbaugh because he goes visiting. God does not love Jeff Amsbaugh because he attends church on a frequent basis. God does not love Jeff Amsbaugh because of how he cuts his hair or how he adorns himself. I am only accepted of God for one reason—the merit of the Lord Jesus Christ. Paul, of course, came to this stark realization when he was on the road to Damascus. He was walking to Damascus full of religious pride and hypocrisy, and then he ran into Jesus. In that moment, he had an epiphany that was very shocking. Paul realized that all of his religious activity was worth nothing.

Paul thought he was pretty good with God because of all the things that he had done, and then he recognized in that moment that it had nothing to do with him. It had everything to do with Jesus. His pride was dealt a death blow that day by the light that shined upon him. That light left him blind, and I believe that his eyesight was permanently affected by it so that every time the apostle Paul picked up a pen, he was reminded again that it was not him, it was God.

I think in our zeal to fight the charismatic movement, we have made an erroneous statement. I've heard people say that when God heals people, it is always complete and instantaneous. I don't think that is accurate. Jesus, you remember, healed a blind man and when he opened the guy's eyes, Jesus asked, "What do you see?" The man said, "I see men as trees walking." The first healing was not complete. The man still saw a blur. I believe that God healed Paul of his blindness, but I still believe there were some problems left behind to teach Paul a lesson.

When I had Friedreich's Ataxia, I couldn't take more than ten steps without falling down. My parents called for the pastors of all the independent churches to come over and anoint me with oil and pray that God would heal me, and I believe that God did. There is only one documented case of healed Friedreich's Ataxia in the history of the United States and it's me. The doctors said that by age thirty-five, I would be completely bedridden and that I would not live to see my fifty-first birthday. When my neurologist released me, the neurologist said, "You've got nerve endings that you didn't even have before. I don't understand this." Well, I understood it completely because I have a great God.

There are still times, however, when I walk around the mall and feel the remnants of Friedreich's Ataxia, however slight, in my legs. There are days when I really battle pain in my legs, and I think that is because when I was sixteen and had that disease, I was arrogant. I cut my hair just right and adorned myself the way all good Baptists do. God was repulsed with my pride and had to teach me a lesson. I recognized that day that I needed Him. I needed the anointing of God on my life—it wasn't my talent; it was His power.

God brought me to that realization, and even though God healed me, He wants me to be reminded of where I could have been had His grace not intervened in my life. Just as the remnants of Paul's eyesight lingered, so the remnants of ataxia remain to some small degree in my life to remind me of my need of Him. It is all vain unless the power of God is upon it.

The message is written to the false teachers, and Paul is writing with big letters to let them know that all they are concerned about is pride, but true Christianity is concerned with humility. It is about His power, not about our pride, and the large print proves it.

It Proves that We Are Not Cowards

There was another reason these false teachers embraced error. It was not merely to make a show of the flesh, but also because they were cowards. They did not want to embrace the reproach of the cross. The cross is the paramount symbol of Christianity. In the first century, crosses were not being sold in local Christian bookstores—people were not buying crosses as pieces of jewelry and wearing them around their necks. In the first century, crosses were not ornamentation. A cross was not anything that anybody gloried in; it was a means of execution. The cross had a stigma. How strange, then, that Paul gloried in the cross (Galatians 6:14)! Think about what the cross was—it was the blood, the sacrifice, the slaughter, and the gore, and it is still an offense to an unbelieving world. That's why liberal denominations take out all reference to blood in their hymnals. The cross in an offense (I Corinthians 1:23).

I had a professor in Bible college who was witnessing to a Jewish man, and the Jewish man looked at him in anger and said, "I'll tell you one thing. When my Messiah comes, He won't be hanging on any cross." You see the reproach and the stigma of it all. In the first century, those who embraced the cross were subject to persecution. It is not as overt today, but it is still there. You go to any secular college campus today and tell them you are a Bible-believing Christian and they will say that you are crazy. There's still a stigma associated with the cross.

Those who embrace the cross are subject to persecution; therefore, people tend to back off and look for another religion that doesn't carry that stigma with it. Paul could have used a secretary to avoid the stigma of Christianity, but he chose not to.

I was at a board meeting once facing a difficult decision. We knew the decision we were about to make was right. We had to assign a messenger boy to communicate the decision, and one board member said, "I don't mind doing it." The board member recognized that there was going to be a stigma attached to the decision, and it would be better if he protected me from that stigma. I appreciated that kind of friendship. Paul could have had a secretary go do something for him so he could have avoided the stigma of saying this with his own hand. Cowards are afraid to embrace the cross, but Paul was no coward. He asked for his pen, and his large print clearly revealed that he was no coward. We need people today who will stand up and say, "I am no coward. I am willing to take the reproach."

It Proves that We Are Not Hypocrites

False teachers try to get people to do what they themselves could not do and that is keep the law. People who are legalists try to get other people to do what they themselves don't do and can't do. Legalism always tries to impose a burden that the legalist himself cannot bear. It is me trying to get you to do something that I myself cannot do (cf. Matthew 23:2).

We are all like that, aren't we? We have great ideas for other people. If you're not going to be part of the solution, don't bring up the problem. You ought to be willing to get involved and help solve whatever the dilemma is, but legalists are not like that. They are always telling you how you can be a better Christian if you do this and that. Don't ask them to do it, but they are willing for you to do it.

In writing this letter, Paul didn't ask his secretary to do it. He gladly took the pen in his hand and said, "I'll take care of this." Unlike the false teachers, he was no hypocrite. We have to be very careful that we are not hypocrites in the things that we do. I think there are many people who are quick to point out things that they themselves are guilty of. I have to be very careful that I don't practice things that I'm condemning. Nothing sticks in people's minds like a hypocrite.

One of the hardest things to be as a pastor and as a

parent is consistent. It's easy to make decisions according to mood rather than principle, and every week people want you to bend a rule. But you have to be consistent. True, authentic Christianity doesn't operate with duplicity and hypocrisy—it is the real deal all the time and doesn't demand stuff of other people when it is not willing itself to engage in it. Any time I stand at the pulpit and lift the Bible to encourage the congregation to do something in their Christian life, I have to make sure that I'm doing the same thing in my Christian life. Every time you are pointing a finger at somebody else, you have three pointing right back at you.

Let's make sure that we get out there with our large-print editions of the Bible, and let's make our own lives large-print editions of the Bible. Let's do it without pride. Let's do it without cowardice. And let's do it without hypocrisy.

I always want my life to be a transparent life. I want my life to be an open book. You are the only Bible that somebody will ever read, and because that's true, you need to make sure that what people see stands out in sharp relief. In large letters, let them see your life as God intended the Christian life to really be seen.

You're writing a gospel, a chapter each day,
By the deeds that you do and the words that you say.
People read what you write, distorted or true.
What is the gospel, according to you?

CHAPTER FORTY-SEVEN

Glorying in the Cross

Galatians 6:14

What a shocking, yet what a tremendous statement, we find in this verse from the pen of the Apostle Paul. We find that great missionary statesman and apostle of the Lord Jesus Christ glorying in the cross. Now we have to remember that when Paul penned these words people were not buying crosses in Christian bookstores. People were not wearing crosses around their necks or on their lapels. For when the Apostle Paul penned these words, a cross was known for only one thing, and that was a means of execution. The Apostle's statement is equivalent to someone today glorying in lethal injection, or in a hangman's noose, or a firing squad, or an electric chair. No one would dare think, let alone say, that he was glorying in a cross.

Why the Bible itself says, "Cursed is everyone who hangs on a tree." And yet my friends that day when the God-man trudged up Calvary's mountain, and had his hands and his feet nailed to the tree, and was suspended between heaven and earth, something that day happened to this terrible and awful means of execution. It was magnified; it was sanctified; it was glorified. So much so, that now the Apostle Paul tells his readers at the church of Galatia that the cross, this terrible, cruel, malicious, form of execution is something we as believers can glory in.

On a hill far away stood an old rugged cross,
The emblem of suffering and shame;
And I love that old cross where the dearest and best
For a world of lost sinners was slain.

So I cherish the old rugged cross,
Till my trophies at last I lay down;
I will cling to the old rugged cross,
And exchange it some day for a crown.

Oh, my friends, let me tell you,

Beneath the cross of Jesus
I fain would take my stand,
The shadow of a mighty rock
Within a weary land;
A home within the wilderness,
A rest upon the way,
From the burning of the noon-tide heat,
And the burden of the day.

I take, O cross, the shadow
For my abiding place;
I ask no other sunshine than
The sunshine of thy face;
Content to let the world go by,
To know no gain nor loss.
My sinful self my only shame,
My glory all the cross.

Let us then take a few moments to glory in the cross.

Because the Cross Is Exalted

The cross is exalted in the Bible. In I Peter 1:11, Peter speaks about the Old Testament prophets who prophesied of the sufferings of Christ. It was the claim of Jesus, in His conversation with the two disciples on the way to Emmaus, that Moses, and all the prophets, indeed, all the Scriptures, dealt with the subject of His death (Luke 24-:27, 44). The atonement is the scarlet cord running through every page in the Bible. Cut the Bible anywhere, and it bleeds; it is red with redemptive truth. One out of every 24 verses in the New Testament deals with this theme. The death of Christ is mentioned 175 times in the New Testament. The cross is exalted in the Bible.

The cross was exalted at Bethlehem. Hebrews 2:14 makes it plain that Jesus became a partaker of flesh and blood in order to die. I John 3:5 says that He was manifested to take away our sins. We are not putting the matter too strongly when we say that Jesus was born to die. You cannot worship the babe in the manger and reject the Christ on the cross. Those little soft hands were fashioned inside Mary's womb in order that one day they might drive nails into them. Those pink baby's feet were fashioned in order that one day they might take a walk up Golgotha's hill. His sweet infant brow was fashioned in order that one day they might rip it apart with thorns. They covered him with swaddling clothes in order that one day He might hang exposed to the world. This baby was born to die. The cross was exalted at Bethlehem.

The cross is exalted in our belief. Paul told the Corinthian church that the very first plank in the Gospel message is the fact that Christ died for our sins according to the Scriptures (I Corinthians 15:3). There can be no gospel story apart from the story of the death of Christ as the redeemer of men.

> Good news, good news, Christ died for me.
> Good news, good news, if I believe.
> Good news, good news, I'm saved eternally.
> That's wonderful extra good news.
> The cross is exalted in our belief.

And then the cross is exalted in the by and by. One of my favorite chapters in the entire Bible is Revelation 5. The chapter opens with the Apostle John weeping because no man was found worthy to open, to read, or even to look upon the book. One of the elders comes over and speaks to John telling him not to weep because the Lion of the tribe of Judah has prevailed to open the book. As John looks through his tear-stained eyes, instead of seeing a lion, he sees a lamb, and not only a lamb, but a bludgeoned lamb. And that abused Lamb takes the book out of the right hand of Him who sits on the throne. That act initiates a spontaneous song, "Worthy is the lamb that was slain." My friends, the theme song of heaven is that of Christ's death.

> I love to tell the story,
> 'Twill be my theme in glory
> To tell the old, old story
> Of Jesus and His love.

The cross is exalted in the Bible, at Bethlehem, in our belief, and in the by and by. I glory in the cross because the cross is exalted.

Because of How the Cross Is Explained

How would you explain what happened that day on Calvary's cross? The Bible uses several descriptive terms to explain the crucifixion of Christ. These terms when understood will definitely cause us to glory in the cross.

First, the cross is explained as a ransom. The Bible tells us in Matthew 20:28 that Jesus came to give His life as a ransom. Now what is a ransom? Leviticus 25:47-49 tells us that a ransom is the act of delivering a person or thing by paying a price. According to Romans 7:14, we were sold under sin. We were in bondage to sin, and we needed deliverance. That deliverance was accomplished by Christ paying the price. And that price was His own precious blood. Nothing less would do. Let us understand this morning that we were not redeemed with corruptible things, but with the precious blood of Christ (I Peter 1:18-19).

All my life I dreamed of good fortune,
And there were times I sought to be honored by men;
And yet if I owned the richest of kingdoms,
Still I could not save myself from my sin.

Too precious by far to be sold
Or ransomed with mere earthly gold.
If wealth were the way, all earth could not pay
The price that could save a man's soul.

Jesus Christ stepped into history to redeem our souls with the shedding of His own precious blood. And that ransom price was not paid to Satan either. God has never owed Satan one thin dime. Galatians 3:13 makes it plain that Christ redeemed us from the curse of the law. The ransom price was paid to the demands of Christ's own righteous, perfect, sinless law. We have been redeemed.

A second term that is used to explain the cross is the word *propitiation*. The Bible tells us in Romans 3:25 that Jesus was set forth to be propitiation. Now what is propitiation? This same word translated *propitiation* in Romans 3:25 is translated *mercy seat* in Hebrews 9:5.

In the Old Testament holy of holies there was the Ark of the Covenant. And in that ark was placed the tables of stone. Over the ark between the two cherubs dwelt the Shekinah glory of God. And that glorious divine presence constantly looked down on that law in the box, a law that Israel had broken many times. And what a contrast! A broken law was in the presence of a holy God. It graphically pictured that all had sinned and come short of the glory of God (cf. Romans 3:23). Consequently, the high priest would come into that holy of holies with his back to the divine presence. And with his hyssop that had been dipped in blood, that priest would sprinkle blood on the top of the box so that God would view that broken law through a shed blood. And that place where the blood was sprinkled, and the divine anger was appeased, was called the mercy seat. And what that Old Testament ritual was in type, Jesus was in reality. He stepped between the holiness of God and the broken law which had been written in our hearts and appeased the anger of God with the application of His own precious blood. He is our propitiation.

Third, Christ's death is explained as reconciliation. Romans 5:10 tells us that when we were enemies to God, we were reconciled to God by the death of his Son. Job prayed for a daysman (an umpire) who would lay hands upon both he and God and settle the dispute between them (Job 9:33). Job needed a mediator between God and himself.

No doubt you have seen a football game where an umpire stepped between two fighting players. And laying his hands on both players, the umpire settled the dispute. That is exactly what Jesus Christ did through His cross. He reconciled me to God. Ephesians 2:16 says that the enmity was slain by the cross. Colossians 1:20 says that he made peace through the blood of his cross. I have been reconciled.

And then the cross of Christ is explained in Scripture as a substitution. Romans 5:8 says while we were still sinners Christ died for us. Now if there is anybody in the universe who should understand that word *for* it is Jeff Amsbaugh. I went to a small Christian school where everyone who went out for the basketball team made the basketball Consequently, I played end, guard, and tackle. I sat at the end of the bench, guarded the water bottles, and tackled anybody who tried to get them. Now if the game was well in hand, if we were ahead by fifty points with 30 seconds left, the coach would say,

"Amsbaugh go in for Smith." I knew what the word *for* meant; it was a word of substitution. So when the Bible says that Jesus died for us, I understand that Jesus was my substitute. Jesus took my place. Jesus bore the penalty of my sin. Jesus died for me. And that substitution, that absorbing of my penalty, took place on the tree (I Peter 2:24).

> Oh can it be, upon a tree
> The Saviour died for me?
> My soul is thrilled, my heart is filled,
> To think He died for me!

Because the Cross Is Essential

The cross is essential because the holiness of God demands it. Jesus said in Matthew 5:20 that our righteousness must exceed the righteousness of the scribes and Pharisees. There were no better rule keepers than the Pharisees, but Jesus says we need a better righteousness than that. Why? All our righteousness is filthy rags (Isaiah 64:6). Every old lady that has been walked across the street, every box of girl scout cookies that has ever been bought, every noble deed that has been done for the charity of your choice is nothing more than a polluted, filthy, puss-filled rag in the sight of a holy God.

We need a better goodness than that, a better righteousness than that. Praise God the Bible tells us in I Corinthians 1:30 that Christ is made unto us righteousness. The only righteousness that is good enough to take us to heaven is the righteousness of Jesus Christ. The holiness of God makes the cross essential.

The cross is also essential because of the sinfulness of man. If sin is regarded as merely an offense against man, as a weakness of human nature, as a mere disease, or alternate lifestyle, there was no reason for Jesus to die. On the other hand, if sin is rebellion, and transgression, and enmity against God, if it is something condemning and punishable, then the atonement is absolutely necessary and essential.

We must see sin as God sees it. It is something which brings wrath, condemnation, and eternal ruin in its train. We must see it as guilt which needs expiation. We confess sin today in such light and easy terms, that it has almost lost its terror. And light erroneous views of the atonement come from light and erroneous views of sin.

The accident theory, and the martyr theory, and the moral-example theory, and the governmental theory, and the love of God theory of the atonement, all suffer from the same weakness. They have watered down the severity of sin. Jesus died for sins. That is what makes his cross so essential.

And then the cross is essential because it fulfills Scripture. In Luke 24:25-27, Jesus made it plain that his death was the fulfillment of Old Testament prophecy. Jesus had to die in the way that He died for Old Testament Scripture to be fulfilled thus making His cross essential.

Because the Cross Is Extended

Let us not think that the death of Christ is only for

a select few. Oh, my friends, He is the propitiation not for our sins only, but also for the sins of the whole world (I John 2:2). The Lamb of God takes away the sin of the world (John 1:29). He gave Himself a ransom for all (I Timothy 2:6). We do not have to wonder if the cross and its offer of salvation has been limited to a select, elect group. The cross is extended to the whole world.

And that means, my friend, it is extended to you personally. Hebrews 2:9 says that He tasted death for every man. I was once told that Jesus died for all sin, but not for all men. That simply is not true. Jesus tasted death for every man. And that means you.

Sometimes we get to thinking that Jesus died for the whole world, and I'm just a little bit of the whole world; therefore just a little bit of Jesus death was for me. My friends, Jesus took all your hell for you. He tasted death for you personally. While it is true that His death extends to the whole world, it is equally true that His death extends to each individual man.

Third, Jesus death extends to sinners. Christ died for the ungodly (Romans 5:6), for those who violently and brazenly refuse to pay their dues to God. He died for sinners (Romans 5:8), those who are in open opposition to God. He died for His enemies (Romans 5:10), those who constantly fight against Him and His cause. He died for the unjust (I Peter 3:18), those who openly violate His laws. Paul said in I Timothy 1:15 that Christ Jesus came into the world to save sinners. Jesus did not come to call the righteous, but sinners to repentance (Matthew 9:13).

Saints are made from sinners,
Out of losers, not from winners,
Out of those who've fallen on their faces,
Last men in in all the races.
Jesus comes a callin'
Not the risen, but the fallen,
Not the strong and the succeeding,
But the broke and bruised and bleeding.
Is that you my friend, oh is that you?
He will not receive you
If you stubbornly conceive you
Have no need of being pardoned,
If your mind and will are hardened.
But if you will now confess
That you are something so much less
Than He designed your life to be
You're on your way to being free.
Let's break the trend my friend,
Let's break the trend.

The cross is extended to sinners.

And then finally, it would compel me to tell you that the cross is only extended efficaciously to those who believe. I Timothy 4:10 tells us that Christ is the Saviour of all men, specially of those that believe. His death is sufficient for all, but efficient for those who believe. The invitation is unlimited, but the application is limited to those who believe. He saves all potentially, but believers alone effectually.

And therefore, my friend, you have a decision to

make. You must place your complete confidence and trust in the finished work of Christ on Calvary's cross.

Tho' millions have found him a friend
And have turned from the sins they have sinned,
The Saviour still waits to open the gates
And welcome a sinner before it's too late.
There's room at the cross for you,
There's room at the cross for you;
Tho' millions have come,
There's still room for one,
Yes, there's room at the cross for you.

Yes, my friends, I glory in the cross today. I glory because the cross is exalted. I glory because the cross is explained. I glory because the cross is essential. I glory because the cross is extended.

In the cross of Christ I glory,
Towering o'er the wrecks of time;
All the light of sacred story
Gathers round its head sublime.

When the woes of life o'ertake me,
Hope's deceive, and fears annoy,
Never shall the cross forsake me;
Lo! It glows with peace and joy.

When the sun of bliss is beaming
Light and love upon my way,
From the cross the radiance streaming
Adds mere luster to the day.

Bane and blessing, pain and pleasure,
By the cross are sanctified;
Peace is there, that knows no measure,
Joys that through all time abide.

I will glory in the cross, in the cross,
Lest His suffering should all be in vain.
I will weep no more for the cross that He bore.
I will glory in the cross.

CHAPTER FORTY-EIGHT

Why Grace Is My Favorite Word

Galatians 6:15-18

Grace is my favorite word. I think it is providential that I have been pastor of two churches that have been called Grace—it's hard to beat that word. The word *grace* is full of meaning. I'm very thankful that there was a day in my life when the grace of God intervened and made a transforming difference in my life.

Grace is so full of meaning, and every day we ought to thank the Lord that there is such a thing as grace. Many times people think that life is not fair, and I'm always thankful that it's not. If life were fair, you and I would be in a hot place in Hell today, but there is something that intervened. I thank the Lord for His grace.

The Reality of Grace

When we place our faith in the Lord Jesus Christ, He makes us new people. We received a new heart that was created to love God and His people. God did a miracle in our hearts. It doesn't matter whether you are circumcised or uncircumcised. What matters is that you've had that heart change when God took away the heart of stone and replaced it with a heart of flesh that beats for the things of God. Circumcision or uncircumcision is not the big deal. The big deal is that you and I have been made new creatures. There is a point in your life where God can actually make something new out of you.

593

Sometimes, you and I wish that we could reboot life. We all from time to time wish that we could start over. Nicodemus asked, "Can a man enter into his mother's womb a second time and be born?" The answer is a resounding yes! There is a way to begin again. If any man is in Christ, he becomes a new creation (II Corinthians 5:17). Praise the Lord there is such a thing as a new birth and this is what matters. It's not whether you've had a religious ritual preformed on you—that doesn't matter—what matters is that your heart has been changed by a divine encounter with the Lord Jesus Christ.

When you become that new creature, you get new desires and new habits, and you do things that you couldn't have envisioned doing in your pre-Christian days. God performs a spiritual heart transplant on the person who exercises faith. God completely changes a person when he becomes saved—He changes us from the inside out. No spiritual gymnastics can accomplish this, no twelve-step program can do this, no weekend seminar that you pay a registration fee for can accomplish this—the only thing that can accomplish this is a personal encounter with the Lord Jesus Christ. Thus, we must place our faith in Him. This is the only thing that can accomplish change.

Years ago after my grandfather had gone through a twelve-step program that had completely reformed his life. He thought he was on his way to Heaven because he had been through this program. My dad, who was witnessing to his father, told him, "Dad, the only thing a self-help program will do for you is send you to Hell sober." No twelve-step program can make you a new person, no seminar can make you a new person, and no conference can make you a new person. What makes you a new person is a personal relationship with the Lord Jesus Christ. Praise God, there is such a thing as grace that can really make us new people.

Every Christian can mark his or her life as BC and AD—this is what I was before Christ and this is what I am now—I'm a different man. When my dad was growing up in his alcoholism, he had two teenage buddies by the name of Jerry and Bob. They did everything together, including drinking. My mom has a picture in an album of Jerry, my dad, and Bob sitting on a couch and you could tell what they were. Over time Jerry, Bob, and dad all became saved. Mom took another picture of them after conversion and put it in the photo album right next to the previous picture. She put "BC" under the first picture and "AD" under the second. Every person who has been to Calvary can so label his life. There is a real change that God makes in a person when that person avails himself of the grace of God. Grace is reality. The grace of God makes new people.

The Results of Grace

At the end of this book, Paul gives a conditional benediction. He doesn't bless everybody. The benediction is not universal; it is a limited benediction to those people who follow the rule. The word *rule* refers to a standard that has been stated. Mercy and peace are only available for those who live up to the standard. What's the standard? The standard is what he mentioned in the previous verse—the standard of having a new birth. You can't know the mercy of God or the peace of God until first of all you've been born again by the grace of God.

At the beginning of this book, Paul began with a conditional curse (1:6). Now we end with a conditional blessing. Paul is not smoothing over the differences between him and the false teachers. Paul is not interested in superficial harmony. If you believe the false doctrine mentioned in chapter one, you are damned, but on the other hand, if you believe the Gospel of grace, you receive mercy and peace. Every person has a choice that they must make concerning the new birth, and what you decide with regard to the new birth will determine whether you are a cursed individual or a blessed individual.

That is why Paul refers to the Israel of God here. What does he mean by that? I don't feel duty-bound to give every one of my children an inheritance. If I have a child who turns out to be a drunk or a drug addict, I don't feel that I should at my death reward her habit. I feel that if she is not going to use that money for good and for God, I am not duty-bound to leave it to her just because she came out of my loins. I will not give one of my children money to go spend in riotous living. Being an Amsbaugh is just not having a name attached to you—being an Amsbaugh is living up to the principles that I have tried to put into the hearts of my children. God is essentially saying the same thing with the Jewish people. There is more to being Jewish than just being a physical descendant of Abraham (cf. Romans 9:6). You could be a physical descendant of Abraham and not live up to what Abraham taught, which is that men are justified by faith alone in God.

If you are a Jew but you are trying to get to Heaven by your works, you are of Israel but you are not really of Israel. You don't understand what it means to be a true heir of Abraham. On the other hand, if you are a Gentile and you understand that a person is made right with God by putting faith in the Lord Jesus Christ, then you have more of what Abraham was about than a Jewish person who is trying to get to Heaven by works. The point that Paul is trying to make here is that it is only those who are the children of faith who truly understand what it means to be a chosen person of God. It is only those people who get the mercy and peace. God does not forgive our sins and grant us peace in daily living because we are involved in religious rituals. The only way we are going to get peace is if we really mean business with God. God gives His mercy and peace through a personal relationship with Christ. A relationship with God bestows the mercy and the peace. He gives mercy and peace only to those who have been authentically born again. The reality of grace is that I am made new, and the result of grace is that God gives His mercy and peace so that I can function in daily life.

The Resilience of Peace

Because God has given me His mercy and peace, I've never found a better offer. If you have forgiveness of sins and peace in your heart, what can the world or any other religion offer you that is better than that? The bottom line is there isn't anything better than that.

Because I have experienced the reality of grace and the results of grace, I can put up with a lot being a Christian because I know what Christianity has done for me. I'm not offended by the people who mock my Christianity. I'm not going to leave Christianity because of the detractors. God forgave my sins and gave me peace in my heart. Do you think a little idle tongue is going to move me from my faith? I have the best deal going. God has done more for me than anyone else ever could. This gives me resilience.

False teachers cannot trouble us. Our most difficult issues have already been resolved by Christ. I'm so blessed in what God has given me that you can't shake me in it. As a matter of fact, Paul faced much more severe opposition than these teachers. He bore in his body the marks of the Lord Jesus.

St. Francis of Assisi actually had nails put into his hands and his feet so he could bear in his body the marks of Jesus. I'm told that throughout history there have been about three hundred people who have actually had nails put in them so they could bear in their body the marks of Jesus. Paul, however, didn't go through some superficial crucifixion act—that is not what he is talking about here. What he is talking about is that when you become saved, you have to take the lumps.

We have the resilience of God's life (II Corinthians 4:10), which leads us to put up with the hatred and persecution that the world throws our way. In Paul's case, the persecution was physical. He was stoned in the area of Galatia (Acts 14: 19). The Galatians knew firsthand what it was for Paul to take his lumps for Christianity. They thought he was a dead man and left him there for dead. But Paul rose up the next day and went right back into the city. What's in your heart is so vital that nothing that happens out in the world can shake what is going on in your heart. The world didn't give it to you, and the world can't take it away. The grace of God that lives in me has done so much in my heart that I don't pay any attention to what the world says about it. Something bigger is going on inside of me. Grace has produced a resilience inside of me that lets me put up with it.

It is interesting that these false teachers boasted about being circumcised in the flesh. Paul is essentially saying here that he has a mark in his flesh that is vastly different. His is the mark of persecution, and it is not self-inflicted but has been inflicted by the world. This mark proves the reality of God's life inside of him, and he's willing to put up with that stigma of the cross. The grace of God gives us the sufficiency to deal with the hatred of the world. If the world is shaking you and you're a scared Christian in the break room, you haven't got hold of what God put inside of you. If you really get hold of what God did on your inside, the outside can't do a thing to you. Because of the reality of what grace has done and because of the result that grace has accomplished, resilience is inevitable.

The Resources of Grace

Paul could put up with what the world was because the grace of God was operative in his spirit. Paul's desire is that the same grace be operative in your spirit and in my spirit. I'm so glad that God's grace can help me with my spirit. The spirit is where I lose it so often. Sometimes little things make us lose our spirit. Little things can easily upset us. Why is it that we get so worked up? The grace of God is not operative in our spirit. I'm so thankful that God's grace is always there to help me with my spirit.

When I decided to do my dissertation, I decided it to do on why we were losing so many missionaries from the mission field—it was something I felt very passionate about. After I put the finishing touches on my dissertation and was sending it off, someone came to me and said, "Have you seen this book?" and it was a book dealing with missionary attrition and the problem of it. I had just finished my dissertation and here is a book that would have helped me tremendously being given to me the day after the dissertation was complete. I wanted to kill the person who gave it to me.

While I was writing my dissertation, I found a resource at just the right time. At the very moment I was writing a chapter on missionary contentment, I found a book dealing with that exact subject. On the other hand, another resource that I found, which could have been of inestimable value, was discovered after I had already defended the dissertation orally. The resource came, but it came too late.

It's always better to find the resource at the time you need it than after you need it. Find the grace of God to help your spirit before it's too late. Some of us lose battles with our spirit. The resource for victory is right at our fingertips, so grab hold of it. Don't wait until you have lost your testimony and then say, "Maybe I should have availed myself of the grace of God." Get the grace of God when it can help you—not when it is too late.

What are you going to do when someone threatens your spirit tomorrow? Avail yourself of the resource of God's grace at the time you need it, not after you need it. This is why the grace of God is so great. It is always available. You can always get your hands on it.

I love the grace of God because it can really make new people out of us. I love the grace of God because of the results—it really does take away my sins and give me peace in my heart. I love the grace of God because it produces resilience in my heart to stand up against the world. And I love the grace of God because every single day its resources are available to me. No wonder Paul says, "Amen!" May it be so! Grace is the most beautiful word in the entire English Language.